Epictetus and Laypeople

Epictetus and Laypeople

A Stoic Stance toward Non-Stoics

Erlend D. MacGillivray

LEXINGTON BOOKS

Lanham • Boulder • New York • London

Published by Lexington Books
An imprint of The Rowman & Littlefield Publishing Group, Inc.
4501 Forbes Boulevard, Suite 200, Lanham, Maryland 20706
www.rowman.com

6 Tinworth Street, London SE11 5AL, United Kingdom

British Library Cataloguing in Publication Information Available

Library of Congress Control Number: 2020934438

ISBN 978-1-7936-1823-8 (cloth: alk. paper)
ISBN 978-1-7936-1825-2 (pbk: alk. paper)
ISBN 978-1-7936-1824-5 (electronic)

♾ ™ The paper used in this publication meets the minimum requirements of American
National Standard for Information Sciences—Permanence of Paper for Printed Library
Materials, ANSI/NISO Z39.48-1992.

To my parents Donald and Margaret MacGillivray,
for all the love, patience, and
wisdom that you have continually shown to me.

*For who can be more truly the benefactors of their children than
their parents, who have not only caused them to exist, but have
thought them to be worthy of food, and after that of education
both in body and soul, and have enabled them not only to live,
but to live well.* Philo of Alexandria, *Spec. Leg.* II.229

Contents

Acknowledgments and Dedication

I owe the University of Aberdeen a great debt for the myriad instances of support and encouragement that I received during my decade-and-a-half association with the institution, but a few people bear particular mention. First of all, my thanks should be offered to Dr. Jutta Leonhardt-Balzer for the integral part that she played in overseeing my academic development over many years. I am also indebted to the encouragement that I received from Professor Grant Macaskill, Dr. Jane Heath, and Dr. Tomas Bokedal, and the various suggestions they made which improved my manuscript. The funding I obtained from the Arts and Humanities Research Council was also paramount in helping me to bring this book to a successful completion, for which I am most grateful. My time at the British School at Athens, and at Tyndale House, Cambridge, also greatly aided my research and provided me with many happy memories.

Beyond academia, I owe particular thanks to my wife Mary Jane. Her patience with my intermittent absences, the presence of innumerable books crowding our home, and her efforts in supporting me through the ups and downs of academic research have been invaluable. My deepest gratitude though should be expressed to my parents, Donald and Margaret MacGillivray, for the love, patience, and wisdom that they have continually extended to me. They have supported me in every way possible and with unstinting resolve. This book would not exist were it not for them, and for this reason I wholeheartedly dedicate this work to them.

Introduction

"You must assume either the stance of a philosopher or that of a layperson," τοῦτ' ἔστι φιλοσόφου στάσιν ἔχειν ἢ ἰδιώτου.

—Epictetus (*Discourses.* III.15.13.)

One of the many legacies that antiquity has bequeathed to later generations is a substantial store of philosophical literature wherein different views on concepts such as ethics, epistemology, anthropology, theology, and logic have been carefully scrutinized and delineated. Modern scholarly interest in ancient philosophy has, perhaps understandably, largely focused upon explicating the theoretical content of the schools' propositions, and to do so by, for instance, attempting to systematize their tenets, reflecting upon where cohesion and tensions between various doctrines lie, and highlighting the varying emphases and philosophical preferences that different generations of thinkers could prioritize. The richness of the intellectual depth that is contained in these texts has, perhaps understandably, tended to obscure the value of studying the schools as a sociohistorical phenomenon and in exploring the stances that their proponents took on topics that lie outside of formal philosophical discourse. In this regard, it is the intention of this book to consider ancient philosophers' attitudes toward a group that would have constituted the largest segment of the society that surrounded them, but which their opinion of has elicited almost no scholarly attention: individuals who lacked philosophical training, laypeople.

To assess the views regarding laypeople that were held across the classical philosophical schools (e.g., Platonic, Peripatetic, Stoic, and Epicurean) and, indeed, even just across an individual philosophical tradition would be a mammoth task, and is not achievable within the space of a single monograph. To render the goal of this book more manageable, its focus will narrow upon exploring the mid-first to early second century CE Stoic philosopher Epictetus' views of them. The reason for selecting Epictetus is that, as will become evident, he mentions laypeople with notable frequency, and so a robust reconstruction of his views of them can, quite uniquely for an ancient philosopher, be obtained.

EPICTETUS

Epictetus (ca. 55–135 CE) led, as one of his recent commentators has reflected, "(perhaps) not a strikingly eventual life, but yet a memorable one."[1] Born in Hierapolis in Asia Minor, Epictetus spent his formative years as a slave in the household of Epaphroditus (ca. 25–95 CE), who was a freedman and secretary to the Emperor Nero. This placed Epictetus close to the heart of the Imperial government, which was an experience that he would sometimes draw upon to help add color to his philosophical explications. For example, when he talking about the misplaced concern for wealth that humans can exhibit, Epictetus recalls that a man had once approached his master in palpable distress because he had only a million-and-a-half sesterces (a sizeable sum) left.[2] Little else is known about Epictetus' early life, and only once in the extant portions of his discussions does he explicitly refer to his previous servile status.[3]

Epictetus would almost certainly have remained in obscurity had his aptitude for philosophical thought, the provision of leisure time that was afforded to him by his master, and the presence of the engaging Stoic philosopher Musonius Rufus in Rome not coincided. Attending Rufus' lectures while he was still a slave,[4] Epictetus seems to have formed a close bond—at least in terms of intellectual deference—with the Stoic scholar. As he would later relay to his own circle of pupils regarding the effect that Rufus had upon his audience:

> He [Rufus] used to address us in such a manner that each of us sitting there imagined that some person had informed on him; such was his grasp of understanding how people behave, and his ability to set each person's private faults before their eyes.[5]

> τοιγαροῦν οὕτως ἔλεγεν, ὥσθ᾽ ἕκαστον ἡμῶν καθήμενον οἴεσθαι, ὅτι τίς ποτε αὐτὸν διαβέβληκεν: οὕτως ἥπτετο τῶν γιγνομένων, οὕτως πρὸ ὀφθαλμῶν ἐτίθει τὰ ἑκάστου κακά.

Epictetus also established himself as a well-regarded and popular philosophical figure during his lifetime, with, for example, several high-ranking political figures, including the procurator of Epirus and the corrector of the free cities in Greece,[6] visiting his school in Nicopolis so they might hear him lecture or to solicit his advice. In addition, if Aelius is to be believed, even the Emperor Hadrian visited Epictetus' school.[7]

With Epictetus never having secured his teachings in written form, his influence would have almost certainly dissipated had one of his pupils, Arrian, not endeavored to document their contents.[8] These exist in a series of books entitled the *Discourses*, which originally spanned eight volumes, but unfortunately only the first four are extant, in which Epictetus' discussions on a variety of philosophical topics are relayed. Arrian also compiled the *Enchiridion*, which is a gnomological text that appears to be a mnemonic aid that was crafted to help Arrian, or his envisaged audience, to apply Epictetus' teachings in a daily life setting.[9] Outside of his lifetime perhaps Epictetus' most famous and influential admirer was the Emperor Marcus Aurelius, whose own philosophical interests are well known.[10] Epictetus' name, and a brief account of his ideas, especially regarding the concept of freedom ἐλευθερία, is also preserved in a second-century epigraph that was constructed by a slave/freedman, or at least someone who adopted the guise of a slave/freedman.[11] Furthermore, and rather beguiling given the topic of this book, the third-century Christian philosopher Origen reflected that Epictetus was the only philosopher who was read by many (πολλοί),[12] a remark that probably indicates the accessibility and popularity of the *Encheiridon*. Post-antiquity during the seventeenth to nineteenth centuries, Epictetus' teachings enjoyed a remarkably wide reception, with, among others, figures such as Thomas Jefferson, René Descartes, Blaise Pascal, Søren Kierkegaard, the third Earl Shaftsbury, and Tolstoy all appealing and favorably referencing him in their writings or speeches.[13]

Regarding Epictetus' views of laypeople, currently no study of extended length exists which explores the issue. Given how frequently Epictetus' remarks upon laypeople punctuate his discussions, this is, I suggest, a surprising lacuna in Epictetan scholarship.

There are a couple of shorter studies in which the presence of lay visitors to his school are noted. In the first, within Ronald Hock's 1992 journal article which seeks to analyze the *Discourses* through the prism of social network analysis, he catalogues the recorded visitors to Epictetus' school.[14] Hock highlights if any of these visitors are nonphilosophers, but aside from arguing that their presence testifies to Epictetus' popularity, as well as observing the often abrasive manner in which he tended to deal with them, Hock is not concerned to explore Epictetus' opinion(s) of laypeople, or to elucidate any broad framework of thought that might have influenced his views regarding them. In addition, within his 2010 book chapter, Gerald Boter notes a few instances where Epictetus interacts with laypeople, and the advice he offers

to his students to not be frustrated when nonphilosophically trained individuals exhibit faltering moral awareness. Boter, however, offers little reflection
on these passages beyond briefly narrating them, and commenting that they
reveal the varied success Epictetus could have when he engaged with philosophically inexperienced individuals.[15]

OUTLINE OF THE BOOK

In chapter 1, it is highlighted that over the past two decades research has
shown that after the rise of Rome in the first century BCE philosophical
schools became evermore decentralized from their traditional bases on the
Attic mainland, and that the autonomy and disparate location of its affiliates
across the now-sprawling Roman Republic becomes increasingly apparent
in our sources. The resulting ambiguity over who was, and who was not, a
legitimate adherent of philosophy and how this status could be affirmed or
contested is probed at length with reference to numerous classical authors'
opinions. It is concluded that the authenticity of a person's claim to be a
philosopher would be determined, firstly, by how faithfully their behavior
conformed with their chosen philosophy's ethical principles, and, secondly,
by the depth of their comprehension and the fluidity of recall they could display in annunciating its central tenets. Finally, that philosophers who were
affiliated with rival traditions of philosophical thought and students who
were being coached in philosophical precepts were both accepted as having a
genuine claim to a philosophical identity is documented.

   In chapter 2, Epictetus' understanding of the extent and enduring nature of
vice in society is explored. This chapter, therefore, highlights the most negative aspect of Epictetus' evaluation of laypeople, and where the differences
he believes exist between them and philosophically observant individuals
are at their starkest. Firstly, it is demonstrated that Epictetus holds that the
body's powerful registering of pain and sensory pleasure often prompts
people to channel their effort and volition in solely securing their physical
comfort, and to consequently let their capacity for introspection, reasoning,
and the freedom of their internal disposition atrophy. Furthermore, while it
is seen that Epictetus affirms traditional Stoic monism and is not (beyond
idiomatic borrowing) influenced by Platonic dualism, his repeated disregard
for the body and advocacy that his students should dislocate their identity
away from their flesh is deliberated at length, and the scholarly conversation
on this topic is reframed. Secondly, Epictetus opines that most children are
mentored by nonphilosophically informed guardians, which systematically
entrenches the embedding and normalization of vice and misunderstanding
across humanity, which an individual can only hope to expunge (although

almost certainly not entirely) by submitting themselves to a laborious philosophical process. It is shown that Epictetus holds that theoretical learning and practical application need to be honed to work together before such a refining effect can take place. His commendation of therapeutic exercises (such as role-playing and memorizing of moral maxims) to help catalyze such a harmony in his students' lives is then documented. Epictetus' position that a philosophical education is limited to a small number of individuals who can apportion extended periods of free time and resources to its study and who need to have previously obtained skills such as literacy is then interacted with.

The question addressed in chapter 3 is if Epictetus perceives that the vast majority of people who surround him to be laypeople, what is his opinion regarding widely communicating philosophical knowledge to them, and in encouraging people to begin philosophical study? After framing the exploration of this question with reference to two competing portrayals of the early Stoics' stance toward public engagement which Diogenes Laertius' *Lives* document, it is seen that Epictetus uniquely signals that a change in his perspective on this issue has occurred, namely that his youthful optimism in the possibility of impacting and enthusing laypeople with philosophical insight has been displaced by the conviction that such attempts are futile and more than likely are counterproductive. With empathy for his students' apparently frequently felt conviction to relay the messages of the lecture room to a wider audience, it is documented that Epictetus instead repeatedly seeks to dissuade them from bringing philosophical deliberation to the public.

In this chapter, it is further established that Epictetus' perspective on public engagement parallels his teacher Musonius Rufus', and can be seen firsthand in the attitude that Epictetus had toward visitors who sought to glean philosophical insight from him. The question is then posed, and which the rest of this book seeks to address: Does Epictetus show any concern for those individuals whom he believes will never obtain philosophical awareness?

In chapter 4, it is noted that Stoic thinkers who claim moral progress is contingent upon the provision of philosophical instruction can also state that nonphilosophical (or layperson-like, ἰδιωτικόν) techniques can be of assistance. Whether such remarks should be understood to articulate a broader schema of thought regarding the possibility that people might gain moral awareness through nonscholastic routes is then explored. In addressing this question, our efforts are primarily centered upon the Stoic philosophers Posidonius' and Seneca's portrayal of primitive humanity, wherein they state that our distant ancestors exhibited uniform moral excellence which required no theoretical or epistemic underpinnings (i.e., they were proto-virtuous nonphilosophers). These Stoics posit that early humanity's remarkable conformity to virtue was due to the absence of vicious and corrupting ideas, and the lack of material comfort which could monopolize our ancestors' attention. Once vice began its slow installation over humanity's affections, however, Seneca and Posidonius depict a second age where wise, although likely still not philosophically aware, leaders moderated the advance of misapprehension in society by offering guidance to people.

In turning to contemporary society, it is argued that the features the Stoics believed prompted primitive humans to live according to virtuous principles are not thought by them to have concluded. Indeed, the adoption of atavistic traits and the observing of legislation that certain wise ancients laid down is held by the Stoics to remain impacting nonphilosophically aware people in contemporary society. In this regard, the correlation between primitive circumstances and the manifestation of preferred indifferent actions in the lives of nonphilosophers is strongly seen in the remarks of Musonius Rufus and Epictetus.

Chapter 5 is prefaced with a discussion of Stoic epistemology, and then brings Epictetus' position regarding preconceptions into focus. In this regard it is noted that several times in his discussions he reflects that people who lack philosophical awareness nevertheless hold that principles such as justice, honor, familial fidelity, and so on are self-evidently good and should hold normative force across society. He further observes that humans have an instinctive sense of shame (αἰδώς), which is often able to compel people to behave correctly without any period of contemplation or self-reflection having to be undertaken. These phenomena are understood by Epictetus within the context of the Stoic doctrine of preconceptions (προλήψεις), which posits that humans have an innate, although largely unrefined, understanding of virtuous principles. His confidence in the furnishing of preconceptions in humanity is also suggested to be observed by his frequent employment of the dialectical/elenctic method: a type of discourse that seeks to induct people through a series of questions that will throw the contradictions that exist between their moral preconceptions and daily praxis into sharp relief. A conversation that Epictetus has with an affiliate of Epicurean philosophy is proposed to have particular salience for understanding his confidence in the efficacy of preconceptions. In their exchange, when Epictetus reflects that his dialogue partner exhibits familial devotion and care, he remarks that with (as he understands it) Epicureanism mandating a range of antisocial commitments from its adherents, his dialogue partner's instinctive sense of family obligations has evidently proved strong enough to incubate him from some of the more damaging influences of Epicurean philosophy.

The limitations that Epictetus holds preconceptions have is then considered—in particular his stance that while concord is easily established between people regarding the importance of concepts such as "justice" or "honor," the implementation of these ideals into legislation or normative customs is evidently frequently fallible and contradictory. It is concluded that in Epictetus' view preconceptions only provide people with a high abstraction of what the good is and that the moral insights they offer should be systematized and elucidated in an intellectually coherent framework, that is, the philosophy of the Stoa. It is argued that although Stoics believe that in the absence of philosophical guidance the ability of preconceptions to help humans structure their lives according to virtue is significantly constrained, they are confident that they maintain a role in mediating error in society and in steering individuals toward performing suitable or appropriate actions.

In chapter 6, it is noted that apprehending Epictetus' attitude toward civic legislation can be challenging. The topic is not made a matter of explicit deliberation in either the *Discourses* or the *Enchiridion*, and it has rarely been the object of sustained scholarly inquiry. In addition, Epictetus' remarks about the law can appear to voice conflicting sentiments. On the one hand, he can deride the value of various pieces of legislation and openly question the integrity of the officials who are charged with enforcing them. Furthermore, he openly avers that his students should focus their concentration on how to live upon the parameters that have been established by philosophical insight, and not to those that have been borne from legal deliberation.

On the other hand, it is seen that Epictetus considers obedience to the law to be a duty that every citizen should assume and to only neglect if a particular piece of legislation is in conflict with their philosophical principles. More significantly, he praises Spartan polity for having been instituted by an ancient wise leader, Lycurgus, and for its expressing ideals that are commensurate with philosophical teachings which he believes successfully engrained themselves into the Spartan people's character. Additionally, while referring to contemporary Roman law, a pronouncement of marriage by the legislator is claimed by Epictetus to laudably restrain men's attempts to acquire another person's wife, and in another passage the connection that exists between civic law and the correct understanding of ownership, material possessions, and marital relationships that are found in its citizenry is observed by him. Furthermore, regarding his friend Agrippinus Paconius' tenure as a governor, Epictetus reflects that he was able to exercise his judicial duties so that he became like a moral physician (ἰατρός), protector (ἐπιμελητής), and guardian (κηδεμών) to the people who were arraigned before him, and that he succeeded in instigating the moral reform of their lives. It is evident, therefore, that it is not just the state's legal doctrines that Epictetus views as having the potential to affect beneficial change in people, but, depending upon the official, also the act of dispensing justice itself. The conclusion reached is that although Epictetus believes civic law is frequently flawed or confused in its logic, he holds that it can have a useful role in highlighting and delimiting what is, and what is not, correct behavior and in influencing individuals to act according to virtuous precepts. It is, therefore, a means whereby he believes that the differences between philosophers and laypeople can be lessened.

The chapter then extends to note that it is often believed that the Stoics held a rather derisory attitude toward the rendering of the divine that was commonly advanced in the myths and rituals of popular Greco-Roman religion. Although Epictetus' opinion of religion has been rarely scrutinized by his modern interpreters at length, several of his remarks on the topic have been highlighted as giving voice to this perspective. This chapter, however, argues that the contours of his thoughts regarding popular religion are more complex than has so far been appreciated by scholars and that it is in need of greater delineation.

Firstly, when isolating statements from Epictetus on religion that are critical in tenor, it should be noted that he ridicules the view that idols have qualities beyond those that are usually inherent to inert matter; he scolds his pupils for their intention to visit Olympia to see Pheidias' famed statue of Zeus when they have still to perfect the divine traits that are within them. Secondly, regarding Epictetus' more accommodating stance toward religion, after cataloguing such remarks, it is observed that he does not usually appeal to traditional religious sentiments in order to negate their worth or to redact them, but as a springboard from which he can launch an explication of Stoic philosophy. It is further highlighted that Epictetus attributes civic religion with having a role in educating and orienting individuals to accept correct patterns of thought, which he significantly holds parallels the intended results of philosophical tuition. In particular, his conviction that the mystery cults were established by wise ancients to provide education and amendment for their participants is noted and used to inform our discussion on the Stoics' perspective regarding primitivism and the potential didactic function of religion. Thereafter Epictetus' reflection that through mere habit Christians are steeled with a disdain for their physical security even to the point of facing death at the hands of the emperor's soldiers, which is a stance that he argues his students should be able to hold through reason, is then commented upon. Finally, Epictetus' conception of divination is probed, and his understanding that the mantic has been used to prompt self-reflection and philosophical inquiry among laypeople is documented. As with civic law, popular religion is, therefore, found to be another mechanism through which Epictetus believes that the differences between philosophers and laypeople can be reduced.

In chapter 7, after providing context regarding the prevalent use of exempla in classical literature, speeches, and pedagogy, the lack of studies that plot Epictetus' (as opposed to Seneca's) employment of exempla is observed, and is a gap in our knowledge that this study proposes to begin to redress. First, it is documented that Epictetus' elucidation of moral principles from the lives of philosophers chiefly pivots around the figures of Socrates (whom Epictetus presents as being the moral exempla par excellence) and Diogenes the Cynic. Aside from these individuals, his general lack of interest in highlighting philosophers, including luminaries from his own school, as having exhibited moments of commendable moral worth is argued to be striking, especially given his privileging of noting actions from some of the most deprived and uneducated groups in society, such as slaves, gladiators, and laborers. In one notable instance, it is observed that Epictetus draws a direct equivalence between the mindset that slaves and menial laborers can assume and those of Socrates, Diogenes, Cleanthes, and what he terms "the legitimate philosophers" (οἱ γνησίως φιλοσοφοῦντες). He then further assesses that both groups (the laypeople and the philosophers) can show the proper exercise of their faculty of choice/will (προαιρέσει)—a key concept in his philosophy. Thereafter the actions of certain city-states; individuals such as Menoeceus of Thebes; an anonymous athlete; and figures from literature and mythology, such as Sarpedon, Odysseus, and Heracles, are seen to be praised by Epictetus and commended as being worthy of his students' emulation and as revealing his belief in commendable lay actions and disposition. Epictetus' conviction that the examples of people, particularly government officials, can help prompt moral advancement across society is then observed. In addition, his advice that philosophers should attempt to leverage the didactic ability of exempla and aim to first disclose their principles to laypeople through their praxis, instead of explicating philosophical doctrines to them, is documented. In the conclusion to the chapter, Epictetus' extensive use of exempla is argued to firstly highlight his belief that laypeople can act and think in morally beneficial ways, and to secondly disclose his position that an individual can be influenced by exempla irrespective of whether they have the ability to correctly parse or comprehend philosophical teachings or not.

SOURCES

Regarding sources, the chief ones for the reconstruction of Epictetus' views are the records that Arrian has left us—namely, the surviving *Discourses* and the *Enchiridion*. Occasionally, other classical authors, such as Aulus Gellius, who make references to Epictetus' views will though be cited. As I noted at the beginning, it is beyond the scope of this book to provide a comprehensive study of the Stoic school and its representatives' perception(s) of laypeople. Other Stoics' thought apart from Epictetus' as well as texts that are accepted to relay information about the school's position will be occasionally referenced to reveal that there are indications that Epictetus' stance is not particular to him, but instead might be reflective of a typical Stoic viewpoint. Where they can add particular clarity to a topic, or to help elucidate the broader architecture of Stoic thought, other Stoics philosopher's opinions will be occasionally discussed at length within the main body of the text, and this is especially so in chapter 4.

KEY TERMS

Finally, it should also be noted that despite the central place that the word "layperson" holds in this study's discussion and the attention that will be directed to understand the word choice of relevant primary sources, this book is not a philological study on the Greek word that is often translated as layperson—ἰδιώτης. The presence of laypeople in Epictetus' discussions (and other relevant classical sources) will instead be considered conceptually, that is, wherever the context implies that a person of little/no philosophical awareness is in view. The primary reason for this conceptual approach is that ἰδιώτης was not the exclusive, or indeed dominant, way in which a classical author could signify a person's lack of philosophical training or knowledge. As it will be observed in chapter 1, other words that have no direct semantic connections to ἰδιώτης could also be used in ancient literature to relay a similar meaning, for example απαίδευτος (uneducated/cultured), αγράμματοι (the uneducated), οἱ πολλοὶ and τὸ πλῆθος (the many/the multitude), ὁ λαός (the people), and so on. In addition, people who lacked philosophical instruction could often be described in a way that meant using a particular appellation to designate them as such would be superfluous. The precise nature of how laypeople are to be defined and their presence be discerned in ancient texts will be considered in the following chapter.

The decision to select the word "layperson" in this study to describe nonphilosophers should also be explained. The English word "layperson" (or "layman") has two primary meanings, both of which relate to a person's lack of technical knowledge or instruction. The first meaning is a nonordained member of a religious, usually mainstream Christian, movement, and, secondly, someone who lacks professional or specialized knowledge of a particular subject. As I will explore in more depth in the next chapter, the Greek word ἰδιώτης also holds dual, although more broader, meanings; firstly, the word is being used to designate a private rather than a political individual, and, secondly, to describe a person who is relatively unskilled or inexperienced in one or more range of activities, skills, or fields of knowledge, for example baking, warfare, oratory, and so on, and also used in a general way to refer to an uneducated or unrefined person.[16] The overlap between the English and Greek terms might allow us to select either word to refer to nonphilosophers in this book. On balance, however, I suggest that the use of the English word "layperson" is preferential.[17] The narrower semantic range of "layperson," which is usually employed in English to describe a person's lack of formal knowledge or training in a technical subject, in comparison with ἰδιώτης, which can be applied in more broader contexts, makes the former the more apt one for us to select given that this book's topic revolves around people's grasp of philosophical knowledge. Moreover, given my conceptual approach to identifying and discussing nonphilosophically trained individuals, and not focusing solely upon where the word ἰδιώτης is used, selecting ἰδιώτης to refer to nonphilosophers throughout the book risks unintentionally implying to its readers that ἰδιώτης is being used in a particular text when it is not. The use of the English word "layperson," however, permits us to discuss individuals who are inexperienced in the technical understanding of philosophy and to highlight the wording in the primary texts without the abovementioned misunderstanding arising.

NOTES

1. Long (2002, 11).

2. *Diss.* I.26.11-12. On Epictetus' reflections on the imperial court, see the valuable study by Miller (2002).

3. *Diss.* I.9.29. Epictetus' lameness, alluded to at *Diss.* I.17.20 has been interpreted by some, including Origen, *Cels.* 7.53, 7.54, as being the result of physical harm that was inflicted upon him by Ephaproditus. For a fuller discussion on this story, see Long (2004, 10).

4. *Diss.* I.9.29. Hollowchak (2008), and the sources that are assembled in Inwood and Gerson (2008).

5. *Diss.* III.23.29.

6. *Diss.* III.1.12; 7.1.

7. *Historia Augusta, Hadrian*, 16.

8. For an extended discussion on Arrian's records of Epictetus' teachings, see Long (2002, 39–43). The *Discourses* though, as Cooper (2007, 10–11) importantly notes, do not record "the formal course of instruction in Epictetus' school. [Rather] they were, with only a few exceptions, ancillary and informal admonishments or protreptics, or bits of practical advice, addressed to his pupils and delivered, it would seem, in the afternoons or evenings, after the main work of the day was already completed. . . . it appears, the main part of the curriculum consisted in the systematic reading out loud of classic 'old' Stoic texts . . . together with Epictetus' oral commentary and interpretation of them—*Diss.* II.14.1, 21.10, III.21.6-7, 23.10-11 at 16." See also Mason (2007a, 2).

9. On the likely purpose and provenance of the *Enchiridion*, see Long (2002, 260), and the important recent study by Boter (2017).

10. For example, see his reference to Epictetus at *Med.* 1.7.

11. See Ahlholm (2017, 60–63).

12. *Contra Cels.* 6.2.

13. See MacMillan (1979), and on the reception of Epictetus see Long (2002, 259–274).

14. Hock (1992).

15. Boter (2010, 330–331).

16. Regarding the nonspecific meaning of ἰδιώτης, consider also the remarks at Galen at *In Hipp. Nat. Hom comment* 3.1. For a useful overview of the definition that ἰδιώτης has within various contexts, the discussion in Pitts (2016, 62–64) is of use.

17. The English word "layperson" largely seems to derive its definition from the Latin *idiotes*, which means (Stock 1983, 28, 29): "someone who was ignorant of a science, a doctrine, or an area of study, and as a corollary one unperfected in a practical discipline."

Chapter 1

Establishing a Philosophical Identity in Antiquity

Although as a formal subject of study philosophy had existed for at least some 600 to 700 years,[1] during the time of the late Roman Republic and Roman Empire philosophy was enjoying one of its, if not *the*, most notable periods of its influence.[2] The concerns and idioms that marked its discourse now found themselves regularly punctuating the conversations of educated/cultured society;[3] mosaics, statues, and coins were eagerly commissioned to celebrate its most famous members; the lecture rooms of its exponents were toured as a matter of routine by the children of the elite; and philosophers were enthusiastically inducted into the client bases of well-connected and aspiringly erudite patrons.[4] Moreover, the increasing provision of resources such as epitomes, gnomologies, doxographies, and public lectures/readings were enabling many of philosophy's ideas to reach people who would, from either a lack of resources or resolve, have otherwise remained ignorant of them.[5]

This influence and diffusion of philosophy in antiquity, as well as the decentralization of the schools as institutions after the rise of Rome,[6] meant that establishing who was, and who was not, a philosopher was perhaps not as easy a distinction to make as it might at first be imagined.[7] Indeed, from the middle of the first century BCE, people apparently felt increasingly able to assert that they were affiliated with one of philosophy's schools, even if they had never been formally instructed in its tenets, or had ever explored its cache of texts.[8] It should be highlighted that the difficulty in classifying an ancient person as a philosopher is not just felt by modern interpreters looking back with hindsight. Numerous classical authors comment, or allude, to the fact that with little formalized means of identifying a philosopher, discerning a genuine philosopher from an inadequate or even fraudulent claimant of the title can be problematic.[9] Dio Chrysostom (ca. 40–115 CE), for instance,

1

remarks: "However, it is possible there is nothing to prevent one's claiming to be a philosopher and at the same time playing the impostor and deceiving himself and everyone else," τὸ δέ γε φῆσαι φιλοσοφεῖν καὶ ἀλαζονεύεσθαι καὶ αὐτὸν ἐξαπατῆσαι καὶ τοὺς ἄλλους οὐδὲν ἴσως κωλύει, and elsewhere he reveals that, in his estimation, most people could be deceived by the mere pretense of philosophical acumen.[10] A similar frustration is shared by Apuleius (ca. 124–170 CE), who at one point declares that he wishes a proc-lamation (*edictum*) could be issued so that people might easily recognize an authentic philosopher, and penalties enacted to dissuade the inappropriate donning of the philosopher's mantle[11]—an innovation that Epictetus also intimates he would like to see.[12]

A further ambiguity, as Harry Hine has highlighted,[13] is that even figures such as Cicero and Seneca, who are highly regarded expositors of ancient philosophy and whose writings we depend upon to help us better map the contours of ancient philosophical thought, appear to have declined to use the title philosopher (*philosophus*) to describe themselves. With regards to Cicero, Hine notes that on several occasions the implications of his remarks are that he believes he can claim the identity of being a philosopher, but that he consistently refrains from doing so.[14] In particular, Hine points out at *Tusc.* 2.1, Cicero opines that individuals who are engaged in the search for wisdom can be called *philosophi*, which implies broadening philosophical identity beyond people who have formal institutional ties with a school, or a professional responsibility to instruct others in philosophical tenets. Such a definition of a philosopher would also, quite naturally, include Cicero within its purview, but again is an implication that Hine notes Cicero leaves for his readers to draw.[15] In addition, it can be noted that at *De Off.* 1.2, a text which Hine does not cite, where Cicero draws a direct equivalence between his philosophical efforts and those of Peripatetic writers, he again deftly avoids using the epithet *philosophus* to describe himself. Similarly with regards to Seneca, Hine highlights that he never applies the title *philosophus* to describe himself within his large body of writing—although it might be highlighted that he does freely describe himself as having a philosophical affiliation to Stoicism.[16]

Cicero's and Seneca's hesitancy to use the title *philosophus* to describe themselves, but to evidently believe and present themselves as being engaged in philosophizing is explained by Hine as being due to the particular socio-economic background that these men had in common. In his study, Hine argues that for high-ranking Roman individuals the title (although not the identity) of philosopher would connote an image of a lower-class, usually Greek figure who was vocationally engaged in coaching young men to under-stand philosophical thought. Hine asserts that a few decades after Seneca's life the reticence from high-ranking Roman individuals to lay claim to the title of *philosophus* disappears, and we see figures such as Aupelius (fl. 150 CE), who was born into a local elite family in North Africa, striving to have their status as a philosopher openly recognized.[17]

Hine concludes his study by asserting: "I am not for one moment suggesting that it is inappropriate for us to call Cicero and Seneca and Romans philosophers,"[18] something that people who have a familiarity with both individual's philosophical efforts, and who do not associate philosophers with individuals of low, Greek birth would doubtless raise little objection to.

If, as has just been argued, people who had little interest in teasing out complex philosophical ideas could attempt to stake their claim to be philosophers, while some of the ancient world's most notable philosophical thinkers had often declined to use the title, how, it might be wondered, was philosophical identity during the Roman period evaluated? Within this chapter I will explore this topic with reference to numerous ancient writers, but given the frequent illuminating remarks that he is recorded as making on the issue, my attention will chiefly focus upon Epictetus. Consideration will also be given to people who were viewed as being decidedly beyond the confines of philosophical identity—namely, laypeople. Finally, sections on whether representatives from rival schools recognized the legitimacy of each other's philosophical status, and if students were acknowledged to be philosophers, will also be explored.

CONDUCT AND PHILOSOPHICAL IDENTITY

With regards to conduct, while instilling ethical behavior in students is (at least within a university setting) largely absent from the formal evaluation of modern philosophical instruction, in antiquity this objective propelled the entire enterprise.[19] As Michael Trapp notes: "[ancient] philosophy, taken as seriously as it showed itself to want to be taken, posed an evangelical challenge, to life-changing commitment of a kind that could make awkward demands on the individual; in particular, it could demand the adoption of values and targets at odds with those of ordinary civic society."[20] This expectation can be seen being repeatedly emphasized across the records of the Stoics' teachings,[21] but note in particular the following passage from Arius Didymus:

> For it is not the person who eagerly listens to and makes notes of what is spoken by the philosophers who is ready for philosophizing, but the person who is ready to transfer the prescriptions of philosophy to his deeds and to live in accord with them.[22]

Οὐ γὰρ τὸν προθύμως ἀκούοντα καὶ ὑπομνη ματιζόμενον τὰ λεγόμενα ὑπὸ τῶν φιλοσόφων ἕτοιμον εἶναι πρὸς τὸ φιλοσοφεῖν, ἀλλὰ τὸν ἑτοίμως ἔχοντα πρὸς τὸ τὰ διὰ τῆς φιλοσοφίας παραγγελλόμενα μεταφέρειν ἐπὶ τὰ ἔργα καὶ κατ᾽ αὐτὰ βιοῦν.

In this passage, it argued that it is not an individual's apprehension of philosophical theory in itself that is considered to be the goal of their education, but rather their successful *application* of philosophical doctrines to their life (or the philosophy's orders/prescriptions—παραγγέλλω). For Arius Didymus, the tenets of philosophy should be transferred (μεταφέρω) to impact a person's deeds (ἔργα) and how they live (βιόω) their life. Meanwhile Seneca, laconically but notably, states: "She [philosophy] is not a thing to be followed at odd times, but a subject for daily practice," *Non est res subsiciva, ordinaria est; domina est.*[23] Moreover, a catalogue of stories regarding individuals whose exposure to philosophy instigated a dramatic, lifelong reorientation of their lives, such as the effect that Plato's philosophizing had upon Speusippus, that Diogenes' had upon Crates, and that Xenocrates' had upon Polemo, is documented in classical literature.[24] In particular though, note Lucian's portrayal of the effect that a lecture on Platonism had upon one audience member:

When he had said this and much more of the same sort, he ended his talk. Until then I had listened to him in awe, fearing that he would cease. When he stopped, I felt like the Phaeacians of old,[25] for I stared at him a long time spellbound. Afterwards, in a great fit of confusion and giddiness, I dripped with sweat, I stumbled and stuck in the endeavor to speak, my voice failed, my tongue faltered, and finally I began to cry in embarrassment; for the effect he produced in me was not superficial or casual. My wound was deep and vital, and his words, shot with great accuracy, clove, if I may say so, my very soul in two.[26]

ταῦτά τε καὶ πολλὰ ἕτερα τοιαῦτα διελθὼν κατέπαυσε τὸν λόγον. ἐγὼ δὲ ᾽τέως μὲν ἤκουον αὐτοῦ τεθηπώς, μὴ σιωπήσῃ πεφοβημένος· ἐπειδὴ δὲ ἐπαύσατο, τοῦτο δὴ τὸ τῶν Φαιάκων πάθος ἐπεπόνθειν πολὺν γὰρ δὴ χρόνον ἐς αὐτὸν ἀπέβλεπον κεκηλημένος εἶτα πολλῇ συγχύσει καὶ ἰλίγγῳ κατειλημμένος τοῦτο μὲν ἱδρῶτι κατερρεόμην, τοῦτο δὲ φθέγξασθαι βουλόμενος ἐξέπιπτόν τε καὶ ἀνεκοπτόμην, καὶ ἥ τε φωνὴ ἐξέλειπε καὶ ἡ γλῶττα διημάρτανε, καί τέλος ἐδάκρυον ἀπορούμενος· οὐ γὰρ ἐξ ἐπιπολῆς οὐδ᾽ ὡς ἔτυχεν ἡμῶν ὁ λόγος καθίκετο, βαθεῖα δὲ καὶ καίριος ἡ πληγὴ ἐγένετο, καὶ μάλα εὐστόχως ἐνεχθεὶς ὁ λόγος αὐτήν, εἰ οἷόν τε εἰπεῖν, διέκοψε τὴν ψυχήν.

In this vivid account, Lucian depicts the recounting of Platonic tenets as having induced an almost-epiphinal moral awakening in this student (eliciting wonder/awe τέθηπα), which produced a wound so deep that it cut his soul in two and manifested itself in his physical distress and immobilization.[27] The significant impact that philosophy could have upon the character of its students is, however, perhaps most effectively relayed by Seneca's profound remark: "I feel, my dear Lucilius, that I am being not only reformed, but transformed (*transfigurari*)," *Intellego, Lucili, non emendari me tantum sed transfigurari.*[28] Descriptions such as these, and others, regarding the reorientation of an individual's values and aspirations because of their introduction to philosophical theory (e.g. see also Seneca's description of the "burning" (*flagro*) desire that new adherents of philosophy can feel for learning all they can about their chosen philosophy and Marcus Aurelius' reflections on the effect that the writings of the Stoic Aristo had upon him[29]) have led some scholars to conclude that "conversion" is often the most apt word in modern parlance to describe an ancient person's decision to commit themselves to a philosophical school, regardless of the particular tradition that they opted to associate with.[30]

Conversely, people who failed to observe the robust moral principles that were advocated by the philosophy they professed to adhere to are censured by numerous classical writers, with particular criticism being made of philosophers who betray an interest in seeking glory and money, in feasting, or in pursuing acts of sexual deviance.[31] Being wary of such duplicitous individuals, potential students (including Stoic ones) are recorded as carefully scrutinizing the conduct of their intended philosophical instructor for any signs of moral laxity before they would entrust their philosophical development to them.[32] Seneca even portrays a friend of his seeking to counter Seneca's attempts to persuade him of the value of the philosophical life by recounting examples of Stoics who chase after money and girls and who are gluttonous.[33] What is of relevance to us here is that such venally oriented people are often asserted in our sources to not just be hypocrites, but to have ended their ability to legitimately identify themselves with their chosen philosophy. For example, this is bluntly stated in Dio Chrysostom's writings,[34] and in Plutarch's account of his attempt to arbitrate between two brothers in a legal dispute, one of whom was reputed to be a philosopher, but—after observing his contemptuous behavior toward his sibling—Plutarch concludes has been assigned a false epithet (ψευδεπίγραφος).[35] In addition, Aulus Gellius documents that a philosopher (of unspecified persuasion) associate of his had a particular dislike of base and idle people whom he judged as seeking to put a cover (*pallium*) over their failings by adopting the dress of a philosopher, and recounted that the sophist and senator Herodes Atticus reproved a man who he had judged falsely (*falso*) laid claim to the title and character of a philosopher.[36] In addition, in a passage that lays bare that gaining knowledge of an individual's good conduct was deemed to be necessary before confidence in their status as a philosopher could be established, Gellius narrates that when a man who was dressed as a Cynic, but who turned out to be of worthless character, approached Herodes and requested money, Herodes replied by asking who he was because "I see, said Herodes, a beard and a cloak; the philosopher I do not yet see." "*'Video' inquit Herodes, 'barbam et pallium, philosophum nondum video.'*"[37]

Strikingly, Gellius also documents that Herodes sought to expose a pompous and self-affected student of Stoicism by appealing to the records of Epictetus' discussions in a way that both disclose the ancient expectation that a philosopher should adhere to a high standard of moral behavior and also reveal a near contemporary of Epictetus framing his stance on this topic in a way that parallels the one that will be supplied in this chapter.

> "Allow me, mightiest of philosophers, since we, whom you call laypeople, cannot answer you, to read from a book of Epictetus, greatest of Stoics, what he thought and said about such big talk as that of yours." And he bade them bring the first volume of the *Discourses* of Epictetus, arranged by Arrian, in which that venerable old man with just severity rebukes those young men who, though calling themselves Stoics, showed neither virtue nor honest industry, but merely babbled of trifling propositions and of the fruits of their study of such elements as are taught to children. Then, when the book was brought, there was read the passage which I have appended,[38] in which Epictetus with equal severity and humor set apart and separated from the true and genuine Stoic, who was beyond question without restraint or constraint, unembarrassed, free, prosperous and happy, that other mob of triflers who styled themselves Stoics, and casting the black soot of their verbiage before the eyes of their hearers, laid false claim to the name of the holiest of sects.[39]

> *'Permitte inquit, philosophorum amplissime, quoniam respondere nos tibi, quos vocas idiotas, non quimus, recitari ex libro quid de huiuscemodi magniloquentia vestra senserit dixeritque Epictetus, Stoicorum maximus' iussitque proferri Dissertationum Epicteti digestarum ab Arriano primum librum, in quo ille venerandus senex iuvenes qui se 'Stoicos' appellabant, neque frugis neque operae probae, sed theorematis tantum nugalibus et puerilium isagogarum commentationibus deblaterantes, obiurgatione iusta incessuit. Lecta igitur sunt ex libro qui prolatus est ea quae addidi; quibus verbis Epictetus severe simul et festiviter seiunxit atque divisit a vero atque sincero Stoico, qui esset procul dubio* ἀκώλυτος, ἀνανάγκαστος, ἀπαραπόδιστος, ἐλεύθερος, εὐπορῶν, εὐδαιμονῶν, *vulgus aliud nebulonum hominum qui se 'Stoicos' nuncuparent, atraque verborum et argutiarum fuligine ob oculos audientium iactal sanctissimae disciplinae nomen ementirentur.*

In the above passage, people who present themselves as being Stoics, and who have the ability to recount the school's doctrines to a great and even irritating length, but who do not concede to follow its ethical principles, are asserted to be false (*ementior*) members of the school, and it is argued that—at least conceptually—they should be separated (*seiungo*) from true (*verus*) Stoics.

Further revealing the force that Epictetus' remarks were understood in antiquity to have in challenging the discordance that exists between many purported philosophers' teachings and their actions, Gellius later remarks that Favorinus (whose own philosophical enterprise it can be noted was vulnerable to charges of sophistry[40]) records that Epictetus declared most individuals who give the appearance of practicing philosophy were: "without deeds, only so far as words," *id significat factis procul, verbis tenus.*[41]

Turning to consider the records of Epictetus' discussions for ourselves, it can first of all be observed that he provides evidence that the wider public were, at least to some extent, aware that to declare a philosophical identity required that the claimant should follow a high level of moral behavior; as he comments to his students: "We cannot bear to have those who meet us say, 'Look, so-and-so has become a philosopher, who was like this or that,'" οὐδὲ φέρομεν τοὺς ἀπαντῶντας καὶ λέγοντας 'εἶδ' ὁ δεῖνα φιλοσοφεῖ, ὁ τοῖος καὶ ὁ τοῖος.'[42] That is, their previous behavior did not suggest a life that would naturally come to be dedicated to philosophical study. Meanwhile, Epictetus depicts a bystander, observing a philosopher who was disturbed by a noise and whose reflexes disclosed his concern for his physical safety, as exclaiming: "Philosopher, what has become of what you were saying? Where did it come from? From your lips only?" ποῦ ἐστιν, φιλόσοφε, ἐκεῖνα ἃ ἔλεγες; πόθεν αὐτὰ προφερόμενος ἔλεγες; ἀπὸ τῶν χειλῶν αὐτόθεν.[43]

Secondly, Epictetus' own high expectation of his students' behavior is repeatedly evidenced; for example, he trenchantly informs one of them:

> Do you think that you can act as you currently do, and still be a philosopher? That you can eat, drink, and burst forth with anger and irascibility as you do now? You must conquer certain desires, must be aloof to your familiars, be derided by a slave, be mocked by the people you meet; come off worse than others in everything, whether that be in power, in honor, in the courts. When you have diligently weighed all these things then, if you think it suitable, come to philosophy, and be willing to exchange all of this for serenity, freedom and an unperturbed mind. Otherwise do not come near.[44]

καίτοι τίς οὕτως δύναται εἰπεῖν ὡς ἐκεῖνος; θέλουσιν καὶ αὐτοὶ φιλοσοφεῖν. ἄνθρωπε, σκέψαι πρῶτον τί ἐστι τὸ πρᾶγμα, εἶτα καὶ τὴν σαυτοῦ φύσιν, τί δύνασαι βαστάσαι. εἰ παλαιστής, ἰδού σου τοὺς ὤμους, τοὺς μηρούς, τὴν ὀσφῦν. ἄλλος γὰρ πρὸς ἄλλο τι πέφυκεν. δοκεῖς ὅτι ταῦτα ποιῶν δύνασαι φιλοσοφεῖν; δοκεῖς ὅτι δύνασαι ὡσαύτως ἐσθίειν, ὡσαύτως πίνειν, ὁμοίως ὀργίζεσθαι, ὁμοίως δυσαρεστεῖν; ἀγρυπνῆσαι δεῖ, πονῆσαι, νικῆσαί τινας

ἐπιθυμίας, ἀπελθεῖν ἀπὸ τῶν οἰκείων, ὑπὸ παιδαρίου καταφρονηθῆναι, ὑπὸ τῶν
ἀπαντώντων καταγελασθῆναι, ἐν παντὶ ἔλασσον ἔχειν, ἐν ἀρχῇ, ἐν τιμῇ, ἐν δίκῃ.
ταῦτα περισκεψάμενος, εἴ σοι δοκεῖ, προσέρχου, εἰ θέλεις ἀντικαταλλάξασθαι
τούτων ἀπάθειαν, ἐλευθερίαν, ἀταραξίαν. εἰ δὲ μή, μὴ πρόσαγε.

In this passage, everything from eating and drinking habits to the conquering of desires are asserted by Epictetus to be under philosophy's oversight.
If the student cannot manage to undertake this effort, he is told that he must
not (μὴ πρόσαγε) come near engaging in the study of philosophy. Epictetus
similarly proceeds to caution that individuals should not consider commenc-
ing philosophical study in the same lighthearted manner as children do when
they envisage their possible future careers, such as vacillating between aspir-
ing to be a wrestler one moment, a gladiator the next, and a trumpet player the
next. In Epictetus' view, philosophy's candidates should instead manifest a
similar disposition to athletes who manage to achieve success at the Olympic
Games: namely, a steely resolve and an unbaiting fixation upon obtaining this
hard-won goal.[45] Furthermore, one of Epictetus' frequently utilized words to
express the training that his students should undertake is ἄσκησις, a word
that holds the sense of a drill, or a routine that entails strenuous physical
exercise.[46]

Additionally, in a discourse that is entitled *To Those Who Take Up the
Teachings of the Philosophers For the Sake of Talk Alone* (Πρὸς τοὺς μέχρι
λόγου μόνον ἀναλαμβάνοντας τὰ τῶν φιλοσόφων), which is the passage
that Aulus records Herodes citing above, Epictetus chides students under his
tuition, and opens his comments in the imperative mood by exclaiming:

Observe how you conduct yourself, and you will find out to what school you
are affiliated with. For most of you, you will find that you are Epicureans, and
some are Peripatetics—although rather inadequate ones. For, how do you show
that you believe virtue is equal, and even superior, to everything else? Show me
a Stoic if there is one among you. Where, or how? . . . Who, then, is a Stoic?
As we say a statue is "Phelidian" if it has been crafted according to the art of
Pheidias, so show me a person who is fashioned in accordance with the judgements that he professes.[47]

Τηρεῖτε οὕτως ἑαυτοὺς ἐν οἷς ἐπράσσετε καὶ εὑρήσετε τίνος ἔσθ' αἱρέσεως.
τοὺς πλείστους ὑμῶν Ἐπικουρείους εὑρήσετε, ὀλίγους τινὰς Περιπατητικοὺς
καὶ τούτους ἐκλελυμένους. ποῦ γὰρ ἵν' ὑμεῖς τὴν ἀρετὴν πᾶσιν τοῖς ἄλλοις
ἴσην ἢ καὶ κρείττονα ἔργῳ ὑπολάβητε; Στωικὸν δὲ δείξατέ μοι, εἴ τινα ἔχητε.
ποῦ ἢ πῶς; . . . τίς οὖν ἐστι Στωικός; ὡς λέγομεν ἀνδριάντα Φειδιακὸν τὸν
τετυπωμένον κατὰ τὴν τέχνην τὴν Φειδίου, οὕτως τινά μοι δείξατε κατὰ τὰ
δόγματα ἃ λαλεῖ τετυπωμένον.

Despite learning Stoicism in his school, because of their actions Epictetus claims that his pupils are actually the adherents of the Epicurean school (i.e., they are seeking pleasure[48]), and he later scolds them for failing to exhibit progress in conquering their desires, or in managing their feelings of jealousy or anger, by asking: "why do you dress in a [philosophical] dress that is not yours, and walk around in it, as thieves and robbers who have stolen titles and properties that do not belong to them?" καὶ περιθέμενοι σχῆμα ἀλλότριον περιπατεῖτε κλέπται καὶ λωποδύται τούτων τῶν οὐδὲν προσηκόντων ὀνομάτων καὶ πραγμάτων.[49] Again, it can be seen from this passage, as well as other similar remarks that could be highlighted,[50] that praxis and philosophical identity are firmly interwoven for Epictetus: it is behavior that he believes truly evinces where a person's philosophical allegiances lie and which reveal what philosophical commitments actually shape/mold them (τετυπωμένον). This connection is also demonstrated by Epictetus' frequently expressed concern to censure individuals who pursue philosophy because they are interested in feasting, impressing a senator or family member, learning witty phrases, or obtaining financial gain.

It is notable that Epictetus even appears to suggest to his students that if they cannot bear to align their behavior with philosophy's standards, then they should vacate his school,[51] and he candidly states that if they are only interested in learning the history and theory of philosophy, instead of how to apply it truths to their lives, then they should realize that they are like children,[52] and are training to become a literary scholar/grammarian (γραμματικός) and not a philosopher (φιλόσοφος).[53] For example, in one passage Epictetus argues whether it is one of his student's habit/custom (ἔθος) to read books without giving recourse to consider how the teachings that are contained within them should impact their life: "I ask him to go home straight away and to not neglect his affairs there, for he has travelled here for nothing," λέγω αὐτῷ αὐτόθεν πορεύεσθαι εἰς οἶκον καὶ μὴ ἀμελεῖν τῶν ἐκεῖ· τοῦτο γὰρ ἐφ᾽ ὃ ἀποδεδήμηκεν οὐδέν ἐστιν.[54] When considering Epictetus' language use, it can be seen that the intended effect of his critique is amplified, as he characteristically uses ἔθος as a way to refer to thinking or an action that is done without reasoned deliberation.[55] Meanwhile, in another passage a hypothetical student who is portrayed as being solely interested in scholastic endeavors likewise has his continued presence in the school challenged, with Epictetus remarking to him: "Speak the truth then, you unfortunate thing, and do not put on airs and claim to be a philosopher. . . . leave this [true philosophy] to those people who are prepared for it, those with confidence. As for you, return to your own affairs, and never depart from them again," λέγε οὖν τὰ ἀληθῆ, δύστηνε, καὶ μὴ ἀλαζονεύου μηδὲ φιλόσοφος . . . σὺ δ᾽ ἐπὶ τὰ σαυτοῦ βάδιζε καὶ ἐκείνων ἀποστῆς μηδέποτε.[56] It should be noted that the word for "claim" here, ἀλαζονεύομα, is not a morally neutral one, but is used to designate misleading, deceptive claims.

Following his teacher Rufus,[57] Epictetus also advocates bringing to light (δείκνυμι) a false philosopher not by having any deficiencies that exist in their *comprehension* of philosophical theory highlighted, but rather by their failure to let its teachings *impact upon their lives*:

> From this conduct it can be observed what sort of person you are; why do you want to display it in any other way? Do you not know that Diogenes showed up one of the sophists in such a manner, by pointing at him with his middle finger, and when the man became enraged at that, Diogenes said: "That is the man; I have pointed him out to you."[58]

> βλέπεται ἐξ αὐτῶν τούτων. τί θέλεις ἐξ ἄλλων δεῖξαι; οὐκ οἶδας, ὅτι Διογένης τῶν σοφιστῶν τινα οὕτως ἔδειξεν ἐκτείνας τὸν μέσον δάκτυλον, εἶτα ἐκμανέντος αὐτοῦ 'οὗτός ἐστιν,' ἔφη, 'ὁ δεῖνα: ἔδειξα ὑμῖν αὐτόν.

In another passage, Epictetus imagines an individual who has not apprehended that improper behavior disqualifies someone from being a philosopher—regardless of whether they style themselves as one or not. Instead of looking to appearances, Epictetus argues that it is a person's *actions* that will reveal if they are a philosopher:

> But he [the person who views an apparent philosopher's misdeeds] should rather have said, on the evidence of the indecent behavior, that he was not a philosopher at all. For, if this is the preconception of what a philosopher is and his profession, namely to wear a cloak and have long hair, they would be correct; but, if it is to keep himself free from faults, why, when he does not meet the demands of his profession, do they not remove the appellation of philosopher from him?[59]

> ἔδει δ᾽ ἀφ᾽ ὧν ἠσχημόνει μᾶλλον λέγειν αὐτὸν μὴ εἶναι φιλόσοφον. εἰ μὲν γὰρ αὕτη ἐστὶν ἡ τοῦ φιλοσόφου πρόληψις καὶ ἐπαγγελία, ἔχειν τρίβωνα καὶ κόμην, καλῶς ἂν ἔλεγον: εἰ δ᾽ ἐκείνη μᾶλλον, ἀναμάρτητον εἶναι, διὰ τί οὐχὶ διὰ τὸ μὴ πληροῦν τὴν ἐπαγγελίαν ἀφαιροῦνται αὐτὸν τῆς προσηγορίας; οὕτως γὰρ καὶ ἐπὶ τῶν ἄλλων τεχνῶν.

It is within this context of prioritizing inner resolve and its accompanying actions, instead of mere appearances, that Epictetus elsewhere approvingly highlights that the Stoic Euphrates did not (as Epictetus appears to have done[60]) adopt the *dress* of a philosopher, but was instead happy to *live* as a philosopher should.[61] Finally, on this topic I suggest that it is worthwhile to give *Discourse* II.23, which is entitled *To Those Who Read and Dispute/ Declaim for Display* (πρὸς τοὺς ἀναγιγνώσκαοντας καὶ διαλεγομένους ἐπιδεικτικῶς), extended consideration. Within this discourse no epithet is used to describe the type of people who Epictetus has in view, but he portrays them as styling themselves in fine robes, speaking from rostrums that are in spacious and well-attended lecture halls, and humoring their audiences' desires in order to obtain praise (ἐπαινέω) and shouts of "bravo" (οὐά) from them.[62] The discourse is lengthy, but its tone and purpose are well summarized in its closing lines:

> But tell me, who, upon hearing you recite or lecture, has come to be anxious about himself, or turns to look upon himself, or has left saying: "That philosopher has really grabbed hold of me: I must no longer behave as I do?" No, to the contrary, for all that you are in high repute, one man says to another "That bit about Xerxes was neatly expressed," to which the other replies, "No, I found the bit about Thermopylae to be better." Is that what it means to listen to a philosopher?[63]

> ἢ εἰπέ μοι, τίς ἀκούων ἀναγιγνώσκοντός σου ἢ διαλεγομένου περὶ αὑτοῦ ἠγωνίασεν ἢ ἐπεστράφη: εἰς αὑτὸν ἢ ἐξελθὼν εἶπεν ὅτι 'καλῶς μου ἥψατο ὁ φιλόσοφος· οὐκέτι δεῖ ταῦτα ποιεῖν;' οὐχὶ δ᾽, ἂν λίαν εὐδοκιμῇς, λέγει πρός τινα 'κομψῶς ἔφρασεν τὰ περὶ τὸν Ξέρξην,' ἄλλος 'οὔ· ἀλλὰ τὴν ἐπὶ Πύλαις μάχην;' τοῦτό ἐστιν ἀκρόασις φιλοσόφου;

Through inference and direct censure, Epictetus seeks to expose the superficial nature of the envisaged speaker's speech. He asserts that no introspection or anxiousness (ἀγωνιάω) is elicited from the audience regarding their behavior (ποιέω), only amusement at considering the figures and events that happened to be mentioned in the talk. Like with Arius Didymus above, Epictetus therefore expects that a person will not just seek to understand the theoretical points that they have encountered when they listened to an explication of philosophical themes, but they will utilize them to impact their life, here expressed through the language of the individual turning his attention onto himself (περὶ αὑτοῦ ἠγωνίασεν ἢ ἐπεστράφη). Given such qualities, it should not be surprising that Epictetus frequently calls the legitimacy of this hypothetical speaker's philosophical status into question. For example, in response to the speaker's professed intention to obtain a large audience, Epictetus mockingly replies: "Here is the language of a philosopher! Behold the frame of mind of a man who wants to benefit his fellow humankind!" ἰδοὺ φωναὶ φιλοσόφου, ἰδοὺ διάθεσις ὠφελήσοντος ἀνθρώπους, and "who ever heard Socrates say, 'I know something and will teach it'? But instead he used to send people to different instructors," διὰ τοῦτο τίς ἤκουσέ ποτε Σωκράτους λέγοντος ὅτι 'οἶδά τι καὶ διδάσκω'; ἀλλὰ ἄλλον ἀλλαχοῦ ἔπεμπεν.[64] In addition, Epictetus castigates the speaker's intention of seeking to entertain an audience with philosophy, by saying: "Was this what Socrates used to do, or Zeno, or Cleathes?," τοῦτο Σωκράτης ἐποίει, τοῦτο Ζήνων, τοῦτο Κλεάνθης.[65] The mentioning of Zeno and Cleanthes gives this critique a decidedly Stoic point of reference and indicates that the lecturer might profess allegiance to the school. Of further interest is that Epictetus portrays an audience member praising the speaker by saying: "This man writes with more artistic style and in a more finessed manner than Dio's," οὗτος ὁ ἄνθρωπος πάνυ τεχνικώτατα γράφει, Δίωνος πολὺ κάλλιον, and later the lecturer himself proudly notes the size of his audience by exclaiming: "Dio never had so great an audience," Δίωνος οὐδέποτ' ἤκουσαν τοσοῦτοι.[66]

The Dio who produces skillful writings, and who attracts a large audience is doubtless none other than Dio Chrysostom, Epictetus' contemporary, who combined eloquent oratory with philosophical content that was largely drawn from the Stoic-Cynic tradition. Given that Dio is (apart from individuals who are cited as historical exempla) the only person who is named within the critique, and the audience and hypothetical speaker are presented as assessing the standards of public declamations and writing style against his example, if this discourse does not intend to directly attack Dio, it certainly includes him within its ambit. This means that the person who it was noted at the start of this chapter voices his irritation at individuals who falsely lay claim to being philosophers, here is cited by Epictetus as being a representative of this very phenomenon.

Although it is not my intention to comment upon whether Epictetus' portrayal of the philosophical depth and purpose of Dio's speeches and writings are warranted, it should be noted that with Dio having begun his career as a sophist and then apparently having a dramatic conversion to philosophy,[67] this made him a sort of hybrid figure whose identity was, and indeed is, notoriously hard to define.[68] Dio's frequent critiques of inadequate philosophers (which will be reflected upon below again in more detail) and his reflection upon the criteria through which they might be exposed probably disclose Dio's sensitivity about *himself* being subject to the type of criticism that Epictetus raises in this passage.[69] This discourse, therefore, has salience both for apprehending the moral dimension of ancient philosophical identity, and also, as per my argument above, in highlighting its often fluid and contested nature.

In conclusion, from the passages that are assembled above, the expectation of suitably moral behavior from adherents of philosophy is hopefully evident, yet despite the injunctions against inappropriate conduct and charges against falsely called philosophers that sound from ancient texts, we should be cautious in understanding how deviation from a philosophical school's teaching would, in reality, determine a person's ability to associate themselves with it. All schools acknowledged that their adherents would have to strive to make moral progress, and (as will be explored in more detail in chapter 2) this stance is particularly prominent in Stoicism: while perfection in disposition and conduct was the prescriptive ideal, they conceded that such an objective was out of reach of many, if not all, people. True virtue was instead believed by the Stoics to alone belong to the sage, a rare and perhaps nonexistent figure, with most of humanity being fortunate if they could make some measure of moral progress. As Epictetus plainly states: "So is it possible to be entirely free from fault? No, that is not possible; but it is possible to strive persistently to not commit faults," τί οὖν; δυνατὸν ἀναμάρτητον ἤδη εἶναι; ἀμήχανον, ἀλλ' ἐκεῖνο δυνατὸν πρὸς τὸ μὴ ἁμαρτάνειν τετάσθαι διηνεκῶ.[70] Meanwhile the academic philosopher Cicero similarly articulates: "Now, the men we live with are not perfect and ideally wise, but men who do very well, if there be found in them but the semblance of virtue," *Quoniam autem vivitur non cum perfectis hominibus planeque sapientibus, sed cum iis, in quibus praeclare agitur si sunt simulacra virtutis.*[71]

It is, therefore, likely that only the most egregious or unashamed vicious behavior would lead to questions being raised over the legitimacy of a person's claimed affiliation with a school. In this regard we might commend in passing Philostratus' gracious comments regarding the Stoic Euphrates, who momentarily lost his temper, and that this should not effecting the renown in which he should be held.[72] Furthermore, although it was noted earlier that Epictetus asserts that because of their misplaced desire for pleasure that most of his students are the devotees of the rival philosophical system of Epicureanism, he raises this not as a reason for them to conclude their studies, but to rather spur them to rededicate themselves to Stoicism.[73] Of further interest, it can be observed that while in several passages Marcus Aurelius associates himself with the study of philosophy,[74] he also discloses that he is free from the conceit that he has succeeded in living as a philosopher should.[75] Correct praxis is, therefore, a vital, although perhaps subjective, criterion through which the legitimacy of a person's adherence to a philosophical school would be determined.

Regarding people who vocationally instructed others in philosophy, it appears, however, that there was a more pressing concern to ascertain whether their teaching was primarily intending to meet their audience's desire for entertainment, or to engender their moral introspection and self-improvement. The latter demands would, as per Epictetus' critique of the hypothetical speaker that was noted above, likely be established on the basis of the tone of the lecture's discussions, the presence of overt exhortations in their speeches for their audience to seek the moral reform of their lives, and in assessing the lasting effects that exposure to their remarks had upon their listeners' behavior. Furthermore, as it will be further clarified when I explore Epictetus' interaction with laypeople, when trying to ascertain if an individual was suited to *begin* receiving philosophical instruction and to commence their efforts to be impacted by it, then the prospective student's willingness and capacity to align their behavior with philosophical principles becomes a key criterion against which their inclusion or exclusion into philosophical circles would be evaluated.

KNOWLEDGE AND PHILOSOPHICAL IDENTITY

Although they were formulated to enable the ethical improvement of people, with the notable exception of Cynicism,[76] ancient philosophies were intellectually rigorous and demanding systems of thought. In ancient culture, and especially within the Greek East, where education was held in high regard, obtaining mastery over a philosophical school's doctrines and texts and especially receiving formal instruction from one of its professional exponents were often held to be the acme of a person's educational career.[77] The means of gaining a high level of education in antiquity, however, extended beyond philosophy, and schools of thought that were devoted to explore subjects such as medicine and rhetoric also vied to attract the desirant erudite.[78] The sense of distinction that people could feel after completing such a high level of training in one of these schools has often been noted by ancient writers and scholars,[79] as is the small number of individuals whose circumstances could permit them to undertake such an extended period of contemplation.[80] The scenario that the rhetorician Dionysius of Halicarnassus (ca. 60–7 BCE) documents, when a man who was unknown to him ventured to outline his opinion regarding a topic in rhetoric in his presence, is also, I suggest, particularly revealing:

> Now initially I supposed that the person who had ventured to make this statement was an ordinary layperson, and I advised you not to pay attention to every paradox you heard.[81]

> κατ' ἀρχὰς μὲν οὖν ὑπελάμβανον τῶν πολλῶν τινα εἶναι τὸν ταῦτ' ἐπιχειρήσαντα λέγειν, καὶ παρῄνουν σοι μὴ πᾶσι τοῖς παραδόξοις προσέχειν.

After first advising his students to largely ignore the visitor, upon apprehending that this man is not actually one "of the many" (τῶν πολλῶν), but that he has received enough education to allow him to discourse knowledgably on this subject, Dionysius gives way to listen to him and intimates that his students can do likewise. Therefore, despite this visitor having no personal connections with Dionysius or his circle of students, once known, his training enabled him to gain a positive reception from this group.

Similarly demonstrating how knowledge can be used to establish or preclude inclusion into intellectual circles, Philostratus records that Polemo (the third head of the Platonic school) likewise had a concern to exclude nonexpert opinion from being voiced within his school,[82] while Lucian describes the situation of a philosopher who bore jealously/ill-will (φθονέω) when someone else became a philosopher because he knew he would have to treat him as his equal (ἴσος) in future disputations. Plutarch meanwhile records that because the associates of the poet Aratus judged that he was inexperienced (ἀπειρία) in philosophical study, they tried to prevent him from publicly dialoguing with others on philosophical themes.[83]

With regards to philosophy and its scholarly expectations, depending upon the particular school of affiliation, over the course of several years[84] a student might have to gain familiarity and openly discourse on a wide range of topics as diverse as epistemology, cosmology, mathematics, and the correct manner of parsing of syllogisms and paradoxes, and show their comprehension of an ever-expanding corpus of texts and commentaries.[85] Memorably, regarding the extended duration of study that philosophy's pupils are expected to undertake, Lucian's *Hermotimus* depicts with satirical license one student of Stoicism bemoaning that after twenty years of learning he has only *just* started traversing the long, infrequently traveled, and sweat-inducing road, and exclaiming that:

> philosophy is unattainable even over a long period, unless you are very much awake all the time and keep a stern glaring eye on her. The venture is for no mere trifle—whether to perish miserably in the vulgar rabble of the common herd or to find happiness through philosophy.[86]

> φιλοσοφία δὲ καὶ μακρῷ τῷ χρόνῳ ἀνέφικτος, ἢν μὴ πάνυ τις ἐγρηγορότως ἀτενὲς ἀεὶ καὶ γοργὸν ἀποβλέπῃ ἐς αὐτήν, καὶ τὸ κινδύνευμα οὐ περὶ μικρῶν, ἢ ἄθλιον εἶναι ἐν τῷ πολλῷ τῶν ἰδιωτῶν συρφετῷ παραπολόμενον ἢ εὐδαιμονῆσαι φιλοσοφήσαντα.

Meanwhile, the first to second century CE Pythagorean and possibly Stoic-influenced[87] allegorical work known as the *Tablet of Cebes* compares philosophical instruction to be like an arduous physical journey. It portrays the road to true education as being a rocky, trackless wasteland that forces its travelers to climb up a high hill that has a narrow ascent and that features dangerously deep precipices on either side.[88] Eventually, the author claims, only if the two sisters named "self-control" and "perseverance" come down and lift the traveler up can those on the journey hope to reach their desired destination.[89]

The speech of philosophical students was also expected to be carefully honed, with, as Allen Hilton has reflected,[90] the reputed proper use of diction and pronunciation being one of the first features that was taken to signify whether a person was educated or not. Hilton, for example, highlights that the poet Ausonius refers to "a scholar's accent" (*doctis accentibus*),[91] and that Sextus Empiricus remarks on the characteristic difference in speech that differentiates the learned (πιλολόγοι) and laypeople (ιδιῶται).[92] It might be further added that Aupelius valuably reflects upon the type of speech that was expected to emanate from a philosopher's lips, stating: "the philosopher's reasoning and speaking are to be continuous in time, solemn to the ear, profitable to the mind, and polyphonous in tone" (*sed enim philosophi ratio et oratio tempore iugis est et auditu uenerabilis et intellectu utilis et modo omnicana*).[93] In addition, the expectation that a philosopher will have been coached to speak in a well-ordered way (εὐφυής), and to clearly (καθαρός) read in the style of the philosopher(s) they are reading or discussing is also highlighted by Epictetus and Seneca.[94]

Given such a demanding series of skills and intellectual requirements, it is no wonder that philosophy's students are frequently portrayed in classical literature as remaining awake throughout the night so they can devote themselves to their studies,[95] and depicted as trembling when they have to speak in front of their fellow students.[96] Epictetus, for example, imagines one of his students sitting in a lecture and reflecting: "What are my people at home saying about me? Right now they are thinking that I am advancing in my studies, and they are saying 'He will come back knowing *everything*,'" τί λέγουσιν οἱ ἐκεῖ ἄνθρωποι περὶ ἐμοῦ; νῦν οἴονταί με προκόπτειν καὶ λέγουσιν ὅτι ἥξει ἐκεῖνος πάντα εἰδώς.[97] In this regard, it can be observed that the complexity of Stoicism in particular is remarked upon by individuals from within as well as from outside of the school (and is reflected upon by modern scholars too[98]). Epictetus himself notes the difficulties that people can have in understanding philosophical thought[99]; for example, regarding discussing philosophical themes, he states: "These are technical terms, which are tiresome for the non-philosopher and difficult for them to comprehend, and yet for our part we are unable to dispense with them," ῥήματα τεχνικὰ καὶ διὰ τοῦτο τοῖς ἰδιώταις φορτικὰ καὶ δυσπαρακολούθητα, ὧν ἡμεῖς ἀποστῆναι οὐ δυνάμεθα, and, so, Epictetus continues to reflect, they are unable to move him.[100] He elsewhere notes that if an individual in his school reveals insufficient comprehension, then they risk exposing themselves to ridicule from their fellow students; refers to the study of philosophy as being serious/demanding work (συσπουδάζω); and notably, after having apprehended what his tuition under Epictetus will entail, one of his pupils is recorded as exclaiming: "But this requires long preparation, and much effort and study." To which the philosopher pointedly replies: "So what? Do you believe that the greatest of arts can be acquired with little study?" ἀλλὰ πολλῆς ἔχει χρείαν παρασκευῆς καὶ πόνου πολλοῦ καὶ μαθημάτων . . . τί οὖν; ἐλπίζεις ὅτι τὴν μεγίστην τέχνην ἀπὸ ὀλίγων ἔστιν ἀναλαβεῖν.[101] Such is the effort that Epictetus is trying to convey to this pupil that he should expend the noun he uses which is rendered as "much effort," πόνος, usually designates hard, painful labor, and even physical distress. Meanwhile, in another passage Epictetus chides a person who has evidently only engaged in the self-study of philosophy, and emphasizes to him that extended periods of learning under a vocational teacher, and a deep rather than a casual knowledge of a school's texts and tenets are required before he can legitimately stake his claim to be a philosopher:

> What did you do at school then, what did you hear? What did you learn? Why do you mark yourself down as being a philosopher when you might have recorded the reality, saying, "I have studied a few introductory works and have read a bit of Chrysippus, but I have never even approached the door of a philosopher."[102]

> τί οὖν ἐν τῇ σχολῇ ἐποίεις, τί ἤκουες, τί ἐμάνθανες; τί σαυτὸν φιλόσοφον ἐπέγραφες ἐξὸν τὰ ὄντα ἐπιγράφειν; ὅτι ʼεἰσαγωγὰς ἔπραξάς τινας καὶ Χρυσίππεια ἀνέγνων, φιλοσόφου δʼ οὐδὲ θύραν παρῆλθον.

The verb above, ἐπιγράφω, "putting down," is commonly used in the sense of someone inscribing something, usually on stone, or, less commonly, to publicly attach one's name to something. It is clear, therefore, that Epictetus is intending to portray this person who has only a passing interest with philosophy, as attempting to formally have their identity as a philosopher be recognized, something that Epictetus strongly contests. Intending to lead someone to reach a similar conclusion, Dio Chrysostom asks an unnamed dialogue partner what he would think of an individual who professes to be a huntsman, but who has no equipment that would allow him to engage in the activity; or a musician who neglects to ever pick up an instrument; or an astronomer who exchanges time contemplating the science to pursue gambling? When Dio's imagined interlocutor replies that he would not believe these people to be genuine practitioners of their proclaimed arts/area of expertise, Dio similarly argues that if a person were to claim that they are a philosopher a thousand times, even in front of a public assembly or kings, it is of no matter, for:

> there are certain words which one who goes in for philosophy must hear, and studies which he must pursue, and a regimen to which he must adhere, and, in a word, one kind of life belongs to the philosopher and another to the majority of mankind.[103]

> Ἀλλὰ δὴ καὶ λόγοι τινές εἰσιν ὧν δεῖ τὸν φιλοσοφοῦντα ἀκούειν, καὶ μαθήματα ἃ δεῖ μανθάνειν, καὶ δίαιτα ἣν δεῖ διαιτᾶσθαι, καὶ καθόλου βίος ἄλλος μὲν τοῦ φιλοσοφοῦντος.

Through the above statement and the analogies he provides, Dio intends to argue that just as being a hunter, musician, or astronomer requires dedication and the use of certain resources, so does being a philosopher: in this case, firstly having access to philosophical teaching and literature, and devoting enough attention to them until its idioms and technicalities become known, and, secondly, adopting a pattern of behavior that is distinct from the bulk of humanity's. Dio's stance that the philosopher should have a different type of life (βίος) to the layperson's is further seen from the phrase which is translated above as "regimen to which he must adhere," δίαιτα ἥν δεῖ διαιτᾶσθαι. When δίαιτα is used in the middle voice, as it is here, it almost always refers to a person having a mode of life in which there are continually operative rules that guide their behavior, not just that they happen to have a particular routine.[104] In this passage there is, therefore, the two requisite criteria for philosophical identity that have been outlined in this chapter being openly reflected upon.

It is perhaps worthwhile at this point to note that the listing of the ethical and intellectual demands for philosophers together is, to my knowledge, expressly commented upon in at least three other classical authors' writings, which, due to space constraints and a fear of laboring what is hopefully an already substantiated point, I will not detail in depth. The first example comes from Apuleius (ca. 124–170 CE), who expresses a wish (that was referenced near the start of this chapter) that an edict regarding the identity of philosophers would be issued so that the (1) inexperienced (*imperitus*) (2) and/or base (*sordidus*) claimants of the title would be exposed for punishment.[105] Alcinous' (ca. second century CE) stipulation that philosophy's students should show a capacity for intellectual endeavor and also be of virtuous disposition provides us with a second relevant text.[106] Finally, for our interest is Lucian's (125–180 CE) portrayal of the competition for the chair of Peripatetic philosophy in Athens during the reign of Marcus Aurelius, where, firstly, the candidates' doctrinal familiarity and, secondly, their actions are portrayed as being held up against their school's teachings.[107] These passages hopefully show that the criteria for philosophical inclusion that have been explored in this chapter are not just evident with hindsight, but were recognized and utilized by people at the time.

Finally, it is worthwhile to note that during the course of this discussion two conclusions have been reached whose ability to sit alongside each other might require some explanation. On the one hand, it has been argued that during the time of the Roman Empire philosophical identity was imprecise and flexible, yet, contrastingly, that obtaining it necessitated that significant and robust criteria should be met. In order to ascertain how this dynamic worked, I suggest that we might consider two types of individuals who could have tried to gain inclusion into philosophical circles. Firstly, if evaluating a person who has an apparent deficiency in their intellectual capacity or moral character, then the criteria by which philosophical communities define themselves would appear to be solid and well defined, indeed almost able to be perfunctorily applied. Secondly, should another candidate for affiliation but whose attributes appear ambiguous, then it is found that the means of determining their inclusion or exclusion within a school appear to lose their power of precision, and the issue suddenly becomes a matter of subjective interpretation. When placed within this context, philosophical identity during the time of the late Roman Republic and Empire should not, therefore, be thought to be nebulous, but it apprehended that when effort is made to plot its boundary lines with exactitude, then they suddenly seem to lose their clarity.

In this regard, it might be usefully highlighted that in her study of Libanius' (314–394 CE) school of rhetoric, Raffaella Cribiore draws upon the work of the classicist Fritz Pedersen, which explores Imperial-era attitudes toward professional qualifications, especially for political and military posts, and wherein Pedersen argues that the evaluation of potential candidates was largely carried out in an informal and person-person basis.[108] Drawing upon insights from Fritz's work and the extant records of Libanius' school, Cribiore argues:

> modern concepts of competence do not apply to the ancient world, and that con-
> siderations of training and efficiency emerge only sporadically and unsystem-
> atically . . . testing [in the schools] was largely informal and thus escapes sure
> detection . . . [there is a] lack of formal examinations and the seeming absence of
> precise and objective criteria of evaluation in ancient [rhetorical] education.[109]

Such a situation should, I propose, be understood by scholars to also characterize the ancient evaluation of philosophical identity.

PHILOSOPHICAL OUTSIDERS

It can be observed that the lengthy process of study that philosophy required and the change in attitudes/worldview that it could provoke in its adherents would often instill a sense of affinity between respective schools' pupils.[110] For example, Dio Chrysostom reflects that philosophers believe themselves to be superior (διαφέρω) in morals to those around them, while Lucian can portray a philosopher (of seemingly Stoic allegiance) promising a prospective student that philosophy could make him one citizen (πολίτης) of many who lived in a different and higher state.[111] Appealing to an equally strong concept, Plutarch asserts that because of their similar training in philosophy, even people who live centuries apart can display a similarity in outlook and behavior that bespeaks of a shared kinship, while, expressing a similar outlook, Apuleius can refer to the *"Platonica familia."*[112] Both Plutarch's and

Apuleius' remarks align with research which has posited that despite the disparate location of Platonic adherents across the Roman Empire, they existed in a "textual community," where their allegiance to Platonic texts and practice of similar intellectual pursuits provided them with a shared identity.[113] In addition, it might be noted that although it has not been widely deliberated in scholarly discussions, there is evidence that some schools' students (including the Stoics') might have adopted a shared dress code.[114]

The feeling of connection to fellow adherents and the exacting scholastic demands of philosophical study naturally created a divide between individuals who were and were not familiar with deep philosophical thought. A frequent way in antiquity to refer to people who were not philosophers was to employ the word ἰδιώτης. Ἰδιώτης has two primary meanings: firstly, a private as opposed to a political person, and, secondly, someone who lacks familiarity or skill in a certain activity or field of expertise.

Regarding the first use, ἰδιώτης is frequently utilized in ancient literature to designate someone who does not hold political office. When used in this sense, ἰδιώτης is obviously being employed in a way that places it outside of the concerns of this book. It should, however, be noted that while ἰδιώτης might be used to signal a person's lesser status in comparison with an individual who holds political office, scholars have noted that it does not often appear to carry derogatory connotations.[115]

With regards to its second meaning, the ignorance or inabilities of ἰδιῶται in relation to, for example, the skills of military officers, physicians, orators, craftsmen, sophists, and philosophers is also frequently described in classical literature.[116] When used in this way ἰδιώτης can again sometimes seem to lack derogatory intention, for example when it is employed to refer to people who were not part of early Christian circles.[117] More often than not, however, when ἰδιώτης is used in ancient literature to negate someone's skill, experience, or knowledge, then demeaning descriptions of their capabilities or intelligence are attendant,[118] and ἰδιῶταί are referenced in order to set up a contrast with and amplify the talents of the skilled or cultured.[119]

As it was noted in the Introduction, aside from ἰδιῶται, words that relate to crowds, the masses, or humanity in general (such as δήμῳ, the people of a country/the general masses; ὄχλος, crowd/throng; οἱ πολλοί, the many) are also frequently used by classical authors as a way to describe people who lack philosophical education or awareness.[120] Regarding Latin, the Greek word ἰδιώτης was transliterated into the language as *idiota*, and was commonly used to designate an individual who was ignorant of a particular area of study, whether that be science, philosophy rhetoric, etc.[121] The language of crowds or the commonality of humanity could also be appealed to by Latin writers to refer to generally (and especially philosophically) uneducated people.[122]

Turning now to explore Epictetus' portrayal of laypeople, where it will be seen that many of the words and concepts that have been earlier looked at are employed, we can note that even a quick perusal of his discussions discloses that he holds there is a marked difference between the lay majority and the few philosophically minded members of society, so, for example, he clearly opines at one stage:

only a small number of us [incline] towards the divine and the blessed. And since every person must by necessity deal with each matter in accordance with the belief that they hold regarding it, the few of us who think that they are born for fidelity, self-respect, and confidence in their use of impressions, will entertain no abject or ignoble thought about themselves, while the majority of people will think the opposite.[123]

ὀλίγοι δέ τινες ἐπὶ τὴν θείαν καὶ μακαρίαν. ἐπειδὴ τοίνυν ἀνάγκη πάνθ᾽ ὁντινοῦν οὕτως ἑκάστῳ χρῆσθαι ὡς ἂν περὶ αὐτοῦ ὑπολάβῃ, ἐκεῖνοι μὲν οἱ ὀλίγοι, ὅσοι πρὸς πίστιν οἴονται γεγονέναι καὶ πρὸς αἰδῶ καὶ πρὸς ἀσφάλειαν τῆς χρήσεως τῶν φαντασιῶν, οὐδὲν ταπεινὸν οὐδ᾽ ἀγεννὲς ἐνθυμοῦνται περὶ αὑτῶν, οἱ δὲ πολλοὶ τἀναντία.

Here the few (ὀλίγοι), namely the philosophers, are openly contrasted against the multitude (πολλοὶ)—the nonphilosophers. Utilizing the same language, Epictetus elsewhere compares philosophers to be like a small (ὀλίγοι) number of people who attend a cattle market to observe and reflect upon the procedures that govern its operation, but who find themselves being laughed at by the bemused multitude (πολλοὶ):

Only a few people come with the purpose of looking at the fair, and observe how it is organized, who set it up and for what purpose. . . . Few are those who attend the fair because they enjoy looking on considering it . . . and what is the result? They are mocked by the multitude.[124]

ὀλίγοι δέ τινές εἰσιν οἱ κατὰ θέαν ἐρχόμενοι τῆς πανηγύρεως, πῶς τοῦτο γίνεται καὶ διὰ τί καὶ τίνες οἱ τιθέντες τὴν πανήγυριν καὶ ἐπὶ τίνι . . . ὀλίγοι δ᾽ εἰσὶν οἱ πανηγυρίζοντες ἄνθρωποι φιλοθεάμονες . . . τί οὖν; καταγελῶνται ὑπὸ τῶν πολλῶν.

Often though Epictetus' estimation of the narrow constitution of philosophically observant/aware members of humanity is relayed through his employment of analogies, such as his appeal for his listeners to consider philosophers to be like the narrow line of purple is in a senatorial toga (the *latus clavus*) in comparison to the color white which that chiefly constitutes the garment, and that he depicts as representing the nonphilosophically minded majority of society.[125]

Although Epictetus cautions that hostility should never be directed toward laypeople as their vices are the result of ignorance,[126] he consistently uses evocative language to describe them, such as referring to them as being confused, ignorant, wretched, miserable, children, slaves and fools, and deluded.[127] He also consistently presents laypeople as being the antithesis of the philosopher,[128] candidly stating, for example, to his pupils: "you must assume either the stance of a philosopher or that of a layperson," τοῦτ᾽ ἔστι φιλοσόφου στάσιν ἔχειν ἢ ἰδιώτου.[129] An important point to highlight here is that his advocacy for his students to assume the same attitude (στάσις, standing state) of either a philosopher or a layperson is framed around moral rather than intellectual attributes, specifically whether his students' ruling faculties (ἡγεμονικόι) and desires are for the things that are inside of them/concerning them (περί), rather than outside (ἔξω), that is, to be focused upon internal attributes rather than external circumstances or appearances. As our preceding discussion would suggest, here it is clearly seen that in Epictetus' estimation being a layperson is not solely based upon whether the individual in view is ignorant of philosophy's doctrines, but also if they neglect to let these principles impact their life.[130] Similarly, it can be observed that he considers the status of being educated, παιδευομένοις, to include a person's successful implementation of philosophical teachings into their daily life, as he defines "to be properly educated," ὄντι παιδευομένοις, to be marked by an individual's possession of "tranquility, fearlessness, freedom," ἀταραξία, ἀφοβία, ἐλευθερία.[131] If readers miss this point, however, they might conclude that Epictetus makes perplexing, perhaps even contradictory, statements, such as that a person who has learned about syllogisms and eythmemes, but who is conceited/puffed up, χαυνόω, is uneducated, ἀπαίδευτος.[132] This position can unfortunately sometimes be obscured in commonly utilized translations. For example, in *Diss.* II.1.2 there is no contextual reason for rendering ἰδιώτης as "illiterate" as Hard does,[133] especially since ἰδιώτης is not synonymous with the word αγράμματος that normally carries this meaning.[134] When we are attuned to Epictetus' perspective that philosophical education incorporates both intellectual and moral criteria, we realize that the ἰδιώτης in this passage in fact might just as easily be a highly schooled individual, but one who does not understand how, or who refuses to let their actions accord with the philosophical principles they have learned.

Returning to consider the broader point about Epictetus' portrayal of laypeople, it can be noted that in another passage he can present a firm distinction as existing between them and philosophers, for instance by averring:

> It is proper that for laypeople to inquire of you philosophers, just as people who come to a strange city do of the citizens who are acquainted with the area, to ask you what is the best thing in the world, so when we have heard what it is we may seek it out and look at it, as visitors to cities do.[135]

ἄξιον, ἔφη, τοὺς ἰδιώτας ἡμᾶς παρ' ὑμῶν τῶν φιλοσόφων πυνθάνεσθαι, καθάπερ τοὺς εἰς ξένην πόλιν ἐλθόντας παρὰ τῶν πολιτῶν καὶ εἰδότων, τί κράτιστόν ἐστιν ἐν κόσμῳ, ἵνα καὶ αὐτοὶ ἱστορήσαντες μετίωμεν, ὡς ἐκεῖνοι τὰ ἐν ταῖς πόλεσι, καὶ θεώμεθα.

In the above passage, philosophers are again pictured as being individuals who look and evaluate the world in a way that differentiates them from the nonphilosopher, a theme that Epictetus reprises in another discourse in which he labels the masses as being deluded (τὸ δ' ἐξαπατῶν τοὺς πολλοὺς τοῦτ' ἔστιν) and, elsewhere, when he reflects that they view philosophy and its paradoxes in a similar light to how an individual who has no medical knowledge might bemusedly look upon a physician who attempts to cure someone's blindness by poking a lancet in their eye.[136] In this regard, Epictetus elsewhere reflects upon the mutual confusion (φύρω) that can arise between philosophers and laypeople (ἰδιῶται) if they enter into dialogue with each other, with, he suggests, the nonphilosopher finding philosophical concepts to be obscure (δυσπαρακολούθητος) and to be vulgar/repulsive (φορτικός), while the philosopher is apt to revile (λοιδορέω) and openly laugh (καταγελάω) at their conversation partner and exclaim: "he is a layperson; there is no making anything of him," 'ἰδιώτης ἐστίν: οὐκ ἔστιν αὐτῷ χρήσασθαι.[137] Bearing this context in mind, it can surely be understood why Epictetus repeatedly feels the need to caution his students against entering into discussions on philosophical topics with laypeople,[138] and at one point argues that if they recognize a person cannot understand or won't accept philosophical truths, then they should hold their silence rather than announcing their views and prompting animus to occur. He similarly advises that they should clap along with laypeople as they enjoy their festivals instead of attempting to prompt a shift in their perception of the world.[139] Epictetus even goes so far, as the following chapter will explore in more depth, to advise his students to limit their contact with nonphilosophically informed individuals, for example stating: "I would advise you to use discretion when involving yourselves with non-philosophers," συμβουλεύω ὑμῖν εὐλαβῶς τοῖς ἰδιώταις συγκαταβαίνειν,[140] and "avoid parties that are hosted by non-philosophers, but if you do have occasion to go, be sure that you don't slip back into a non-philosopher's frame of mind," ἑστιάσεις τὰς ἔξω καὶ ἰδιωτικὰς διακρούου: ἐὰν δέ ποτε γίνηται καιρός, ἐντετάσθω σοι ἡ προσοχή, μήποτε ἄρα ὑπορρυῇς εἰς ἰδιωτισμόν.[141]

Notably, one of Epictetus' students is also depicted as admitting that he is reluctant to conform to the behavior that Epictetus expects from him because of the opposition that this could arouse in members of the public (as later Marcus Aurelius will also reflect upon[142]), arguing:

Yes, but if I should place the good here, amongst things that lie within the sphere of choice, everyone will mock me. Some grey-haired old man with his fingers covered with gold rings will come up and shake his head, saying: "Listen to me, child, yes you should practice philosophy, but do not get carried away. This is ridiculous. You learn syllogisms from the philosophers, but you know better than they how you should act in life."[143]

ναί: ἀλλ᾽ ἂν ἐνταῦθά που θῶ τὸ ἀγαθόν, ἐν τοῖς προαιρετικοῖς, πάντες μου καταγελάσονται.ἥξει τις γέρων πολιὸς χρυσοῦς δακτυλίους ἔχων πολλούς, εἶτα ἐπισείσας τὴν κεφαλὴν ἐρεῖ "ἄκουσόν μου, τέκνον: δεῖ μὲν καὶ φιλοσοφεῖν, δεῖ δὲ καὶ ἐγκέφαλον ἔχειν: ταῦτα μωρά ἐστιν. σὺ παρὰ τῶν φιλοσόφων μανθάνεις συλλογισμόν, τί δέ σοι ποιητέον ἐστίν, σὺ κάλλιον οἶδας ἢ οἱ φιλόσοφοι.

Finally, when his students raise their concern that people who lack a background in philosophy might judge them to be impious, Epictetus responds (in strikingly similar language to others philosophers,[144] including one who was on trial a few decades later in this very circumstance[145]) by again contrasting the value of philosophical and lay thought, and arguing for the latter's redundancy:

So, who is this person who has been given the power to pass such a judgement on you? Does he know what piety or impiety actually is? Has he studied and learned of it? Where? From whom? . . . The truly educated person is under no obligation to pay any heed to the uneducated one when he passes judgement on what is religious or irreligious, just and unjust.[146]

οὗτος οὖν τίς ποτε ὁ ἔχων ἐξουσίαν τοῦ ἀποφήνασθαί τι περὶ σοῦ; οἶδεν τί ἐστι τὸ εὐσεβὲς ἢ τὸ ἀσεβές; μεμελέτηκεν αὐτό; μεμάθηκεν; ποῦ; παρὰ τίνι; . . . ὁ δὲ ταῖς ἀληθείαις πεπαιδευμένος ἀνθρώπου ἀπαιδεύτου ἐπιστραφήσεται ἐπικρίνοντός τι περὶ ὁσίου καὶ ἀνοσίου καὶ ἀδίκου καὶ δικαίου.

It is important to highlight that the sense of division between philosophers and laypeople could be apprehended and even reinforced by the latter. Epictetus frequently portrays people (including slaves) who lack philosophical education as laughing (καταγελάω) at philosophers, being repelled if they hear that they are ignorant (ἀγνοέω) of what the good (ἀγαθός) is, openly reviling (λοιδορέω) philosophers—even having the propensity to become violent if they are confronted with philosophical exposition.[147] As he warns one of his students:

If you commit yourself to philosophy, prepare from the beginning to be ridiculed and laughed at, to have many people jeering at you and to hear them say, "Look, he has returned to us a philosopher all of a sudden!"[148]

εἰ φιλοσοφίας ἐπιθυμεῖς, παρασκευάζου αὐτόθεν ὡς καταγελασθησόμενος, ὡς καταμωκησομένων σου πολλῶν, ὡς ἐρούντων ὅτι 'ἄφνω φιλόσοφος ἡμῖν ἐπανελήλυθε'.

Less threateningly, Epictetus also notes that laypeople can conclude that philosophy scholars know nothing and speak gibberish (βαρβαρίζω) and advance nonsense (φλυαρέω), or accuse them of adopting a supercilious (ὀφρύς) look,[149] and state that people say, "Nobody gets any benefit from going to [a philosophy] school," οὐδεὶς ὠφελεῖται ἐκ τῆς σχολῆς.[150]

The opinion that laypeople have toward philosophers is a topic that is also frequently reflected upon by a wide range of classical thinkers, such as by the Epicurean Philodemus, Persius (the satirist and one-time pupil of the Stoic philosopher Cornutus), the rhetorician Quintillian, and numerous other authors, who record that people might consider philosophers to be objectionable, miserable, effeminate, fixated upon boring and pointless speculations, believe that philosophical schools provide no benefit and lead people away from right thinking,[151] and, in rather memorable phrasing, hold that each tradition is "dwelling in a separate word-maze of its own construction," καὶ διαφόρους λόγων λαβυρίνθους ἐπινοήσαντες.[152] Furthermore, laypeople are recorded as believing that many of philosophy's students "have assurance and a pose and a gait, and a countenance that is filled with arrogance and a disdain which spares nobody," ἔχοντες θράσος ἔχουσι καὶ σχῆμα καὶ βάδισμα καὶ πρόσωπον ὑπεροψίας καὶ ὀλιγωρίας μεστὸν ἀφειδούσης ἁπάντων.[153]

Because of such derision from certain portions of society, and perhaps especially within a Roman context, Seneca reflects that people are often hesitant to start imitating philosophers in some areas of their life, in case they feel compelled to follow them in everything and end up a fully observant philosopher.[154] This attitude is also documented by Epictetus, and to remarkably involve an individual who apparently did harbor philosophical pretensions:

If you want to know what Romans think of philosophers, just listen to this. Italicus, who was reputed to be amongst the greatest of them as a philosopher, once became angry with his friends in my presence. Claiming that his situation was desperate he proclaimed: "I cannot bear it!" "You are killing me. You will make me just like him"—and he then pointed to me![155]

Πῶς ἔχουσι Ῥωμαῖοι πρὸς φιλοσόφους ἂν θέλῃς γνῶναι, ἄκουσον. Ἰταλικὸς ὁ μάλιστα δοκῶν αὐτῶν φιλόσοφος εἶναι παρόντος ποτέ μου χαλεπήνας τοῖς ἰδίοις, ὡς ἀνήκεστα πάσχων, "Οὐ δύναμαι," ἔφη, "φέρειν: ἀπόλλυτέ με, ποιήσετέ με τοιοῦτον γενέσθαι," δείξας ἐμέ.

Such an attitude is also apparent in the frequently documented phenomenon of Roman parents who attempt to prevent their children from either studying, or from becoming overly preoccupied with philosophy.[156]

Describing a more combative approach, and in one particularly extended portrayal of a layperson's views, Seneca describes someone directly challenging the austere moralizing of philosophers by staunchly advocating that better benefits can be obtained through sensual pleasure such as gluttony, drinking, and adopting a lax attitude toward the disposal of money, that is, the inversion of usual philosophical convictions.[157] Meanwhile, in a depiction of lay opinion Persius notes that the schools' students were widely believed by the public to be fixated upon arcane and useless theories; with him imagining one layperson's withering response after the details of Epicurean cosmology had just been detailed as being:

> "What I know is enough for me. Personally, I have no desire to be like Arcesilas or those troubled Solons with their heads bent, eyes fixed on the ground, while they gnaw their mumbles and rabid silences to themselves and weigh words on their stuck-out lips, repeating the fantasies of some aged invalid: that nothing can come from nothing, that nothing can return to nothing. Is this why you're so pale? Is this the reason for missing lunch?" These jibes make the rabble laugh, and with wrinkled nose the muscular youths redouble their quivering cackles.[158]

> *"quod sapio, satis est mihi. non ego curo esse quod Arcesilas aerumnosique Solones obstipo capite et Agentes lumine terram, murmura cum secum et rabiosa silentia rodunt atque exporrecto trutinantur verba labello, aegroti veteris meditantes somnia, gigni de nihilo nihilum, in nihilum nil posse reverti, hoc est quod palles? cur quis non prandeat hoc est?" his populus ridet, multumque torosa iuventus ingeminat tremulos naso crispante cachinnos.*

A similar reaction to the one above, but with the added threat of violence to ensure that the speaker would refrain from continuing to enunciate philosophical thought, is also described by Tacitus when Rufus apparently tried to introduce ideas of cosmopolitanism to Roman soldiers.[159] Worthy of note is also Dio Chrysostom's comments that the crowds "seize the initiative and abuse and jeer at them [philosophers] as being wretched and foolish, knowing that if they establish them as senseless and mad, they will prove themselves to be self-controlled as intelligent/of sound mind," οὐκοῦν προκαταλαμβάνουσιν αὐτοὶ λοιδοροῦντες καὶ τωθάζοντες ὡς ἀθλίους καὶ ἀνοήτους, εἰδότες ὅτι, εἰ μὲν τούτους ἀποφανοῦσιν ἄφρονας καὶ μαινομένους, ἅμα καὶ αὐτοὺς ἀποδείξουσι σωφρονοῦντας καὶ νοῦν ἔχοντας.[160] The verb προκαταλαμβάνω holds the sense of seizing, or occupying beforehand, and is usually employed in a military context. The sense in this passage is, therefore, of laypeople who attempt to stake out ground to combat and critique philosophers, before the philosophers have a chance to critique them. This two-way derision between philosophers and laypeople is a dynamic that classical authors could directly reflect upon, such as Sextus Empiricus, who states: "Just as the scholar (ὁ φιλόλογος) is ridiculed by laypeople (οι ιδιῶται), so is the layperson (ἡ ἰδιωτική) ridiculed by scholars (οἱ φιλόλογοι)."[161] People who conceived of philosophy and those with an interest in it in the manner that the above sources portray, would doubtless find it a matter of little concern if they found themselves prevented from being able to lay claim to the identity of the philosopher.

Of final interest for us in this section is Lucian's portrayal of someone asking a student of Stoicism to relay philosophical truths to him, but to request that he do so simply, and by adopting the character of a layperson (ὁποῖος τότε ἦσθα ἰδιώτης, "now do so as a layperson"), for he is an outsider (οὕτως ἀπόκριναι) and so cannot easily comprehend the ideas that the student has been coached in.[162] With the use of the verb ἀποκρίνω (to be set apart), we notably have an example of an ancient source which frames the philosopher/layperson divide explicitly in the language of the insider/outsider.

PHILOSOPHERS FROM OTHER SCHOOLS

One topic that has not been touched upon, but which should be mentioned in a discussion of philosophical identity in antiquity is the stance that philosophers took toward people whose allegiances belonged to rival schools of thought, such as Platonic, Peripatetic, Stoic, or Epicurean ones (etc.), and specifically whether they consider such individuals to be genuine philosophers or not. Understanding cross-school opinions of each other is, however, complex for it is rarely a directly addressed topic in ancient texts, and our understanding of respective philosophers' attitudes toward other schools and their members is largely an inferred one.[163] Of potential help for this discussion though are studies which highlight that after the decentralization of the schools as institutions in the first century BCE[164] the historical record often reveals individuals who, while assured and ready to defend the veracity and superiority of their chosen school's viewpoints,[165] are prepared to constructively engage with other philosophies' ideas and writings.[166]

Scholars have frequently observed that this relatively open stance toward other schools' thought is particularly strongly expressed within the Stoic tradition,[167] and that it can be traced back at least as far as Panaetius' and his student Posidonius' (ca. 185–109 BCE/135–51 BCE) apparent respect for and proclivity to cite Platonic and Peripatetic thought.[168]

Exploring this issue firstly with reference to Seneca, numerous studies have also recognized the potential that his large volume of writings have for revealing a member of the Stoic school's attitude to, and possible impact from, other philosophies' propositions.[169] It is not, however, my intention to opine upon Seneca's stance regarding other philosophical schools' thought, which is a debated point and is beyond the scope of this book to address, but to rather highlight that he views them as being a legitimate part of the philosophical community. One helpful indication of his use of other philosophers as dialogue partners that can be profitably drawn attention to is Tuen Tielemans' catalogue of citations that Seneca makes to philosophers, which reveals (with the exclusion of Socrates) that a substantial 170 out of 277 of them are to non-Stoic thinkers, and that Plato and Epicurus (and to a lesser extent Aristotle) receive especially heavy reference.[170]

Given the lack of explicit reflections on the attitude toward other philosophies in our sources, two passages in Seneca's writings are of particular value. In the first, *Ep.* 21.9, after quoting Epicurus counselling his student Idomeneus that he should restrain his desires (*cupiditates*), Seneca remarks that he feels able to appeal to Epicurus' words because he considers them to be "public property" (*publicae sunt*).[171] Seneca then helpfully proceeds to liken this situation to the liberty he has to vote for a senator's motion that he agrees with, without this compelling him to vote for a second that he does not.[172] In other words, if approached with discernment and selectivity, Seneca believes that Epicurus' philosophy can be a resource wherein insight and the useful articulation of truth might be found—or at least in the way that Seneca believes he can constructively frame them.[173]

In the second passage for our interest, *Constant.* 1.1, Seneca asserts that Stoicism and other philosophies make an equal (*tantusdem*) contribution to society (*societas*), but that because of their soft (*mollis*) nature non-Stoic traditions should be compared to females, while the Stoic school is of recognizably manly (*virilis*) character.[174] From this passage it is apparent that Seneca differentiates other schools from Stoicism, and likely considers them to be less effective in their philosophizing, but so too is his belief that they are, in theory, engaged in the same enterprise as Stoicism—namely, philosophical deliberation.[175]

Turning to Marcus Aurelius' *Meditations*, direct reflections on other philosophical schools do not feature within the text, but scholarly interest on whether its contents have been shaped by alternative streams of thought to those of Stoicism have been regularly piqued. The most recent studies that have explored this topic conclude that the influence of other schools upon Marcus' thinking is largely idiomatic and not substantive in nature.[176] No catalogue of the references he makes to non-Stoic philosophers, to my knowledge, exists, but it can be observed that he positively cites the opinions of Epicurus four times, Heraclitus three, Pythagoras and Plato twice, and the Platonist Phocion and Pre-Socratic Empedocles once.[177] This allows us to suggest that Marcus' approach toward other philosophies mirrors Seneca's: both have evidently invested considerable effort to learn about the opinions of other schools, and they consider them to be useful dialogue partners when they deliberate upon philosophical themes, but neither attempts to utilize this interest to try and effect a substantial syncretic or eclectic refashioning of Stoic philosophy.

Regarding Epictetus, compared to Seneca and Marcus there has been less evaluation of his engagement and interaction with different philosophical schools. Deliberation over whether his understanding of theology, psychology, or philosophical contemplation reveals a Platonic imprint can, however, be drawn upon, and where the weight of scholarly opinion rests upon the conclusion that while there is idiomatic influence, Epictetus' views firmly align with traditional Stoic ones.[178] With regards to direct references that Epictetus makes to other schools, the value of Epicurean and Academic strains of thought are particularly heavily critiqued by him,[179] and his brief mention of Peripatetic and Pyhrronic philosophy is also critical in tone.[180] Stephen Williams has noted Epictetus' positive assessment of non-Stoic proponents from ten references he makes to Plato (whom it can be observed Epictetus' teacher Rufus is also recorded as praising[181]) and five to Xenophon.[182] To this list it can be added that Epictetus cites Pythagoras and the Neopythagorean Apollonius approvingly,[183] and in chapter 7 of this book the high estimation he has for several Pre-Socratic thinkers will also be outlined. Comparing Epictetus' interaction with other schools to that of his Stoic counterparts who have been considered above, there is notable congruence in his appreciation of Platonic, Pythagorean, and Pre-Socratic thought, but not Epicurean or Peripatetic philosophy. The differing philosophical preferences that the Stoic thinkers considered above display likely reveals the flexibility they had—which was mentioned at the start of this discussion—to choose what schools or thinkers they could favor to employ as profitable interlocutors in their deliberations.

Although Epictetus does not explicitly expound upon his perception of the identity of non-Stoic philosophers, despite his firm misgivings about Epicurean philosophy that have just been noted, he does refer to a member of the Epicurean school as being a philosopher (φιλόσοφος), and challenges him for (at least in Epictetus' opinion) not properly adhering to the behavior that his school would expect of him.[184] Elsewhere, Epictetus also asks one of his students whether Plato was a philosopher or Hippocrates a physician, with the anticipated reply being an unhesitating yes.[185] Therefore, along with his practice of portraying philosophy in broad terms rather than within scholastic boundaries,[186] and in keeping with the prevailing expectation of the time that value might be extracted from other schools' postulations, it does not appear that Epictetus delimits the identity of being a philosopher only to individuals who are associated with the philosophy of the Stoa.

PHILOSOPHICAL STUDENTS

Before our discussion of philosophical identity is concluded, consideration of philosophical students, whose status is obviously more ambiguous than that of professional teachers should also be briefly addressed. To my knowledge only Michael Trapp has directly addressed this topic,[187] when he suggests (although without further deliberating upon it) that provided that the schools' students abided by their philosophy's ethical standards, they could lay claim to the identity of being philosophers during and after the completion of their philosophical training without much contestation:

> The cohorts of pupils they [professional philosophical teachers] send out into the world, moreover, are "fellow professionals" not primarily in the sense that they will themselves claim the status of educators in their own right (though some of course will), but in taking with them a shared dedication to a style of life, and one that claims to provide the governing framework for everything else that they are and do.[188]

I suggest that Trapp's proposal is indeed correct. Certainly, with regards to Epictetus it has been established here that he regularly frames his students as being included within the confines of philosophy vis-à-vis laypeople who are outside of its boundaries.[189] Furthermore, it has been noted that Epictetus' concern to include students in his school only if they have more than scholastic aims in mind and his frequent advice to them on how they can continue to live according to philosophical principles once their training has ceased certainly implies his expectation that they will have an enduring affiliation with philosophy.[190] On the latter point, he will talk about the moral behavior and philosophical disposition that he expects should mark a person who has come out (ἐκ) of his school.[191] Of additional importance, several remarks in the *Discourses* can be catalogued that reveal Epictetus' students freely identified themselves as being philosophers, which Epictetus does not protest. For example, they are portrayed as discussing who among them is the best philosopher (τίς ἄριστός ἐστι τῶν φιλοσόφων), and Epictetus can even use their self-identifying as philosophers to spur them to evaluate whether they are truly acting as philosophers should,[192] and he notes their frustration if members of the public do not recognize them to be philosophers.[193] Finally, relaying his own stance, Epictetus refers to his being in front of his students to be standing in the company of philosophers (φιλόσοφοι) where the easy relaying of truths can be conveyed.[194]

It would seem, therefore, that for Epictetus provided that a student retains a depth of knowledge about a philosophy's teachings and behaves in-line, or at least not in an notably discordant manner with its moral expectations, then he would view them as being on the philosophical side of the philosopher–layperson divide.

CONCLUSION

In conclusion, with their inability to depend upon institutional or formalized means of verification, the criteria by which philosophers, at least after the rise of Roman power, would usually judge the authenticity of another person's philosophical status are, firstly, their depth of knowledge of their chosen school's tenets, and, secondly, their faithfulness in adhering to its ethical demands. There was, however, no agreed-upon schema that a person could employ to reveal if someone else was a philosopher or not; instead, this evaluation would be decided on a person-person basis and would be prone to variance and be vulnerable to contestation.

Furthermore, a firm distinction is found to have been made by philosophers between people who do, and who do not belong within philosophy's ranks. Some evidence that laypeople could reciprocate by negatively evaluating the characteristics of philosophy, and that they hold philosophers to be engaged in a largely pointless and needlessly austere pursuit has also been found. Finally, it has been revealed that philosophy's students, and adherents from rival schools appear to have been widely held to be legitimate claimants of a philosophical identity.

NOTES

1. See Papas (2015).

2. With regards to the Romans' varied, and occasionally hostile, reception of philosophy, see the discussion in Trapp (2007, 226–257; 2014) and Rivière (2017).

3. Scholarly reflection on this area is, of course, substantial, but in particular see the useful discussions in Rawson (1985, 282–297) and MacGillivray (2012). Sedley (2003a, 186) also asserts: "It is difficult to think of a society where members of the upper class were more generally aware of philosophy than seems to have been the case in Imperial Rome."

4. On philosophical sculpture and art, see Zanker (1995); the touring of philosophical schools, Cicero *Fam.* 13.1.2, *Fin* 1.16, *Brut.* 89.306-91.316, Lucian *Menipp.* 4-5, cf. *Diss.* II.14; and on Roman patrons of philosophy, see Damon (1997,

235–252). On the diffusion of philosophy across Roman society, see the important collection of essays in Vesperini (2017).

5. On abridged philosophical texts, consider Thom (2012), MacGillivray (2015), as well as numerous studies of interest in Horster and Reitz (2010). Regarding the popularity of public talks on philosophy, see the extensive and insightful discussions in Maxwell (2006, 11–41) and Wright (2017, 63–115).

6. See Sedley (2003b).

7. That identifying an ancient philosopher should be done on a case-by-case basis, see Curnow (2006, 1), Trapp (2008, 1, 21), Goulet (2013, 13), and the discussion in Lauwers (2015, 183–190).

8. On this, consider the excellent discussion from (Glucker 1978), as well as from Trapp (2014, 45–47). Ahlholm (2017, 7–15) remarks upon the difficulty we have in establishing whether many epigraphs which depict people as having a philosophical identity were intending to portray themselves as being professional philosophers, or, in Ahlhom's words (2017, 10), rather "intellectual laypeople." For similar reflections, consider also Dillon (2002, 29, 33), Haake (2008, 151), and Lauwers (2015, 27, 265). See also Cicero *Off.* 2.5 and *Tusc.* 1.1 along with the comments of Hine (2015, 15). Barnes (2002, 304) argues that in antiquity the title of philosopher could be used to: "designate non-professionals . . . part-time amateurs, men of diverse talents," while Goulet (2013, 38) notes that poets, musicians, historians, architects, and even shoemakers and barbers (etc.) could identify themselves as being philosophers. Regarding Stoic philosophy, Rist (1982, 23) claims: "Many Stoics had merely read their Stoicism or talked to Stoicizing individuals, and then claimed to be Stoics or desiderant Stoics." In this regard, see also Mann's (2011, 89) insightful comments on the Stoic astronomer Manilius (fl. first century CE).

9. For example, see Lucian *Fug.* 4.14, *Peregr.* 24, *Pisc.* 31; Philostratus *VA* 2.29, 6.3.

10. Respectively, *Or.* 70.10, and 49.12, 70.8, cf. Lucian *Pisc.* 42.

11. *Flor.* 7.9-10.

12. See *Diss.* III.24.41 and also IV.8.16-17.

13. Hine (2015).

14. *Att.* 1.18-31, *Acad.* 1.10, *Fam.* 9.17.2, Hine (2015, 19).

15. Hine (2015, 13).

16. On Seneca presenting himself as a Stoic, see Conradie (2010, 103–105), along with *Constant.* 2.1, and the commentary in Asmis (2015, 224).

17. Hine (2015, 22). See a recent study, Ahlholm (2017), which might cast Hine's proposal into doubt.

18. Hine (2015, 29).

19. On this topic, see especially the reflections of Hadot (1995), Pavie (2012), and Sharpe (2014); and on this aim in the Stoic tradition, see in particular Sellars (2003). Sellars (2007, 117) also usefully states: "For a Stoic such as Epictetus, it seems that philosophy is not merely a matter of words or arguments, but also a matter of deeds or actions. This suggest a conception of philosophy which is quite different from the implicit conception that seems prevalent today." Meanwhile, Reydams-Schils (2010, 567) argues: "Presumably Epictetus would measure his own success as a teacher by the actual moral progress of his pupils."

20. Trapp (2014, 55).

21. E.g. *Diss.* I.1.25; 8.10-16; 12.17.

22. *Epit.*11k, trans. Pomeroy (1999, 81, 83).

23. *Ep.* 53.9, trans. Gummere (1917, 359). See also *Ep.* 106.12, and *Med.* 12.9. On the Stoics' belief in the interconnectedness of contemplation (δόγμα), reason (λογικός), and action (πρακτικός), consider also Diog. Laert. 9.130, along with the comments of Reydams-Schils (2017, 188).

24. Regarding Plato's reputed effect upon Speusippus see *Plut. De frat. Amor* 491f-492a; on Diogenes' effect upon Crates *Apul. Flor.* 14, and *Ep. Diog. Ep.* 9; and on Xenocrates' impact upon Polemo *Diss.* III.1.4, III.11.30, Seneca *Ep.* 108.23, *Horace Sat.* 2.3.253-257, and Diog. Laert. 4.16.

25. On Odysseus holding the Phaeacians spellbound, see *Od.* 2.333-334.

26. *Nigr.* 35, trans. Harmon (1913, 135).

27. See also Plutarch's comments at *Max. princ.* 776c.

28. *Ep.* 6.1, trans. Gummere (1917, 25).

29. *Ep.* 108.1, *Ad Marc.* 4, 13.

30. The most complete consideration of this topic is still Nock (1933, 164–186). Consider as well more recent discussions in Rousseau (1996, 386–387) and Stowers (2011, 231–232), cf. Sedley (1989).

31. For critiques of philosophers who were interested in money, see for example Plutarch *De Tuenda* 16 and Galen *San. Tu.* 16; regarding feasting *Att.* 2.55.d, 3.103.d, 4.163-164, 13.607; sexual deviance Martial *Ep.* 7.58, Juvenal *Sat.* 2.8 13, and Seneca *Ep.* 123.15.

32. See *Ep.* 6.6, and Lucian *Herm.* 21.

33. *Ep.* 29.5-6.

34. For example, *Or.* 31.3 "For no-one is a philosopher who belongs among the unjust and wicked" trans. Cohoon and Crosby (1940, 339): οὐ γάρ ἐστιν οὐδεὶς φιλόσοφος τῶν ἀδίκων καὶ πονηρῶν.

35. *De Frat.* 479E.

36. Respectively *Att.* 13.8.1,4, and 9.2.1.

37. *Att.* 9.2.5.

38. The passage that will be mentioned is actually found at *Diss.* II.19, and not in the first volume of the *Discourses* as Gellius intimates.

39. *Att.* I.2.7-8.

40. Lauwers (2015, 35–36).

41. *Att.* 17.19.

42. *Diss.* III.16.11.

43. *Diss.* II.9.17.

44. *Diss.* III.15.10-12.

45. *Diss.* III.15.1-6. From this passage, as well as *Diss.* I.15.7-8, Hock (1992, 139) argues that Epictetus: "discourages other visitors and students from coming back with warnings about the amount of time it takes to become a philosopher." On the need for prospective philosophers to consider whether they have the stamina to live philosophically, see also *Diss.* IV.8.34-36 and *Ench.* 51.

46. For example, see *Diss.* II.9.13-14 and the study by Hijmans (1959).

47. *Diss.* II.19.20-21, 23. Glucker (1978, 184) remarks on this passage: "The true test of affiliation to a philosophical αἵρεσις, says Epictetus, is whether or not one follows its moral precepts in everyday behaviour—and such a test is true Stoic practice, which would entitle a man to be properly called a Stoic, is described [in this passage]." See also a similar discussion in Sellars (2007, 116–117).

48. For Epictetus's perception that Epicureans seek after hedonism, consider, for example, *Diss.* III.7.2-9.

49. *Diss.* II.19.28.

50. For example, *Diss.* I.8.14, where he appeals to his students: "Why will you not perceive and distinguish what are the things that make men philosophers and what belongs to them on other accounts?": οὐ θέλεις αἰσθάνεσθαι καὶ διακρῖναι κατὰ τί οἱ ἄνθρωποι γίνονται φιλόσοφοι καὶ τίνα ἄλλως αὐτοῖς πάρεστιν. See also *Diss.* IV.9.8, where Epictetus discusses an individual who has exchanged philosophy for a life of vice. Regarding *Diss.* III.15.10-13, Sorabji (2007, 143) reflects that for Epictetus: "If you choose to be a philosopher, then you must change your whole way of life and cannot live like a tax gatherer, an orator, or a procurator of Caesar." Consider also Epictetus' comments at *Fr.* 10.

51. *Diss.* II.13.23, III.5.1-4, 12-17, and 24.78-80.

52. *Diss.* II.21.10.

53. For example, *Diss.* I.28.9; II.17.3; III.10.10-19, 22.66; 23.22, 37-38; IV.4.3, 4.42.

54. *Diss.* I.4.22.

55. See *Diss.* II.914, III.19.4-6, and the discussion in Hijmans (1959, 64–65).

56. *Diss.* II.13.23, 25-26. See also *Diss.* I.1.31.

57. See *Att.* 9.2.8.

58. *Diss.* III.2.11. See the wider discussion at *Diss.* III.2.8-15, and also Epictetus' comments at *Diss.* III.22.80 regarding Cynics, who fail to live up to their calling, as well as similar critiques at Dio. *Or.* 32.9, Lucian *Pisc.* 48, Apuleius *Apol.* 39.39, Julian *Or.* 6.

59. *Diss.* IV.8.5-6. See also Epictetus' comments at *Diss.* IV.8.15-16, Seneca' at *Ep.* 76.31-32, and Dio's comments at *Or.* 49.11, and 70.6.

60. For example, see *Diss.* I.2.24.

61. *Diss.* IV.8.17-20.

62. *Diss.* III.23.1,19,23, 24 27, 35.

63. *Diss.* III.23.37-38.

64. *Diss.* III.23.20, 22.

65. *Diss.* III.23.32.

66. *Diss.* III.23.17, 19.

67. Syn. *Dio* 2-3.

68. For relevant discussions, see Swain (2000 *passim*), Van Sijl (2010, 183–187), and Lauwers (2015, 46–52).

69. For a similar point being made, consider Lauwers (2015, 49).

70. *Diss.* IV.12.19, see also the comments on this passage from Brunt (2013, 169). Consider also Epictetus' comments at *Diss.* I.2.36-37 and III.7.15 in particular, as well as at I.2.34-37; 8.14, II.8.24-25, III.16.9, and *Ench.* 12;13; 48.2-3. Long (2002, 109) comments on Epictetus' "insistence on choosing between the stance of

philosopher or layperson . . . but his purpose in doing so is not to select a philosophical elite or to adopt a censorious attitude toward ordinary people. He acknowledges that he himself is no Socrates, and at the end of this chapter [*Diss.* III.15.8-13]." See also the discussion in Tsalla (2014, 110). From *Diss.* III.25.1-4, Long (2002, 112) also importantly remarks: "When Epictetus speaks in this vein, he mitigates the philosopher/layperson contrast. He includes himself and everyone else in the intermediate category of progressives or aspirants to the ideal happiness promised by philosophy."

71. *De Off.* 1.46, trans. Walsh (2000, 18). See also *Ep.* 6.1, 116.5, *Tranq* 7.4, *Const.* 7.1, Stob. 2.66.14-67,4, Diog. Laert. 7.83, 120, *Fin.* 1.15, *De Off.* I.xv-46, and especially Marcus Aurelius' comments at *M. Aur. Med* 5.10. On Seneca's tripartite division of people who are making progress, see *Ep.* 75.8-18, along with the discussion in Ware (2008, 270) and Brunt (2013, 168). Consider also the fascinating recent study by Jones (2014) that explores Seneca's portrayal of himself as being a hypocrite, wherein she argues that in their discourse Stoics realize that they are describing philosophical ideals to which they have not yet attained.

72. *VA* 1.488.

73. See also a similar passage at *Diss.* II.19.21-28.

74. See my discussion further in this chapter, as well as the discussion in Rist (1982).

75. *M. Aur. Med* 8.1.

76. On Cynicism's lack of sophisticated intellectual content, and the debate in antiquity over whether it should be classed as a αἵρεσις or not, see, for example, Diog. Laert. 1.19, 6.103, *Julian Or.* 6.186B, and the discussion in Branham (2018, 597–602). Regarding Plato's critique of the Cynics, see Papas (2016, 55–57).

77. For example, see Morgan (1998) and Bénatouïl (2006).

78. On such schools consult, for example, Von Staden (1982) and Cribiore (2007). On the competition between philosophy and rhetoric, as well as the Stoic critique of it, see the useful overview in Reydams-Schils (2015, 126), and on Epictetus' criticism of rhetoric *Diss.* III.23.33-38, cf. III.1. On the variance of opinions in antiquity regarding the status of physicians Mattern (2013, 21–27) is useful.

79. On the propensity of education in antiquity to establish a "them and us" divide, see especially the comments from Watts (2006, 1–7) and Johnson (2010, 166–170).

80. See Cicero *De. Part. Orat.* 90; *Tusc.* II.1.4; *Contra Cels.* 1.27.13; *Adv Prax* 3; Lactantius *Div. inst.* 3.25. Carrier (2016, 11–31) estimates that 0.4 percent, or 1 in 250 people in the early Roman Empire would have undertaken higher education. Meanwhile, Brookins (2014, 132–146) argues that at least in urban areas 7–10 percent of the population would have undertaken training in a gymnasium, wherein some limited instruction in philosophy would have likely taken place.

81. *Amm.* 1.1.

82. *VS* 529, and *Herm* 21. See also Dio. *Or.* 32.8 and comments from Eshleman (2012, 44).

83. *Arat.* 5.2.

84. See the discussion in Dillon (2004, 409) and also comments at *Att.* 3.102.a and *Ep.* 108.5.

85. Barnes (2002, 306) briefly avers that a philosopher in antiquity can be recognized from their interest in "logic, physics and ethics and you would recognize them by the congruence between their intellectual interests and those of the Greek masters." On philosophical schools as institutions, and their relationships with their pupils, see, among others, Dorandi (1999), Snyder (2000, 14–121), and Dillon (2002, 2004). See also the fascinating study from Goulet (2013, 33–39). On the range of topics that would likely be included in a Stoic education (and the division between logic, ethics, and physics), and in particular under Epictetus' tutelage, see Long (2002, 97–128) and Cooper (2007, 9–15). On the place of logic especially within Epictetus' school, see *Diss.* I.7.9-12, II.21.20-21, II.25 (*passim*). On Epictetus' students practice of openly deliberating on philosophical themes with each other, see also *Diss.* II.17.34, and 21.11.

86. Lucian *Herm.* 1.

87. See Trapp (1997).

88. *Tab. Cebes* 14.2-3.

89. *Tab. Cebes* 14.3-5.

90. Hilton (2018, 71).

91. *Idyll.* 4.18.22.47-50.

92. *Math.* 233-235.

93. *Flor.* 13.3.

94. *Diss.* III.23; III.21. Seneca. *Ep.* 80.10-11, and see the discussion in Dupont (2017, 171–173).

95. *Pers.* 5.63, *Diss.* II.21.19; IV.4.41, cf. *Diss.* III.15.11.

96. For example, see *Diss.* II.6.4, 17.34.

97. *Diss.* II.21.13.

98. On Manilius' comments at *Astron.* 3.38-39 and his stated satisfaction regarding the impenetrableness of his work, consider the valuable discussion in Bartsch (2015, 166–167). Consider also reflections on the complexities of Stoicism at Cicero *Parad.* 2, Plutarch *De virt. mor.* 449AB, Gellius *Att.* 12.5.6, and discussions at Gowers (1993, 180–181) and Roskam (2005, 16).

99. See *Diss.* I.25.33, II.11.7-14.

100. *Diss.* II.12.10-12.

101. *Diss.* I.20.13. See, respectively, *Diss.* I.26.13-14; 10.13; 20.13. See also *Diss.* I.7.5-12, 30, along with the comments of Dobbin (2007, 115).

102. *Diss.* II.16.34. Regarding Epictetus' frustration at people who cannot properly identify a philosopher, consider *Diss.* I.8.14.

103. *Or.* 70.1.

104. See the useful discussion on the use of δίαιτα in antiquity in Bartoš (2015).

105. *Flor.* 7.9-10.

106. *Epit.*1.52.11-22. On this point, see the discussion in Lauwers and Roskam (2012, 185).

107. *Eun.* 4-5, 9. Regarding this passage, see the useful commentary in Frede (1999, 792) and Eshleman (2012, 36). Consider also *Pl. Sym.* 174 on the selection of Xenocrates to be Speusippus' successor in the academy.

108. Pedersen (1976).

109. Cribiore (2007, 198).

110. On this, see also the reflections of Haake (2015, 76, 78).

111. *Herm.* 21. On the Stoic idea of belonging to a city consider Schofield (1991).

112. *Dion* 1.1. On this passage, see also Trapp (2007, 15), cf. Apul. *Apol.* 64, 536, and Galen *Aff. Pecc. Dig.* II.68.9-10.

113. Boys-Stones (2018, 10) and Baltzly (2014).

114. On this practice with regards to Bion's school, see the valuable comments at Dorandi (1999, 62). At *Herm.* 82, 86, Lucian implies that students of Stoic philosophy might grow their beards to mark themselves out as being philosophers. On the importance of uniforms and shared symbols for social identity theory, see Jenkins (1994, 145).

115. For example, see Plut. *Demetr.* 45, Jos. *BJ* 1.209, *Ath.* 6.78, and Dio *Or.* 1.43.

116. Respectively, *Polyb* 1.69.11, *Thuc* 2.48.3, *Isocr* 4.11, Plato *Theag.* 124c, Xenophon *Hiero* 6, Plu. *Symp* IV.2.3, and Sextus *adv Theag.* 124c.

117. For example, see 1 Cor. 14.16, 23, 24. For further uses of ἰδιώτης that are not derogatory, see also Galen *Affect.* 1 and the discussion in Kraus (1999).

118. For example, see *De Anima* 81.27 and Plut. *Cic.* 26.6.

119. Luc. *Dom.* 2, Plut. *Compar.* 1, and *Ath.* 9.20.

120. For example, respectively, Ps.-Xenophon *Const. Ath.* 1.5, *Rep.* 6.494, 489, *Med.* 11.23. As Maxwell (2006, 16) notes: "aristocratic condescension toward ordinary people is often cited as an indication of the gulf separating elite and mass culture . . . Remarks about 'masses' usually indicate an unquestioned sense of superiority over ordinary people."

121. Stock (1982, 28–29).

122. For example, at *Parat. Orat* 90 Cicero contrasts the *indocti* (uneducated) and *agrestes multi* (uncultured/rustic majority) with the *humani* (well educated) and *politi boni* (good/refined men).

123. *Diss.* I.3.3-4.

124. *Diss.* II.14.23, 25, 39. This analogy appears to have been first used by Pythagoras (Diog. Laert. 8.8, Iamblichis, *V.P.* 12.58-59), from which Fitzgerald (2013, 136) argues that Pythagoras must have "believed that 'philosopher' was sufficient to distinguish the minority who devoted themselves to the contemplation and discovery of nature from the majority who gave themselves to other pursuits."

125. *Diss.* I.2.22. Stephens (2007, 120, 121) significantly comments: "this quotation is essential for establishing that Epictetus believes Stoicism is for the few, not the many. . . . His judgment, which probably derives from empirical observations, is that the multitude judge themselves wretched because they judge their physical condition to be wretched . . . only a rare few, as it turns out, have the prowess to stand out from the crowd like this." See also Epictetus' remarks at *Diss.* III.1.18-19.

126. See. *Diss.* I.18.

127. *Diss.* II.17.5, 21.8, III.23.28, IV.7.32.

128. *Diss.* I.12.35, 27.5; 29.22-23; II.14.2; 17.4; III.16.6-7, *Ench.* 51, and consider especially *Diss.* III.19, a discourse that is entitled "What is the Position of the Layperson, and What That of the Philosopher?" Τίς στάσις ἰδιώτου καὶ φιλοσόφου.

129. *Diss.* III.15.13. Eshleman (2012, 73–74) comments in this regard are worth quoting at length: "Echoing Socrates, he [Epictetus] repeatedly cautions against chasing after the meaningless approval of lay people, which no specialist heeds when it

comes to his own art (2.13.3; 14.2; 4.1.117, 5.22, 12.14). Why would a philosopher care if he is admired by non-philosophers (1.21.3-4; cf. 2.7.4-7, 13.16-19, 2.9.50-4) or despised by the ignorant (4.5.22), whose behavior betrays their incomprehension of true moral value? . . . [For Epictetus] exclusion of lay voices serves to marginalize inappropriate (sophistic, crowd-pleasing) modes of philosophy." See also the discussion in Hock (1993, 139) and Boter (2010, 327–331) and similar comments to Epictetus' from Seneca at *Ep.* 5.6, 7.1-8, 10.5, 20.3, 23.8, 25.7, as well as *Muson.* 18b. Okell (2005, 193), also notes that in Seneca's play *Hercules*: "Hercules is struggling to save mankind from the restriction of fear and tyranny, but mankind (in the form of the chorus) is clearly not interested in being saved or in being heroic."

130. See also *Ench.* 51.

131. *Diss.* II.1.21.

132. *Diss.* I.8.8-7, and I.19.1-2. That Stoics could even characterize philosophers as being ignorant (or ἄγνοια), but due to their lack of consistently upheld correct behavior/mindset, and not because of any epistemic failings, see Cuany (2015).

133. Gill and Hard (1995, 101).

134. See Kraus (1999).

135. *Diss.* III.7.1. See also *Diss.* III.15.8-13 along with the discussion in Hoof (2010, 103).

136. *Diss.* II.17.5, I.25.32-33.

137. *Diss.* II.12.2.

138. Consider especially *Diss.* IV.8.17-24, and *Ench.* 46, 47, cf. *Diss.* II.1.36-39 and 13.22-23. For comments on some of these passages, see Oakes (1993, 53).

139. *Diss.* I.29.31; 26.30-31, see also II.22.36.

140. *Diss.* III.16.9.

141. *Ench.* 33.6.

142. *Med.* 6.35.

143. *Diss.* I.22.18-19.

144. For example, see *Ep.* 91.19, where Seneca approvingly notes that the Cynic Demetrius compares the speech of laypeople to be like the grumbling of the digestive tract. See also the strong language used regarding the views of nonphilosophers' judgments at *Med.* III.4, and Apuleius *Apol.* 39.1.

145. Apuleius *Apol.* 3.6, 27.1.

146. *Diss.* I.29.52, 54. Eshleman (2012, 36 n.63) also draws attention to this passage. See also a similar statement from Epictetus at *Diss.* IV.5.22. Meanwhile, Wildberger (2014b, 309–310) argues from *Ep.* 95.56: "Like Socrates and like his fellow Stoics, Seneca is clearly an intellectualist. For him this means that one must not only practice ethical behavior but seriously study philosophy in order to become a good person." See also *Herm.* 1.

147. Regarding laypeople laughing at philosophers, see *Diss.* I.11.39, III.15.11; III.20.18; on them being repelled II.14.21, III.23.28-30, cf. *Diss.* II.13.4 and IV.8.34-36; and regarding the thread of violence from nonphilosophers, see II.12.24-25, and IV.1.7.

148. *Ench.* 22.

149. Respectively, *Diss.* II.21.11, III.9.14, 20.19; 21.22; *Ench.* 22.

150. *Diss.* II.21.15.

151. For example, Philodemus *Rhet. Fr.* 3, *Pers.* 5.86, Quintillian *Inst.* 12.3.11, *Constant.* 3.1, *Ep.* 73.1, 76.4, Aristoxenus *Harm.* 2.102, Dio *Or.* 66.25, 72.8, *Vit. Auct.* 7.10, *Symp.* 34, *Fug.* 14-15, *Pisc.* 12, 37, *Merc. Cond* 25, *Juv.* 2.8-9, 14-15, and *Diod. Sic.* 2.29.5-6.

152. Lucian *Icar.* 29.

153. Plut. *Virt. prof.* 81.B.

154. *Ep.* 5.3.

155. *Diss.* III.8.7.

156. Horace *Sat.* 1.4.109, Seneca *Ep.* 108.22, Muson. Rufus *Fr.* 16.10, and Tacitus *Agric.* 4.3.

157. *Ep.* 123.10-11.

158. *Pers.* 3.80-89.

159. Tacitus *Hist.* 3.81.1.

160. Dio *Or.* 72.7-8.

161. See also the discussion in Hilton (2018, 27).

162. *Herm.* 15.

163. See though my comments here at p. 14 n.76, regarding the debate over classifying the Cynic school as a philosophical school or not.

164. See again Sedley (2003a).

165. For instance, in his *Epistles* Seneca, to my count, depicts objections being raised to Stoic philosophy on at least five occasions: *Ep.* 74.22, 92.21, 102.8, 121.1, 124. It is hard to ascertain whether his imagined interlocutor belongs to a particular, or any, philosophical school, but informed debates range over topics such as empiricism and the Stoic understanding of *oikeiosis*. For a description, although likely overemphasized for satirical purposes, of philosophers from different schools who turn away from each other in disgust at a dinner party, see *Symp.* 6.

166. For example, see Frede (1999, 783–790) and Hatzimichali (2011, 1–5, 14–20).

167. On this, see in particular Boys-Stones (2001, 99–122), along with the studies of Reydams-Schils (2011) and Long (2013b) and comments by Sellars (2014, 106–108).

168. See Cicero *Tusc.* 1.79, *Fin.* 4.79, Philodemus *Stoic Hist.* 61.2-6, Galen *Php* 4.7, and the discussions in Frede (1999, 777–778) and Tieleman (2007).

169. In recent years, a broad agreement in scholarship has been reached that even if Seneca was idiomatically influenced his philosophy, he does not in any substantive sense borrow from rival philosophies such as Platonism; see Reydams-Schils (2010), Donini (2011), Boys-Stones (2013), and comments from Graver (2015, 192), and especially the studies that Graver cites at 192 n.3.

170. Tieleman (2007, 137). On Seneca's habit of considering Plato's position on a certain topic, see, for example, *Ep.* 58.1 and the discussion in Long (2017, 216–217).

171. *Ep.* 21.9. See also his comments at *Ep.* 12.11, 33.2.

172. For instances where Seneca critiques Epicureanism, see *Ben.* 3.3.4, 4.18.19, *Firm.* 16.5, and *Vit. Beat* 2.4, 3.1.

173. For some debate over Seneca's purpose of regularly citing Epicurus in the early sections of his *Epistles*, and whether we should take his expression of finding

value in Epicurus' remarks at face value, see page n. For similar statements to those at *Constant.* 1.1, see also *Ep.* 12.11, 16.7.

174. *Constant* 1.1. Regarding Seneca's belief in the rigors of the Stoic school, consider also his comments at *Helv.* 12.4 and *Nat. Quest* 2.35.1.

175. *Ep.* 44.2-3, 64.9-10, and on this later passage, see remarks from Conradie (2010, 101–102).

176. On this, see Gourinat (2012, 75–82) and Bénatouïl (2013).

177. Epicurus: *M. Aur. Med* 7.64, 9.41, 11.26; Heraclitus: 4.46, 6.47, 8.3; Pythagoras 6.47, 11.27; Plato: 7.48, 10.23; Phocion: 11.13; Empedocles: 12.3.

178. Long (2002, 156–179), Algra (2007), and Bénatouïl (2013).

179. For example,see *Diss.* I.5; 1.23; 2.20; and 3.7 (*passim*).

180. See *Diss.* II.9.20, 22; 19.20-22, 20 (*passim*), and the discussion in Stanton (1973, 361–363), Snyder (2000, 21), and Boter (2010, 331–333).

181. *Muson.* 10.

182. (Stephens 2002, n.18). For some representative remarks, see *Diss.* I.17.2, II.18.20; and 22.36.

183. *Diss.* III.10.2-5, 12.16.

184. *Diss.* III.7.1, 17-18.

185. *Diss.* I.8.11.

186. For example, see *Diss.* I.1.25; 2.29; and 4.1.

187. Although Glucker (1978, 122) argues: "the title 'Academic philosopher' implies 'a philosopher who has studied at the Academy'—and who, presumably, used this epithet as something similar to our M.A. (Oxon.) or PhD. (Lond.)."

188. Trapp (2008, 9).

189. For example, see *Diss.* I.27.5, 29.22-23, II.12.2-8; 13.3; III.16.6-8, and *Ench.* 51.

190. For example, see *Diss.* I.25.26; 29.33; 30.5, II.1.29.

191. *Diss.* II.1.35-46.

192. Respectively, *Diss.* I.26.15, III.2.10, 15.10.

193. *Diss.* IV.8.23.

194. *Diss.* IV.1.138.

Chapter 2

Limitations on Moral Advancement

In understanding Epictetus' stance regarding the low moral awareness of lay-people, the first topic that I will consider in this chapter is the body. I will then explore his views of the pervasiveness of vice in society, and the significant effort that he believes transitioning from lay status requires.

THE BODY

As is well known, the Stoics believe that human beings are constituted by a blending (ἐγκαταμίγνυμαι) of body and soul, which they hold are both corporeal.[1] For the Stoics, the cosmos can be divided between πνεῦμα (which can be given alternative names such as λόγος, Μοῖραι, θεός, etc.), which is the active, divine, sentient part of the universe, and passive inert matter, which the πνεῦμα structures and sets into motion[2]; or, to use other language, the constituent matter is the substance or substrate through which the πνεῦμα extends. The Stoics hold that the πνεῦμα pervades the entire cosmos,[3] but that it varies from low to high degrees of tension depending upon the type of matter that it is blended with.[4] For example, water and earth are viewed by them to be almost entirely inert, flora and fauna as having a higher degree of pneumatic tension, and matter which displays intelligence and autonomy, that is, animals, to have an even higher pneumatic tension.

Stoics hold that it is within human beings where the highest pneumatic tension in the cosmos can be found (although they believe the outer regions of the cosmos are essentially pure pneuma[5]), and who are uniquely furnished with a rational ruling faculty (the ἡγεμονικόν), which provides us with our ability to exercise reason and to engage in intellectual and introspective thought. The human ἡγεμονικόν is, in fact, understood to be consubstantial with the divine and is defined as being the soul.[6] Whether upon the soul's dislocation from the body upon death it retains, or is aware of the identity it had in its embodied state was a matter of dispute within Stoicism. Cleanthes, Seneca, and Marcus Aurelius appear to be unsure about the issue, but others such as Chrysippus, Cornutus, and Epictetus assert that it is indeed lost, and this position appears to have become associated with the school by its commentators.[7] In this view, how the πνεῦμα reacts or is able to function is believed to depend upon the type of body in which it is blended. For example, as has been recently explored,[8] Chrysippus was of the opinion that should the πνεῦμα of a human happen to be transferred into the body of an animal such as a donkey, the πνεῦμα would animate the donkey, but would be limited to only enable its new host to fulfill the characteristics that cohere with its physical frame, that is, to function as a donkey. The previous capabilities of reasoning and philosophizing that the πνεῦμα was able to fulfill when it was within its human host is understood to be lost.

From the above discussion, it can be seen that the πνεῦμα is responsible for structuring and animating matter, yet that the identity and capabilities of a particular object (be that largely inert matter like soil or highly sophisticated creatures like human beings) also has a material basis, or, in other words, everyone is a composite of their substance/substrate (ὑποκεμενον/οὐσια), and the πνεῦμα which extends throughout it and makes us a peculiarly qualified (ἰδίως ποιόν) thing. This, perhaps confusing, interplay between πνεῦμα and matter, and the resulting characteristics of the objects/creatures they constitute can, I suggest, be profitably clarified by way of an analogy. If we consider that electricity, the energy that activates so many of our modern appliances, is restricted in the effects that it can produce by the physical object it happens to flow through (e.g., the electrons that move through a light bulb filament will produce light and heat, while the electrons that power a radio will permit the reception and conversion of radio waves into sound), we can perhaps get some basic sense of how the Stoics believe the πνεῦμα functions vis-à-vis matter. What the πνεῦμα is able to produce is dependent upon the object in which it happens to find itself blended with. Or as Aiste Celkye notes, "Personal identity, or to use a Stoic term, being a peculiarly qualified individual is grounded in being a compound of a body and a soul."[9] This belief might also, I propose, be disclosed by the Stoics' affirmation of physiognomy, whereby they hold that individuals who have certain physical traits, such as having a broad chest (where some Stoics believe the ἡγεμονικόν resides[10]), find that they have greater control of their emotions.[11]

Narrowing our concentration upon the Stoics' perception of what our existence as embodied human being upon earth entails, it appears that at least for Epictetus the flesh offers the first impediment to peoples' possible moral progress. So he argues:

For since we are on earth, and confined/shackled to an earthly body, and among earthly companions, how could it be possible that, in view of all this we should not be limited by external things? . . . But as things are, you must not forget that this body does not belong to you, but it is only cleverly fashioned clay. Since, then, I could not give you this, I have given you a certain portion of myself, this faculty of exerting the impulse to act and not to act, of desire and aversion, and, in a word, the power of making good use of impressions.[12]

ἐπὶ γῆς γὰρ ὄντας καὶ σώματι συνδεδεμένους τοιούτῳ καὶ κοινωνοῖς τοιούτοις πῶς οἷόν τ᾽ ἦν εἰς ταῦτα ὑπὸ τῶν ἐκτὸς μὴ ἐμποδίζεσθαι; . . . νῦν δέ, μή σε λανθανέτω, τοῦτο οὐκ ἔστιν σόν, ἀλλὰ πηλὸς κομψῶς πεφυραμένος. ἐπεὶ δὲ τοῦτο οὐκ ἠδυνάμην, ἐδώκαμέν σοι μέρος τι ἡμέτερον, τὴν δύναμιν ταύτην τὴν ὁρμητικήν τε καὶ ἀφορμητικὴν καὶ ὀρεκτικήν τε καὶ ἐκκλιτικὴν καὶ ἁπλῶς τὴν χρηστικὴν ταῖς φαντασίαις.

Note his association of the body with the hindering effects it has upon people and the careful language of disassociation he utilizes, especially with regards to conceiving it as an object. He informs his interlocutor that we are bound (συνδέω) to the body, that he should conceive of it as being like finely mixed clay (ἀλλὰ πηλὸς κομψῶς πεφυραμένος), and that it is not really his (τοῦτο οὐκ ἔστιν σόν). It should also be noted that the phrase νῦν δέ employed here usually in classical literature refers to an unreal condition, but is characteristically used by Epictetus as a means of censure, so here is being used to reinforce his critique of his dialogue partner for his erring conception of the body.[13]

Continuing this theme, elsewhere Epictetus remarks:

but since these two elements have been mixed together within us since our creation, a body which we have common with the animals, and reason and good judgement which we have in common with the gods. Many of us tend towards the former kinship, miserable as it is and wholly mortal. . . . Feeble indeed, but you have also something that is better than this paltry flesh. So why do you turn away from this and attach yourself to what is mortal? Because of this kinship with the flesh, some of us tend towards it and become like wolves, faithless, vicious and treacherous; others, like lions, are wild, savage and untamed; but most of us become like foxes, the most unscrupulous of living creatures, or something even less dignified.[14]

ἀλλ᾽ ἐπειδὴ δύο ταῦτα ἐν τῇ γενέσει ἡμῶν ἐγκαταμέμικται, τὸ σῶμα μὲν κοινὸν πρὸς τὰ ζῷα, ὁ λόγος δὲ καὶ ἡ γνώμη κοινὸν πρὸς τοὺς θεούς, ἄλλοι μὲν ἐπὶ ταύτην ἀποκλίνουσιν τὴν συγγένειαν τὴν ἀτυχῆ καὶ νεκράν, . . . τὰ δύστηνά μου σαρκίδια. τῷ μὲν ὄντι δύστηνα, ἀλλὰ ἔχεις τι καὶ κρεῖσσον τῶν σαρκιδίων. τί οὖν ἀφεὶς ἐκεῖνο τούτοις προστέτηκας; Διὰ ταύτην τὴν συγγένειαν οἱ μὲν ἀποκλίναντες λύκοις ὅμοιοι γινόμεθα, ἄπιστοι καὶ ἐπίβουλοι καὶ βλαβεροί, οἱ δὲ λέουσιν, ἄγριοι καὶ θηριώδεις καὶ ἀνήμεροι, οἱ πλείους δ᾽ ἡμῶν ἀλώπεκες καὶ ὡς ἐν ζῴοις ἀτυχήματα.

Through its continuous needs and its vulnerability to register pain and to be placed under subjection,[15] Epictetus believes that the body competes for our attention and obscures our realization that the locus of our concentration should be upon maintaining the freedom of our internal disposition and in furthering the appropriately beneficial aspects of our character. In Epictetus' view, the sensory pleasure that the body registers often compels people who lack philosophical insight to direct their talents, labor, and volition to maximize their physical comfort, and to let their god-given capacity for introspection and reasoning atrophy. It is within this context that Epictetus articulates his opinion that some people resemble unreasoning animals more than they do humans.[16] It is also within this context that he describes the flesh as being wretched, δύστηνος; a little bit of flesh, σαρκίδιον; and to be like a corpse, νεκρός, a word that it is unusual in classical texts to compare the body to, apart from its similar employment in the New Testament corpus.[17] For Epictetus, our flesh has the capacity to make us like a wild (ἄγριος), untamed (θηριώδης), and misfortunate (ἀτύχημα) animal (with the latter being an analogy he frequently employs[18]), and after death we will return to what is akin (συγγενής) to us, in other words our more divine nature, a statement that also seems to significantly imply Epictetus' belief in some incorporeal existence of the soul after death.[19]

From these passages, it can be observed that Epictetus expects his students will conceptualize the body in quite negative terms, emphasizing that, unless they are steeled with the appropriate philosophical training, it will prove to be an inimical force that will act against their desired moral progress. Indeed, at almost every reference that Epictetus makes to the body, he seems to disparage it. For example, when mentioning it instead of using the word σῶμα, he uses the diminutive σωμάτιον, "paltry body," some nineteen times,[20] and he notably recoils at the suggestion that the true constitution of god (οὐσία θεοῦ) is flesh (σάρξ).[21]

What is more significant, though, are passages where Epictetus appears to locate human identity outside of it. So, we can observe his claims: "Our body, therefore, is not our own, its parts are not our own," οὐκοῦν τὸ σῶμα ἀλλότριον, τὰ μέρη αὐτοῦ ἀλλότρια,[22] "my poor body is nothing to me; its parts are nothing to me," τὸ σωμάτιον δὲ οὐδὲν πρὸς ἐμέ: τὰ τούτου μέρη οὐδὲν πρὸς ἐμέ,[23] and his description of a person who is full of vice as merely being a corpse with a pint of blood.[24] Moreover, he asserts that Diogenes of Sinope managed to obtain his laudable stance toward life because he did not consider his body to be his own,[25] and to a student who commented upon Socrates' fate at the hands of the Athenians, Epictetus pointedly replies:

Slave! Why do you say "Socrates"? State the matter as it really is and say: the poor body of Socrates should be arrested and dragged away to prison by those who were stronger than he: that someone should administer hemlock to the paultry body of Socrates; and that it should grow cold and die?[26]

ἀνδράποδον, τί λέγεις τὸ Σωκράτης; ὡς ἔχει τὸ πρᾶγμα λέγε: ἵν᾽ οὖν τὸ Σωκράτους σωμάτιον ἀπαχθῇ καὶ συρῇ ὑπὸ τῶν ἰσχυροτέρων εἰς δεσμωτήριον καὶ κώνειόν τις δῷ τῷ σωματίῳ τῷ Σωκράτους κἀκεῖνο ἀποψυγῇ;

Here, again, the difference between the true identity of a person and the body is made clear in Epictetus' thought: it was the body (little/poor body σωμάτιον) that Socrates inhabited which was afflicted by hemlock—not Socrates himself. At this juncture, we can perhaps draw attention to the fact that Epictetus' chosen word for "slave" for his student is not the more generic δοῦλος, but ἀνδράποδον, a person who has been taken captive and enslaved, usually as a spoil of war. The implication is that Epictetus is wrestling to free his student from an enemy that has imprisoned him, or, using the language of the previous text, the student has lost a fight and has been dominated by their animalistic nature. It is the following remark by Epictetus though (which is preserved in Marcus Aurelius' *Meditations*) by which he seems to most strikingly detach human identity from the body by stating: "'You are a little soul, carrying a corpse,' as Epictetus used to say," ψυχάριον εἶ βαστάζον νεκρόν, ὡς Ἐπίκτητος ἔλεγεν.[27]

Before attempting to understand how, or if, the above statements fit with the Stoic position that humans are a synthesis of body and soul, it is important to note that the appeal to dualistic-sounding language from a Stoic proponent at this time is not unique to Epictetus. Indeed, most of the major Imperial Stoic writers repeatedly issue scornful descriptions of the body. Note, for example, the resonance between Epictetus' and Seneca's claims regarding the body in the following passages:

For this body of ours is a weight upon the soul and its penance; as the load presses down the soul is crushed and is in bondage, unless philosophy has come to its assistance and has bid it take fresh courage by contemplating the universe and has turned it from things earthly to things divine . . . so the soul, imprisoned as it has been in this gloomy and darkened house, seeks the open sky whenever it can, and in the contemplation of the universe finds rest.[28]

Nam corpus hoc animi pondus ac poena est; premente illo urgetur, in vinclis est, nisi accessit philosophia et illum respirare rerum naturae spectaculo iussit et a terrenis ad divina dimisit . . . sic animus in hoc tristi et obscuro domicilio elusus, quotiens potest, apertum petit et in rerum naturae contemplatione requiescit.

This vesture of the body which we see, bones and sinews and the skin that covers us, this face and the hands that serve us and the rest of our human wrappings—these—are but chains and darkness to our souls. By these things the soul is crushed and strangled and stained and, imprisoned in error, is kept far from its true and natural sphere. It constantly struggles against this weight of the flesh in the effort to avoid being dragged back and sunk; it even strives to rise to that place from which it once descended. There eternal peace awaits it when it has passed from earth's dull motley to the vision of all that is pure and bright.[29]

Haec quae vides circumdata nobis, ossa nervos et obductam cutem vultumque et ministras manus et cetera quibus involuti sumus, vincula animorum tenebraeque sunt. Obruitur his, offocatur, inficitur, arcetur a veris et suis in falsa coiectus. Omne illi cum hac gravi carne certamen est, ne abstrahatur et si dat; nititur illo, unde demissus est. Ibi illum aeterna requies manet ex confusis crassisque pura et liquida visentem.

The body is not a permanent dwelling, but a sort of inn (with a brief sojourn at that) which is to be left behind when one perceives that one is a burden to the host.[30]

nec domum esse hoc corpus, sed hospitium, et quidem breve hospitium, quod relinquendum est, ubi te gravem esse hospiti videas.

In these passages, among other things, the body is said to be a weight (*pondus*) that strangles (*offocatur*) and encloses (*arcetur*) the soul in a darkened house, and that the soul strives for open sky but that it remains enfettered. Like Epictetus, Seneca also disdainfully describes the body, portraying it as being like an inn in which the soul is only resident for a brief period, and he finds the language of prisons and chains to be particularly apposite in articulating the impact that he believes the body's presence has upon humans.[31]

In trying to comprehend remarks such as those that are listed above, scholars have argued that they should not be understood to be articulating a form of Platonic dualism, wherein the soul is believed to be noncorporeal, in contrast with the physical, fleshy body. The Stoics' frequent pronouncements that denigrate the flesh, and the placing of the body and soul/mind in the language of dichotomy has rather been understood to be making assessments on where a person's ethical orientation lies. That is to say whether someone feels more affinity to fulfilling the irrational animalistic impulses of the flesh through sensory pleasure, or to honing the talents of their internal (although still physically constituted) divine spark through which their intelligence and rational capabilities are enabled.[32]

While accepting this position, Tad Brennan has, however, persuasively argued that the Stoics could conceptualize the body as being separate from their identity and still hold to their understanding of body-soul holism. Additionally, he has suggested that this concept of our relationship to the body and soul, far from being an Imperial-age innovation and an indication of encroaching Platonism or eclecticism within the school, can be traced back to around the philosophy's inception.[33] So Brennan asserts that in Stoicism the idea of the composition of a person (*systatis*) is

> a principle of composition, a cause of the compounding, or rationale for the structure of the compound . . . and *this* is our self. Not the soul and the body, but rather the soul as a principle of composition for the soul-body compound.[34]

He proceeds to clarify this position by stating:

> When we ask who we are, what our selves are, then the answer is that we are a purely psychic thing, the *systasis* . . . true while the soul is incorporated, it plays the role of organizing the soul-body compound that is the animal, and that is when we call it a *systasis*. But that is to describe it as relatively disposed towards something else, not to say what it is in essence. The body is not part of the *anthropos*, any more than the knife is part of the shoemaker; it is just something that the shoemaker can pick up and put down. The shoemaker has some reason to keep it in good shape—it would surely be irrational for him to neglect or abuse his tools—but the good of those tools is no part of his good since they are no part of him.[35]

If Brennan's suggestion is correct, then it can be seen that the Stoics could sustain the proposition that humans are a mixture of both soul and body along with the assertion that our identity should be solely located with the soul/ πνεῦμα. As will be seen below, Brennan's suggestion finds a lot of textual support. But the question might be rightly raised, if the Stoics hold that our identity should be solely fixed upon our divine, rational ruling center, does this conflict with the conclusion that was reached at the start of this chapter, that they view an individual's characteristics and identity to be the result of the interplay between the πνεῦμα and the body? Such a question would, I suggest, however be to conflate two separate meanings of "identity."

There is the question of how the particular identity we have upon earth is established, and the question of what identity we should conceptualize as being truly ours. As we have seen, for the Stoics what makes us *us* is our ability to employ reason and philosophical insight, qualities that the πνεῦμα retains after its release from the body. The various capabilities and attributes that every individual has which lies outside of their ἡγεμονικόι, and the particular individuals we happen to be, or have been, for example, a male Babylonian-era agrarian laborer, a female member of the first-century Roman nobility, or a twenty-first-century academic, with their various predilections and social contexts in which they lived, are *not* what we should understand as being really ours.

The above viewpoint can also, I suggest, be usefully seen in a passage from Rufus which is not referenced by Brennan, in which he remarks:

> Since a human being happens to be neither soul alone nor body alone, but a composite of these two things, someone in training must pay attention to both. He should, rightly, pay more attention to the better part, namely the soul, but he should also take care of the other part, or part of him will become defective. The philosopher's body also must be well prepared for work because often virtues use it as a necessary tool for the activities of life.[36]

> ἐπεὶ τὸν ἄνθρωπον οὔτε ψυχὴν μόνον εἶναι συμβέβηκεν οὔτε σῶμα μόνον, ἀλλά τι σύνθετον ἐκ τοῖν δυοῖν τούτοιν, ἀνάγκη τὸν ἀσκοῦντα ἀμφοῖν ἐπιμελεῖσθαι, τοῦ μὲν κρείττονος μᾶλλον, ὥσπερ ἄξιον, τουτέστι τῆς ψυχῆς. καὶ θατέρου δέ, εἴ γε μέλλει μηδὲν ἐνδεῶς ἔχειν τοῦ ἀνθρώπου μέρος. δεῖ γὰρ δὴ καὶ τὸ σῶμα παρεσκευάσθαι καλῶς πρὸς τὰ σώματος ἔργα τὸ τοῦ φιλοσοφοῦντος, ὅτι πολλάκις αἱ ἀρεταὶ καταχρῶνται τούτῳ ὄντι ὀργάνῳ ἀναγκαίῳ πρὸς τὰς τοῦ βίου πράξεις.

If not intending to communicate the position that has been outlined above, Rufus' remarks are, at the very least, consonant with it. He asserts that a person is composed of both body and soul, yet he describes the body using decidedly distant terms of reference: according to him, humans are to consider it as being part of us and should seek its maintenance—but only, he cautions, as we would take care of a necessary tool (ὄργανον).[37] If our hypothesis is accurate, then this is precisely the type of imagery we should expect to find proponents of Stoicism utilizing: one that affirms the body is part of us, but that carefully places our identity away from it.[38] Our body just happens to be the transient tool in which the πνεῦμα flows.

This understanding, which separates our true identity from the body, but does not subscribe to Platonic dualism can, I suggest, also be observed in several of Marcus Aurelius' remarks. Like Epictetus and Seneca, he appears to comfortably hold the belief that humans are a composite of soul and body[39] alongside with his evident, and frequently stated, disregard for the flesh and advocacy that we dislocate our true identity away from it.[40] In particular, in the following passage he seems to outline a similar stance to Rufus' above:

> There are three things of which you are composed: body, breath, and mind. Of these, the first two are your own in so far as it is your duty to take care of them; but only the third is your own in the full sense. So if you will put away

from yourself—that is to say, from your mind—all that others do or say, and all that you yourself have done or said, and all that troubles you with regard to the future, and all that belongs to the body which envelops you, and to the breath conjoined with it, or is attached to you independently of your will, and all that the vortex whirling around outside you sweeps in its wake, so that the power of your mind, thus delivered from the bonds of fate, may live a pure and unfettered life alone with itself doing what is just, desiring what comes to pass, and saying what is true—if, I say, you will put away from your ruling center all that accretes to it from the affections of the body.[41]

Τρία ἐστὶν ἐξ ὧν συνέστηκας: σωμάτιον, πνευμάτιον, νοῦς. τούτων τἄλλα μέχρι τοῦ ἐπιμελεῖσθαι δεῖν σά ἐστι, τὸ δὲ τρίτον μόνον κυρίως σόν. ὃ ἐὰν χωρίσῃς ἀπὸ σεαυτοῦ, τουτέστιν ἀπὸ τῆς σῆς διανοίας, ὅσα ἄλλοι ποιοῦσιν ἢ λέγουσιν ἢ ὅσα αὐτὸς ἐποίησας ἢ εἶπας καὶ ὅσα ὡς μέλλοντα ταράσσει σε καὶ ὅσα τοῦ περικειμένου σοι σωματίου ἢ τοῦ συμφύτου πνευματίου ἀπροαίρετα πρόσεστιν καὶ ὅσα ἡ ἔξωθεν περιρρέουσα δίνη ἑλίσσει, ὥστε τῶν συνειμαρμένων ἐξῃρημένην καὶ καθαρὰν τὴν νοερὰν δύναμιν ἀπόλυτον ἐφ᾽ ἑαυτῆς ζῆν, ποιοῦσαν τὰ δίκαια καὶ θέλουσαν τὰ συμβαίνοντα καὶ λέγουσαν τἀληθῆ ἐὰν χωρίσῃς, φημί, τοῦ ἡγεμονικοῦ τούτου τὰ προσηρτημένα ἐκ προσπαθείας.

Again, the belief that humans are an amalgamation/blending (συνίστημι) of body and soul (on his tripartite division of body, breath, and mind see the comments from Gill[42]) is affirmed at the same time as our relation to the body is distanced. Only the soul, Marcus stresses, is ours in the truest sense, and the body merely envelops (περίκειμαι) it.

With this perspective having been clarified, in order for us to form a properly rounded understanding of Epictetus' stance regarding the body, two more remarks from him warrant particular attention.

In the first passage, he describes the body as being like a fetter (δέσμα), and he reveals his concern that, upon gaining cognizance of where their *true* identity lies, his students will attempt to commit suicide (or throw off/reject ἀπορρίπτω their body):

But he should strive that there may not be among you young men who, when they learn of their kinship to the gods, and that we have, as it were, these fetters attached to us, namely the body and its possessions, and all that is required for the management and persistence of life, may throw them aside as being both burdensome and useless, and to depart to their kind.[43]

ἀλλὰ μή τινες ἐμπίπτωσιν τοιοῦτοι νέοι, οἳ ἐπιγνόντες τὴν πρὸς τοὺς θεοὺς συγγένειαν καὶ ὅτι δεσμά τινα ταῦτα προσηρτήμεθα τὸ σῶμα καὶ τὴν κτῆσιν αὐτοῦ καὶ ὅσα τούτων ἕνεκα ἀναγκαῖα ἡμῖν γίνεται εἰς οἰκονομίαν καὶ

ἀναστροφὴν τὴν ἐν τῷ βίῳ, ὡς βάρη τινὰ καὶ ἀνιαρὰ καὶ ἄχρηστα ἀπορρῖψαι
θέλωσιν καὶ ἀπελθεῖν πρὸς τοὺς συγγενεῖς.

Upon death we, that is, the soul, are pictured as being unshackled and
unbound from the body and being loosened from the personality identity
that it held upon earth and to return to its true kindred. The latter, rather
oblique statement, seems to suggest that Epictetus holds that our segment of
the divine will return to the upper parts of the cosmos where it will reside
with other portions of unembodied πνεῦμα.[44] This passage also notably discloses that Epictetus fears that so emphatically expressed were his attempts
to have his students dislocate their identity from their body that they might
attempt to commit suicide. Such a concern does not speak of a philosopher
who is merely using rhetorical flourish when he denigrates the body, or one
who should be understood to be appealing to language that distinguishes the
body and the spirit merely as a way to frame where a person's ethical goals
should be directed—an interpretation that Allan Girdwood has also sought
to critique.[45] When Epictetus, and other Stoic philosophers, assert that our
identity should not to be associated with the body and that we should consider
our flesh to fetter and bind us, they are, in fact, speaking plainly regarding
their views. Additionally, however, his worry that his students might commit
suicide reveals that while Epictetus understands the body to be an inhibiting
and obscuring force, he expects that people will learn to tolerate and struggle
to *overcome* its negative consequences, not (as he fears some might) attempt
to liberate themselves from it by seeking death.

The above lines of thought are also present in another passage where
Epictetus asserts (although in an evidently begrudging tone):

> At any rate we love and take care of our body, which is the most unpleasing
> and the foulest of all things. . . . Truly, it is amazing that we should love a thing
> which demands such daily maintenance. I stuff the sack, then I empty it again.
> What is more troublesome? But I have to serve god, so I remain and put up with
> washing, feeding, and sheltering this miserable body.[46]

> τὸ γοῦν σῶμα, τὸ πάντων ἀηδέστατον καὶ ῥυπαρώτατον, στέργομεν καὶ
> θεραπεύομεν . . . τῷ ὄντι θαυμαστόν ἐστι φιλεῖν πρᾶγμα, ᾧ τοσαῦτα
> λειτουργοῦμεν καθ᾽ ἑκάστην ἡμέραν. νάττω τουτονὶ τὸν θύλακον: εἶτα κενῶ:
> τί τούτου βαρύτερον; ἀλλὰ θεῷ δεῖ με ὑπηρετεῖν. διὰ τοῦτο μένω καὶ ἀνέχομαι
> λούων τὸ δύστηνον τοῦτο σωμάτιον, χορτάζων, σκέπων.

This section of text depicts the body as being a firmly impeding force
and to be filthy (ἀηδέστατον καὶ ῥυπαρώτατον). Furthermore, the body is
again framed in language of dissociation with it described as being like a

sack (θύλακος), and again implicated in catalyzing the spread of vice within humanity. Again, however, notably the conclusion that Epictetus' draws is not that we should ignore our bodily needs, or adopt a position of abject derision or neglect toward the flesh, but rather (and in line with Musonius Rufus and Seneca's advice[47]) that his students should take care of their bodies and keep them clean.

Before concluding my deliberation of the Stoics' view of the body, it is worthwhile to consider how their view of its deleterious effect upon humanity's moral constitution and philosophical awareness might impact some of their other philosophical commitments. In particular, it might be wondered how they could sustain their belief in a providentially ordered and created cosmos.[48] In this regard, following some previous scholarship,[49] James Ware in particular has recently highlighted a strain of thought that existed within Stoicism which acknowledges the negative effects of the flesh and accounts for it as being the result of limitations that constrain divine creativity and its providential intent. Ware observes that this stance can be witnessed in remarks from Chrysippus in his *De Providentia*, wherein the concept of physical evil is explained by him as being a concomitant (κατὰ παρακολούθησιν), or necessary by-product, of divine creation,[50] and also by Seneca, whose remarks across several treatises envisage there being constraints upon divine creativity with regards to the body, and through which he explain its various frailties and the hindering effect it has upon humanity.[51] Significantly, this line of reasoning is also attested in Epictetus' remarks:

> But what does Zeus say? If it were possible Epictetus, I would have made both your little body and your possessions free and unrestricted. As it is though do not be ignorant of this: this body is not really yours, rather it is cleverly fashioned clay. And since I could not give you what I have just said, I have given you a small portion of myself.[52]

> ἀλλὰ τί λέγει ὁ Ζεύς;"Επίκτητε, εἰ οἷόν τε ἦν, καὶ τὸ σωμάτιον ἄν σου καὶ τὸ κτησίδιον ἐποίησα ἐλεύθερον καὶ ἀπαραπόδιστον. νῦν δέ, μή σε λανθανέτω, τοῦτο οὐκ ἔστιν σόν, ἀλλὰ πηλὸς κομψῶς πεφυραμένος. ἐπεὶ δὲ τοῦτο οὐκ ἠδυνάμην, ἐδώκαμέν σοι μέρος τι ἡμέτερον.

Such a view can also, I suggest, be witnessed in Epictetus' remarks that our kinship with the body is unfortunate (ἀτυχέω).[53] These texts reveal that one stance[54] the Stoics took to resolve the tension that existed between their holding to the providential creation of the cosmos and their acknowledgment of the detrimental effects of the body was to posit that there are constraints upon divine creative ability—namely that *god could not but have* created us with our faulty and hindering fleshly constitution. It might be noted that although this position regarding the recalcitrant nature of matter receives explicit textual warrant and resolves how the Stoics maintained their view regarding the encumbering effects of the body with their belief in divine providence, it is unfortunately often not raised in modern accounts of Stoic philosophy.[55]

THE PERVASIVENESS OF VICE

In addition to each member of the human race finding themselves incorporated into flesh, according to Stoicism every individual is destined to proceed through a state of childhood, which is devoid of the guidance of a functioning reasoning faculty,[56] and to emerge with engrained vices and misunderstandings that can only be expunged by conscious exertion.[57] Epictetus frequently reiterates the view that childhood deadens and habituates everyone to enact inappropriate actions/assumptions, and he uses childhood as a cipher for ignorance and irrationality,[58] by, for example, commenting that "we have been long accustomed to do the opposite of what we should, and the opinions that we hold are the opposite of the correct ones," πολλῷ γὰρ χρόνῳ τὰ ἐναντία ποιεῖν εἰθίσμεθα καὶ τὰς ὑπολήψεις τὰς ἐναντίας ταῖς ὀρθαῖς χρηστικὰς ἔχομεν.[59] Elsewhere he remarks:

> We have taken a different route from the beginning. Already when we were still children, if we ever happened to absent-mindedly wander and bump into something, our nurse did not chide us, but instead would strike the stone. Why, what had the stone done? Should it have moved out of its location because of the silliness of a little child? . . . Thus even when we are adults, we resemble infants. For it is a child to be unrefined in matters of culture, unlettered in literary matters, and uneducated in how to live.[60]

> ‘νῦν δ' ἄλλην ὁδὸν ἐξ ἀρχῆς ἐληλύθαμεν. εὐθὺς ἔτι παίδων ἡμῶν ὄντων ἡ τιτθή, εἴ ποτε προσεπταίσαμεν χάσκοντες, οὐχὶ ἡμῖν ἐπέπλησσεν, ἀλλὰ τὸν λίθον ἔτυπτεν. τί γὰρ ἐποίησεν ὁ λίθος; διὰ τὴν τοῦ παιδίου σου μωρίαν ἔδει μεταβῆναι αὐτόν . . . οὕτως καὶ αὐξηθέντες φαινόμεθα παιδία. παῖς γὰρ ἐν μουσικοῖς ὁ ἄμουσος, ἐν γραμματικοῖς ὁ ἀγράμματ[ικ]ος, ἐν βίῳ ὁ ἀπαίδευτος.

Here the negative effects of childhood wherein moral misunderstanding is reinforced by guardians is laid bared, as is the disposition of people who have not educated/trained (ἀπαίδευτος) themselves to reach maturity, and are, in Epictetus' view, therefore in a state of persisting infancy. Such a position was described by Cicero as being as if we drink in error within our nurse's milk.[61] It should be noted, however, that given Epictetus' understanding of the poor moral condition of the surrounding society, it seems he believes that even when people emerge out of childhood with the capacity to use reason, the habits of vice that are now rooted so deeply within them will act to restrict their possible progression, and will require sustained therapeutic action:

> If you apply no remedy, it will no longer return to its previous state, but when it is aroused again by a corresponding impression, it will become inflamed by desire more quickly than before, and through frequent repetitions it will finally become callous. By this infirmity the love of money becomes permanent. For if someone had a fever and then recovered, unless he is perfectly cured he would not be in the same state as before. Something similar happens with the sickness of the mind.[62]

> ἐὰν δὲ μηδὲν προσαγάγῃς εἰς θεραπείαν, οὐκέτι εἰς ταὐτὰ ἐπάνεισιν, ἀλλὰ πάλιν ἐρεθισθὲν ὑπὸ τῆς καταλλήλου φαντασίας θᾶττον ἢ πρότερον ἐξήφθη πρὸς τὴν ἐπιθυμίαν. καὶ τούτου συνεχῶς γινομένου τυλοῦται λοιπὸν καὶ τὸ ἀρρώστημα βεβαιοῖ τὴν φιλαργυρίαν. ὁ γὰρ πυρέξας, εἶτα παυσάμενος οὐχ ὁμοίως ἔχει τῷ πρὸ τοῦ πυρέξαι, ἂν μή τι θεραπευθῇ εἰς ἅπαν. τοιοῦτόν τι καὶ ἐπὶ τῶν τῆς ψυχῆς παθῶν γίνεται.

The effective power of vice, though, is amplified in Epictetus' view by the ease in which people can fall into degradation and the destructive habits.[63] Bad decisions seem to be conceived by Epictetus to set patterns of behavior that people then effortlessly follow, and a vice might become fixed (βεβαιότης) in a person's character, a word that is usually employed in Stoic writings to refer to *virtues* that are fixed, but here used by Epictetus to refer to philosophically suspect modes of conduct. In this regard, as I will explore in chapter 5, it should be noted that the Stoics believe each impression that an individual gives assent to is a conceptual building block which is stored in their memory and effects the tension (τόνος) of their ruling faculty, and, as a result, comes to influence their use of future impressions—either for the better or for the worse.[64] Epictetus memorably reflects upon this by comparing instances of mistaken assent to a person who is being flogged which at first causes weals, but then wounds which cannot always be healed.[65] In this light we can understand why he reinforces to his students the need they have to be constantly vigilant against slipping into error by comparing them to a ship's captain, whose only momentary lapse in concentration could result in the destruction of what has been entrusted to his care.[66]

The conception that vice is a pervasive and largely unchallenged presence in society also explains Epictetus' consistently iterated advice to his students that it would benefit them if they removed themselves from various aspects of the surrounding world, and in particular from their circle of friends and from associating with laypeople.[67] In this context, Epictetus relays the story of one of his students who came to reject philosophy and who replaced his copies of the works of Zeno and Chrysippus for the poetry of Aristides and Euenus, and the esteem he once had for Socrates and Diogenes to admire the serial seducers of women.[68] Upon his previous student's transition, Epictetus bemoans: "But formerly you did not ever think of any of these things, but only where you could locate a decent discourse, a person of merit, a noble thought," πρότερον δ' οὐδὲ ἐνεθυμοῦ τι τούτων, ἀλλὰ ποῦ εὐσχήμων λόγος, ἀνὴρ ἀξιόλογος, ἐνθύμημα γενναῖον.[69] In another passage, we also learn of Epictetus' correct prediction that a person would renege from their professed philosophical commitments upon his return to Rome.[70] We can, therefore, perhaps better apprehend Epictetus' regularly stated concern that his students will descend into immoral behavior once they vacate his classroom,[71] his begrudging acceptance that new students of philosophy will find they are unable to refuse the advances of a pretty young girl,[72] and why he presents his students with the ultimatum to choose between their compatriots or their devotion to philosophy:

> Formerly, by setting your heart entirely on worthless pursuits, your friends found you agreeable. But you cannot excel in both courses, for in so far as you engage in one, you will necessarily fall short in the other. If you no longer drink with the people whom you drank with before, you cannot appear equally agreeable to them. Decide, then, whether you want to be a drunkard and pleasing to those people, or sober and unpleasing to them.[73]

> πρότερον γὰρ εἰλικρινῶς ἐφιέμενος τῶν οὐδενὸς ἀξίων ἡδὺς ἦς τοῖς συνοῦσιν. οὐ δύνασαι δ' ἐν ἀμφοτέρῳ τῷ εἴδει διενεγκεῖν: ἀλλ' ἀνάγκη, καθόσον ἂν τοῦ ἑτέρου κοινωνῇς, ἀπολείπεσθαί σ' ἐν θατέρῳ. οὐ δύνασαι μὴ πίνων μεθ' ὧν ἔπινες ὁμοίως ἡδὺς αὐτοῖς φαίνεσθαι: ἑλοῦ οὖν, πότερον μεθυστὴς εἶναι θέλεις καὶ ἡδὺς ἐκείνοις ἢ νήφων ἀηδής.

Implicit in this demand is the divergence he holds exists in the ethical positions of people who are undergoing philosophical education and laypeople, with the latter, of course, constituting the largest section of society, and whose behavior and customs he believes are competing to gain his students' attention.[74] For Epictetus, those pupils who wish to keep their development secure must, it seems, take firm steps to incubate themselves from the surrounding corruption and temptations of society which are so marred by error.

THE NEED FOR STUDY AND APPLICATION

As will be explored in more depth in the following chapter, the stance in Stoicism regarding the installation of reason in humanity does not signify belief in the immutable and continuing awakening of right reasoning in people, but only the *capacity* for it.[75] This is a crucial distinction for, properly understood, the Stoics' stance regarding humanity's possession of reason and rationality tells us little about their opinion of the effectuation of it across society. This fact is clearly outlined when Epictetus informs a father who had accompanied his son to one of his lectures that wisdom cannot be obtained by merely desiring its possession, but instead by committing oneself to a lengthy period of learning and reflection:

> Probably, then, it is not sufficient in this case to merely want to become a wise and virtuous person, but in addition it is necessary to learn certain things. So we must endeavor to ascertain what these things are.[76]

> μή ποτ' οὖν καὶ ἐνθάδε οὐκ ἀπαρκεῖτὸ βούλεσθαι καλὸν καὶ ἀγαθὸν γενέσθαι, χρεία δὲ καὶ μαθεῖν τινα; ζητοῦμεν οὐντίνα ταῦτα.

From this passage, and others,[77] it is again evident that although Epictetus believes that humanity has been invested with the preconceptions and capacity that are needed for leading a virtuous life, actualizing this potential depends upon the volition and resolve of each individual. It can be noted, as I will detail at some length in chapter 5, that at *Diss.* I.22.1-8 Epictetus indeed argues that the noticeably vacillating and contradictory positions that are adopted by individuals and societies on what is good and beneficial demonstrate that innate preconceptions on their own are insufficient to enable people to reach correct opinions. They rather need to be augmented and exercised by an accurate philosophical schema before they can be appropriately utilized. For Epictetus, a prerequisite for establishing this architecture in an individual's mind is their acquisition of logical skills; so, he remarks:

> You must learn how one thing follows from a single thing, and sometimes from several premises together. It is also necessary that a person should gain this skill if he is to conduct himself intelligently in discussion, to enable him to establish each of his points in succession, to comprehend the demonstrations of others, and to not be deceived by people who put forward sophistries as if they were proof? This has given rise among us the study and practice of inferential arguments and logical figures, both of which have proven themselves to be indispensable.[78]

> δεῖ δὲ μαθεῖν πῶς τί τισιν ἀκόλουθον γίνεται καὶ ποτὲ μὲν ἐν ἑνὶ ἀκολουθεῖ, ποτὲ δὲ πλείοσιν κοινῇ. μήποτε οὖν καὶ τοῦτο ἀνάγκη προσλαβεῖν τὸν μέλλοντα ἐν λόγῳ συνετῶς ἀναστραφήσεσθαι καὶ αὐτόν τ' ἀποδείξειν ἕκαστα ἀποδόντα καὶ τοῖς ἀποδεικνύουσι παρακολουθήσειν μηδ' ὑπὸ τῶν σοφιζομένων διαπλανηθήσεσθαι ὡς ἀποδεικνυόντων; οὐκοῦν ἐλήλυθεν ἡμῖν περὶ τῶν συναγόντων λόγων καὶτρόπων πραγματεία καὶ γυμνασία καὶ ἀναγκαία πέφηνεν.

Epictetus' belief that facility in logic and analytical dexterity are required for undertaking philosophical study highlights that, for him, philosophy extends beyond mere rote learning, or the comprehension of various speculative theorems. It is instead, as A. A. Long notes, a "hermeneutic activity,"[79] and one that depends upon numerous skills, insights, and dispositions being honed to work together before appropriate actions or thoughts can be hoped to be accurately apprehended.

As for where, and from whom, instruction on obtaining this skill set might be gleaned, we should not be surprised given Epictetus' vocation as a professional teacher of philosophy that he stipulates it should be handed on/transmitted (παράδοσις) and dispensed through words (λόγοι).[80]

Meanwhile, when responding to someone who asked why it was that progress in his philosophical training was alluding him, Epictetus relays that advancement in philosophy depends both upon a person's ability and, further, the guidance of a skilled teacher who can coach them to maturity. From this passage, it can be again seen that the philosophical process is thought by Epictetus to be one that requires instruction from a teacher to be given. Elsewhere, he remarks upon the necessity of being educated through the spoken word and instruction,[81] and he appeals to an unknown addressee to: "instead of attending on a rich old man, attend a philosopher, and be seen around his doors. You will not get any shame by being seen there, and you will not return unedified or empty, provided that you approach him as you should," θεράπευσον ἀντὶ γέροντος πλουσίου φιλόσοφον, περὶ θύρας ὄφθηται τὰς τούτου· οὐκ ἀσχημονήσεις ὀφθείς, οὐκ ἀπελεύσῃ κενὸς οὐδ᾽ ἀκερδής, ἂν ὡς δεῖ προσέλθῃς.[82] His belief that philosophical training is pivotal in establishing a life that is lived in consonance with nature, in fact, led Epictetus at one point to almost deify the role of the philosopher when he advises his audience to provide as much attention to their utterances as they would to an oracle's pronouncements.[83]

The structure and contents of the course of pedagogy that we might expect a student in Epictetus' school to have undergone is hard to ascertain. Arrian's recollection of Epictetus' teachings demonstrates his evident emphasis on delivering practical and exhortative discourses,[84] but many of the features that are common in classical philosophical treatises are notably absent.[85] There are, for example, no lengthy excursions that detail or appraise intricate theories of cosmology, theology, or societal/political structures. As most commentators on Epictetus are, however, apt to caution,[86] concluding that he holds the more technical aspects of philosophical tuition to be superfluous would almost certainly be a mistake. Throughout the *Discourses*, there are numerous allusions and references to conventional facets of philosophical instruction that took place within the school, such as the exegeting of the works of prominent Stoic thinkers,[87] solving syllogisms,[88] committing philosophical precepts to memory,[89] and reflecting upon the lives of the morally upright.[90]

A key pedagogical concern for Epictetus though seems to be to furnish his students with the techniques (or exercises, γυμνάζομεν[91]) that they need to allow them to apply philosophical principles to their lives. So, when confronted with a corrupting impression (φαντασία), that is to say an idea or perception that can either be assented to or denied, Epictetus argues that assent should not be given:

> but rather, you should introduce some fair and honorable impression to replace it, and cast out this improper and sordid one. If you become habituated to this type of exercise, you will see what shoulders, what muscles and what stamina you will acquire.[92]

> ἀλλὰ μᾶλλον ἄλλην τινὰ ἀντεισάγαγε καλὴν καὶγ ἐνναίαν φαντασίαν καὶ ταύτην τὴν ῥυπαρὰν ἔκβαλε. κἂν ἐθισθῇς οὕτως γυμνάζεσθαι, ὄψει, οἷοι ὦμοι γίνονται, οἷα νεῦρα, οἷοι τόνοι.

To understand the importance of this concern, we need, as was noted in the introduction, to realize that Epictetus (and, indeed, most philosophers of the Classical world) would hold that philosophy would be distorted if it is reduced to merely center around the retention of knowledge, and that its therapeutic power would be accordingly emasculated. As was noted in the opening chapter, its success was instead to be evaluated by its ability to effect a change in its adherents' behavior. This meant that to be properly formed by philosophy its pupils needed to possess skills that went beyond mere analytical aptitude, with them being expected to be able to continually observe and interpret how to apply the school's principles in their lives and to maintain an unbaiting level of introspection.[93] It was, in fact, thought vital that students learn to internalize and apply philosophy's teachings throughout every event and thought of their life. In this regard, Epictetus comments on the need for both learning and practical application to work in conjunction:

> This is why philosophers recommend that we be not content with mere learning but that we should add practice too. For we have grown accustomed for a long time to practice the opposite of what we should, and the opinions we maintain and apply are the inverse of the right ones. If, therefore, we do not adopt and apply the correct opinions, we will be nothing more than the interpreters of other peoples' judgements.[94]

> διὰ τοῦτο παραγγέλλουσιν οἱ φιλόσοφοι μὴ ἀρκεῖσθαι μόνῳ τῷ μαθεῖν, ἀλλὰ καὶ μελέτην προσλαμβάνειν, εἶτα ἄσκησιν. πολλῷ γὰρ χρόνῳ τὰ ἐναντία ποιεῖν εἰθίσμεθα καὶ τὰς ὑπολήψεις τὰς ἐναντίας ταῖς ὀρθαῖς χρηστικὰς ἔχομεν. ἂν οὖν μὴκαὶ τὰς ὀρθὰς χρηστικὰς ποιήσωμεν, οὐδὲν ἄλλο ἢ ἐξηγηταὶ ἐσόμεθα ἀλλοτρίων δογμάτων.

To avoid merely being an interpreter (ἐξηγητής) of philosophical thought, a person should, Epictetus advises, be prepared to exercise and practice putting philosophical principles into action. It should be noted that the later verb (μέλω) usually holds the meaning of "give attention to," but when used in the infinite, as it is here, it holds the idea of "practice," but connotes the idea of doing so with due care. As was noted in the previous chapter, Epictetus consistently rebukes pupils who chose to determine their success by how much of Chrysippus they have read,[95] or how well they can impress guests at banquets by their fluid recitation of philosophical theories.[96] As he states to an unnamed dialogue partner:

> Never have you desired to achieve serenity, impassibility, and peace of mind; never have you approached any teacher with this as your goal, but instead approach many for the sake of learning about syllogisms. Never have you examined any of these impressions by asking yourself, "Can I bear this, or not?" "What have I still to face?" . . . Should you not have begun by acquiring something from reason and securing it?[97]

> οὐδέποτε δ᾿εὐσταθείας ὠρέχθης, ἀταραξίας, ἀπαθείας: οὐδένα τούτου ἕνεκα ἐθεράπευσας, συλλογισμῶν δ᾿ ἕνεκα πολλούς: οὐδέποτε τούτων τινὰ τῶν φαντασιῶν διεβασάνισας αὐτὸς ἐπὶ σεαυτοῦ ῾δύναμαι φέρειν ἢ οὐ δύναμαι; τί μοι τὸ λοιπόνἐστιν; . . . οὐκ ἔδει προσκτήσασθαι πρῶτον ἐκ τοῦ λόγου, εἶτα τούτῳ περιποιεῖν τὴν ἀσφάλειαν;

According to Epictetus, it is not the learning of syllogisms that should concern this person, but rather how he should live his life. Epictetus' intention is to prevent the situation that Cicero describes where people listen to lectures on Stoic thought, come to understand and voice support for them, but leave being morally unchanged.[98] Attempting to meet this challenge, schools from across the dogmatic divide developed exercises to help their students align themselves with the practical implications of their philosophy's teachings.[99] Many of these techniques are referred to in the records of Epictetus' discussions, such as the use of mnemonic maxims and aids (of which the *Enchiridion*, a collection of maxims, is probably the best example from within the Stoic tradition),[100] role-playing,[101] and the selection of role models.[102] In this light, Epictetus' comments at *Diss.* III.26.39, where he mentions exercises alongside discourse and reading as being components of his students' education might be usefully cited.

After setting out this context, we can perhaps appreciate why Epictetus so readily compares the effort that is needed to successfully undertake a philosophical education to the training that is required to become a soldier or an athlete.[103] We are also, perhaps, in a better position to comprehend his remarks in several places where he opines that in order to become a philosopher, individuals should have expendable leisure time, such as his statement that "Whose concern is it, then, to examine these matters? The person who has leisure," ταῦτα οὖν τίνος ἐστὶ θεωρεῖν; τοῦσχολάζοντος.[104] An idea that he restates when he argues that the learning of philosophy must be done by one who has the ability and the leisure to do so (ἀλλὰ τὸν δυνάμενον τὸν σχολάζοντα).[105] With reference to the Stoic school more broadly, although its members held that virtue is in theory open to everyone,[106] the recognition that given the intellectual effort and time that was required to pursue a philosophical education meant that wealth/resources (χορηγία) were usually required was stated since at least the time of Panaetius and Posidonius, of whom Diogenes Laertius records: "Yet Panaetius and Posidonius say that virtue is not self-sufficient, claiming that strength, health, and material resources are also needed," ὁ μέντοι Παναίτιος καὶ Ποσειδώνιος οὐκ αὐτάρκη λέγουσι τὴν ἀρετήν, ἀλλὰ χρείαν εἶναί φασι καὶ ὑγιείας καὶ χορηγίας καὶ ἰσχύος.[107] There is evidence that Seneca was, at least in principle, reluctant to accept this, as is seen by his statement that virtue can be gained by kings and slaves, as well as by people who are not materially well-off such as Cleanthes, who did menial jobs to support himself while he learned philosophy—which I should note Epictetus does also reference in passing.[108] In exploring this issue, Peter Brunt surely correctly concludes that Seneca's remarks "can hardly be taken as realistic, especially given Seneca's own description of the knowledge the wise man will possess . . . we get the practical conclusion that wisdom and virtue are only thing the reach of those who can afford education."[109]

As Brunt intimates, the position of Stoics such as Panaetius, Posidonius, and Epictetus should not be taken to be a concession to elitism, but to rather express their pragmatic assessment, which mirrored the largely settled conclusion in the Roman era,[110] that philosophy is only accessible to a slender minority of people who have the time and financial means which are required to successfully consider its detailed theorems and texts. In this regard, the association between Stoicism and the materially rich is a phenomenon that, for instance, the Roman satirist Horace pokes fun at with his reference to Stoic books that rest upon the silk cushions of the elite.[111] Indeed, judging from the concerns and activities of Epictetus' student base and those of his visitors, which revolve around advising and frequenting with Caesar (*Diss.* IV.1.6, 47), visiting gymnasiums (*Diss.* III.16.14), their intention to gain reputation (*Diss.* I.1.14), their ownership of slaves (*Diss.* IV.7.39-40), fearing the weight of responsibility that will fall upon them when they gain public office (*Diss.* I.19.24, IV.4.19), and their having been raised by nurses, pedagogues, and cooks, and being disappointed at the quality of baths in Nicopolis (*Diss.* II.16.39, III.19.4-5, II.21.15), it is obvious that Epictetus was tutoring some of the empire's most privileged individuals. Also of relevance in this regard is that his critique of contemporary Cynics as being charlatans, has recently been profitably assessed by Marie-Odile Goulet-Cazé as testifying to Epictetus' position "against the uneducated who didn't have the benefit of παιδεία."[112] At this point, it should be noted that Epictetus' background as a slave, although sometimes raised by commentators to show the accessibility of Stoic philosophy outside of elite circles is, of course, questionable. Epictetus was a member of one of the most influential household of the empire, and he appears to have been afforded significant free time, education, and the ability to frequent and comprehend philosophical lectures while he was still a slave.[113] In this light we should note that the existence of highly trained slaves who assisted in the managing of aristocratic households and estates is well attested in antiquity, as is the high status that this position afforded them.[114] This makes Epictetus decidedly not an individual who can be referenced as representing an underprivileged stratum of Roman society,[115] and their inclusion within philosophical education.

In conclusion, Epictetus holds that the challenge of the pervasive presence and the normalization of vice across society, which is aided by the body and the acceptance of childish misapprehension, and the difficulty in obtaining a philosophical education that can counter these deleterious influences, makes gaining moral progress hard to achieve. Whether those people who do not or cannot gain philosophical awareness through which they might modify their lives are believed by Epictetus (and the Stoics more broadly) to be left without any moral direction or aid is an issue that I shall now turn to consider. It is a question that is, to my knowledge, best articulated and left open by Peter Brunt, when, with reference to the opinions of Seneca, he pondered that in the Stoic view:

> if philosophical instruction is the one path to virtue, it is [then] barred to the illiterate, and indeed to all who lack the leisure required. Moreover, others too may be so circumstanced that they do not encounter men whose example and teaching might put them on the right path; they may be irretrievably subject to the corrupting influences which Seneca himself regarded as prevalent in society . . . if some, and indeed most men, are destined to be wicked and therefore miserable, and it is only by divine caprice that others are virtuous and happy, how can we claim that the world is ordered for men's good? . . . It was an inescapable contradiction in their conception of nature that in a world totally controlled, as they held, by nature that is divine and rational men are continually thinking and acting in ways that they can describe as "contrary to nature."[116]

Whether the Stoics did indeed reflect upon this topic, as Brunt characterizes, will hopefully be clarified in the proceeding sections of this book.

NOTES

1. *Diss.* I.3.3: "since in our birth we have these two [the body and our divine soul] elements mingled within us," δύο ταῦτα ἐν τῇ γενέσει ἡμῶν ἐγκαταμέμικται. See also Chrysippus *apud SVF* 2.473, Hierocles *Elem.* IV.30-50, and the discussion in Mansfeld (1983), Long (2001, 224–249), and Ramelli (2009, 45).

2. Diog. Laert. 7.134.

3. Clem. *Strom.* V. 8.

4. See Sellars (2006, 88–89), and *Plut. De Comm. Nat.* 1085d, *Alex. Aphr. De mist.* 223, 54, and Galen *De plac. Hipp et. Plat.* IV.5.5.

5. Diog. Laert. 7.148.

6. See Long (2017, 228–229), and relevant remarks from Epictetus at *Diss.* I.1.12; 14.6; and 2.8.10-12. On the ἡγεμονικόν, see Sextus Empiricus, *Math.* 7.234.

7. On the Stoics' belief that upon separation from the body the soul loses its identity with the person it was blended with, see Algra (2009, 371), Long (2017, 227–228), and Celkyte (2018); and on Cornutus and the understanding in antiquity regarding the Stoics' position on postmortem identity, see Boys-Stones (2018, 32), and on Epictetus' *Diss.* III.24.94, and the discussion in Long (2019, 157, 170). On the debate over this issue, see the excellent discussion in Long (2019, 152–173).

8. See the profitable discussion of this idea in Celkyte (2018), and also Epictetus' comments at *Diss.* I.6.13-21; III.1.3-6, and Chrysippus' *apud* Plut. *Mor.* 1063F-1064B, along with the remarks of Stephens (2014a).

9. Celkyte (2018, 15).

10. See Diog. Laert. 7.55, 110, 159.

11. See Galen *PHP* 459-465, and on the position of Zeno, Posidonius, and Seneca regarding physiognomy, see the discussion in Grahn-Wilder (2018, 123–124).

12. *Diss.* I.1.9, 11-12.

13. See the relevant discussion in Dobbin (1998, 159).

14. *Diss.* I.3.3, 6-8.

15. See *Diss.* I.1.9;9.14-15.

16. This thought is additionally outlined at *Diss.* I.3.3-8 and IV.7.32. On these passages, Stephens (2014, 214) comments: "But why should it be the case that only a few human beings will excel in rationality and become virtuous? If reason is a natural endowment of all human beings, why do only a few realize this potential? The explanation Epictetus offers is that . . . . Because of our kinship with the flesh, he explains, some of us incline towards the body and become like wolves, faithless, treacherous, and harmful. Others incline towards the body and become like lions, wild, savage, and untamed. But most of us incline towards the body and become like foxes." See also *Muson.* 11.3.

17. See Dobbin (1998, 176).

18. For example, *Diss.* II.9.2-8, III.23.4, IV.5.21.

19. *Diss.* I.9.11.

20. *Diss.* I.1.11; III.1.43; 6.6; 10.5, 15, 16; 18.3; 22.33, 101; 24.71; IV.1.72,151, 153, 158, 163, 6.34; 7.18; 11.13, 23. On this, see Stephens (2012, 62), and, for other instances where Epictetus appears to diminishes the value of the body, consider *Diss.* I.29.6; II.1.19, and III.18.3.

21. *Diss.* II.8.2. On the Stoic belief that god has a body *sui generis*, and is not composed of any of the four basic material elements of fire, air, water, and earth, consider the insightful discussion in Cooper (2004, 219–222).

22. *Diss.* IV.1.130.

23. *Diss.* III.22.21.

24. *Diss.* I.9.34. On the difference between humans and animals in relation to this point, see *Diss.* I.6.12-14; on the Stoic understanding of the position of animals, see Wildberger (2008) and Stephens (2014), and in wider Greco-Roman thought consider Newmyer (2011).

25. *Diss.* IV.1.158.

26. *Diss.* I.29.16.

27. *Fr.* 26. Brennan (2009a, 390), comments that this passage "identifies the human being with the soul alone, to the exclusion of the body. It does not say that you are a living body, or a body that is animated by a soul, or a body together with a soul, or a combination of the body and soul. You are simply a soul. . . . Epictetus is making the body a burden, an encumbrance, an alien weight constantly perceived as impeding the soul's freedom."

28. *Ep.* 65.16, 18, trans. Gummere (1917, 453, 455).

29. *Cons. Mar* 24.5, trans. Basore (1932, 89).

30. *Ep.* 120.14 trans. Gummere (1925, 391). See also *Ep.* 70.17.

31. Asmis, Bartsch, and Nussbaum (2014, xix) comment: "Drawing inspiration from Plato, Seneca tells us there is a god inside; there is a soul that seeks to free itself from the dross of the body."

32. On this, see especially Reydams-Schils (2010, 199–207), Asmis (2015, 227), and Long (2017, 215–217; 225–229), and the references to relevant secondary literature that Long makes (2017, 217). Long (2002, 158) also remarks: "What he [Epictetus] wants to emphasize is a duality in our human constitution that gives us the option of deciding whether we shall be godlike (by identifying with our minds) or merely animals (by identifying with our bodies)"; Reydams-Schils (2010, 202): "The Platonic language and imagery in Seneca is meant to emphasize the importance of the turn inwards"; Gill (2012, 387): "Taken on its own, this [Marcus'] phraseology suggests Platonic-style rejection of the body or a Cynic desire to shock by rejecting conventional norms." See also Huttunen (2009, 109) and Russell (2012, 166). The only studies, to my knowledge, apart from Brennan (2009a), that consider the Stoic disdain for the body without attempting to frame it in this way are Trapp (2007, 101–103) and Stephens (2011, 62, 131). Others have argued that Seneca, Epictetus, and Marcus Aurelius' view of the body is due to their drawing upon the Platonic rather than the Stoic tradition, for example see Engberg-Pedersen (2010a, 10–11).

33. Brennan (2009a, 398, 400–401).

34. Brennan (2009a, 401, 403), emphasis mine.

35. Brennan (2009a, 404, 405).

36. *Muson.* 6.4, trans. King (2011, 36–37).

37. Reydams-Schils (2010, 200) cites this passage as having the hallmarks of Platonism.

38. See also Rufus' comments at *Muson.* 19.1, where he compares the body to be like a horse that has been entrusted to our care. Supporting this, we might also note

that Hierocles refers to our instinctive (and appropriate) sense of affinity to ourselves as only being directed to our mind, or our body, so see Stob. *Anth.* 4.84.23.

39. See *M. Aur. Med* 5.26, 11.20.

40. Stephens (2011, 13) notes that at *M. Aur. Med* 3.3: "Marcus describes his body as a 'battered crate.' Its substance he calls 'garbage.' He repudiates pleasure and pain as dangerously annoying distractions to the superior art of him, his mind and spirit. Marcus is clearly tired of having to pay so much attention to his 'battered crate.' He looks forward to no longer being forced to expend mental energies serving bodily demands."

41. *Med.* 12.3, trans. Gill and Hard (2011, 114–115). See also similar remarks at *M. Aur. Med* 2.2.

42. Gill (2013, 89).

43. *Diss.* I.9.11.

44. See the discussion in Long (2017, 225).

45. Girdwood (1998, 106, 107): "Epictetus tells us that this [separating our identity away from the body] is not simply a moral orientation or determination of priority, but actually a way of delineating the self. I, says Epictetus, 'am not a body or property or reputation, but a rational animal' (4.6.34) . . . Thus far, we might get the impression that Epictetus is concerned only with locating a sense of self, rather than its true location. But Epictetus has elsewhere insisted that we are *prohairesis*, so that the seat of selfhood lies in the *hegemonikon* and its disposition and activity."

46. *Fr.* 23.

47. *Muson.* 19.1, Seneca *Ep.* 14.2, 15.17, see also Apuleius *Apol.* 15.4-6, and Epictetus' further remarks at *Ench.* 41.

48. Regarding the Stoics belief in providence, see Wildberger (2018, 45–51).

49. See, for example, Rosenmeyer (2000, 111–116) and Algra (2003, 172).

50. Ware (2017, 291), citing *SVF* 2.1170, 2.1176, 1178.

51. Ware (2017, 290, and n.27 and 28). In particular, see *Ep.* 58.27, 65.10, 66.3, *Ben.* 2.29.3.

52. *Diss.* I.1.10-12.

53. *Diss.* I.3.3.

54. For other options, see Inwood (2018, 57–58).

55. See for example, Sellars (2016, 13), who considers this issue in relation to Chrysippus' remarks *apud* Plutarch *Stoic Rep.* 1051C and *Comm. Not.* 1065b, upon which I concur with Sellar's caution over using these texts to support the above hypothesis.

56. On this, see *Aet.* 4.11.1-4, Seneca *Ep.* 121.13-19, and 124.9.

57. As Van Sijl (2010, 92–93) usefully explains: "At the very first moments of their [humans] lives they have not yet developed preconceptions, let alone knowledge. If uncorrected, such confusions of pleasure with the truly beneficial lead to bad habits and extended mistaken beliefs. These initial misconceptions subsequently find their way into the education of new generations of children and thus grow and spread among people and throughout human history."

58. For example, *Diss.* II.1.16, and IV.7.32. See also Seneca. *Ep.* 4.2.

59. *Diss.* II.9.14.

60. *Diss.* III.19.4,6. See also *Ep.* 60.1, 115.11, *Muson.* 6.6, and Dio *Or.* 11.2.

61. *Tusc.* III.2-3.

62. *Diss.* II.18.9-11. On the perniciousness of vice according to the Stoics, see Brunt (2013, 16–17).

63. At *Or.* 11.1 Dio also clearly and eloquently argues this point.

64. Philo *Leg All.* 1.30, Cicero *Acad.* 2.31, Plutarch *Comm. Not.* 1084f. See also Shogri (2018), Diog. Laert. 7.54, and *Nat. D.* 2.14.

65. *Diss.* II.18.11. On this, see Girdwood (1998, 162, 175–176, 185). On Epictetus' belief that it is difficult, and in some cases likely impossible to impact people with philosophical insight, see, for example, *Diss.* I.5.1-3; II.15.14; 17.1; 18.11-12; 20.37. On Epictetus' stance regarding precipitancy, see Salles (2005, 92, 103, 106–108), and on whether the Stoics viewed everyone as being equally teachable, see, for example, *Stob. Anth.* 2.11, Diog. Laert. 7.115, Seneca *De Ira* 2.19, *Ep.* 11.6, 108.12, and Cicero *De Fin.* 4.56, and on their perception that some people have inherent moral weaknesses see the useful study of Ranocchia (2012).

66. *Diss.* IV.3.4-7.

67. *Diss.* III.16.16: "Fly from all laypeople, if you ever want to make a start on becoming somebody," φεύγετε τοὺς ἰδιώτας, εἰ θέλετε ἄρξασθαί ποτέ τινες εἶναι. See similar comments at *Diss.* III.16.9-10, IV.2.1, *Ench.* 33.6, *Ep.* 23.7-9, 31.2, 32.2, 52.9, 69.4-5, *Vit. Beat.*1.2-5, 2.2.1, *De Ira* 3.8.1, and *Tranq.* 6.1. Schafer (2009, 86), also comments on Seneca's belief that "the pernicious effect of corrupt values is self-reinforcing ([*Ep.*]94.54) . . . we are contaminated by the opinions of people of lesser status as well as of greater status; my vices make you worse and you make me worse in turn." See also the useful discussion in Gloyn (2014, 237–238). On the importance of choosing virtuous friends according to Stoic thought, see Long (2013, 220), and consider comments from Eshleman (2012, 43). Reymans-Schils (2010, 571) also notes: "Epictetus' *Discourses* explicitly address the challenge of the transition from the school to everyday life (as in *Diss.* 4.1.132-143, 4.5.37, 4.12.12; cf. also 1.29.34-35, 2.9.15-16, 2.10.29-30, 2.16.2, 3.3.17, 3.20.18). As they point out, it is quite a bit easier to display the correct attitude and behaviour among like-minded people and peers than to hold on to what one has learned outside the school environment (*Diss.* 2.16.20-21)." On Seneca's warning regarding the negative influences that can come from friends and family members, see also Gloyn (2014, 237–240).

68. *Diss.* IV.9.6.

69. *Diss.* IV.9.8.

70. *Diss.* I.10.2-6.

71. For example, see *Diss.* II.8.15,16, III.20.18, IV.1.138, 5.36-37. Marcus Aurelius also, *M. Aur. Med* 10.9, comments: "Cheap comedy, war, excitement, lethargy, servitude—day by day these will wipe away those sacred principles of yours, which you form and retain with the help of natural philosophy," trans. Gill and Hard (2011, 96): Μῖμος, πόλεμος, πτοία, νάρκα, δουλεία: καθ᾽ ἡμέραν ἀπαλείψεταί σου τὰ ἱερὰ ἐκεῖνα δόγματα, ὁπόσα ἀφυσιολογήτως φαντάζῃ καὶ παραπέμπεις. See also Diog. Laert. 7.89, Cicero *Tusc.* 3.2-3, and especially Seneca *Ep.* 31.2.

72. *Diss.* III.12.12.

73. *Diss.* IV.2.6-7. See also *Ench.* 33.

74. He also comments at *Diss.* III.16.3: "Since, then, the danger is so great, caution must be used in entering into these familiarities with laypeople; remembering that

it is impossible to rub up against a person who is covered with soot without getting some of the soot on oneself," ἐπεὶ ὅρα οἷον ἦν ἡμᾶς φροντίζειν μὴ περὶ αὐτῶν μόνον ἀλλὰ καὶ περὶ τῶν προβάτωνκαὶ τῶν ὄνων, πῶς ἐνδύσηται καὶ πῶς ὑποδήσηται, πῶς φάγῃ, πῶς πίῃ.

75. So Belliotii (2008, 208) notes: "accordingly, the Stoic life is not natural to human beings in the biological sense. We must work hard to attain it and doing so is crucial to achieving what is natural in the normative sense, our own well-being."

76. *Diss.* II.14.10.

77. *Diss.* I.11.37-38, 12.17, 20.13-16; II.14.14-15; III.7.14-15, IV.1.170, *Fr.* 16.

78. *Diss.* I.7.10-12. Long (2006, 99 argues that according to Epictetus: "Human beings are innately equipped to achieve this by reason of their own intellect and sensory faculties, but these require training in (we may interpret) the subject-matter and methodology of dialectic; hence what Epictetus calls elsewhere the 'necessity of logic'" (*Discourses* II.25).

79. Long (1996, 276)—made in reference to Epictetus' comments at *Diss.* I.6.12-20.

80. *Diss.* II.23.40. See also *Diss.* I.4.1 and III.9.6-7, and Salles (2005, 105) comments: "They [the exercises Epictetus lists at *Diss.* II.18.8-9, 12-14, 23-24] implicitly presuppose the availability of a specific kind of teacher—one who is able to instruct the precipitate agent what the exercise consists in. The performance itself of the exercises can be carried out by the precipitate agent on its own. But he cannot get started, as it were, without the help of this sort of teacher. At this initial stage, his guidance will be crucial." See also similar remarks from Copper (2007, 17).

81. *Diss.* II.23.38-41.

82. *Diss.* IV.1.177.

83. *Diss.* II.21.10: "Do I go to my teacher, as though to an oracle, prepared to obey": ἔρχομαι πρὸς τὸν διδάσκαλον ὡς ἐπὶ τὰ χρηστήρια πείθεσθαι παρεσκευασμένος. See also *Diss.* III.9.6-7.

84. Barnes (1997, 44).

85. Cooper (2007, 9–11).

86. See Long (2002, 44), and Cooper (2007 *passim*).

87. *Diss.* I.4.6-10, 28; 12.13-25; II.16.34;17.34, 40;19.14; 23.44; III.2.13; 21.6-7, IV.4.11, and *Ench.* 49.

88. *Diss.* I.26.1; II.13.21; 17.27; III.2.6, 21.10, and IV.4.14.

89. *Diss.* II.21.17.

90. For example, *Diss.* I.29.57 and IV.1.152, 169. Snyder (2000, 29) reasonably conjectures: "the curriculum in Epictetus' classroom was most likely structured around a series of topics proposed by Epictetus, rather than a set of texts. To elucidate and illustrate these topics, Epictetus would have used texts—more than anecdotally, to be sure but in such a way that texts were conformed to curricula, not vice versa."

91. On these exercises, and the argument over whether they represent noncognitive aspect of Epictetus' philosophy, see the excellent thesis Trembley (2016).

92. *Diss.* II.18.25-26. See also *Diss.* IV.12.7.

93. So Brunt (2013, 337) comments: "Book learning was not enough; it had not be supplemented by continuous moral training, by the formation of habits in taking

the correct decisions." While commenting on *Diss.* III.2.1, see also Cooper (2007, 17), and general remarks from Long (2004, 208) and Sharpe (2014, 17, 22).

94. *Diss.* II.9.13-14. See also *Diss.* I.26.3. Sellars (2003, 110) states: "Epictetus' clear affirmation of the necessity of both exercise (*askesis*) and theory (*logos*) for philosophy. Philosophical exercises cannot replace theory; rather they supplement theory. Theory—such as the ethical theory one finds in Hierocles' treatise the *Elements of Ethics*, roughly contemporary with Epictetus—remains a necessary condition and, for Epictetus, the point of departure for philosophical progress. For that, both *logos* and *askesis* are required."

95. *Diss.* I.4.5-8.

96. *Diss.* I.26.9.

97. *Diss.* III.26.13-14, 15. See also *Diss.* I.29.56, III.21.1-3, 24.78-87, and IV.4.14, 16.

98. *Fin.* 4.7.

99. So Sorabji (2002, 212), notes: "Ancient philosophical therapy relied heavily on exercises . . . many exercises were free of doctrinal presuppositions, and were consequently interchangeable among schools." On the exercises and their role in the teaching of philosophy see Nussbaum (1994) and Hadot (1995). Following Tsouna (2007, 79 n.7), I will refer to "therapeutic exercises" rather than Hadot's preferred designation of "spiritual exercises." For a useful study on Epictetus' employment of them, see Braicovich (2014).

100. On this, see Sellars (2003, 143–144).

101. For example, consider *Ench.* 3.

102. *Ench.* 33.1,12.

103. See *Diss.* I.14.15; 16.4, 18.21-23; II.18.22-28; III.10.6-7, and 24.34. In a study that compares Stoicism and modern practices of cognitive behavioral therapy, see Robertson (2010, 86).

104. *Diss.* I.29.58.

105. *Diss.* I.27.20-21.

106. See, for example, Seneca *Ep.* 88.31, *De Ben.* 3.18.2.

107. Diog. Laert. 7.128, trans. Miller and Mensch (2018, 356).

108. *Ep.* 44.3-4, *Diss.* III.26.23.

109. Brunt (2013, 166). See also his remarks (2013, 167; 179). Consider *De Otio* 1.1, where Seneca argues that leisure is needed to obtain virtue.

110. See Varro *apud De Civ.* 6.5, Cicero *Tusc.* II 1.45, Galen *Aff. Pec. Dig.* 2.2, Manilius *Astron.* 2.135-140, *Div. inst.* 3.15, and *Contra Cels.* 6.2.

111. Horace *Ode* 8. That Stoicism seems to not have spread widely beyond the elite consider the remarks in Brunt (2013, 110, 336).

112. Goulet-Cazé (2019, 82, 83). See also Bosman (2017, 45).

113. *Diss.* I.9.29.

114. See Booth (1979) and remarks from Robertson (2016, 72, 117, 181–182, 206) with reference to Epictetus' likely background.

115. As Dobbin (1998, iv) remarks that Epictetus was "a slave on the one hand, but also a privileged member of the emperor's inner circle." Consider also Miller (1965) regarding the close proximity that Epictetus had to people in power.

116. Brunt (2013, 496, 497).

Chapter 3

The Selective Engagement
of Laypeople

In Diogenes Laertius' account of two of the leading figures in the early Stoic school, Zeno of Citium (ca. 334–262 BCE) and Chrysippus of Soli (ca. 279–206 BCE), he portrays two contrasting stances toward engaging the public with philosophy. Regarding Zeno, Diogenes explains that his custom of pacing up and down (ἀνακάμπτω) while he expounded upon philosophical themes, and his locating his school in the Stoa Poikile, which had the macabre association as having been the site of the murder of several hundred Athenians a few decades before, was because "his object was to keep the place clear of crowds," διετίθετο τοὺς λόγους, βουλόμενος καὶ τὸ χωρίον ἀπερίστατον ποιῆσαι.[1] Diogenes continues to recount that whenever more than two or three companions would assemble around Zeno, he would bluntly ask them to remove themselves from the vicinity so their presence would not annoy him. To bolster his portrayal Diogenes continues to cite Zeno's successor to the school, Cleanthes, in his now lost work *On Bronze,* Περὶ χαλκοῦ, as recalling that Zeno would request money from bystanders not in order for his pecuniary benefit, but so that "the people" (οἱ πολλοί) would be dissuaded from gathering around him, and that in addition his contemporary/near-contemporary Antigonus of Carystus (fl. 240 BCE) noted that Zeno even selected what seat to take in order to be near to as few people as possible.[2]

Aside from strategizing to ensure that he only had a small number of people around him, Zeno's selectivity in engaging with individuals who came to receive philosophical instruction from him is also narrated in Diogenes' *Lives,* namely that, first of all, Zeno made a visitor sit on a dust-covered bench so he would soil his woolen cloak, and that he made him sit over where the beggars sat so their ragged clothing would directly rub up against him, which resulted in the visitor's withdrawal.[3] Furthermore, Diogenes records that when another young man ventured to pose a deep question, Zeno led him to a mirror and tersely asked him whether he thought it appropriate for someone who looked like him to make such an inquiry.[4] This portrayal of Zeno's stance is markedly different from that of Chrysippus', who Diogenes notes the first century BCE biographer Demetrius of Magnesia records was the first, πρῶτος, Stoic to deliver lectures in the open air/publicly, ὕπαιθρος, in the Lyceum.[5]

While the citation of numerous earlier sources lends some credibility to Diogenes' depiction of these luminary Stoics' attitudes toward public engagement, beyond the issue of these passages' possible historicity they should, I suggest, naturally pique our interest about the extent to which these two differing approaches might be represented in the school's extant literature, which I will attempt to explore here regarding Epictetus.

To my knowledge, the attitude that the Stoics assumed toward public engagement has only received passing attention in scholarship, and has been largely centered upon the "minor Stoics" Manilius and Persius. With regards to Manilius, in his 2011 book chapter Wolfgang-Rainer Mann argues that his *Astronomica* can occasionally express an "exclusionary tone . . . [by] addressing only a chosen few,"[6] which is evidenced in Manilius' remarks such as the following: "Not in the crowd nor for the crowd shall I compose my song [i.e., the *Astronomica*], but alone," *nec in turba nec turbae carmina condam, sed solus.*[7] Meanwhile, in her 2015 book Shadi Bartsch shows (although without connecting it to him) that Persius expresses a similar standpoint to Manilius', with him envisaging only one or two readers benefiting from his work,[8] and by portraying his philosophical mentor Cornutus as having a selective approach to gathering students and maintaining an aversion to conveying philosophical advice to crowds.[9]

Within the remit of exploring "public engagement," I will consider actions where Epictetus envisages philosophical information being relayed outside of the philosopher-student relationship (whether to crowds or to individuals), and the attitude he has to laypeople who express an interest in familiarizing themselves with philosophical teaching. First though, in order to provide context for my proceeding discussion, I will explore Epictetus' opinion about the role of the philosopher.

THE DIVINE CALL OF THE
VOCATIONAL PHILOSOPHER

Epictetus' belief that philosophers should monitor and spur their students' moral reformation is repeatedly evidenced in the *Discourses*. For instance, he describes philosophers as having a "care of the young,"[10] ἐπιμεληθῆναι νέων and portrays them saying, "I am him who must take care of human beings,"[11] οὗτός εἰμι, ᾧ δεῖ μέλειν ἀνθρώπων, and describes their vocation as being to aid, ὠφελέω, others.[12] Similarly, Epictetus' concern for others is also disclosed when he recounts a visit that he made to an individual who, because of his awareness of certain philosophical principles, had wrongly concluded that he should put an end to his life,[13] a scenario upon which Epictetus' remarks: "with some difficulty, it proved possible to change this man's mind," ἐκεῖνος μὲν οὖν μόγις μετεπείσθη.[14]

It is striking though that whenever Epictetus' students indicate that they harbor a desire to emulate him and come to eventually follow in his footsteps an formally instruct others in philosophy, he consistently challenges this aspiration. He does so by chiefly asking them to reflect upon whether their progress in philosophy is sufficiently secure for them to assume such a weighty task, and if their ambition is the result of careful deliberation or of whimsy.[15] In addition, as others have already been explored, Epictetus repeatedly asserts that becoming a philosopher requires divine sanction.[16] For example, he describes the philosopher as being a witness (μάρτυς) summoned by god,[17] and in response to a student's query "But so-and-so keeps a school; why shouldn't I also?," 'ἀλλ' ὁ δεῖνα σχολὴν ἔχει· διὰ τί μὴ κἀγὼ σχῶ', Epictetus demurs: "Slave, these things are not done carelessly or haphazardly, but one should be of a particular age, and lead a certain kind of life, and have god as his guide," οὐκ εἰκῇ ταῦτα γίνεται, ἀνδράποδον, οὐδ' ὡς ἔτυχεν, ἀλλὰ καὶ ἡλικίαν εἶναι δεῖ καὶ βίον καὶ θεὸν ἡγεμόνα.[18] He then provides a lengthy discussion wherein he equates the calling of a philosopher to the criteria that the mystery cults employ before they sanction one of their members to relay its tenets to others:[19] namely that they should be a person of a particular age and physique, that they have purified their body and mind, and that they display a deep cognizance of and reverence for the mystery's contents.[20] Epictetus then speaks directly regarding the role of the philosopher and avers: "This is a great undertaking, a solemn mystery, not to be lightly accorded to all who come. Indeed, even wisdom is perhaps not even an adequate qualification for taking care of the young," μέγα ἐστὶ τὸ πρᾶγμα, μυστικόν ἐστιν, οὐχ ὡς ἔτυχεν οὐδὲ τῷ τυχόντι δεδομένον. ἀλλ' οὐδὲ σοφὸν εἶναι τυχὸν ἐξαρκεῖ πρὸς τὸ ἐπιμεληθῆναι νέων; and furthermore: "above all else, you must have a calling from God to discharge this function," πρὸ πάντων τὸν θεὸν συμβουλεύειν ταύτην τὴν χώραν κατασχεῖν,[21] and "If, however, the theorems of philosophy amuse you, sit down and mull them over in your mind by yourself," ἀλλὰ εἴ σε ψυχαγωγεῖ τὰ θεωρήματα, καθήμενος αὐτὰ στρέφε αὐτὸς ἐπὶ σεαυτοῦ· φιλόσοφον δὲ μηδέποτ' εἴπῃς σεαυτὸν μηδ' ἄλλου ἀνάσχῃ λέγοντος.[22] We can note in passing that this perspective on the philosopher's task is replicated with some symmetry in another passage in the *Discourses*, although with reference to the budding of vegetation instead of the conventions of mystery cults.[23] Through such unyielding remarks, Epictetus makes it apparent to his students the exacting duties that he believes the professional philosopher's position entails, and the specific call they should establish they have from God/nature before they attempt to assume its mantle.[24] Attempting to vocationally relay philosophy to others is not, Epictetus labors, an easy task, or one which his students should feel they can assume without undertaking strenuous preparation and reflection.

EPICTETUS AND THE RECOMMENDATION
OF PHILOSOPHICAL ENGAGEMENT

Regarding communicating insights to people who lack philosophical awareness, to my knowledge only in one remark does Epictetus provide a qualified affirmation that this might be advisable. This occurs when he responds to a student who states: "But my mother grieves at not seeing me," ἀλλ' ἡ μήτηρ μου στένει μὴ ὁρῶσά με, by replying:

> Then why hasn't she learned these principles? And I'm not saying it is wrong to take care that she does not grieve, but rather that we should not hope absolutely for things that are not our in our power. My own grief is, I will, therefore, certainly put an end my own grief at all cost, because that is within my power; but regarding the lamenting of another, I will endeavor to put an end to it to the extent that I am able, but I will not labor to do so at all costs, otherwise I will be battling God, opposing Zeus, and be positioning myself against him in the governing of the universe.[25]

> διὰ τί γὰρ οὐκ ἔμαθεν τούτους τοὺς λόγους; καὶ οὐ τοῦτό φημι, ὅτι οὐκ ἐπιμελητέον τοῦ μὴ οἰμώζειν αὐτήν, ἀλλ' ὅτι οὐ δεῖ θέλειν τὰ ἀλλότρια ἐξ ἅπαντος. λύπη δ' ἡ ἄλλου ἀλλότριόν ἐστιν, ἡ δ' ἐμὴ ἐμόν. ἐγὼ οὖν τὸ μὲν ἐμὸν παύσω ἐξ ἅπαντος, ἐπ' ἐμοὶ γάρ ἐστιν· τὸ δ' ἀλλότριον πειράσομαι κατὰ δύναμιν, ἐξ ἅπαντος δ' οὐ πειράσομαι. εἰ δὲ μή, θεομαχήσω, ἀντιθήσω πρὸς τὸν Δία, ἀντιδιατάξομαι αὐτῷ πρὸς τὰ ὅλα.

Here Epictetus recommends that if a student wants to lessen his mother's sorrow because of his absence, he should convey philosophical principles, λόγοι, which would counsel her against placing her attachment onto things which are beyond her power to control—such as, in this instance, the proximity of her friends and family. Whether Epictetus envisages that this would consist of a plotted introduction to formal philosophy thought, or (perhaps more likely) the relaying of simply stated advice or precepts that might soothe her distress cannot be firmly stated. It is noticeable, however, that the focus of Epictetus' comments center upon cautioning the student that any such efforts should be done in a measured manner, namely that they should not be expended at all costs, ἅπαντος δ᾽ οὐ πειράσομαι, and that the student should recall his mother's actions and beliefs are not "in my power," δύναμις. In further elucidating this last remark, Epictetus asserts that this student's desire to end his mother's distress by in some form relaying philosophical advice to her is to place himself into a battle against God, θεομαχία, by which Epictetus is referring to his conviction (which he often articulates in a theological parlance) that each person's *prohairesis* is solely and inviolably under their own agency. This position is perhaps most usefully clarified by Epictetus' comments elsewhere that "He [God] has commended me to myself, and has made it that my choice should be subject to myself only," ἐμὲ ἐκεῖνος συνέστησεν ἐμαυτῷ καὶ τὴν ἐμὴν προαίρεσιν ὑπέταξεν ἐμοὶ μόνῳ; and "You fail to comprehend that a judgement can only conquer itself, cannot be conquered by someone else."[26]

THE FUTILITY AND DISTRACTING NATURE OF PUBLIC ENGAGEMENT

Regarding engaging others with philosophy, this is a topic where Epictetus uniquely signals that a shift in his stance has occurred. This is evinced in a statement where he reflects upon the difficulty of communicating philosophical ideas to laypeople[27] by stating: "consequently, being aware of this inability, we give up the attempt, or at least those of us who have a measure of caution do so," λοιπὸν εἰκότως συναισθανόμενοι ταύτης ἡμῶν τῆς ἀδυναμίας ἀπεχόμεθα τοῦ πράγματος, ὅσοις γ᾽ ἐστί τι εὐλαβείας.[28] He then proceeds to depict a hypothetical exchange that occurs between a philosopher and a layperson, but which only results in the latter's frustration and his throwing a punch at his educated interlocutor.[29] Epictetus then proceeds to bolster this point with a biographical sketch by informing his students that when he had been in Rome (and so presumably prior to Domitian's expulsion of philosophers from the capital[30]), he used to attempt to engage passersby in dialectical exchanges, until he apprehended that this only seemed to result in his engendered intended dialogue partners' hostility, and to even provoke their physical aggression toward him.[31] With implied empathy for his students' compulsion to follow in such exploits, Epictetus then remarks: "This was an activity that I too had been enthusiastic about, until I met with such troubles/adventures," τούτου τοῦ πράγματος ἤμην ποτὲ ζηλωτὴς καὶ αὐτός, πρὶν εἰς ταῦτα ἐμπεσεῖν.[32]

Secondly, with reference to the individual whom Epictetus persuaded to refrain from killing himself that I noted above, he continues to remark that unlike this man's pliable disposition, "there are some people today who cannot be persuaded. So, I now realize what I couldn't before, the meaning of the saying 'A fool can be neither bent nor broken,'" τῶν δὲ νῦν τινας οὐκ ἔστι μεταθεῖναι. ὥστε μοι δοκῶ ὃ πρότερον ἠγνόουν νῦν εἰδέναι, τί ἐστι τὸ ἐν τῇ συνηθείᾳ λεγόμενον· μωρὸν οὔτε πεῖσαι οὔτε ῥῆξαι ἔστιν.[33] This statement again highlights that Epictetus is aware, and is prepared to highlight that a change in his thinking has occurred, and that his earlier optimism about engaging people with philosophical reasoning has been displaced by a more pessimistic perspective.

It is within this context that we can understand why when Epictetus usually broaches the issue of engaging others with philosophy, his stance appears to be overwhelmingly negative. For example, he mocks the idea that a philosopher should attempt to gather an audience by stating, "Does a philosopher invite people to a lecture?," φιλόσοφος δ᾽ ἐπ᾽ ἀκρόασιν παρακαλεῖ, and sarcastically framing such a proposal as being: "I invite you to come and hear that you are in a dire way, and that you are interested in anything but that which you should be, and that you are uninformed about what is good and evil, and that you are unfortunate and miserable. What a beguiling invitation!," παρακαλῶ σε ἐλθόντα ἀκοῦσαι, ὅτι σοι κακῶς ἐστι καὶ πάντων μᾶλλον ἐπιμελῇ ἢ οὗ δεῖ σε ἐπιμελεῖσθαι καὶ ὅτι ἀγνοεῖς τὰ ἀγαθὰ καὶ τὰ κακὰ καὶ κακοδαίμων εἶ καὶ δυστυχής. κομψὴ παράκλησις.[34] He also twice commends for his students' emulation Socrates and once the Stoic philosopher Euphrates for, in his view, them not promoting themselves as being philosophers, and Socrates specifically for his directing people who were interested in philosophical deliberation to others instead of attempting to gather an audience around himself.[35] In several other passages Epictetus is recorded as encouraging his students to disregard any interest that they might have to convey philosophical truths to people around them, and instead advises them that they should keep their philosophical commitments concealed[36]; for example, he argues:

> This is the proper display of a young man who has come from school. Leave other things to others; do not let anyone ever hear anything from you about them [philosophical ideas], nor, if someone lauds you for them, accept it, but let yourself be considered to be a nobody and that you are ignorant.[37]
>
> αὕτη ἐπίδειξις νέου ἐκ σχολῆς ἐληλυθότος. τἆλλα δ᾽ ἄλλοις ἄφες, μηδὲ φωνήν τις ἀκούσῃ σου περὶ αὐτῶν ποτε μηδ᾽, ἂν ἐπαινέσῃ τις ἐπ᾽ αὐτοῖς, ἀνέχου, δόξον δὲ μηδεὶς εἶναι καὶ εἰδέναι μηδέν.

Furthermore, when Epictetus' students express an interest in conveying the results of philosophical reasoning to laypeople, he remarks that convincing (πείθω) the multitude (πολύς) of the foolishness of seeking riches, reputation, and so on, is "ineffectual and tedious—to attempt the very thing that

Zeus himself has not been able to do, namely to persuade everyone of what the good and what the evil is," ἀνήνυτος καὶ μακρά, ὃ ὁ Ζεὺς οὐκ ἠδυνήθη ποιῆσαι, τοῦτο αὐτὸ ἐπιχειρεῖν, πάντας ἀνθρώπους πεῖσαι, τίνα ἐστὶν ἀγαθὰ καὶ κακά. μὴ γὰρ δέδοταί σοι τοῦτο; ἐκεῖνο μόνον σοι δέδοται, σαυτὸν πεῖσαι. καὶ οὔπω πέπεικας; and he concludes by reiterating: "Why, that has not been accorded to you, has it? No, this alone has been accorded—to convince yourself . . . Will you not, then, let other people alone and become your own pupil and your own teacher?" οὐ θέλεις οὖν ἀφεὶς τοὺς ἄλλους αὐτὸς σαυτῷ γενέσθαι καὶ μαθητὴς καὶ διδάσκαλος.[38] It is, to my knowledge, only this passage with its blunt disavowal of the effectiveness, and even possibility of successfully engaging members of the public with philosophical insight that has drawn the notice of Epictetus' modern interpreters, namely in passing by John Yueh-Han Yieh,[39] and in a more extended manner from Julia Annas, who asserts:

> For a Stoic in Epictetus' position, trying directly to make the world conform to Stoic theory is unrealistic to the point of delusional. . . . For Epictetus, one of the things that Stoicism teaches us is a sense of our own limitations, and the limitations that our circumstances put on us and our ability to change things . . . the possibilities for guided social change are far larger than any that he could envisage.[40]

Numerous passages can be turned to where Epictetus expresses a similar perspective. When the issue of parents who display errant attitudes is again broached (now regarding their potential to show a preference to individuals who are not part of their family), he does not respond with a qualified recommendation that his student might consider proffering philosophical principles to them, but he instead trenchantly remarks:

> Well then, was it you who brought about this state of affairs, who made your father the sort of man he is? Or is it in your power to transform him? Is that granted to you? So then, should you desire to change what isn't granted to you, and to be ashamed if you don't get what you want? And is this the habit you have learned from studying philosophy: to look to others and hope for nothing from yourself?[41]

> σὺ οὖν ἐποίησας τοῦτο, τὸν πατέρα τοιοῦτον; ἢ ἔξεστίν σοι ἐπανορθῶσαι αὐτόν; δίδοταί σοι τοῦτο; τί οὖν; δεῖ σε θέλειν τὰ μὴ διδόμενα ἢ μὴ τυγχάνοντα αὐτῶν αἰσχύνεσθαι; οὕτως δὲ καὶ εἰθίζου φιλοσοφῶν ἀφορᾶν εἰς ἄλλους καὶ μηδὲν αὐτὸς ἐλπίζειν ἐκ σεαυτοῦ;

Here Epictetus isolates and presses the argument that his student is proposing to exert an influence over something that is not possible, ἔξεστι, for him to reform/correct, ἐπανορθόω, and that his proposed redirection of focus from his own conformity to philosophical principles to those of another's is not a concern that his time under Epictetus' instruction should have inspired.

In another passage, Epictetus voices similar sentiments when he states to his students that:

> We should approach our education with this order of things in mind, not to change the existing order (which is not granted to us, nor would it be better if it were) . . . Is it possible to change people if we frequent with them? And who has given such an ability to me? What is to be done then, what technique might we discover that can be used when dealing with them? . . . Well, what have you been made responsible for? Only for that which lies within your own power: the correct use of your impressions. Why, then, do you make yourself accountable for things that you are not responsible for? You are just creating trouble for yourself.[42]

> ταύτης οὖν τῆς διατάξεως μεμνημένους ἔρχεσθαι δεῖ ἐπὶ τὸ παιδεύεσθαι, οὐχ ἵν᾽ ἀλλάξωμεν τὰς ὑποθέσεις (οὔτε γὰρ δίδοται ἡμῖν οὔτ᾽ ἄμεινον) . . . τί γάρ; ἐνδέχεται φυγεῖν ἀνθρώπους; καὶ πῶς οἷόν τε; ἀλλὰ συνόντας αὐτοῖς ἐκείνους ἀλλάξαι; καὶ τίς ἡμῖν δίδωσιν; τί οὖν ἀπολείπεται ἢ τίς εὑρίσκεται μηχανὴ πρὸς τὴν χρῆσιν αὐτῶν; . . . τίνος οὖν ὑπεύθυνόν σε ἐποίησαν; τοῦ μόνου ὄντος ἐπὶ σοί, χρήσεως οἵας δεῖ φαντασιῶν. τί οὖν ἐπισπᾷς σεαυτῷ ταῦτα ὧν ἀνυπεύθυνος εἶ; τοῦτό ἐστιν ἑαυτῷ παρέχειν πράγματα.

Here the conviction that we can alter the constitution, order of things ἀλλάξωμεν τὰς ὑποθέσεις, is discounted by Epictetus, as is the belief that we are invested with the ability to change other people's opinions. Continuing to stress this point, Epictetus sarcastically inquires of his pupils what new method they propose might be able to fashion which would allow them to modify other peoples' views. It is significant to note that Epictetus does not just restrict this incapacity to his still maturing students, but he includes himself, ἡμῖν, as also being affected by this limitation. Epictetus then reminds his students that they are only, μόνος, accountable, ὑπεύθυνος, for their *own* handling of impressions, and that for them to be interested in prompting *others* to apprehend their need for philosophical awareness is to dedicate themselves to a cause (which the verb ἐπισπάω holds in its metaphorical sense) that is decidedly not theirs to advance.

Furthermore, in an extended discourse Epictetus twice imagines a student expressing a desire to marry philosophical explication with broad scale public engagement, in the first instance wondering: "What, must one say this to the many?," τί οὖν; λέγειν δεῖ ταῦτα πρὸς τοὺς πολλούς, and then later similarly inquiring: "What, then, are we to proclaim these truths to everyone?" τί οὖν;

κηρύσσειν δεῖ ταῦτα πρὸς πάντας.[43] In response to the first iteration of this query, Epictetus answers *by orienting the student's focus upon themselves* and undercutting the appropriateness of the question by asserting that they should be monitoring their *own* philosophical advancement: "To what end? Is it not enough to be persuaded in one's own mind?," ἵνα τί; οὐ γὰρ ἀρκεῖ τὸ αὐτὸν πείθεσθαι. Turning to consider the second question, Epictetus again bluntly negates the value of attempting to bring the deliberations of the lecture room into a broader public context, but this time he draws the focus upon what his students', and seemingly also his, *attitude toward members of the general public should be*: "No, we should accommodate ourselves to non-philosophers," οὔ, ἀλλὰ τοῖς ἰδιώταις συμπεριφέρεσθαι.

Epictetus continues to defend the adoption of this attitude by drawing upon an example from Socrates' life, noting that when Socrates observed his jailor's distress at his impending fate with the cup of hemlock, instead of attempting to instigate a shift in the man's judgment that death is an evil, Socrates instead inclined him to leave the room. Regarding this scenario, Epictetus approvingly remarks: "he conducted himself to him, as one would to a child," ἐκείνῳ δὲ συμπεριφέρεται ὡς παιδίῳ.[44] Epictetus' advocacy of such a non-confrontational reaction to lay misapprehension about death is reprised in the *Enchiridion*, wherein (unlike in the passage above regarding the student's mother) he is portrayed as recommending that his students should *not* express a philosophically informed response to people who are in grief. Indeed, he proposes that they might mask their true convictions by outwardly manifesting symptoms of angst, arguing: "as far as words go, however, don't hesitate to sympathize with him, or even, if the occasion arises, to join in his lamentations; but watch that you do not likewise lament deep within yourself," μέχρι μέντοι λόγου μὴ ὄκνει συμπεριφέρεσθαι αὐτῷ, κἂν οὕτω τύχῃ, καὶ συνεπιστενάξαι· πρόσεχε μέντοι μὴ καὶ ἔσωθεν στενάξῃς.[45] Several other passages where Epictetus outlines this position can be turned to, but I will avoid commenting upon for fear of laboring what is hopefully an already-established point.[46]

In reflecting upon Epictetus' remarks that have been considered so far, he appears firm in his resolve to persuade those around him of the inappropriateness and futility of public engagement. Yet, as was seen in one passage, he importantly provides a heavily circumscribed affirmation that it might be appropriate to relay information of some sort to a distressed mother. Our extant source material unfortunately fails to provide us with any clear-cut answer on how Epictetus established whether a person should be philosophically engaged with or not. One reasonable conclusion that might be drawn is that his advice on the appropriateness of engaging an individual or not with philosophy would depend upon whether they would likely prove to be amenable, or have the capacity to constructively respond to any exhortation that is

directed to them, or whether attempting to impact them with philosophically
derived wisdom would require an "at all cost" effort.

I propose that considering this topic in relation to Marcus Aurelius'
Meditations (which reveal a notable Epictetan influence[47]) might provide
more clarity on this issue. Within this work we can see Marcus reflect that
he should attempt to instruct people in his daily life who display errant
understandings,[48] but, as John Sellars has in part also recently drawn attention to,[49] he reminds himself that impelling a change in others is an external,
potentially distracting issue, and one that is ultimately beyond his power to
control.[50] Furthermore, in one passage he dwells upon many of the themes
that I have explored in this chapter with reference to Epictetus:

> So set to work, if you are able, and *do not look around you to see if anyone will
> notice. You should not hope for Plato's ideal state, but be satisfied to make even
> the smallest advance*, and regard such an outcome as nothing contemptible. *For
> who can change the convictions of others?* And without that change of convic-
> tion, what else is there than the slavery of people who grumble away while
> making a show of obedience? Go on, then, and talk to me of Alexander and
> Philip and Demetrius of Phalerum [rulers who attempted to combine politics and
> philosophy]. If they saw what universal nature wishes and trained themselves
> accordingly, I will follow them; but if they merely strutted around like stage
> heroes, no one has condemned me to imitate them. *The work of philosophy is
> simple and modest: do not seduce me into vain ostentation.*[51]

Marcus' remarks above have occasioned some scholarly interest, particularly as he maintained his Stoic convictions while he wore the imperial purple.[52] Aside from the issue of how far Marcus might have attempted to render
his philosophical convictions into state policy, of interest to me is his opinion
that he should express his philosophically informed actions beyond the gaze
of others, to bear in mind the independence of other peoples' judgemnts, to
conceptualize philosophy as having modest aims, and to remind himself that
grand ideas about effecting a change in the constitution of things to be impossible to achieve. These sentiments all, I suggest, find resonance in Epictetus'
thought.

EPICTETUS' DISCOURAGING STANCE
TOWARDS LAYPEOPLE

As far as we can tell, while Epictetus did not, like most Roman-era Stoics,
base his school in a public space,[53] visitors appear to be able to frequent
his lectures if they wanted to. Thanks to Arrian's attention to inform the

Discourses' readers about these guests, we have a remarkably valuable resource through which we can explore firsthand the attitude that Epictetus took toward laypeople who sought to familiarize themselves with philosophical thought, and to test whether the above portrayal of his stance I have outlined in this chapter is indeed accurate. I will briefly survey these passages here to see what themes emerge. By their order in the *Discourses* they are:

1. *Diss*. I.11. A lengthy and profitable exchange is portrayed as taking place between Epictetus and a government official (whose reasons for being at the school are not delineated), regarding what is right, ὀρθός (1-37). Epictetus then (39) cautions, and claims that he believes his dialogue partner already comprehends that such issues can only be understood if he is prepared to lay aside all other concerns and commit himself to an extended period of study: "You can see, then, that it is necessary for you to become a student, that creature who everyone laughs at, if you really want to subject your opinions to suitable examination. But that is, as you know, not the work of a single hour or day," ὁρᾷς οὖν, ὅτι σχολαστικόν σε δεῖ γενέσθαι, τοῦτο τὸ ζῷον οὗ πάντες καταγελῶσιν, εἴπερ ἄρα θέλεις ἐπίσκεψιν τῶν σαυτοῦ δογμάτων ποιεῖσθαι. τοῦτο δ᾿ ὅτι μιᾶς ὥρας ἢ ἡμέρας οὐκ ἔστιν, ἐπινοεῖς καὶ αὐτός (39).

2. *Diss*. I.15. In this passage an individual is recorded as approaching Epictetus in the hopes of obtaining wisdom from him which he can convey to his brother, in order to draw a fractious family feud to a close. In response, Epictetus highlights the problematic nature of this man's request by comparing the results of philosophical education to the harvesting of figs: "Now if the fruit of even a fig-tree is not perfected all at once and in an hour, how can you expect to obtain the fruit of a man's mind in so short a time and so straightforwardly? Do not suppose it, not even if I should tell you so," εἶτα συκῆς μὲν καρπὸς ἄφνω καὶ μιᾷ ὥρᾳ οὐ τελειοῦται, γνώμης δ᾿ ἀνθρώπου καρπὸν θέλεις οὕτως δι᾿ ὀλίγου καὶ εὐκόλως κτήσασθαι; μηδ᾿ ἂν ἐγώ σοι λέγω, προσδόκα (8). Just as fig trees need to be planted and carefully tended over time before they can bear fruit, so Epictetus argues that philosophy requires the patient investment of labor before its teachings can yield results in a person's life. This man's hope of acting as an intermediary through which discrete philosophical advice will abate his brother's anger is, therefore, firmly discounted by Epictetus.

3. *Diss*. II.14. A father and son are visiting the school and Epictetus begins to explain the manner of his teaching to them, but then falls silent (1). When he is prompted by the father to continue to outline his pedagogical approach, Epictetus instead informs him that numerous professions or interests, such as shoemaking or learning to play a musical instrument, at first offer no pleasure, or are tedious/troublesome (ἀνιαρός) to people who lack familiarity with them, and that in this regard philosophy is similar (2-6). Epictetus then argues that laypeople (ἰδιῶται) need to be instructed before they can benefit

from philosophy (7-9), and tersely states: "it is not sufficient to *desire* to be wise and good but it is essential to *learn* certain things," μή ποτ᾽ οὖν καὶ ἐνθάδε οὐκ ἀπαρκεῖ τὸ βούλεσθαι καλὸν καὶ ἀγαθὸν γενέσθαι, χρεία δὲ καὶ μαθεῖν τινα (10). Epictetus proceeds to labor the (in his view) jejune nature of the request by again utilizing an analogy, this time comparing it to an illiterate person who asks him for a word to write, that is, the visitor is requesting information that he has no capacity or training to properly utilize (14-15). Epictetus then remarks that the man's demeanor indicates that he is impervious to reason and that he will likely feel affronted if he is exposed to detailed philosophical discussion, in much the same way as an ugly person would be repelled if they are confronted with a mirror (16-21). The passage concludes with Epictetus asserting that only a few people have an interest in, and the time that allows them to consider philosophical issues, and that if they do so they will be laughed at by the multitude (28).

4. *Diss.* II.24. In this passage, we are informed that an individual has been frequenting Epictetus' school with the hopes of engaging him in conversation, but that he has not been able to realize this aim (1). After pleading to speak with him, Epictetus explains that their lack of interaction has not been an oversight on his part—Epictetus has been evading him on purpose. The man is then informed that listening to a philosopher requires skill/experience (ἐμπειρία) that Epictetus judges he does not possess (2-11) and that, with him lacking the ability to discern what truth or error is, attempting to hold a discussion with him on topics of philosophical debate would, he states, be a waste of time (13-18). Epictetus then proceeds to state that the man's appearance did not rouse him to excitement (ἐρεθίζω) as a thoroughbred horse should make a horseman excited, for his body is shamefully overattended, his clothing is effeminate, and even his facial expression is objectionable (28). At this point, the record of their interaction unsurprisingly ceases.

5. *Diss.* III.1. A student of rhetoric is conversing with Epictetus about what should be considered beautiful (καλός) or not (1-10). It is, however, relayed to him that were they to explore this subject any further Epictetus fears that he will cause his finely dressed interlocutor to be offended. After maneuvering to bring their discussion to a close, Epictetus then apparently vocally remonstrates with himself that what if this youth should come later in life to his senses and wonder why a philosopher had not shown more interest in coming to his aid when his errors had been so visibly displayed (11-24). A long and seemingly largely effective dialogue then takes places between them over whether human beauty can be found in aesthetic qualities, or in the substance of our character (25-45), wherein Epictetus again reflects that he is not in the habit of speaking with anyone (36). The ultimate reaction of this visitor to Epictetus' attempts to reason with him are not recorded.

6. *Diss.* III.4. The Procurator of Epirus approaches Epictetus and explains that he has been mocked by a theater audience because of the partiality he displayed toward a certain comic actor. Instead of offering sympathy or advice regarding this public humiliation, Epictetus asserts that the crowd was merely mirroring the official's own vices back to him. Beyond this no direct interaction is recorded as taking place between them and this passage's importance for our concern is minimal.

7. *Diss.* III.9. A rhetorician who is in Nicopolis before he travels onto Rome to attend a lawsuit visits Epictetus' school in the hopes of gleaning some advice from him about his forthcoming trial (1). Again pivoting the discussion to speak on a subject that he has not been asked to directly address, Epictetus enquires whether his guest has ever reflected on how he forms judgments (δόγματα) (2-6) and if he has ever set aside time to reflect upon, or has ever approached someone to help him with this task (7-10). He leads the inquirer to concede that properly understanding philosophy is of the greatest (μέγας) importance, and to exclaim to him: "Well then, does that require only a short time, something you can pick up in passing? . . . the fact is that you've seen me and nothing more," τί οὖν; ὀλίγου χρόνου χρείαν ἔχει καὶ ἔστι παρερχόμενον αὐτὸ λαβεῖν . . . εἶδες γάρ με καὶ πλέον οὐδέν (11-12). He admonishes the visitor for desiring a transitory, passive exposure to philosophy, and informs him that he will refuse any appeal to "help me out with this matter," βοήθησόν μοι εἰς τὸ πρᾶγμα, for "you haven't come here as you should come to a philosopher, but as one would to a greengrocer or a cobbler," ὡς πρὸς φιλόσοφον ἐλήλυθας, ἀλλ᾽ ὡς πρὸς λαχανοπώλην, ἀλλ᾽ ὡς πρὸς σκυτέα (10). Epictetus then (14) mockingly characterizes the casual manner in which the visitor has sought to gain familiarity with philosophy as being: "We are passing through and while we are waiting to charter our ship we can go and see Epictetus as well. Let us see what he is saying," οὔ: ἀλλὰ ᾽πάροδός ἐστι καὶ ἕως τὸ πλοῖον μισθούμεθα, δυνάμεθα καὶ Ἐπίκτητον ἰδεῖν: ἴδωμεν, τί ποτε λέγει.[54] Epictetus also reflects that this man must think that meeting him has been like visiting a stone or a statue (12).

Two themes that emerge from this survey are of particular interest for me. Firstly, Epictetus discounts the benefit of passingly engaging others with philosophy, and emphasizes that for a person to profit from its insights they should commit themselves to an extended period of study. Secondly, he declines to enter into, or tries to quickly end conversations with individuals who, even from just a visible inspection, he believes lack the skill or disposition to respond to philosophical insight. Indeed, only in one passage (#1) is a positive exchange between him and a visitor to his school portrayed as occurring throughout (and wherein Epictetus intimates that the person should return to the school for further studies), and once (#5) his willingness to dialogue in depth about philosophical matters is stated partway through a conversation that he had otherwise been expressing a desire to cease. As Ronald Hock notes, Epictetus' characteristic response seems to be to "drive away," "discourage," and issue "warnings" to visitors,[55] and this is a stance that, I suggest, Epictetus himself reflects upon when he remarks on his stone/statue like disposition (*Diss.* III.9.12) his and habit of not talking to many people (*Diss.* III.1.36).

EPICTETUS ON THE NATURAL DRAWING OF PHILOSOPHERS

I propose that two passages can help us better comprehend Epictetus' rationale for adopting this discouraging approach toward visitors to his school. In the first passage for our concern, returning to the text that I considered earlier in this chapter, Epictetus mockingly inquires: "Does a philosopher invite people to a lecture?," φιλόσοφος δ᾽ ἐπ᾽ ἀκρόασιν παρακαλεῖ; he proceeds to explain: "Is it not rather the case that, as the sun draws sustenance to itself, so the philosopher draws to himself those to whom he is to do good? What physician ever invites a person to come and be cured by him?,"[56] οὐχὶ δ᾽ ὡς ὁ ἥλιος ἄγει αὐτὸς ἐφ᾽ ἑαυτὸν τὴν τροφήν, οὕτως δὲ καὶ οὗτος ἄγει τοὺς ὠφεληθησομένους; ποῖος ἰατρὸς παρακαλεῖ, ἵνα τις ὑπ᾽ αὐτοῦ θεραπευθῇ. In the first analogy, Epictetus draws upon Stoic cosmological theory and notes that the sun is able to maintain its light and heat by drawing, ἀγάω, rays to itself,[57] and in the second he observes that physicians do not seek the sick, but instead people who are afflicted by illness search them out and request their assistance. Epictetus uses both analogies to press the same point: his students have misunderstood and inverted where the onus for philosophical engagement should lie, as well as the process through which laypeople should come to philosophy. Epictetus believes that individuals who can benefit from philosophy will be unstoppably drawn toward it, and will purposefully pursue the philosopher.

Epictetus states this position more concretely in the following passage, which, I suggest, also provides an important insight into his rationale for assuming a challenging stance toward lay inquirers in his school:

> It is not easy to gain young men for philosophy, any more than one can get hold of soft cheese on a hook; but those who are naturally gifted, even if one tries to move then away, hold themselves fast all the more strongly to reason. And so Rufus usually tried to turn people away, using that as a test to discern the gifted from the ungifted. For he used to say "Just as a stone, even if you throw it aloft, will fall down to earth by virtue of its own nature, so it is with the gifted

individual: the more one tries to beat him off, the more he inclines towards the object that is natural to him."[58]

τῶν νέων τοὺς μαλακοὺς οὐκ ἔστι προτρέψαι ῥᾴδιον: οὐδὲ γὰρ τυρὸν ἀγκίστρῳ λαβεῖν: οἱ δ᾽ εὐφυεῖς, κἂν ἀποτρέπῃς, ἔτι μᾶλλον ἔχονται τοῦ λόγου. διὸ καὶ ὁ Ῥοῦφος τὰ πολλὰ ἀπέτρεπεν τούτῳ δοκιμαστηρίῳ χρώμενος τῶν εὐφυῶν καὶ ἀφυῶν. ἔλεγε γὰρ ὅτι ʻὡς ὁ λίθος, κἂν ἀναβάλῃς, ἐνεχθήσεται κάτω ἐπὶ γῆν κατὰ τὴν αὐτοῦ κατασκευήν, οὕτως καὶ ὁ εὐφυής, ὅσῳ μᾶλλον ἀποκρούεταί τις αὐτόν, τοσούτῳ μᾶλλον νεύει ἐφ᾽ ὃ πέφυκεν.᾽

In this passage Epictetus restates the concept that individuals who can benefit from philosophy, or who are naturally gifted, εὐφυεῖς, for its study will (seemingly irresistibly) hold fast, ἔχω, and incline, νεύω, themselves toward it—a perspective that it can be noted Seneca also alludes to.[59] Epictetus' comments also indicate that the selective stance he takes toward laypeople (ἀποτρέπω, to turn away) is not the result of misanthropy, but is a strategy/test, δοκιμαστήριον, that he has adopted from his philosophical teacher Rufus' practice, whereby he interacted with visitors in such a way so that those individuals who lacked the skill, disposition, and unshakeable resolution to undergo philosophical instruction would be prompted to leave. In this light I should note that there is also a possibility that a strain of thinking within Stoicism which held that some that people are intended by nature to be laypeople has exerted an influence over Epictetus' view, but we lack any statement from him which would allow us to state this with any certainty.[60]

The understanding that people who can benefit from philosophy will be naturally drawn toward it and be identifiable is, I suggest, key in revealing how Epictetus resolved the possible tension of him being hesitant about actively engaging *laypeople* with philosophical explication, but his maintaining the acceptability of and indeed himself vocationally pursuing the instruction of *student*s. As we have seen, his objection to impacting laypeople with philosophy rests upon three convictions: firstly, that attempting to convey philosophical wisdom to nonphilosopher is troublesome and ineffective; secondly, that other peoples' judgments are solely theirs to direct; and thirdly, the focus of an individual's efforts should be upon monitoring and refining their own, likely vacillating and fragile, adherence to virtue. The challenging, almost intimidating, stance that Epictetus and Rufus adopt toward lay visitors to their respective schools seem to intend to exclude individuals whom it would be a distraction or waste of effort to engage with.[61] This vetting process seems to address the first two objections that we have seen Epictetus raise regarding the futility of public engagement.

Regarding the third reason, to not divert our focus onto the moral advance of others, Epictetus' position on the specific calling and equipping of the philosopher which I explored at the opening of this chapter would, I suggest, seem to excuse them from this restriction. That is to say, Epictetus considers philosophers to be mature enough, and as having been specifically tasked by nature to be capable of routinely considering and supervising the moral awareness of others, but that individuals who are not professional philosophers should refrain from laboring in any dedicated manner upon refining the disposition and actions of others.

One contemporary writer who, I suggest, reflects upon the perspective that is delineated above is Dio Chrysostom. Dio, who we saw in the first chapter was censured by Epictetus for directing his philosophical speeches to large audiences, in turn expresses his disapproval about more restrictive methods of philosophical instruction in a passage where he surveys prevailing attitudes toward philosophical engagement. He begins his appraisal by remarking that robust and beneficial forms of philosophy are "not often heard," οὐ πολλάκις ἀκηκόατε, because:

> For some among that company [of philosophers] do not appear in public at all and prefer not to make the venture, possibly because they despair of being able to improve the masses; others exercise their voices in what we call lecture-halls, having secured as hearers men who are in league with them and tractable.[62]

> οἱ μὲν γὰρ αὐτῶν ὅλως εἰς πλῆθος οὐκ ἴασιν οὐδὲ θέλουσι διακινδυνεύειν, ἀπεγνωκότες ἴσως τὸ βελτίους ἂν ποιῆσαι τοὺς πολλούς: οἱ δ᾽ ἐν τοῖς καλουμένοις ἀκροατηρίοις φωνασκοῦσιν, ἐνσπόνδους λαβόντες ἀκροατὰς καὶ χειροήθεις ἑαυτοῖς.

This portrayal seems to match with Epictetus' stance, namely a form of philosophizing that does not seek to place itself within a public setting or to better (βελτίους) the morals of crowds, and in which supervision is offered to students who have proved themselves to be tractable/amenable, χειροήθεις.[63] We should, of course, bear in mind Dio's purpose in this passage, which becomes apparent as he continues to assert that contemporary Cynics are largely concerned with jokes and trivialities; other philosophers articulate an inoffensive version of philosophy in order to win acclaim; and a small number of philosophers who do speak frankly regarding philosophical tenets only manage to express a few sentences before they fall silent in case they have caused their audience offense.[64] Through these remarks Dio is, of course, presenting himself as being a uniquely commendable figure who succeeds in conveying authentic philosophical thought within a public context. His account is, therefore, doubtless an exaggerated one, but in order to draw benefit from it he must have believed he was relaying a broadly recognizable portrayal to his audience. Certainly, regarding the first category of philosopher he does appear to be voicing a genuine perspective.

CONCLUSION

Epictetus' selective stance regarding public engagement seems, I suggest, to resonate with Diogenes' portrayal of Zeno's approach, by noting of which I noted at the opening of this chapter. Regarding the Stoic movement more broadly, I have observed that previous scholarly inquiry has highlighted the apprehension that Persius and Manilius display toward public engagement, and I have raised evidence here which suggests that Rufus' and Marcus' views on the topic correspond with Epictetus'. Moreover, the lack of evidence for any popularizing movement within Stoicism, for example of the sort that marked out philosophies such as Epicureanism,[65] might be taken to imply that the selective perspective I have traced here was broadly characteristic of the school as a whole. On this point, I propose that scholarship, which has probed and seemingly largely discounted suggestion that philosophical schools provide a precedent for the early Christian missionary practices, has the potential to help situate Epictetus' and the wider Stoic movement's apparent disinterest in engaging in overt "missionary" activities within its historical context.[66]

The contrary position of a Stoic who relays philosophy in an openly public space is only attested by the one-sentence remark to this effect from Diogenes regarding Chrysippus' activity in the Lyceum. In addition, Epictetus' recollection that in his youth (although we cannot know if this was while he was definitely under the influence of Rufus and Stoicism) he had indiscriminately approached people to engage in philosophical deliberation, and the frequency with which he felt he should address his students' compulsion to involve themselves in such activities surely implies that some Stoics would deviate from the normative approach that their school adopted toward discouraging public engagement.

In the rest of this book, I will probe the question as to whether we should conclude that Epictetus not only declines to communicate philosophy to laypeople, but he actively discourages such attempts: Does he show any concern or awareness for these people who he believes will never obtain philosophical awareness?

NOTES

1. Diog. Laert. 7.5. Regarding the mix of public and private activities that were held in the Stoa Poikile, see the useful discussion in Millet (1988, 215).

2. Diog. Laert. 7.14.

3. Diog. Laert. 7.22.

4. Diog. Laert. 7.19.

5. Diog. Laert. 7.185. On the large audiences that the Lyceum could hold, see Diog. Laert. 5.37, and comments from Natali (2013, 88). On Chrysippus' subsequent lecturing in the Odeon, see Diog. Laert. 7.184.

6. See wider discussion by Mann (2011, 87), including on Persius' Stoicism (2011, 87–88; 102–103).

7. *Astron.* 1.137. See also *Astron.* 3.38-39.

8. *Sat.* 1.4.

9. Bartsch (2015, 115, 127) notes that in Persius' *Satires*: "Cornutus is depicted as focusing deeply on the needs of a single student, rather than directing his attention to the citizens at large. . . . Cornutus stays in his house tutoring a single disciple. We hear of no lectures or displays of philosophical learning, and in fact those philosophers who do circumambulate the city . . . are shown to be frauds through and through." Bartsch (2015, 125, 179) further characterizes the perspective in the *Satires* as being: "Don't aim at others, but take a look at yourself. . . . like his Stoic contemporaries, he evinces a total lack of interest in this [public] forum" and (179) "Persius' extravagantly sensual figural language is not put to the service of Stoic proselytizing." For a fuller discussion, see Bartsch (2015, 125–126, 179).

10. *Diss.* III.21.18.

11. *Diss.* III.1.22.

12. *Diss.* III.23.8. See also III.19.29.

13. On the Stoic position that suicide can be appropriate in certain circumstances, see Stephens (2014).

14. *Diss.* II.15.4-13.

15. E.g. *Diss.* III.13.22, and III.21.23.

16. E.g. *Diss.* III.22.82; 26.28; IV.8.32. On Epictetus' view that philosophers require a call from God, see Ierodiakonou (2007), Yieh (2008, 192–195), and MacGillivray (2020).

17. *Diss.* I.29.46. See also *Diss.* III.24.112-113.

18. *Diss.* III.21.10, 11.

19. That an individual who divulged the mysteries to the uninitiated was viewed as being guilty of impiety, see for example Diog. Laert. 7.186.

20. *Diss.* III.21.14-16.

21. *Diss.* III.21.17-18.

22. *Diss.* III.21.23.

23. *Diss.* IV.8.36-43.

24. Yieh (2008, 197, 205) comments: "because teaching moral philosophy is a divine appointment, there is little wonder that Epictetus mentioned divine calling so frequently in his discourses to justify his role as a moral teacher. . . . He believed that a man needed a divine calling to be a philosopher."

25. *Diss.* III.24.22-24. Regarding Epictetus' understanding of personal and communal responsibility, see Dunson (2011, 92–107).

26. *Diss.* IV.12.12, and I.29.12. See also *Diss.* II.8.21-23. See also I.17.23-26 and remarks from Sorabji (2006, 187–192).

27. For useful discussions over whether the records of Epictetus' philosophy, and especially the *Enchiridion*, were structured for outsiders, consider Sellars (2007, 135–138).

28. *Diss.* II.12.12.

29. *Diss.* II.12.2-24.

30. See Gellius *Att.* 15.11.3-5, and Suet *Dom.* 10.3.

31. *Diss.* II.12.10-16.

32. *Diss.* II.12.25.

33. *Diss.* II.15.13.

34. *Diss.* III.23.27, 28.

35. *Diss.* III.23.22-23, see also IV.8.17-23.

36. See *Diss.* III.24.118, and *Ench.* 46 and 47.

37. *Diss.* II.1.36-38.

38. *Diss.* IV.6.3, 5-6, 11.

39. Yieh (2008, 205): "Epictetus seemed to consider it futile to try to convert the general mass because not everybody could live a philosopher's life."

40. Annas (2007, 151).

41. *Diss.* III.26.10.

42. *Diss.* I.12.17-19, 34-35.

43. *Diss.* I.29.30, 64.

44. *Diss.* I.29.66.

45. *Ench.* 16.

46. *Diss.* III.24.18, and *Ench.* 46, 47.

47. On the influence of Epictetus' philosophy upon Marcus, see Stephens (2013, 59–70).

48. For example, *Med.* 8.17: "For if you can, you should put the person right; or if you are unable to, at least put the matter itself right." See also *Med.* 5.28, 6.27, 8.17, 8.59, 9.11.

49. Sellars (2019, 10, 11) comments that Marcus insists "that we ought to pay less attention to what goes on in the souls of other people and instead focus our attention on taking care of our own soul (e.g., *Med.* 2.8, 2.23). . . . Where he differs from Socrates is that his concern is almost exclusively with taking care of himself rather than exhorting others to do the same." Sellars also (2019, p.11 n.34) notably argues: "Compare [Marcus' inward focus] with Epictetus, *Diss.* 1.15, where Epictetus also focuses attention on self-care, and discourages excessive concern about the mental states of others." Regarding this passage, see the discussion below.

50. E.g. consider especially his remarks at *Med.* 4.18 and 8.56, and also at *Med.* 2.6, 8, 13; 5.25. Regarding *Med.* 6.50, see note 53.

51. *Med.* 9.29.

52. For example, Reydams-Schils (2005, 110): "If we connect this passage [*Med.* 6.50] to his doubts about the possibility of changing the conviction of others (9.29), we realize again how modest he had to be in his expectations. The outcome of this analysis, then, is that the Roman Stoic who is the most committed to political action because he has the most power to affect outcomes also emphasizes reservation the most strongly." This point is stated even more strongly in Wildberger (2018, 184–186). See also Annas (2007, 151).

53. See *Diss.* II.14.20, and 16.2, Seneca *Ep.* 76.4, Persius *Sat.* 5, S.H.A. *Marcus Aurelius* 3.1.

54. *Diss.* III.9.10, 14.

55. Hock (1992, 139).

56. *Diss.* III.23.27.
57. See the discussion in Oldfather (1928, 178 n.2).
58. *Diss.* III.6.9-10.
59. See also Seneca's comments at *Tranq.* 3.6.
60. On this perspective see, for example, Plut. *Mor.* 1050 C-D *Med.* 6.42, 7.70, 9.42, and comments in Brunt (2013, 476), and Gill (2013, 159).
61. See Epictetus comments *Diss.* II.21.10: "Do I go to my teacher, as though to an oracle, ready to obey," ἔρχομαι πρὸς τὸν διδάσκαλον ὡς ἐπὶ τὰ χρηστήρια πείθεσθαι παρεσκευασμένος.
62. *Or.* 32.8.
63. Although not with his passage in mind, Long (2002, 122) has noted about Epictetus and Dio that "their lives and styles went in very different directions. Dio the courtier and the modern equivalent of a media personality, Epictetus shunning fame and teaching in provincial Nicopolis."
64. *Or.* 32.9-12.
65. MacGillivray (2015). Consider also the popularizing effort of the second century CE Epicurean Diogenes of Oenoanda.
66. For example, see Goodman (1994, 1–5, 32–37), who, 32, notes: "The search for universal proselytizing will prove equally unproductive in a scrutiny of the process by which philosophical ideas were diffused in the Roman empire. This may seem surprising, for it has been quite widely supposed that philosophers in Hellenistic period and after were eager to convert to the tenets of their philosophy as many individuals as they could reach." Méndez-Moratalla (2004, 58, 60) likewise remarks: "In the endeavour to relate the worlds of philosophy and conversion, it should be borne in mind that modern presuppositions about the importance of the wide diffusion of ideas and of gaining as many adherences as possible could be misleading . . . the majority of the philosophical schools perceived their role as one of improving people's lives within their own social spheres, and not as one of persuading them to join a given community or of inviting them to live in solitude." See also the comments from Annas (2017, 211).

Chapter 4

Nonscholastic Instruction and Primitive Humanity

In this chapter I will explore two interlinked topics. The first regards remarks in Stoic literature that suggest they believe there are nonphilosophical mechanisms that can incline people to act and think in appropriate/suitable ways. The second relates to the Stoics' conception of primitivism and its potential to provide insights to us on how they might perceive that people can be beneficially influenced independently of intellectual enterprise.

THE STOICS AND NONPHILOSOPHICAL DIRECTION

As I have explored in the first chapter, it should not be a matter of surprise that individuals who labored to advance along the long and demanding road of philosophical study believed that there was a substantial benefit that philosophy could supply to them. As Marcus Aurelius, for instance, asserts:

> So what can serve as our escort and guide? One thing and one alone, philosophy; and that consists in keeping the guardian-spirit within us inviolate and free from harm, and ever superior to pleasure and pain.[1]

> τί οὖν τὸ παραπέμψαι δυνάμενον; ἓν καὶ μόνον φιλοσοφία: τοῦτο δὲ ἐν τῷ τηρεῖν τὸν ἔνδον δαίμονα ἀνύβριστον καὶ ἀσινῆ, ἡδονῶν καὶ πόνων κρείσσονα.

In this chapter I will, however, consider whether the Stoics conceive that routes apart from philosophical instruction can offer some insight to people—a topic that has been left unexplored by the interpreters of the school's thought. One notable exception though comes from an observation that Christopher Gill makes regarding the Stoics' propensity to credit the lives of figures who did not belong to their school as exhibiting exemplary moral behavior. His reflections regarding this are worth quoting at length:

> For committed Stoic students and teachers, of course, the projected route to wisdom must lie in the combination of philosophical understanding, based on the integration of the three branches of knowledge, and ethical progress, as embodied both in character development and in practical action. But the tendency in Stoicism to present as candidates for wisdom pre-Stoic thinkers such as Socrates and Diogenes the Cynic, and also non-philosophers such as Odysseus and Hercules, points towards a broader view. This is that, as stressed elsewhere, all human beings as such have the natural capacity to make progress towards perfect wisdom, a belief which also implies a confidence that this progress is possible despite wide varieties in social, cultural, and intellectual contexts of developments.[2]

Gill has also more recently drawn attention to the presence of this phenomenon in Marcus Aurelius' *Meditations*,[3] but again he does not seek to explore this insight in any further detail, and so is a task that I will attempt to undertake in the rest of this book.

Before I consider this issue in relation to the extant records of Epictetus' discussions, there are, I suggest, additional indications of the Stoics' belief in the existence of nonphilosophical means of making moral advancement that should be highlighted. In particular, we can note that the same thinkers who claim moral progress is contingent upon the provision of philosophy can also on occasions appear to credit nonphilosophical/nonscholastic techniques as being of some assistance. For example, in *Epistle* 94 Seneca argues at length that precepts (*praecepta*) are able to partially awaken peoples' natural understanding of goodness, asserting: "They [precepts] need no special pleader; they go straight to our emotions, and help us simply because Nature is exercising her proper function," *adfectus ipsos tangunt et natura vim suam exercente proficient.*[4] He proceeds to liken the exposure to precepts to that of being in the company of a wise (*sapiens*) person, and the passive manner in which their presence can, without them even speaking, help *(juvo)* the people around them to cease doing wrong; with Seneca noting: "Just how this happens would be hard for me to tell you, but I am sure that it has happened. . . . You will not realize how or when it helps you, but you will realize that it has," *Nec tibi facile dixerim quemadmodum prosit, sicut illud intellego profuisse . . . non deprehendes, quemadmodum aut quando tibi prosit, profuisse deprendes.*[5] Significantly for our concerns, regarding the scope that precepts have to impact the ignorant, Seneca reflects: "Who would deny that even quite ignorant people are indeed struck by certain precepts," *Quis autem negabit feriri quibusdam praeceptis, efficaciter etiam inperitissimos*, and he cites precepts that speak against excess, greed, and selfish living, and continues to comment upon the nontechnical manner in which they are able to impact others: "So strongly, indeed, does mere truth, unaccompanied by reason, attract/lead us," *adeo etiam sine ratione ipsa veritas ducit.*[6] Further defending his views regarding the ability that precepts have to shape (*formo*) the lives of individuals who are not known to have pursued philosophical instruction, Seneca highlights Marcus Agrippa's (apparently well-known) dependence upon a precept which commended concord, which, Seneca remarks, helped Agrippa to be a more faithful brother and friend.[7]

Furthermore, for our interest Marcus Aurelius argues:

> An unphilosophical but none the less effective aid to attaining contempt for death is to review in your thoughts those who have clung tenaciously to life. (For how are they any better off than those who died a premature death?)[8]

> Ἰδιωτικὸν μέν, ὅμως δὲ ἀνυστικὸν βοήθημα πρὸς θανάτου καταφρόνησιν ἡ ἀναπόλησις τῶν γλίσχρως ἐνδιατριψάντων τῷ ζῆν.

Here, and in a similar passage,[9] he proposes that a simple nonphilosophical but nevertheless effective (ἀνυστικός) exercise can help people to overcome their fear of death. It is important to highlight that the word that is translated here as nonphilosophical is the adjective form of ἰδιώτης—ἰδιωτικόν, or literally a "layperson-like" method of gaining accurate insights. That Marcus believes laypeople have a means of gaining moral improvement seems to be explicitly reflected upon here.

Turning to Epictetus' discussion with this theme in mind, he can be found opining thus:

> If one has to learn by means of deception that external things which lie outside of the sphere of choice and are nothing to us, for my part I would be willing to undergo such a fiction if it would allow me to live in peace of mind and to be free from troubles from that time onward. What condition you desire for yourself is for you to consider.[10]

> εἰ γὰρ ἐξαπατηθέντα τινὰ ἔδει μαθεῖν, ὅτι τῶν ἐκτὸς καὶ ἀπροαιρέτων οὐδέν ἐστι πρὸς ἡμᾶς, ἐγὼ μὲν ἤθελον τὴν ἀπάτην ταύτην, ἐξ ἧς ἤμελλον εὐρόως καὶ ἀταράχως βιώσεσθαι, ὑμεῖς δ' ὄψεσθ' αὐτοὶ τί θέλετε.

Here Epictetus argues that even by means of deception people can learn (μανθάνω) the lack of value that should be attached to things that fall outside of their internal control.[11] The implication of Epictetus' remarks here (which also find attestation in the records of Chrysippus' opinions, and perhaps also in Seneca's appeal to Epicurean literature in the earlier sections of his *Epistles*[12]) are that even if erroneous ideas or doctrines result in the moral progress of their recipient he would support this—although he would doubtless countenance that if possible accurate grounds upon which such principles can be secured should be found.

Might these passages be interpreted as being indeterminate or casual remarks that should not have any particular interpretive weight placed upon them? Or should they be understood to articulate some broader schema of thought, and one that has a bearing on how Stoics such as Epictetus view laypeople, and the means through which they might be influenced? To begin to answer this question, and to suggest the possibility of the latter, we can note Gretchen Reydams-Schils' remarks upon the Stoics' conception of the place that their expositions of philosophical thought hold:

> The Stoics, for their part, do not recognize "theory" as a form of pure contemplation and engagement in an intelligible, higher-order reality; for them, even though they do value contemplation of the divine order manifested in the universe, theory is primarily what we would call the theoretical aspect of philosophy, which makes sense only to the extent that it informs concrete actions and one's overall disposition in life. As Musonius Rufus puts it [*Fr.* 14], "philosophy is nothing else than to search out by reason what is right and proper, and by deeds to put it into practice."[13]

For the Stoics, as Richard Beniston has also briefly argued,[14] theoretical discussions are only important as long as they can aid the formation of correct understanding and conduct in people. Their concern is (at least in principle) not concentrated upon the theories themselves, but rather the universal/natural truths they are thought to disclose.[15] The importance of this distinction can, I suggest, be profitably seen in a remark that Seneca offers in one of his *Letters* on how a wise man can be benefited by the company of a fellow sage:

> For the wise man is not all-knowing. And even if he were all-knowing, someone might be able to devise and point out short cuts, by which the whole matter is more readily disseminated.[16]

> *non enim omnia sapiens scit. Etiam si sciret, breviores vias rerum aliqui excogitare posset et has indicare, per quas facilius totum opus circumfertur.*

It is apparent that it is not the delineation of philosophical theories that are of value for Seneca, but rather the principles that are inherent to them. Indeed, we see that he advocates jettisoning an argument if a new, more effective rendering of its propositions can be ascertained. In this regard, on his understanding that continuing advances in human knowledge might be made, see also his comments at *Nat. Quest.* 7.25-26.

The above perspective might also explain the notable lack of expository concern that is manifested in the ancient Stoic literary tradition,[17] and provide additional context for understanding Epictetus' consistently voiced concern that his students will confuse familiarity with the school's texts to be the goal of their tuition, rather than the refinement of their character.[18] So, we can note, for instance, that when a pupil asks Epictetus to observe his expert handling of Chrysippus' *On Impulse*, the philosopher responds trenchantly:

That is not what I am looking for, slave, but how you are exercising your impulse to act and not to act, and how you managing your desire and aversions, how you approaching all things, how you apply yourself to them, and prepare for them, and whether in harmony with nature or out of harmony.[19]

ἀνδράποδον, οὐ τοῦτο ζητῶ, ἀλλὰ πῶς ὁρμᾷς καὶ ἀφορμᾷς, πῶς ὀρέγῃ καὶ ἐκκλίνεις, πῶς ἐπιβάλλῃ καὶ προστίθεσαι καὶ παρασκευάζῃ, πότερα συμφώνως τῇ φύσει ἢ ἀσυμφώνως.

Moreover, he elsewhere remarks:

Is this, then, the important and commendable thing, to be able to understand and interpret Chrysippus? Who says that it is? . . . What right has [the competent interpreter] to be proud of himself? Even Chrysippus himself has no reason, if he only interprets the will of nature, but does not follow it himself; how much less his interpreter. For we do not need Chryippus on his own account, but we only need him to help us follow nature.[20]

ἆρ' οὖν τοῦτό ἐστι τὸ μέγα καὶ τὸ θαυμαστὸν νοῆσαι Χρύσιππον ἢ ἐξηγήσασθαι; καὶ τίς λέγει τοῦτο; . . . ποία οὖν ἐνθάδ' ὀφρὺς τοῦ ἐξηγουμένου; οὐδ' αὐτοῦ Χρυσίππου δικαίως, εἰ μόνον ἐξηγεῖται τὸ βούλημα τῆς φύσεως, αὐτὸς δ' οὐκ ἀκολουθεῖ· πόσῳ πλέον τοῦ ἐκεῖνον ἐξηγουμένου; οὐδὲ γὰρ Χρυσίππου χρείαν ἔχομεν δι' αὐτόν.

In this passage, the role of the school's key texts are laid bare. There is no sense of the infallibility or divine-like revelation of Chrysippus' writings; rather (and unlike many other philosophical schools' stances toward their key texts[21]) they are viewed in a perfunctory manner. The understanding in Stoicism that their texts and arguments are only conduits for natural law, means, I suggest, that they are less likely to conclude that the tools of moral progress can only be found within the confines of their school, and are more likely to consider that other avenues might relay some valuable insights to people.

THE STOICS AND ΚΑΘΗΚΟΝΤΑ

In further orienting our discussion, an exploration of the Stoic conception of virtue and the nature of its attainment should also be briefly undertaken. Of first importance, it should be highlighted that for the proponents of the Stoa, virtue does not consist of degrees which would allow a quantifiable evaluation of an individual's virtue to be obtained, for example whether they are modestly, partially, or almost completely virtuous. Instead, virtue and viciousness are held in Stoicism to exist in binary opposition to each other, and the sole assessment that can be made is whether a person is either virtuous or vicious. In this regard, until every part of an individual's character and their outlook is brought to securely accord with nature, it is understood that they cannot claim to have achieved virtue. As A. A. Long notes: "In Stoic ethics a miss is as bad as a mile . . . until a man is good he is bad."[22] In clarifying this viewpoint by way of analogy, the Stoics memorably observed that pondering over the depth at which a person is drowning is irrelevant: whether they are one foot or one fathom under water, they are nevertheless drowning and are perishing.[23]

This perspective regarding the bifurcation of humanity into either nonvirtuous or virtuous status holds particular significance in Stoic thought given their belief in the scarcity of people who achieve the latter state, that is, the elusive sage.[24] The consequential perspective is that they hold almost every individual, even those who dedicate themselves to achieve philosophical reform, belong ultimately in the ranks of the vicious.[25]

This conclusion does not, however, signify despondency in Stoicism. Even if a person does not reach perfection, the commending of progressing toward virtue is well attested in Stoic works, and, as I noted in the first chapter, is a theme that has particular prominence in Epictetus' discussions. Furthermore, the Stoics observed that the actions of the nonsage could, from an external vantage point, mirror those of the sage, for example both individuals could be involved in providing benefaction and support to their wider community and families in an indistinguishable manner. In this regard, members of the Stoa differentiated the conduct of the nonsage, which they view as being actions that *accord* with virtue (an appropriate/suitable action—κάθηκον), but which ultimately rests upon their fallible and vacillating understanding, and the actions of the sage which *are* virtuous (a perfect action—κατόρθωμα), and which emanate from their stable and perfected understanding.[26]

Usefully, Diogenes Laertius documents that the Stoics hold that καθήκοντα are not contingent upon the philosophical cognizance of an agent, such as when plants and animals perform actions which accord with their nature, despite them not having any comprehension of the underlying teleological purpose that prompts their instincts/actions.[27] Regarding humans, Diogenes proceeds to document that "actions belonging to duty are those that reason prescribes our doing, as is the case with honoring one's parents, brothers, country, and spending time with one's friends," παρὰ τὸ καθῆκον δέ, ὅσα μὴ αἱρεῖ λόγος, ὡς ἔχει τὰ τοιαῦτα, γονέων ἀμελεῖν, ἀδελφῶν ἀφροντιστεῖν, φίλοις μὴ συνδιατίθεσθαι, πατρίδα ὑπερορᾶν καὶ τὰ παραπλήσια.[28] Whether the Stoics would hold that humans who, unlike plants and animals, *are* invested with rationality, require some level of *philosophical* awareness before they can perform καθήκοντα (such as in engaging in actions that honor their parents or community) is, I suggest, a topic that warrants extended discussion. In part I will do so by highlighting Seneca's and Posidonius' position on primeval humanity,[29] and argue that this topic discloses their belief that certain situations can allow some people to achieve a form of proto-virtue without engaging in epistemic reflection upon good and evil.

EARLY HUMANITY AND PRIMITIVISM

The broadly held presumption in antiquity that human society in its earliest epoch observed a level of appropriate behavior and nobility that subsequent generations have failed to adopt has long been recognized,[30] as has the impact that this understanding had upon the philosophical schools, especially after the first century CE.[31] In Stoicism in particular, we can note that their confidence in primitivism, the belief that the earliest stage of human history was superior in a meaningful way (either intellectually, materially, or morally) to those that followed it, was augmented and informed by their conviction that the world has been providentially fashioned by nature/god,[32] and that every individual has the capacity to obtain moral perfection. We can, for instance, witness these two presumptions being clearly expressed in the writings of Marcus Aurelius, who reminds himself of the providential organization of early human society,[33] and who further reflects:

> Do not suppose that if you personally find that something is hard to achieve, it is therefore beyond human capacity; rather, if something is possible and appropriate for human beings, assume that it must also be within your own reach.[34]

> Μή, εἴ τι αὐτῷ σοὶ δυσκαταπόνητον, τοῦτο ἀνθρώπῳ ἀδύνατον ὑπολαμβάνειν, ἀλλ᾽ εἴ τι ἀνθρώπῳ δυνατὸν καὶ οἰκεῖον, τοῦτο καὶ σεαυτῷ ἐφικτὸν νόμιζε.

Utilizing the paths that had already been tracked by primitivistic thought, some Stoics sought to understand the pervasive presence of vice, which they hold scars contemporary society, by reasoning that humanity must have descended from an original state, where conformity to moral excellence was more uniform, and perhaps an easier quality to obtain.[35] With no extended or systematic treatise that outlines the Stoics' position on the features of early human society being extant, gaining an appreciation of their stance on this topic is challenging.[36] A profitable resource though can be found in Seneca's *Epistles* 90, where he interacts at length with the otherwise lost Golden Age myth that the Stoic philosopher Posidonius advanced.[37] Although focused upon countering Posidonius' assertion that the various technologies which humanity enjoy owe their provenance to the resourcefulness of philosophers/ sages,[38] throughout the letter—and especially in the introduction (§3-5), an excursus (§37-39), and the conclusion (§44-46)—numerous insights into the circumstances that they believe enabled the Golden Age to exist and the processes that led to its cessation are relayed.

First of all, in the opening of the discussion, Seneca approvingly cites Posidonius' understanding that primeval humanity's success was at least partially secured because of the presence of wise (*sapientes*) leaders:

> The first men and those who sprang from them, still unspoiled, followed nature, having one man as both their leader and their law, entrusting themselves to the control of one better than themselves. For nature has the habit of subjecting the weaker to the stronger. . . . Accordingly, in that age which is maintained to be the golden age, Posidonius holds that the government was under the jurisdiction of the wise. They kept their hands under control, and protected the weaker from the stronger. They gave advice, both to do and not to do; they showed what was useful and what was useless.[39]

> *Sed primi mortalium quique ex his geniti naturam incorrupti sequebantur, eundem habebant et ducem et legem, commissi melioris arbitrio. Naturae est enim potioribus deteriora summittere . . . Illo ergo saeculo, quod aureum perhibent, penes sapientes fuisse regnum Posidonius iudicat. Hi continebant manus et infirmiorem a validioribus tuebantur, suadebant Dissuadebantque et utilia atque inutilia monstrabant.*

These sages are envisaged as having inclined people to conform to correct behavior, not by any means of threat or menace, but because of the compliance of the population to follow their advice: with the most severe punishment that the leaders could propose apparently being that they would cease from supervising humanity's actions. The aspect that chiefly dominates Seneca's attention in *Ep.* 90, however, is that these first people emerged uncorrupted and ignorant of any other conditions than those that nature had instituted they should follow.[40] The characteristics of this society are outlined in both *Ep.* 90 and *Phae.* 480-558, a parallel account of the Golden Age that seems to have evaded comment in previous discussions of Seneca's views of early humanity.[41] In these passages, our forebears are credited with, for example, having avoided acquiring riches or wealth (*Ep.* 90.9, 24, 36, 40, 45/*Phae.* 490, 496-497, 528-531); having no understanding of the concepts of war, murder, or fear (*Ep.* 90.41, 43, 45/*Phae.* 492, 495-496, 531-535); depending upon the natural productivity of the land rather than looking to agricultural or farming methods to supplement their diet (*Ep.* 90.21/*Phae.* 502, 515-517, 535-539);[42] and as having resided in simply constructed and furnished houses—even comfortably sleeping under open skies (*Ep.* 90.10,17/*Phae.* 487).[43]

So beneficial were the first conditions of humanity that Seneca argues that no system or institution can be devised that will be able to surpass it,[44] which is strikingly discordant with numerous assessments from scholars who claim that, because of the lack of broad philosophical knowledge, Seneca believed this was an inferior environment for humanity to have existed in.[45] Seneca in fact continues to further exclaim that this first generation of humanity were blessed beyond all other subsequent generations of humanity:

> What race of men was ever more blest than that race? They enjoyed all nature in partnership. Nature sufficed for them, now the guardian, as before she was the parent, of all; and this her gift consisted of the assured possession by each man of the common resources. Why should I not even call that race the richest among mortals, since you could not find a poor person among them?[46]
>
> *Quid hominum illo genere felicius? In commune rerum natura fruebantur; sufficiebat illa ut parens ita tutela omnium, haec erat publicarum opum secura possessio. Quidni ego illud locupletissimum mortalium genus dixerim, in quo pauperem invenire non posses?*

What is remarkable is that even in this heavily idealized world, Posidonius and Seneca do not conceive of the success of primeval society as being due to any greater provision of moral insight that existed within the populace (i.e., they are of lay status). Its inhabitants were not thought to have the ability to comprehend or articulate the concepts of virtue or vice, but to have existed in a sort of proto-virtuous state. As Seneca proceeds to clarify, they "were not wise, even though they did what wise men do," *Non erant illi sapientes viri, etiam si faciebant facienda sapientibus*[47]; and that "Justice was unknown to them, unknown prudence, unknown also self-control and bravery; but their rude life possessed certain qualities akin to all these virtues," *seerat illis iustitia, deerat prudentia, deerat temperantia ac fortitudo. Omnibus his virtutibus habebat similia quaedam rudis vita.*[48] The excellence of their age was assured because they adhered to the counsel of the sages[49]—who we likewise cannot be certain were believed to have had a technical understanding of philosophy[50]—and so led lives that were closely aligned with nature's purposes.

The ability of the Stoics to conceive of the existence of such a world is, I believe, dependent upon their understanding that their philosophy expresses the accurate preconceptions of the good that every individual naturally holds (although does not necessarily understand), and would follow were they not beset by misapprehension, an idea that I have explored in the previous chapter at some length. The first humans' purity was, therefore, not thought to have been enabled on any epistemic basis, but because they lived in a world where their preconceptions could influence them without faulty ideas competing for acceptance and drawing them into vice.[51]

Seneca, however, continues to relay that the Golden Age came to a close after the emergence of greed and the lust for power in human society, stating at *Ep.* 90 that "avarice broke in upon a condition so happily ordained,"[52] *inrupit in res optime positas avaritia*, and in the *Phaedra*: "This peaceful compact was broken by the unholy madness for gain, by hasty anger and by lust which goads inflamed minds,"[53] *rupere foedus impius lucri furor et ira praeceps quaeque succensas agit libido mentes*. One notable effect of this incursion of greed that is recorded at *Ep.* 90.6 was that tyrants arose and supplanted the sages, and so compounded humanity's slide into degradation. Thereafter people embraced conditions that were the inverse of the ones they had previously enjoyed; with construction, fashion, glass-blown trinkets, weapons, and agricultural techniques, and so on, now monopolizing their attention.[54] Epitomizing the transformation of the circumstances and mindset of post–Golden Age humanity, Seneca tersely remarks: "a thatched roof once covered free men; under marble and gold dwells slavery,"[55] *culmus liberos texit, sub marmore atque auro servitus habitat*, a thought that he similarly expresses in the *Phaedra*.[56]

What allowed this violation of the natural order to occur is not recounted by Seneca,[57] but other passages in Seneca's writings indicate that he believes people have always been assailed by the temptation to err. So, at one juncture in his *Epistles*, he reflects:

> You are mistaken, my dear Lucilius, if you think that luxury, neglect of good manners, and other vices of which each man accuses the age in which he lives, are especially characteristic of our own epoch; no, they are the vices of mankind and not of the times. No era in history has ever been free from blame.[58]

> *Erras, mi Lucili, si existimas nostri saeculi esse vitium luxuriam et neglegentiam boni moris et alia, quae obiecit suis quisque temporibus; hominum sunt ista, non temporum. Nulla aetas vacavit a culpa.*

This passage, and another in his *Natural Questions*,[59] suggests that in Seneca's view vice was not (with perhaps the exception of its very first moments) absent from early human society,[60] but that it existed at a far-less amplitude than today where it is established as a pervasive and corrupting force. This understanding is, I propose, attested by Seneca's comments at *Ep.* 90, in which he remarks upon the increasing dominance that luxury has gained for itself over humanity's affections from age to age.[61]

With our ancestors' innocence having only been established by their ignorance and the lack of corrupting influences, when avarice continued its advance they would in Seneca's view have little effective means at their disposal to counter it. An analogy used by Epictetus is perhaps instructive in this regard:

> The soul is like a bowl that is filled with water; and impressions are like a ray of light that falls upon the water. If the water is disturbed, the light will appear to be disturbed along with it, though in reality it is not. So whenever someone is seized with vertigo, it is not the arts and virtues that are thrown into confusion, but the spirit that contains them; and, if this comes to rest, so will they too.[62]

> οἷόν ἐστιν ἡ λεκάνη τοῦ ὕδατος, τοιοῦτον ἡ ψυχή, οἷον ἡ αὐγὴ ἡ προσπίπτουσα τῷ ὕδατι, τοιοῦτον αἱ φαντασίαι. ὅταν οὖν τὸ ὕδωρ κινηθῇ, δοκεῖ μὲν καὶ ἡ αὐγὴ κινεῖσθαι, οὐ μέντοι κινεῖται. καὶ ὅταν τοίνυν σκοτωθῇ τις, οὐχ αἱ τέχναι καὶ αἱ ἀρεταὶ συγχέονται, ἀλλὰ τὸ πνεῦμα, ἐφ᾽ οὗ εἰσιν· καταστάντος δὲ καθίσταται κἀκεῖνα.

Taking this to apply to our discussion, primeval peoples' minds (i.e., the cup of water) remained at ease not because of their inherent resilience or stability, but because there were no forces to unsettle them. Once disturbed/set in motion (κινέω) a means to allow them to return to rest though needed to be found, and it is within this context that the Stoics find the reason for their philosophy's inception. Through *it* they believe that the natural order/principles the first humans had passively observed have been faithfully delineated and can be followed again—although now significantly only after intellectual exertion has been expended. This understanding is, I suggest, further outlined and clarified by Seneca in another letter, where he comments:

> It was once more simple because men's sins were on a smaller scale, and could be cured with but slight trouble; in the face, however, of all this moral topsy-turvy men must leave no remedy untried. . . . Against this overmastering and widespread madness philosophy has become a matter of greater effort, and has taken on strength in proportion to the strength which is gained by the opposition forces. It used to be easy to scold men who were slaves to drink and who sought out more luxurious food; it did not require a mighty effort to bring the spirit back to the simplicity from which it had departed only slightly.[63]

Fuit aliquando simplicior inter minora peccantes et levi quoque cura reme-
diabiles; adversus tantam morum eversionem omnia conanda sunt. Et utinam
sic denique lues ista vindicetur! . . . *Adversus tam potentem explicitumque late*
furorem operosior philosophia facta est et tantum sibi virium sumpsit, quantum
iis, adversus quae parabatur, accesserat. Expeditum erat obiurgare indulgentes
mero et petentes delicatiorem cibum; non erat animus ad frugalitatem magna vi
reducendus, a qua paullum discesserat.

Here Seneca argues that at first only a slight remedy was required to be
given to conduct people back to their original simple or temperate state.
However, with the increase of misapprehension in humanity, a more robust/
sophisticated solution had to be developed, and effort (*vis*) expended, that is,
philosophical thought, which itself has had to be reinforced with ever more
complexity to counterbalance the strengthening grip that error/vice has over
humanity.[64]

But what about the circumstances and mechanisms that prompted these
nonphilosophical people to live in a proto-virtuous way? Was their ability to
operate dependent upon the continuing existence of the Golden Age, or might
they be thought to remain impacting humanity through some—perhaps more
muted—avenues? An indication of the latter can be found within the account
of *Ep.* 90, in which Seneca approvingly refers to Posidonius' belief that the
role of the sages was not wholly obviated by tyranny, but:

A need arose for laws; and these very laws were in turn framed by the wise.
Solon, who established Athens upon a firm basis by just laws, was one of the
seven men renowned for their wisdom. Had Lycurgus lived in the same period,
an eight would have been added to that hallowed number seven. The laws of
Zaleucus and Charondas are praised; it was not, in the forum or in the offices
of skilled counsellors, but in the silent and holy retreat of Pythagoras, that these
two men learned the principles of justice which they were to establish in Sicily
(which at that time was prosperous) and throughout Grecian Italy.[65]

Sed postquam subrepentibus vitiis in tyrannidem regna conversa sunt, opus esse
legibus coepit, quas etipsas inter initia tulere sapientes. Solon qui Athenasaequo
iure fundavit, inter septem fuit sapienia notos. Lycurgum si eadem aetas tulisset,
sacro illinumero accessisset octavus. Zaleuci leges Charondaeque laudantur.
Hi non in foro nec inconsultorum atrio, sed in Pythagorae tacito illosanctoque
secessu didicerunt iura quae florenti tunc Siciliae et per Italiam Graeciae
ponerent.

By assuming the responsibility for the crafting of state law, the wise men
are envisaged by Seneca as at least to some extent being able to continue

to help direct humanity's actions and establish firm and just foundations for society in law. We should note, however (as we observed at n.48), that most of the individuals listed as belonging to this group are not credited with having any philosophical background, indicating that the wisdom they were thought to have might be a broad, rather than a technical or philosophical one. Furthermore, judging by the varying time periods and locations that these legislators inhabited, it is apparent that their role was not thought to have been a passing or isolated one, as Van Nuffelen and Van Hoof have briefly, but importantly, suggested:

> sages are thus a continuous presence in the history of mankind and not restricted to the Golden age. What makes the Golden age stand out is that wisdom and leadership fully coincided, creating a community that fully lived in line with nature. . . . Posidonius seems to see culture [including laws, political structures and arts] as a whole as the product of the reaction by the sages to the degeneration they witness. . . . This suggests that there may always be sages and philosophers who can adjust culture so as to bring mankind more in line with nature . . . [to] stem the tide of vice.[66]

I will explore the Stoics', and particularly Epictetus', understanding of civic law later in this book, but it is worth noting here that there is evidence which indicates Posidonius and Seneca believe that the law can still help to excise vice from society.

In another record of Posidonius' writings that has been preserved by Seneca, he remarks that for laws to be effective at persuading people to adhere to their decrees, concision and an authoritative, almost denouement-like, expression needs to be utilized.[67] Within this assertion, the emphasis on attempting to incline people to adopt correct patterns of behavior, and not to induct them into wise or higher ways of thought (i.e., to change them from being laypeople to philosophers) is again manifest, and is a concern which is made explicit when Posidonius concludes by portraying a person appealing to the legislator: "Warn me, tell me what you wish me to do; I am not learning but obeying," *Mone, dic, quid me velis fecisse; non disco, sed pareo.*[68]

Through the law we can see that humanity was not believed to have been left without any guidance until philosophy was formulated and students be gathered to be nurtured by its tenets.[69] But what about the other factor that I argued impelled people to act appropriately—their simple and uncorrupted environment? Is this dynamic also thought by Seneca to have retained its capacity to influence humanity? Seeming to confirm this, we can observe that his description of primeval society that he provides in the *Phaedra* is predicated on the scenario of someone relocating to the countryside where, removed from urban excess and debasement, they find they are able to live according to primitive principles again.[70] Furthermore, at *Ep.* 90 Seneca explicitly asserts that the characteristics of the Golden Age are replicated in Scythian (central Asian) and Syrtes (a desert region on the coast of Libya, whose people are presented as moral exempla by several classical authors[71]), specifically because of their apparent awareness that maintaining (ἔχω) the body does not require much labor, and because they dress themselves in the skins of foxes, mice, and live in simple houses dug out of the earth, which Seneca presumes parallels the actions of our first ancestors.[72] In this regard, evidence that suggests Posidonius believes aspects of the Golden Age persist in Mariandynian society (inhabitants of the South Black Sea coast) can also be usefully highlighted.[73] Meanwhile, we can note that in his *On Providence*, Seneca's description of the conditions that Germanic and nomadic tribes who live across the Danube laudably endure likewise mirrors these features.[74]

Significantly it is not just distant tribes or "noble savages"[75] who Seneca depicts as being positively impacted by their environment. Various scenarios and even occupations, I propose, are believed by him to function in a similar manner. For instance, in one passage Seneca argues that people should:

> Flee from delights, flee from good fortune that drains your strength. In good fortune your minds are dissolved, and unless something intervenes to *remind you of your lot as human beings*, your minds fade as if put to sleep in an unending drunkenness. . . . Because all things are harmful that have exceeded due measure, an excess of good fortune is exceedingly dangerous. It disturbs the brain. It lures our thoughts into baseless fantasies. It infuses a great deal of fogginess between fiction and truth.[76]

> *Fugite delicias, fugite enervantem felicitatem, qua animi permadescunt et nisi aliquid intervenit quod humanae sortis admoneat, manent velut perpetua ebrietate sopiti . . . Cum omnia quae excesserunt modum noceant, periculosissima felicitatis intemperantia est: movet cerebrum, in vanas mentes imagines evocat, multum inter falsum ac verum mediae caliginis fundit.*

The resonance with his description of the characteristics of the Golden Age, where technologies and luxuries are credited with having diverting humanity from their observance of self-restraint, is evident. Here though Seneca continues to outline his belief that misfortune can remind (*admoneo*) people of their more natural and appropriate disposition, that is, the apprehension that possessions and comfortable conditions do not help to engender a steady mindset,[77] and it can be observed throughout his writings that he conveys his belief that suffering can prompt people to behave and think more appropriately.[78] Drawing upon this concept of the dangers of abundance, Seneca elsewhere suggests that his ancestors had led more contented lives because they only knew of the resources that nature had laid in close prox- imity to them. Now, however, he demurs, ships with expansive manifests crisscross oceans and arouse a longing in people to obtain more possessions than they can ever hope to sate.[79]

Finally, with regard to Seneca, his account of Mucius Scaevola, a Roman soldier who was seized during a conflict with the Etruscans and who famously held his hand in a fire until it had burned away so that his desire to win glory at any cost would be evident to his captors, should also bear special attention:[80]

> Mucius put his hand into the fire. It is painful to be burned; but how much more painful to inflict such suffering upon oneself! Here was a man of no learning, not primed to face death and pain by any words of wisdom, and equipped only with the courage of a soldier.[81]
>
> *Mucius ignibus manum imposuit. Acerbum est uri: quanto acerbius si id te faci- ente patiaris! Vides hominem non eruditum nec ullis praeceptis contra mortem aut dolorem subornatum, militari tantum robore instructum.*

Here, Seneca labors that although Mucius had no education, his training as a soldier had instilled enough courage in him to allow him to rightly place obtaining honor above his physical well-being.

Turning to the records of Epictetus' discussions, although we do not know if he shares a similar conception of early humanity as Seneca and Posidonius do (although I will highlight evidence in chapter 6 that suggests he does), we can see a similar understanding of the impact that conditions can have upon nonphilosophically trained people. For example, at one point Epictetus asserts that, because of the brutal training their state forced upon them, the Spartans learned that injury can be dispassionately endured.[82] Furthermore, recalling Posidonius and Seneca's stance that Golden Age humanity had conducted themselves correctly because of the absence of corrupting influ- ences, we can note Epictetus' comment regarding his school being located at Nicopolis rather than at Rome:

> For, in truth, it is there at Rome where the great resources are, and the fortunes here in Nicopolis would appear like child's play there. That is why it is difficult for a person to be in control of his own impressions there, where the things that disturb them are so powerful.[83]
>
> ἐκεῖ γὰρ τῷ ὄντι αἱ μεγάλαι ὗλαί εἰσι καὶ οἱ ἐνθάδε πλοῦτοι ἐκεῖ παίγνια δοκοῦσιν. διὰ τοῦτο ἐκεῖ δύσκολον κρατῆσαι τῶν αὑτοῦ φαντασιῶν ὅπου τὰ ἐκ σείοντα μεγάλα.

Nicopolis, an insignificant city when compared to the sprawling capital that lay across the Adriatic, had fewer literary resources on hand to distract students, and also, I might add, displays of affluence (e.g., see his students' complaints regarding the standards of the baths at Nicopolis[84]) which, in Epictetus' estimation, meant that his pupils would be less likely to be tempted to slacken from the observance of their principles. Of relevance to this latter point, while Epictetus' move to Nicopolis appears to have been prompted by the expulsion of philosophers from Rome in 95 CE, the reason for his continued residency in the city long after the edict's effect would have lapsed is unknown. The stance that is expressed in the above text, along with those of other passages—and particularly the contents of the discourse entitled *To Those Who Have Devoted Their Efforts to Advancement at Rome*, πρὸς τοὺς περὶ τὰς ἐν Ῥώμῃ προαγωγὰς ἐσπουδακότας, where he states that as soon a a person got a smell of Rome he would forget his philosophical principles[85]—might, I suggest, provide us with the reason. In this regard we might profitably consider Marcus Aurelius' comments at *Med.* 11.20 on the different constitutions he believes marks rural and urban mice, with the latter, he argues, now showing signs of alarm at any hint of disturbance or threat.

More frequently, we can note Epictetus' belief of the benefits that some circumstances can provide to people is relayed when he references groups or scenarios that would be familiar to his students from their everyday experiences. For example, he advises them that they should learn how those who are healthy (ὑγιαίνω) live by looking at slaves and laborers,[86] argues that the training that wrestlers undergo leads them to be patient (ἀνεκτικός) and free from anger (ἀόργητος),[87] and suggests that having obnoxious neighbors can help people understand what it is to be considerate (εὐγνώμων).[88]

It is, however, Musonius Rufus, in a text that is worth quoting at length, who perhaps most clearly asserts that conditions can prompt people to adhere to correct behavior, a position which is, in part, no doubt motivated by his appreciation of Cynic asceticism.[89] After remarking upon an individual who has been raised in opulent surroundings, he comments:

Compare this young man with another one brought up in a somewhat Spartan manner, not accustomed to live in luxury, but trained to endure and inclined to listen to correct reasoning. If we then were to make these two young men listen to a philosopher speaking about death, pain, poverty, and such things—that they are not evil—and again in turn about life, pleasure, wealth, and things similar to these—that they are not good—will both young men accept the conclusions in the same way and would each one be equally persuaded by them? Certainly not. The first young man—the duller one—barely and slowly pried loose, as it were, by a thousand words, perhaps would agree. The other young man, though, will quickly and readily accept the conclusions as natural and suitable for himself without needing many arguments or more study. Is not this second young man like the Spartan boy who asked Cleanthes the philosopher if pain was not a good? That boy seems to have been so naturally good and to have been trained so well towards virtue that he considered pain to be closer to the nature of a good than of an evil. He asked if pain happened to be a good, since the argument that it was not an evil was understood by him already.[90]

τὸν δ᾽ αὖ Λαχωνιχῶς τως ἡγμένον χαὶ τρυφᾶν οὐχ εἰθισμένον χαὶ χαρτερεῖν μεμελετηχότα χαὶ τῶν λεγομ ένων ὀρθῶς εὐήχοον ὄντα. εἶτα τοὺς δύο τούτους νεανίας εἰ θείημεν ἀχούοντας φιλοσόφου λέγοντος περὶ θανάτου, περὶ πόνου, περὶ πενίας, περὶ τῶν ὁμοίων, ὡς οὐ χαχῶν ὄντων, πάλιν δ᾽ αὖ περὶ ξωῆς, περὶ ἡδονῆς, περὶ πλούτου, περὶ τῶν παραπλησίων τούτοις, ὡς οὐχ ἀγαθά ἐστιν, ἆρά γε ὁμοίως ἀμφω προσήσονται τοὺς λόγους χαὶ παραπλησίως ἑχάτερος <ἂν> πίθοιτο τοῖς λεγομένοις οὐχ ἔστιν εἰπεῖν. ἀλλ᾽ ὁ μὲν μόγις χαὶ βραδέως χαὶ ὥσπερ μοχλευόμενος ὑπὸ μυρίων λόγων τάχ᾽ ἂν ἐπινεύσειεν, ὁ νωθέστερος. ὁ δ᾽ αὖ ταχέως χαὶ ἑτοίμως δέξεται τὰ λεγόμενα ὡς οἰχεῖα χαὶ προσήχοντα αὐτῷ, μήτε ἀποδείξεων δεόμενος πολλῶν μήτε πραγματείας μείζονος. ἢ οὐ τοιοῦτος παῖς ἐχεῖνος ὁ Λάχων, ὃς Κλεάνθην τὸν φιλόσοφον ἠρώτησεν, εἰ ἀγαθὸν ὁ πόνος ἐστίν οὕτω γὰρ ἐχεῖνος φαίνεται φύσει πεφυχὼς χαλῶς καὶ τεθραμμένος εὖ πρὸς ἀρετήν, ὥστε ἐγγύτερον εἶναι νομὶ νομίζειν ειν τὸν πόνον τῆς τἀγαθοῦ φύσεως ἢ τῆς τοῦ χαχοῦ. ὅς γε ὡς ὁμολογουμένου τοῦ μὴ χαχὸν ὑπάρχειν αὐτόν, εἰ ἀγαθὸν τυγχάνει ὤν, ἐπυνθάνετο.

Unlike his counterpart who will require extensive coaching, because of the second young man's familiarity with poverty, pain, and death, before he is introduced to philosophical insight he has, Rufus argues, already (imperfect tense) come to apprehend a key principle that Stoic philosophy seeks to disclose: namely that discomfort and the lack of material success is not an evil or a reason for melancholy. This passage, therefore, continues to indicate that there is an understanding in Stoicism that certain circumstances can allow people who have no apparent exposure or interest in philosophical thought to partially return to the dynamic that was exhibited in the Golden Age; namely when humans were able to conform to virtuous behavior even though they lacked a theoretical or conceptual framework to understand why. In this regard we can perhaps note that the verb Musonius elects to use to encapsulate this youth's understanding (ἐπυνθάνετο "understood already by himself") is not the more usual verb that is employed for learning, μανθάνω, which often connotes formal means of learning through tuition or instruction, but instead means to glean information by asking questions or through general inquiry, that is, an altogether less formal means of gaining awareness.

NOTES

1. *Med.* 2.17. Similar comments can be found being expressed at *Muson.* 4.88, 8.8-9; *Diss.* I.4.1, 7.10-12, II.23.40; and *Ep.* 16.1, 37.3, 53.9.

2. Gill (2006, 389).

3. Gill (2012b, 46, 47): "If Antoninus [his adoptive father] represents such an all-embracing ideal for Marcus, what role remains for philosophy? . . . The combined implication of the two passages [*Med.* 1.16, 1.17] is that Antonius had achieved by non-philosophical means the same qualities of character which, in others, such as Socrates and perhaps Maximus, were the result of philosophy. . . . These passages in [*Med.*] 1.16 seem to suggest that the contribution of philosophy towards ethical development is limited, or at least that it can be achieved by other means, such as engagement in social or political life." See also his comments at (2013, lxxix). I shall explore the Stoics' use of exempla in chapter 7.

4. *Ep.* 94.28.

5. *Ep.* 94.41.

6. *Ep.* 94.43.

7. *Ep.* 94.46-47. On this Schafer (2009, 8, 88, 94), notably asserts that Seneca holds that "many people can attain great moral progress without any indoctrination at all" and that "the means by which this influence takes place of course, are not strictly cognitive ones. Seneca, then, has laid the theoretical basis for a program of moral therapy that includes non-technical pedagogical methods . . . [that are] non-rational and pre-rational."

8. *Med.* 4.50.

9. *M. Aur. Med* 9.3.

10. *Diss.* I.4.27.

11. Wildberger (2013, 431–432) usefully comments on this passage: "If Epictetus' students let themselves be nudged away from taking false pride in their intellectual achievements, they recoil from a real evil, however unsound the reasoning may have been that motivated them. If a fool in progress fears a purposive evil for the wrong reasons, even such an irrational fear can be successful and lead to something beneficial."

12. See Chrysippus *apud* Plut. *St. rep.* 1057A, and the discussion in Dobbin (1998, 97). Consider also Epictetus' comments at *Diss.* IV.6.33. Regarding Seneca, Boys-Stones (2013) and Wildberger (2014a) account for his frequent appeal to Epicureanism in his early *Epistles* as being a tactic that he employed to help ease his purported epistolary dialogue partner into accepting certain philosophical truths, but that later in their exchange the pretense of using Epicurean philosophy is abandoned.

13. Reydams-Schils (2011, 319–320). Gill (2008, 50) also similarly and importantly argues that the Stoics "do not distinguish between practical and intellectual wisdom in a way that is normal in Platonic-Aristotelian thought. . . . The role of philosophy is not to serve as the unique pathway to human perfection. Rather, philosophy analyses with unique clarity—for instance—human progress toward ethical perfection, though this process is not itself necessarily depended on philosophy as its instrument."

14. Beniston (2017, 151) argues that we should cease to understand that the Stoics believe their philosophy was "a body of knowledge that one needs to know in order to become virtuous. For this is not, as it happens, how the Stoics themselves thought about philosophy. Rather, the Stoics believed that the purpose of philosophy was to restore us to a state of accord with nature, from which we have departed because of the corrupted state of our rationality. What we gain from philosophy is not knowledge as such, but therapy."

15. On the idea that their philosophy reflects universal/natural law, see in particular Diog. Laert. 7.87, *Diss.* I.29.19; IV.3.11-12, *Ep.* 30.11; 45.9; 66.39, and, for example, the discussion at Striker (1996, 209–297), Vander Waerdt (2003), and Klein (2012).

16. *Ep.* 109.5. See also his comments at *Ep.* 33.11.

17. On the relative lack of Stoic commentaries and apparent concern to codify and assign authority to their texts, see Snyder (2000, 41) and Reydams-Schils (2011, 306–309), who (308) remarks: "For the Stoics, by contrast [to other schools], it is clear that at best the foundational texts are instrumental, or pointers . . . to help human beings unfold and apply correctly the notions which nature has equipped them." We should note though that Frede (1999, 784–785) argues that there is some evidence of commentary efforts in Stoicism, which Snyder and Reydams-Schils do not allow to weigh upon their conclusions.

18. For example, *Diss.* II.16.34; 17.34-40; 19.5-15; 23.44; III.2.13-18; 9.20-22; 26.6-7; 24.89; *Ench.* 49.

19. *Diss.* I.4.14. On this point, see also the comments at Simplicius *In Ench.* 134.10-24.

20. *Diss.* I.17.13,17-18.

21. On this, see Sedley (1989) and Snyder (2000).

22. Long (1986, 204).

23. Plut. *Comm. Notit.* 1053ab. See also *Ep.* 95.57.

24. On the sage in Stoic thought, see Brouwer (2014).

25. On this, consider the particularly useful discussion in Korstange (2017).

26. See *De Off.* 1.8, 3.3.13, *De Fin.* 4.15, Diog. Laert. 7.106-107, and Arius Didymus *Epist.* 8.5-10. That the καθήκοντα of the nonsage are preferred indifferents, see Arius Didymus *Epit.* 7b, *De Fin* 3.56, and Diog. Laert. 7.107.

27. Diog. Laert. 7.106.

28. Diog. Laert. 7.108.

29. MacGillivray (2017, 2020).

30. For example, Lovejoy and Boas (1935) and Gruen (2011, 223–351). See also the studies that are noted at Van Sijl (2010, 77–78 n.68).

31. For example, consider Lovejoy and Boas (1935, 117–191, 222–286), and particularly Boy-Stones (2001) and Van Nuffelen (2011, 1–98). Drawing upon the work of Boys-Stones, Richter (2011, 183–184) usefully explains: "Prior to the Cynics, the goal of philosophy was progress towards wisdom and virtue through successively higher stages of philosophical knowledge. Philosophy, in other words, was an endeavour that involved the gradual improvement over time of the individual and, indeed the slow enlightenment of mankind in general. In the Hellenistic period,

however, certain intellectuals developed the idea that primitive man somehow possessed knowledge of the truth and that the philosopher need only unearth and decipher it."

32. On Zeno's belief that the first humans were created through divine aid, see Tieleman (1996, 226). Additionally, on the connection between primitivism and providence, see the discussion in Boys-Stones (2001, 7–8).

33. *M. Aur. Med* 11.8. See also *M. Aur. Med* 2.3, 2.11, Seneca. *Ep.* 90.18, 94.56, *Nat. Quest.* 5.18.13, Diog. Laert. 7.135-136, 142, and Cicero *Nat. D* 2.133.

34. *M. Aur. Med* 6.19, trans. Gill and Hard (2011, 49).

35. There is some evidence that Stoic thinkers could credit early people as having had superior intellectual capacity or rationality in comparison with contemporary members of humanity; for example, see Sextius *Math.* 9.28, *Ep.* 90.44 and the discussion in Tieleman (1996, 226), and Van Sijl (2010, 78–79). We should note that we do not know the time frame that is implied; however, when Epictetus was asked (*Diss.* III.6.1-3) why, when more effort is currently being devoted to philosophy that more progress was made in earlier times, he does not reply by positing that any variance exists between modern humanity's character/intellect and those of previous generations, but rather by averring that contemporary attention is being unhelpfully directed onto realizing less profitable aims.

36. As Algra (2009, 236), notes: "It is unfortunate that the evidence we have on the Stoic view, or views, of cultural development is scare and controversial. One thing is certain, however, is that some kind of original moral corruption was assumed to have occurred in the course of the development of civilization: a corruption subsequently to be remedied by philosophy."

37. We can also note the Golden Age myth that is outlined in Cornutus' *Epidrome*. On this, see Boys-Stones (2001, 49–59).

38. *Ep.* 90.7-35. Seneca argues, *Ep.* 90.11-13, 24, that while having ingenuity (*sagacitas*), these inventors cannot be credited as having possessed wisdom (*sapientia*). See also his comments at *Ep.* 90.26. On this dispute, see the overview in Boys-Stones (2001, 20, 37), Van Sijl (2010, 80–81), and Van Nuffelen and Van Hoof (2013, 190–191, 193–194).

39. *Ep.* 90.4, 5, trans. Gummere (1920, 397).

40. *Ep.* 90.4, 16-19, 46.

41. *Phae.* 483–558. He introduces these circumstances as being, §484, "former/ancient ways" and later, §526-527, comments: "This was the way of life, I think, of those who burgeoned in the primal age and mingled with gods" trans. Fitch (2002, 491): *hoc equidem reor vixisse ritu prima quos mixtos deis profudit aetasthen.* To my knowledge, this passage has only been highlighted in this regard by its inclusion at Lovejoy and Boas (1935, 282–286).

42. We can note that this position differs from Seneca's contemporary Musonius Rufus, who, at *Muson.* 11, defends farming as being a worthy pursuit for a philosopher to undertake.

43. Note particularly his comments at *Ep.* 90.43: "Such a dwelling was in accordance with nature" trans. Gummere (1920, 427): *Haec erat secundum naturam domus.*

44. *Ep.* 90.37.

45. For example, Blundell (1984, 218, 219): "Here [*Ep.* 90] we have a classic illustration of the reason why most philosophers cannot be whole-hearted primitivists, since for them virtue can only be acquired intellectually. . . . *For Seneca, the high point of civilization had been reached at the point when the Greek masters of the Stoic school had discovered the essential moral truths,* which thus required no further investigation" (emphasis mine); Boyle (2014, 215): "Seneca expresses reservations about the wisdom and morality of the Golden Age in which innocence stemmed from ignorance."

46. *Ep.* 90.38 trans. Gummere (1920, 423, 424).

47. *Ep.* 90.36.

48. *Ep.* 90.46, trans. Gummere (1920, 429).

49. On the Stoics', and particularly Seneca's, belief that advice or exhortation can prompt people to behave correctly, we can note Schafer's study on their use of precepts, wherein (2009, 56) he concludes that the Stoics hold them to be "an educational method whereby a moral guide at least sometimes, tells her students what to do instead of explaining how one discovers what to do." He further (2009, 57) comments that "they are [considered to be] shortcuts, useful when such an agent, who wants to follow nature, lacks the time and the capacity to figure out nature's demands on the spot." Of importance for the wider purpose of this book, Schafer also (2009, 82), argues the Stoics believe that through precepts "many people can attain great moral progress without any indoctrination at all. Implicit in that last point is that ordinary goodness or wisdom is both a real phenomenon and something of great value; this rules out a doctrinaire insistence on the misery of all non-sages, and frames the debate in a very practical way: how can we make more people 'good' in the way that many people in fact are good." Supporting his argument, we can observe Marcus Aurelius' belief expressed at *M. Aur. Med* 5.12 that proverbs have the potential to help anyone, as well as the comments on this passage from Gill (2013, 153–154).

50. To fully explore this issue would result in a prohibitively lengthy digression from our main concern here; however, we can note Seneca's initial use of the more general term *sapientes* at *Ep.* 90.5-6, rather than the language of *philosophia* to describe these leaders, and the inclusion of nonphilosophers within their ranks, such as the Seven Sages (with the exception of the sage Thales, who was a pre-Socratic philosopher), and Lycurgus of Sparta. On this, see the discussion in Blankert (1941, 100), Frede (1989, 2089), Van Sijl (2010, 78, 80 n.74, 85), and, in particular, Van Nuffelen and Van Hoof (2013). See, though, Boys-Stones (2001, 21–24), who argues that philosophers are indeed in view, along with Van Nuffelen and Van Hoof's (2013, 192–193) response. Boys-Stones' suggestion that the view that the ancient sages had intentionally hidden their philosophy in poetic verse was an idea that later Stoics such as Cornutus developed. This can, I suggest, be challenged by the presence of this theory in Plato's writings, for example *Theaet.* 180d. We should also note that, as Nuffelen (2011, 110) observes, this vision differs from the ideal state that Zeno envisages where every individual can comprehend and follow natural law.

51. On this, see Algra's (2009, 237) brief remarks. When considering the Stoics' use of allegory, Ramelli (2014, 495) also valuably comments: "It must be stressed

that the Stoics valued antiquity, and the ancient cultural heritage, *not instead of*, or *at the expense of*, philosophy, but precisely because antiquity *expressed* philosophy. In the Stoic view, antiquity is a source of philosophy—if opportunely decoded—and the proof of the naturalness of philosophy (emphasis mine)." I suggest this understanding removes the tension that Russell (1974, 91) highlights; namely, that while Seneca argues that philosophy requires significant effort to be expended by its students, here he presents individuals as having apparently passively achieved probity. This is something that Russell later (1974, 92) refers to as being a "difficulty" or "problem" that he leaves unresolved.

52. *Ep.* 90.38, trans. Gummere (1920, 425).

53. *Phae.* 540-542.

54. See especially *Ep.* 90.9-16, 20-25, 31-32, 40-43, 45, and *Phae.* 484-500, 517-558.

55. *Ep.* 90.10, trans. Gummere (1920, 403).

56. *Phae.* 520-521, Fitch (2002, 489).

57. We can note that Boys-Stones (2001, 46–48) argues that Posidonius might have thought error was caused by the irrational part of the soul, an aspect of Platonism that it has been normally understood he adopted. This position, though, has subsequently been challenged, for example see Tieleman (2003, 220–230).

58. *Ep.* 97.1.

59. *Nat. Quest.* 3.15.7-9.

60. Consider also Epictetus' comments at *Diss.* II.24.20: "Is there anything new in all this? Is not this ignorance the cause of all the errors and misfortune that have arisen since the origins of mankind?": νῦν γὰρ πρῶτον τοῦθ᾽ οὕτως ἔχει; οὐχὶ ἐξ οὗ γένος ἀνθρώπων ἐστίν, ἐξ ἐκείνου πάντα τὰ ἁμαρτήματα καὶ τὰ ἀτυχήματα παρὰ ταύτην τὴν ἄγνοιαν γεγένηται;

61. *Ep.* 90.19.

62. *Diss.* III.3.20-22.

63. *Ep.* 95.29, 32, trans. Gummere (1925, 77, 79).

64. Cf. *Diss.* I.20.14-19.

65. *Ep.* 90.6, trans. Gummere (1920, 399).

66. Van Nuffelen and Van Hoof (2013, 194, 195). See also Van Nuffelen (2011, 27–28).

67. *Ep.* 94.38.

68. *Ep.* 94.38, trans. Gummere (1925, 37). We should note, though, that Seneca argues that preambles can be of some use, so see *Ep.* 94.39.

69. There is also an ongoing and extensive debate over whether Stoics consider themselves to be issuing rules of conduct for their adherents to follow, or whether they are attempting to lead them to conform to a more generalized virtuous disposition that they hold cannot be distilled into fixed guidelines. For a useful overview of the competing conclusions that scholarship offers on this issue, read Sorabji (2012, 133, n.19).

70. *Phae.* 482-483.

71. For example, see Horace *Carm.* 3.24.8-16, Strabo *Geog.* 7.3.9, Pliny *HN* 6.53, and Pompeius Trogus *Just. Epit* 2.2.

72. *Ep.* 90.16, 18. Gummere (1920, 405, 407). See also *Prov.* 4.13 for a similar claim. On the perception of the harsh landscape of the Syrtes, consider especially *Luc.* 9.431-453. Lucan also, *Luc.*1.498-502, describes the Senate as having fled from Julius Caesar with as much urgency as they would from a shipwreck on the Sytres, an image that Seneca also appeals to at *Phae.* 570.

73. See *Deip* 6.263. That Posidonius might hold they are adhering to the pattern of the Golden Age society, see some brief remarks by Reydams-Schils (2005, 88).

74. *Prov.* 4.14-15. From this passage Stephens (2013, 42) notes that for Seneca those people who try "to escape the gravitational pull of Nature's norms, are relieved of their misery by simply letting to and returning home to Her. Those habits in accord with the best parts of our human nature deliver us to this happy reunion."

75. On the image of the noble savage/rustic in antiquity, consider, for example, Gruen (2011, 159–178).

76. *Prov.* 4.9,10, trans. Fantham et al. (2014, 291).

77. Note as well *Prov.* 3.3: "Among the many magnificent sayings of our Demetrius [a Cynic philosopher] is this—I heard it recently and it still rings and echoes in my ears: 'Nothing seems to me more unhappy,' he said, 'than someone to whom nothing adverse has ever happened'."

78. *Ep.* 67.6, 10, 14-15; *Virt. Beat.* 7.1, 15.6-7, 25.6, *Tranq.* 10.1-3, and *De Ira* 1.6.1. On the damaging effects of luxury upon the human constitution, consider also *Ep.* 17.3, *Constant.* 10.3, and *Prov.* 4.9-10.

79. *Med.* 329-334. Seneca also critiques the invention of ships at *Ep.* 90.24, which is a sentiment that is echoed at Ovid *Met.* I.89-150.

80. So see *Liv.* 2.11-13, and *Plut. Publ.* 17.1-5.

81. *Ep.* 64.5, trans. Gummere (1974, 169). See also the account at *Livy, Ab Urbe Cond.* 2.12-13.

82. *Diss.* I.2.2. I will consider the Stoics' attitude toward the Spartans later in this book.

83. *Diss.* I.26.10.

84. *Diss.* II.21.14.

85. *Diss.* I.10.3.

86. *Diss.* III.26.23. See also *Diss.* I.29.37.

87. *Diss.* III.20.9.

88. *Diss.* III.20.11.

89. See Goulet-Cazé (2019, 102–103). On the Cynic position that poverty can teach people by practice what philosophy does through reasoning, see Stobaeus *Anth.* 4.32.11.

90. *Muson.* 1.4, 5. See also Musonius Rufus' comments, *Muson.* 9.4, on exile as benefiting individuals because it removes luxury from them, and where he credits exile as having turned Diogenes of Sinope from being a layman into a virtuous philosopher par-excellence.

Chapter 5

Preconceptions

A vital doctrine that informs Stoic epistemology and moral psychology is their theory of impressions. Within Stoicism an impression (φαντασία) is understood to be a sensory stimulus or a thought that presents itself to an agent as supplying them with information about their surrounding environment or how things are, and which is temporarily imprinted on their ruling faculty (ἡγεμονικόν). Epictetus, for instance, gives examples of impressions such as that it is daytime, or that someone's son has been disinherited.[1] While animals and children are believed to respond with an instinctive impulse to follow or accept impressions (which are called nonrational, ἄλογοι), the Stoics hold that adult human beings are furnished with a rational ruling faculty that grants them critical distance from their impressions and the ability to analyze and select between them (the so-called rational impressions, λογικαί).[2] So, in the first example noted above, an adult human being could appraise a range of competing scenarios that might account for the presence of light outside their window and give assent (συγκατάθεσις) to the cause that they deem to be the most probable.

The goal within Stoic philosophy is to assent to as many true impressions and to avoid (ἔκκλισις) giving assent to as many mistaken impressions as possible. They believe that the errant judging of impressions is the cause of passions (πάθη), which are irrational and unnatural movements of the soul that cause humans harm, usually by them having fixed their desire (ὄρεξις) onto indifferents such as health, wealth, or prestige which they wrongly think to be goods and to be within their control. In this light, Epictetus is unequivocal about the importance that the judging of impressions should hold within the philosophical enterprise, with him characterizing it as being the beginning (ἀρχή) of philosophy, and the task (ἔργον) that should define it.[3] In this light he approvingly recalls an anecdote from his time as a student when he was upbraided by Rufus for his failure to notice an omission in a syllogism. When Epictetus responded that it was not as if his error was to have burned down the capitol building, Rufus witheringly retorted: "Slave, here the missing clause was the Capitol! Are the only errors in life to burn down the Capitol and murder one's father, or rather that to make use of one's impressions recklessly and foolishly and at random." 'ἀνδράποδον,' ἔφη, 'ἐνθάδε τὸ παραλειπόμενον Καπιτώλιόν ἐστιν.' ἢ ταῦτα μόνα ἁμαρτήματά ἐστι τὸ Καπιτώλιον ἐμπρῆσαι καὶ τὸν πατέρα ἀποκτεῖναι, τὸ δ᾽ εἰκῇ καὶ μάτην καὶ ὡς ἔτυχεν χρῆσθαι ταῖς φαντασίαις.⁴ The seemingly hair-splitting attention that is given in the Stoic lecture room to evaluating syllogisms and impressions are, Rufus and the now matured Epictetus insist, of vital importance, being the skills that should be employed to inform every aspect of life—on this, see especially Epictetus' comments at *Diss.* III.8.1.

The impressions that are assented to by individuals are held by the Stoics to be retained within their respective ruling faculties, and to build up and form the basis of their notions or common conceptions (κοιναὶ ἔννοιαι). For instance, to use an example that Epictetus will draw upon, when a person experiences different musical notes and instruments and gives assent to notions about their qualities and purpose, their mind assembles these various cognitions and forms them into their concept of "music." Concepts such as these, as well as, Epictetus adds, mathematical theories, should be differentiated from moral concepts such as justice which are ubiquitously present within human beings without any instruction or introduction being required.⁵ In Stoic philosophy, these privileged intuitions are called "preconceptions" (προλήψεις), and it is Epictetus' stance regarding them which I will explore within this chapter.

Before beginning this task, I should highlight that whether respective members of the Stoa held that humans are innately equipped with preconceptions, or instead are physiologically structured to inevitably form them, as well as the precise relationship between their theory of preconceptions (προλήψεις) and conceptions (ἔννοια), are topics that will likely remain contested within scholarship.⁶ With regards to Epictetus though the scholarly consensus is more settled, and it is widely held that he did indeed hold that preconceptions are, at least in some sense, innate.⁷ This debate though is largely irrelevant for my concerns here. Whether they are innate or predisposed, Epictetus and other Stoics concur on the universal presence of preconceptions within humankind once adulthood has been reached.

In this chapter, I will argue that a vital component which informs the Stoics' conviction that humans have the ability to make moral advancement is their stance that every individual has accurate preconceptions (προλήψεις) of what the good and virtuous are. As they observed, their fellow citizens who have no familiarity or even respect for philosophical thought do not need to be persuaded by philosophy's advocates that people should act in accordance with principles such as justice, honor, familial affection, and so on. For example, Epictetus comments that preconceptions are common to all people:

> For, who among us does not assume that the good is advantageous and desirable, and that in every circumstance we should seek and pursue it? And who of us does not assume that the honorable is fair and appropriate?[8]

> καὶ πρόληψις προλήψει οὐ μάχεται. τίς γὰρ ἡμῶν οὐ τίθησιν, ὅτι τὸ ἀγαθὸν συμφέρον ἐστὶ ἐστι καὶ αἱρετὸν καὶ ἐκ πάσης αὐτὸ περιστάσεως δεῖ μετιέναι καὶ διώκειν; τίς δ᾽ ἡμῶν οὐ τίθησιν, ὅτι τὸ δίκαιον καλόν ἐστι καὶ πρέπον.

And elsewhere he can opine:

> But who among us came into the world without having an innate conception of what is good and evil, right and wrong, becoming and unbecoming, and what happiness and misery are, and what we are obliged to do, and what constitutes our lot in life, and what we ought to do and what we ought not to do?[9]

> ἀγαθοῦ δὲ καὶ κακοῦ καὶ καλοῦ καὶ αἰσχροῦ καὶ πρέποντος καὶ ἀπρεποῦς καὶ εὐδαιμονίας καὶ προσήκοντος καὶ ἐπιβάλλοντος καὶ ὅ τι δεῖ ποιῆσαι καὶ ὅ τι οὐ δεῖ ποιῆσαι τίς οὐκ ἔχων ἔμφυτον ἔννοιαν ἐλήλυθεν;

It is this latter passage where Epictetus' position on preconceptions being innate (ἔμφυτος) is most emphatically stated. His perspective on the privileged position of our preconceptions is also relayed in another passage where he notes that they furnish every individual with the ability to understand ideas such as "fortunate" or "unfortunate," "just" or "unjust," in marked contrast with the technicalities of the arts and sciences (such as geometry or music) where instruction is required before an understanding of them can be obtained.[10] In our task of comprehending Epictetus' views of laypeople and their moral awareness, understanding his opinion of preconceptions is, therefore, important.

Aside from their wide institution across humanity, Epictetus also holds that preconceptions enable nonphilosophers to be to some extent morally aware and capable of exercising ethical evaluations over their actions and mindset.[11] In one passage in the *Discourses*, Epictetus even appears to suggest to a layperson, who had hoped to glean some rules from the philosopher that he might apply to his life, that his instinctive conception of right and wrong obviates any advice that he might be able to offer to him:

> What directions then did you arrive with when you came from that other world to this? You should guard by every means what is yours, but should not desire

what belongs to others, and that your trustworthiness is your own. Who can deprive you of these? Whenever you care about what is not your own, you lose what is truly yours. Having such advice and instruction from Zeus, what more advice do you want from me? Am I better than he, or more trustworthy? If you observe the orders from him, what others do you need?[12]

τίνα οὖν ἐντολὴν ἔχων ἐκεῖθεν ἐλήλυθας, ποῖον διάταγμα; τὰ σὰ τήρει ἐκ παντὸς τρόπου, τῶν ἀλλοτρίων μὴ ἐφίεσο. τὸ πιστὸν σόν . . . τίς οὖν ἀφελέσθαι δύναταί σου ταῦτα; τίς κωλύσει χρῆσθαι αὐτοῖς ἄλλος εἰ μὴ σύ; σὺ δὲ πῶς; ὅταν περὶ τὰ μὴ σαυτοῦ σπουδάσῃς, τὰ σαυτοῦ ἀπώλεσας. τοιαύτας ἔχων ὑποθήκας καὶ ἐντολὰς παρὰ τοῦ Διὸς ποίας ἔτι παρ᾽ ἐμοῦ θέλεις; κρείσσων εἰμὶ ἐκείνου, ἀξιοπιστότερος; ἀλλὰ ταύτας τηρῶν ἄλλων τινῶν προσδέῃ;

At least in theory, Epictetus argues that this layperson has located within himself all the advice and direction that he needs to follow if he wishes to lead a virtuous life. Additionally, when he is recorded as being in a conversation with another nonphilosopher, Epictetus recommends that the man should reflect upon the decisions he has made over the course of his life: "in your own mind, if you are ashamed to do so in my presence," ἔπελθέ σου τοὺς χρόνους, εἰ ἐμὲ αἰσχύνῃ, αὐτὸς πρὸς σαυτόν.[13] Importantly, as Rachana Kamtekar has noted, Epictetus' guidance here seems to imply that there is some equivalence between what this layperson is able to achieve by inwardly evaluating his life, moderated as this is by his understanding of right and wrong, and what Epictetus can initially bring him to apprehend by way of a philosophical exchange.[14]

We can also note that Epictetus' belief that our shared sense of shame (αἰδώς) helps to regulate our actions informs the pedagogical strategies that he chooses to deploy in his school.[15] For example, he advises his students that they should strengthen their ability to refrain from committing vice by maintaining the idea that god is observing their actions constantly before their minds,[16] and he recommends that when they are faced with a decision, they should ask themselves what they will receive in exchange for following a particular course of action: namely, "a good action for a little money, a *properly settled mind for idle talk, or decency for indecent talk*," οὐδ᾽ ἀντὶ κέρματος πρᾶξιν καλήν, οὐδ᾽ ἀντὶ ψυχρολογίας ἡσυχίαν οἵαν δεῖ, οὐδ᾽ ἀντὶ αἰσχρολογίας αἰδῶ.[17] This suggests that, at least on some occasions, considering whether an action might induce feelings of shame or provoke an unsettled mind can, without any detailed philosophical deliberation being enacted, lead a person to establish what the appropriate course of action they should pursue is. This is important because, as Epictetus notes, the universal nature of shame in the human constitution can be seen by our propensity to blush when we have knowingly violated our, or our society's, ethical standards.[18] Seneca too considers the ability that shame has to restrain vice, observing that its presence makes those individuals who have knowingly erred hesitant to appear in public and that even when they are left in solitude, a guilty individual will continue to be haunted by feelings of guilt.[19] Seneca further remarks that there is hope for one of his associate's possible restoration to morality, for despite him having fallen prey to numerous vices, he still, Seneca observes, has enough modesty to blush when he has contravened his once stated principles.[20] Consequently, Seneca also advises that people should help to moderate their behavior by envisaging that they are being continually observed, specifically by acting as if the entire world is privy to their actions.[21]

Epictetus' confidence that preconceptions of the good are widely instilled in humanity can also be seen by his frequent employment of the dialectical/elenctic method,[22] a type of discourse (which he credits his moral exemplar Socrates as instituting[23]) that presumes that even individuals who lack a rudimentary grasp of philosophical concepts are nevertheless capable of recognizing that they have moral failings.[24] The method attempts to prompt people to begin to exercise this ability by having a philosophical interlocutor lead them through a series of questions that intend to throw the disconnections that exist between their actions and their deeply held, though often unexplored, moral preconceptions into sharp relief. Once this divergence is exposed, it is hoped that the errant dialogue partner will be compelled to try to bring them into harmony,[25] and that they will chiefly look to utilize the resources that philosophy can offer in this regard.[26]

A good example of this method at work can be seen in a lengthy exchange that is recorded as taking place between Epictetus and a layperson, who, unlike Epictetus,[27] evidently apportioned significant effort to beautify himself.[28] Epictetus attempts to correct the man's mistaken understanding of beauty by engaging him in a dialectical dialogue:

> So what is it, then, that makes a dog beautiful? The presence of a dog's excellence. What about a horse? The presence of a horses' excellence. . . . If you want to appear beautiful, young man, you should labor for this: the excellence that characterizes a human being. . . . Reflect, when you praise people without partiality, do you praise the just or the unjust person? "The just." The moderate or the immoderate? "The moderate." The self-controlled or the dissolute? "The self-controlled." Then, if you make yourself such a person, you can know that you will make yourself beautiful; but while you neglect these things, whatever methods you employ to appear beautiful, you will by necessity be ugly.[29]

> τί οὖν ποιεῖ κύνα καλόν; ἡ ἀρετὴ ἡ κυνὸς παροῦσα. τί ἵππον; ἡ ἀρετὴ ἡ ἵππου παροῦσα . . . ὅρα, τίνας αὐτὸς ἐπαινεῖς, ὅταν δίχα πάθους τινὰς ἐπαινῇς: πότερα

τοὺς δικαίους ἢ τοὺς ἀδίκους;—τοὺς δικαίους.—πότερον τοὺς σώφρονας ἢ
τοὺς ἀκολάστους;—τοὺς σώφρονας.—τοὺς ἐγκρατεῖς δ᾽ ἢ τοὺς ἀκρατεῖς;—
τοὺς ἐγκρατεῖς.—οὐκοῦν τοιοῦτόν τινα ποιῶν σαυτὸν ἴσθι ὅτι καλὸν ποιήσεις·
μέχρις δ᾽ ἂν τούτων ἀμελῇς, αἰσχρόν σ᾽ εἶναι ἀνάγκη, κἂν πάντα μηχανᾷ ὑπὲρ
τοῦ φαίνεσθαί σε καλόν.

Epictetus encourages the young man to reflect upon what the features are
that he truly holds makes people commendable and, consequently, to evaluate what the qualities he should be laboring to realize in himself are. During
the discussion, the man concedes that he believes human excellence is to be
found in the virtuous constitution of our character and not, where his attention has been directed, in our physical appearance. From this discussion, we
can observe that a simple series of questions and this man's basic cognitive
skills and instilled ethical principles have allowed him to articulate what
is (at least, according to Stoic thought) a fundamental insight into human
teleology.[30] It should be highlighted, however, that without Epictetus' adroit
management of the conversation it is unlikely that the man would have been
motivated, or, indeed, would have been capable of reaching this conclusion
by himself.[31] Furthermore, we do not know if this layperson has understood
what the implications of this deduction are, or whether he has apprehended
that any insight he has received into his moral condition is only the start of the
long refining process that philosophy intends to conduct its students through.
This point is laid particularly bare in a conversation that is recorded as taking
place between Epictetus and another layperson, who has visited Epictetus'
school in order to illicit some advice from him. After a dialectical exchange
with Epictetus, the man expresses an openness to continue to examine his life
according to philosophical principles (*Diss.* I.11.37-38). Epictetus, however,
emphasizes (39-40) that this objective cannot be fulfilled by depending upon
dialectical dialogue alone, but by him committing himself to philosophical
training. He further cautions: "But this, as you are quite aware, is not the
work of a single hour or day," τοῦτο δ᾽ ὅτι μιᾶς ὥρας ἢ ἡμέρας οὐκ ἔστιν,
ἐπινοεῖς καὶ αὐτός.[32]
It is worthwhile at this juncture to consider whether the understanding of
right and wrong, which the Stoics posit, is instinctively apprehended by all
human beings constitutes what we might call a "conscience." In many passages, the language that Epictetus employs might indeed appear to suggest
that he believes such a function is being fulfilled by our preconceptions[33]; and
this is an aspect of his thought that is probably best observed in the following
passage:

Why, does anyone say to you that you have powers that are equal to Zeus? No!
but even so he has assigned to each man a guardian, his own personal daemon,

and had entrusted us to his guardianship, a director who never sleeps and who can never be deceived. For to what better and more careful/vigilant guardian could he have entrusted us than this? So, whenever you close your doors and have darkened your room, remember to never say to yourself that you are alone; for you are not. God is inside, and your daemon is inside and neither of them need light to see what you are doing? To this god you should swear allegiance such as soldiers do to Caesar.[34]

τοῦτο δέ σοι καὶ λέγει τις, ὅτι ἴσην ἔχεις δύναμιν τῷ Διί; ἀλλ᾽ οὖν οὐδὲν ἧττον καὶ ἐπίτροπον ἑκάστῳ παρέστησεν τὸν ἑκάστου δαίμονα καὶ παρέδωκεν φυλάσσειν αὐτὸν αὐτῷ καὶ τοῦτον ἀκοίμητον καὶ ἀπαραλόγιστον. τίνι γὰρ ἄλλῳ κρείττονι καὶ ἐπιμελεστέρῳ φύλακι παρέδωκεν ἡμῶν ἕκαστον; ὥσθ᾽, ὅταν κλείσητε τὰς θύρας καὶ σκότος ἔνδον ποιήσητε, μέμνησθε μηδέποτε λέγειν ὅτι μόνοι ἐστέ· οὐ γὰρ ἐστέ, ἀλλ᾽ ὁ θεὸς ἔνδον ἐστὶ καὶ ὁ ὑμέτερος δαίμων ἐστίν. καὶ τίς τούτοις χρεία φωτὸς εἰς τὸ βλέπειν τί ποιεῖτε; τούτῳ τῷ θεῷ ἔδει καὶ ὑμᾶς ὀμνύειν ὅρκον, οἷον οἱ στρατιῶται τῷ Καίσαρι.

Here, Epictetus compares humanity's instinctive conception of morality to be like a guardian who continually evaluates the suitability of a person's actions. There is, however, an important distinction that must be highlighted between Epictetus' stance on the ability that our preconceptions have to regulate our actions and the properties which are perhaps more readily attributed to the conscience in modern thought. Preconceptions are only thought by Epictetus to furnish people with a high abstraction of what the good is, and to not elucidate what the correct implementation of these principles are in practice. So, for instance, while individuals might espouse with some ease the importance of concepts such as "justice," "propriety," "affection," and "honor," their interpretation of these values is frequently fallible. As Epictetus comments, everyone agrees with high abstract notions of right and wrong, but in the implementation of them irresolvable contradictions emerge:

for this is the cause of all human ills, that people are not capable of applying their general preconceptions to particular cases. Instead, some of us think one thing, and some another . . . For who does not have a preconception of evil, that it is harmful and to be avoided, and that it is something that we must get rid of by every means? One preconception does not conflict with another—conflict emerges when it comes to be applied.[35]

τοῦτο γάρ ἐστι τὸ αἴτιον τοῖς ἀνθρώποις πάντων τῶν κακῶν, τὸ τὰς προλήψεις τὰς κοινὰς μὴ δύνασθαι ἐφαρμόζειν. τοῖς ἐπὶ μέρους. ἡμεῖς δ᾽ ἄλλοι ἄλλο οἰόμεθα . . . ἐπεὶ τίς οὐκ ἔχει κακοῦ πρόληψιν, ὅτι βλαβερόν ἐστιν, ὅτι φευκτόν ἐστιν, ὅτι παντὶ τρόπῳ ἀποικονόμητόν ἐστιν; πρόληψις προλήψει οὐ μάχεται, ἀλλ᾽ ὅταν ἔλθῃ ἐπὶ τὸ ἐφαρμόζειν.

In order to highlight the obviously inconsistent or vacillating manner in which humans are prone to handle their preconceptions, Epictetus frequently draws attention to the contrasting regulations that different human cultures have instituted.[36] Furthermore, in an exchange with a layperson, he compares the individual's ability to appeal to preconceptions to be like an illiterate who can fluently recite the principles of writing, but who patently cannot have any understanding or functional use for them, and in another discussion he informs his lay dialogue partner that, despite his protestations, he does not understand what either god, or good, or evil truly are.[37]

For Epictetus he believes that concerted and laborious effort must be expended before our preconceptions can more reliably disclose what the appropriate course of action that we should pursue is.[38] They hold that without systematizing and refining the general principles that our preconceptions supply to us and without placing them into a coherent framework, their ability to help us render our lives according to virtue will lie perpetually dormant. This is an aspect of Stoic thought that Cicero usefully outlines in the following passages:

> It is true she bestowed an intellect capable of receiving every virtue, and implanted in it at birth and without instruction embryonic notions of the loftiest ideas, laying the foundation of its education, and introducing among its endowments the elementary constituents, so to speak, of virtue. But of virtue itself she merely gave the germ and no more.[39]

> *etsi dedit talem mentem, quae omnem virtutem accipere posset, ingenuitque sine doctrina notitias parvas rerum maximarum et quasi instituit docere et induxit in ea, quae inerant, tamquam elementa virtutis. sed virtutem ipsam inchoavit, nihil amplius.*

> Therefore it rests with us (and when I say with us, I mean with our science), in addition to the elementary principles bestowed upon us, to seek out their logical developments, until our full purpose is realized.[40]

> *Itaque nostrum est—quod nostrum dico, artis est—ad ea principia, quae accepimus, consequentia exquirere, quoad sit id, quod volumus, effectum quod.*

Seneca, meanwhile, avers that nature gives us "not a good, but the start of good," *non dico bonum, sed initium boni*, and that "for the attainment of this benefit but not in the receipt of it, were we born," *Ad hoc quidem, sed sine hoc nascimur.*[41]

In two passages, Epictetus is recorded as drawing upon a particularly effective analogy to underscore his stance on the necessity of evaluating the content of our preconceptions.[42] He observes that people apprehend the foolishness of attempting to ascertain the weight, or the straightness of certain items at random, and that they instead depend upon established standards (i.e., scales and rulers) when they make such deductions. Epictetus then reflects, with stated amazement (θαυμάζω), that people routinely do not hold their ethical positions against any such canon and instead act upon each impression that they have without reservation.[43] In this light, Epictetus informs his dialogue partner: "Let us have recourse to our standard, produce your preconceptions," ἔλθωμεν ἐπὶ τοὺς κανόνας, φέρε τὰς προλήψεις,[44] which they can then appraise. Similarly, in another passage he notes that the most important task of the philosopher is to evaluate their impressions, in a similar way to how an assayer depends upon their art/skill (τέχνη) to test the authenticity of coins.[45]

The ability for preconceptions to ground humans in ethical thought, yet for them to still require extensive philosophical training in order to begin to properly employ them, is perhaps best expressed in a dialogue that Epictetus conducts with an Epicurean commissioner. Within this exchange Epictetus argues:

> But even if you were to tell me that you do desist [from appropriate behavior that seeks one's good] I would not believe you. For, as it is impossible to assent to an apparent falsehood, or to turn away from what appears to be true, so it is impossible to abstain from an apparent good. . . . What is in our nature? To be free, noble-minded, self-respecting. For what other animal blushes? What other has a sense of shame?[46]

> ἀλλ᾽ οὐδ᾽ ἂν λέγῃς μοι, ὅτι ἀπέχῃ, πιστεύσω σοι. ὡς γὰρ ἀ . . . πεφύκαμεν δὲ πῶς; ὡς ἐλεύθεροι, ὡς γενναῖοι, ὡς αἰδήμονες. ποῖον γὰρ ἄλλο ζῷον ἐρυθριᾷ, ποῖον αἰσχροῦ φαντασίαν λαμβάνει;

In this passage, Epictetus recounts how this man has evidently refrained from acting against his naturally held social values by, for example, not stealing from his neighbors, not committing adultery, and (at least as Epictetus frames it), contrary to his Epicurean principles, raising a family and engaging in public affairs. Epictetus' argument, that he also usefully articulates elsewhere, is that humans have instilled within them a "natural sense of honor" and a "natural disposition to mutual service, [and] to mutual restraint," οὐδὲν ἔχομεν αἰδῆμον φύσει; . . . φύσει ὠφελητικόν, ἀλλήλων φύσει ἀνεκτικόν[47]; It is this instinctive understanding of social obligations that, Epictetus suggests, has prompted some of this man's most notable decisions in his life, and not his professed allegiance to Epicureanism. From Epictetus' vantage preconceptions appear, therefore, to have mitigated other, and often corrupting, influences in this man's life.[48] Importantly, though, Epictetus continues to address the commissioner and impress upon him the need he has to adhere to a philosophy that is concomitant with such social principles:

You should search for doctrines that are in harmony with that pattern of behavior and with them to guide you, you will gladly be able to refrain from things that are able to attract and overpower you. But if to the seductiveness of these things we add some philosophy such as this, which help propel us towards them and encourage us in this, what will be the result?[49]

τούτοις σύμφωνα δόγματα ζήτησον, ἀφ᾽ ὧν ὁρμώμενος ἡδέως ἀφέξῃ πραγμάτων οὕτως πιθανῶν πρὸς τὸ ἀγαγεῖν καὶ νικῆσαι. ἂν δὲ πρὸς τῇ πιθανότητι τῇ ἐκείνων καὶ φιλοσοφίαν τινά ποτε ταύτην ἐξευρηκότες ὦμεν συνεπωθοῦσαν ἡμᾶς ἐπ᾽ αὐτὰ καὶ ἐπιρρωννύουσαν, τί γένηται.

From this passage it is evident that while Epictetus holds that this individual's preconceptions (and *oikeiosis*) have laudably guided him some way toward appropriate behavior and, in particular, in instituting his social awareness,[50] he cautions that they need to be augmented and further elucidated by a suitable intellectual framework. Without this process, Epictetus believes that the man's preconceptions cannot suffice to provide him with an appropriately composite and resilient understanding of what the virtuous truly is. With similar thoughts, Seneca plainly comments:

> Virtue is not given to a soul unless that soul has been trained and taught by unrelenting practice led to perfection. . . . [Even] the best of men, before you refine them by teaching, there is but the stuff of virtue, not virtue itself.[51]

> *virtus non contingit animo nisi instituto et edocto et ad summum adsidua exercitatione perducto . . . Ad hoc quidem, sed sine hoc nascimur Ad hoc quidem, sed sine hoc nascimur et in optimis quoque, antequam erudias, virtutis materia, non virtus est.*

The training and practice that are required before a person can properly articulate what their preconceptions of the good are, as I have explored in previous chapters, understood by Stoics proponents to be unavoidably rigorous. A further point in this regard is Epictetus' conviction that individuals who have not completed such preparation should not depend upon their preconceptions to reliably disclose what is truly virtuous or not. This is apparent from his recommendation to his students that they should suspend their attempts to pursue the good (which for him is a particular type of impulse, namely ὄρεξις), and instead employ their impulse (ὁρμή) to what they think is appropriate (καθῆκον) and to use reservation (ὑπεξαίρεσις) while doing so. Only when they have completed the third division of instruction at the conclusion of their studies, which comprises logic and assent, does Epictetus advise that they should seek to pursue the good.[52]

In conclusion, it has been seen that preconceptions are an important part of Epictetus' system of thought. Through them he believes that a latent understanding of right and wrong is present within every person, and that preconceptions have a role in mediating error and in steering individuals toward appropriate actions and attitudes. Regarding Epictetus' opinions of laypeople and their capacity for moral conformity, this is, therefore, a topic of some importance.[53] Preconceptions on their own however are not held by him to be able to conduct people, or to even lead them to arrive in proximity to perfection. The benefits preconceptions provide—although noteworthy—can only be concluded to be moderate in Epictetus' view.

NOTES

1. *Diss.* I.28.3, III.8.2.
2. Diog. Laert. 7.51.
3. *Diss.* II.11.14, I.27.2; see also I.20.7.
4. *Diss.* I.7.32-33.
5. *Diss.* II.11.5.
6. See the warnings in this regard from Gould (1970, 170), and approaching five decades later from Colish (2014, 96–98). Highlighting this contestation it can be observed that the most recent spurt of scholarly attention on this topic in the last decade; two PhD theses, Dyson (2009) and Hagland (2010), three articles/book chapters, Fisher (2014), Hadot (2014), and Orlando (2014), explore these topics in some depth, and independent of each other reach different conclusions.
7. See the discussion in Fisher (2014, 2015). See also Girdwood (1998, 62), Long (2004, 82), Inwood (2005, 301; 2018, 66; 2019, 158), and Hadot's (2014, 19).
8. *Diss.* I.22.1.
9. *Diss.* II.11.3. See also *Diss.* III.20.1, and the comments in Long (2002, 80), Vogt (2008, 58), and Dyson (2009, xviii).
10. *Diss.* II.11.5. On the range of topics that Epictetus believes people can have preconceptions about, see Fisher (2015, 26).
11. See the brief, but astute, comments from Tsalla (2005, 60) and Dyson (2009, 148). Atherton (2007, 115) also briefly argues that the Stoics believe preconceptions provide people with "some measure of truth."
12. *Diss.* I.25.4-5. See also *Diss.* IV.12.12.
13. *Diss.* III.9.7.
14. See Kamtekar (1998, 155).
15. On Epictetus' understanding of shame (αἰδώς), which the Stoics held was a subcategory of caution (ευλάβεια), see Kamtekar (1998) and Sorabji (2014, 16). Within this latter study, Kamtekar argues, 136, 137, that through his concept of shame Epictetus has proposed: "something like the notion of a conscience, an internal self-judging standard, which enables a Stoic to make progress and approach virtue by living according to her conscience."

16. *Diss.* I.14, II.8.12-14, cf. 1.30.1. On this, see the respective discussions in Fisher (2014, 81) and Sorabji (2014, 26). See also *Ep.* 41.2.

17. *Diss.* IV.3.2.

18. *Diss.* III.7.26-27, "What is our nature? To be free, noble-spirited, self-respecting. (For what other animal blushes? What other has the idea of shame?)": πεφύκαμεν δὲ πῶς; ὡς ἐλεύθεροι, ὡς γενναῖοι, ὡς αἰδήμονες. ποῖον γὰρ ἄλλο ζῷον ἐρυθριᾷ, ποῖον αἰσχροῦ φαντασίαν λαμβάνει. See also *Fr.* 14 and Johnson (2013, 71–72).

19. Seneca. *Ep.* 43.4-5. See also *Benef.* 4.7.4; 17.21, *Ep.* 97.12, 14, 15, 105.7-8 and the discussions in Colish (2014, 104–105), who argues (105) that according to Seneca: "They [the malefactors] cannot escape knowledge of the truth of their situation and the fact that they have brought their own punished upon themselves."

20. *Ep.* 25.2.

21. *Beata vita* 20.4.

22. On the importance of the dialectical/elenctic method for Epictetus, see Long (2002, 74–93) and Tsalla (2005, 41–52).

23. *Diss.* III.10.9. On the contested origins of the dialectic method, consider Fink (2012, 2–3 n.3).

24. Regarding the differences between the Platonic and Stoic understanding of the dialectical method, see the useful discussion in Tsalla (2005, 51–52).

25. This belief is most notably expressed at *Diss.* II.26.4-5.

26. From the exchange between Epictetus and a skeptic at *Diss.* I.3.3-5, Kamtekar (1998, 145) also importantly highlights that for Epictetus: "the recognition of logical inconsistency or contradiction does not by itself lead one to revise one's beliefs in the direction of consistency. Revision requires, in addition, the intervention of αἰδώς," which, as I have noted at n.15, can cease to function if a person has inured themselves to vice. See also *Diss.* II.24.9-20, 28-29.

27. See *Diss.* III.1.24, along with the commentary of Sidebottom (2009, 82–84).

28. That this visitor is likely styling himself as a rhetorician, see Eshleman (2012, 45). It can be observed that at *Or.* 9.14-20 Dio has a similar conversation with an athlete regarding whether training to be fast at running is truly virtuous.

29. *Diss.* III.1.6-7, 8-9.

30. We might note regarding *Diss.* I.6.19-22 that Tsalla (2005, 39) states: "the fact that one [i.e., a layperson] is willing to blame a philosopher for committing adultery or gluttony or any act that shows no restrain, but not, for example a carpenter or a musician for the same fault, shows that an understanding of the concept [of virtue] is already in place. The confused concept will become knowledge after it has been examined. This is the appropriate function of dialectic."

31. That Epictetus believes the success of this method largely depends upon the competence and experience of the philosophical interlocutor, see *Diss.* I.7.28-29 and II.12.6.

32. *Diss.* I.11.39. Consider also *Diss.* I.7.4-7.

33. See Kamketar (1998, 157) and Sorabji (2007, 96), citing *Diss.* II.23.15, III.22.94-96, and *Ench.* 34. For a discussion on the history of the debate over whether Epictetus has developed a theory of the conscience, see also Huttunen (2009, 44–45). On the various theories of the conscience in antiquity, see Bosman (2003, 49–105)

and Sorabji (2015, 11–96). Schinkel (2007, 187) also usefully notes the lack of division in the ancient mind between consciousness and the conscience, which is a distinction that problematizes modern attempts to define ancient authors' positions. Schinkel, though, valuably comments (2007, 187): "If Stoicism did make a distinctive contribution to the overall meaning of *syneidesis*, it was probably through an unconscious identification with conscience of the ability of every man to know the law of reason."

34. *Diss.* I.14.11-15. See also *Diss.* II.23.15, and if one can affirmatively assign it to Epictetus, *Fr.* 97.

35. *Diss.* IV.1.42, 44-45. Furthermore, note the exchange that is portrayed as taking place between Epictetus and a layperson at *Diss.* II.11.7-8: In this passage, Fisher (2014, 82) comments: "this layperson who, at II.11.7, claims to have knowledge (*eidenai*) of the noble and the base, and Epictetus in his own person agrees that he, in fact, does." See also *Diss.* II.21.3-4, *Leg.* 1.47, Diog. Laert. 7.89 and *SVF* 3.519, and the comments from Aktins (2013, 175–176), as well as Meinwald (2011, 364), who argues that the Stoics hold: "It would be a hopeless strategy for avoiding error to tell someone to assent only to what is true. We are not able to tell, concerning each impression that may arise, whether or not it is true."

36. For example, *Diss.* I.11.12-15 and II.11.15-18.

37. *Diss.* II.14.14-15; and II.14.19.

38. See *Diss.* I.1.12; 6.19-22; 20.14-16; 22.9-10; II.8.23; 11.13, and IV.1.51-52, as well as Aetius *apud SVF* 2.83, and Cicero *Leg.* 1.30. As Horowitz (1998, 25, 26) states: "The Stoics believe that the mind is born predisposed to certain ideas that are not yet held. These ideas are evoked and developed through the stimulus of sense impression and the development of reason. . . . Philosophy thus builds on the foundation of human preconceptions. . . . Our notions need to be analyzed, systematized, and classified in proper relation to observed facts." Consider also the discussions from Dyson (2009, xviii) and Fisher (2014, 84).

39. *Fin.* 5.59, trans. Rackham (1914, 461). See also *Leg* 1.26.

40. *Fin.* 5.60, trans. Rackham (1914, 461, 463).

41. *Ep.* 124.7, 90.46, trans. Gummere (1920, 439, 429, 431). At *De Tranq.* 3.2, he also comments: "For inborn in our constitution are the seeds of virtue, which, if they were permitted to grow, would lead us by nature itself to happiness of life." See also *Ep.* 49.12, *Clem.* 2.2.2, and *Att.* 12.5.7.

42. *Diss.* I.17.10; 28.28-30, and II.11.13.

43. *Diss.* I.28.-30.

44. *Diss.* I.28.28.

45. *Diss.* I.20.7-11.

46. *Diss.* III.7.14-15, 26-27.

47. *Diss.* II.10.22, 23.

48. See also Fisher (2014, 86), who comments regarding *Diss.* III.8.2-4: "What this passage tells us, then, is that applications are cognizable. They need not always go through a preconception test in order to be known—some applications can be known because they carry a 'token from nature.'" It is also profitable to highlight the comments from Schafer (2009, 88–89) regarding Seneca and precepts: "Seneca, then,

has laid the theoretical basis for a program of moral therapy that includes nontechnical pedagogical methods. How can it do so? Because, Seneca claims, the moderately bad person retains her natural impulse to goodness, which precepts stimulate. At [*Ep.*]94.28 Seneca gives several examples of solemn apothegms remarking that they don't need any defense."

49. *Diss.* III.7.22-23.

50. Of relevance to this passage is the Stoic conception of οἰκείωσις. Trying to find a suitable translation for this term is hard; however, in her influential study on the topic, Striker (1996, 281) has usefully defined it as being the: "recognition and appreciation of something as belonging to one . . . coming to be (or being made to be) well disposed toward something." In essence, through *oikeiosis* the Stoics believe that every individual is born with an impulse for self-preservation and has an affinity for themselves. Soon after birth, however, and what Reydams-Schils (2005, 129), calls: "the primordial transition from self-centeredness to social behavior," as individuals expand their social awareness to incorporate the people that surround them, and in particular their family members. Hierocles *apud* Stob. *Anth.* 4.84.23 likens the bonds of affection in humanity to a ring of concentric circles; starting with oneself at the center (where the feelings of affinity are most strong), immediate family in the next circle, distant family in the next, with this extending out to fellow country members and, finally, every person who belongs to the human race and to whom we feel the least connection with. The Stoics believe that through the use of reason we should contract these circles until we feel the same attachment to every individual as we do to ourselves, regardless of their distance from us. On Epictetus' belief that humans cannot help but have a sense of affection for each other, see relevant passages at *Diss.* I.13.5, 19.13-15, 23.2, II.10.21-22; 20.18-21, III.7.14-16, 20-23, and IV.1.122. Regarding his stance, however, that people often fail to uphold or to properly understand their social obligations, see *Diss.* II.4.1-5, 22.4.9-10, 18-19, and IV.5.10-12. On the Stoic understanding of *oikeiosis* and cosmopolitanism, see, for example, further discussions at Reydams-Schils (2005), Ramelli (2009), and Salles (2012).

51. *Ep.* 90.46, trans. Gummere (1920, 429, 431). He also notably argues, *Benef.* 4.7.4: "Of all the benefits that we have from Nature this is the greatest, the fact that Virtue causes her light to penetrate into the minds of all; *even those who do not follow her see her*," trans. Basore (1935, 241): *Maximum hoc habemus naturae meritum, quod virtus lumen suum in omnium animos permittit; etiam, qui non secuntur illam, vident.* On this, Graver (2012, 123) usefully comments that the Stoics hold that preconceptions do not offer: "virtue in themselves, nor even fully formed concepts, but they point us in the direction of virtues that we may develop was we mature."

52. See Inwood (1985, 115–125), and on the three-topic program of Epictetus' school see *Diss.* II.17.29-34, III.2.1-5, *Ench* 2, and 48.3.

53. As Girdwood (1998, 205) notes: "The considerable faith which he has in preconceptions as a permanently available criterion to guide our thinking is not new to the Stoa, but Epictetus clearly goes out of his way to emphasise what he regards as a providentially provided guarantee of the human capacity to think rightly."

Chapter 6

Civic Religion and Law

RELIGION

Civic religion is another means I suggest through which Epictetus holds that people can be morally benefited without them having to engage in philosophical study. As we shall see, religion was an important and pervasive feature in the world in which Epictetus lived and thought. The stance that Epictetus took toward civic religion has to my knowledge, however, not been extensively studied. This lack of attention, therefore, necessitates a somewhat lengthy introduction to his views of civic be supplied, after which I will consider Epictetus' understanding of the potential it has to morally influence laypeople.

The Stoic Attitude toward Civic Religion

While Stoic philosophy was undergirded by firm theological foundations, its theology largely diverged from the understandings of the divine that prevailed in ancient society.[1] Instances of Stoicism's positive interaction with civic religion has been largely credited by scholarship as being due to its features serving as a conduit through which Stoics proponents found they could profitably express their philosophy: an end that was chiefly achieved by filtering religion's contents through etymological or allegorical speculation, as can be seen in particular from Chrysippus, Cicero's Balbus, and Cornutus.[2]

Apart from such instances, it might be thought that the Stoics held a somewhat ambivalent stance regarding the renderings of the divine were characteristically expressed in civic Greco-Roman religion. In particular it has been held that the cults that suffused ancient society were thought by the Stoics to be inimical to humanity's perception of god because of their placing of deities into external assets such as statues, or by orienting their followers to approach the divine through rituals rather than through the exercise of their minds and moral volition. Aligning with this view ambivalence and muted criticism toward religious practices can be seen being expressed in early Stoic sources, and in Seneca's writings in particular.[3]

Several passages from Epictetus' writings can be assembled which seem to accord with this perspective. Indeed, one passage might appear to allow casting him as an ancient iconoclast:

> You carry god about with you, poor fool, but you know nothing of it. Do you presume I mean some external deity that is crafted from gold or silver? It is within yourself that you carry him and that you defile him without knowing it by your impure thoughts and unclean actions.[4]

> θεὸν περιφέρεις, τάλας, καὶ ἀγνοεῖς. δοκεῖς με λέγειν ἀργυροῦν τινα ἢ χρυσοῦν ἔξωθεν; ἐν σαυτῷ φέρεις αὐτὸν καὶ μολύνων οὐκ αἰσθάνῃ ἀκαθάρτοις μὲν διανοήμασι, ῥυπαραῖς δὲ πράξεσι.

This theme of the misleading or usurping role that was played by Greco-Roman religion is reprised in another section, where Epictetus comments upon the notable time and effort that his students apportion to travel to Olympia to view Pheidias' statue of Zeus, while they are slow to consider god who is continually present within them, that is, their rational mind.[5]

Epictetus' Positive Assessment of Civic Religion

While the above pronouncements might be catalogued to support the contention that Epictetus opposes and challenges the legitimacy of traditional Greco-Roman religion,[6] the contours of his stance toward civic religion are, I believe, more complex than has so far been acknowledged in scholarship.[7] The method of reinterpreting civic religion is only explicitly utilized once in the records of his discussions, when, again drawing upon his students' familiarity with Pheidias' statue of Zeus, Epictetus describes the statue as being an anthropomorphized depiction of the appropriate action that he is attempting to instill in his pupils: namely remaining emotionally steady (ἀτάρακτος), faithful, modest, noble, and unperturbed (πιστόν, αἰδήμονα, γενναῖον, ἀτάραχον).[8] Yet, despite the frequent allusions in the *Discourses* to the religious milieu and cultic practices of the first-century CE world, Epictetus seldom provides his audience with further interpretations of religion using this method. When he does introduce religion, he largely approvingly references it, and he does not tender any qualifications on its worth. We even learn of Epictetus' own embrace of its rituals. For example, when explicating his belief in the true value of possessions which he draws from his encounter with a thief, we learn of his ownership of a household shrine,[9] and we can witness him exhorting his students to follow his practice of offering a sacrifice of thanksgiving to the gods when they succeed in jettisoning a stubborn vice from their character.[10] In the *Enchiridion*, Epictetus meanwhile opines that it is appropriate to present sacrifices in accordance with traditional religious practices, so long as it is done in a properly pious and moderate manner.[11]

Often, though, Epictetus provides space for Stoic theology to inform his pupils' understanding of religion by *appending* the results of Stoic philosophy onto religion's features, not by *redacting* them to fit/represent the school's conclusions. For instance, when he cites the numerous cultic exercises that can convey gratitude to the gods, he adds that thanks should also be proffered to them because of the endowment of a reflective and capable intellect in humanity.[12] In another section, he crafts, and then proceeds to comment upon, a hymn to god:

> If we had any sense, what else should we to do, whether in public and in private than sing hymns and proclaim the deity and recount the benefits that he has given to us? Should we not as we dig, plough, or eat sing this hymn of praise to god? "Great is god, that he has supplied us with these tools to till the earth: great is god, that he has given us hands, the ability to swallow and a stomach: and he has given us the power to grow without being conscious of it, and to breathe in our sleep." This is what we should sing on every occasion, and also regarding the greatest and most divine hymn: that he has given us the capacity to understand these things and to use them methodically?[13]

> εἰ γὰρ νοῦν εἴχομεν, ἄλλο τι ἔδει ἡμᾶς ποιεῖν καὶ κοινῇ καὶ ἰδίᾳ ἢ ὑμνεῖν τὸ θεῖον καὶ εὐφημεῖν καὶ ἐπεξέρχεσθαι τὰς χάριτας; οὐκ ἔδει καὶ σκάπτοντας καὶ ἀροῦντας καὶ ἐσθίοντας ᾄδειν τὸν ὕμνον τὸν εἰς τὸν θεόν; 'μέγας ὁ θεός, ὅτι ἡμῖν παρέσχεν ὄργανα ταῦτα δι᾽ ὧν τὴν γῆν ἐργασόμεθα: μέγας ὁ θεός, ὅτι χεῖρας δέδωκεν, ὅτι κατάποσιν, ὅτι κοιλίαν, ὅτι αὔξεσθαι λεληθότως, ὅτι καθεύδοντας ἀναπνεῖν.' ταῦτα ἐφ᾽ ἑκάστου ἐφυμνεῖν ἔδει καὶ τὸν μέγιστον καὶ θειότατον ὕμνον ἐφυμνεῖν, ὅτι τὴν δύναμιν ἔδωκεν τὴν παρακολουθητικὴν τούτοις καὶ ὁδῷ χρηστικήν.

Here again we see that Epictetus appeals to traditional religious sentiments not to critique or redact them, but as a springboard that he can launch an explication of Stoic philosophy from. While Stoic philosophy is argued to be the superior object of his students' concern and devotion,[14] and it is certainly expected to be the prism that informs their perception of the purpose of such practices, he does not directly present it as supplanting or excluding civic religion.[15]

The Didactic Function of Civic Religion and Laypeople

Of significance for my purposes here is that at several junctures in the *Discourses* Epictetus moves beyond merely citing civic religion to attributing it with a role in educating and orienting individuals—including people who have no evident exposure to philosophy—to accept correct patterns of thought, and which he claims has some parallel with the results that can come from undergoing philosophical tuition. So, while plotting the varying skills and circumstances that need to be harmonized before a student can assume the role of coaching others to live philosophically rendered lives, Epictetus contrasts this preparation with the efforts that are expended by mystery cult devotees:

> Are the same proceedings beneficial if they are conducted at the wrong place and at the wrong time? No, a person should come with sacrifices and prayers after having been purified, and with their mind predisposed to the thought that they will be approaching sacred and ancient rites. It is in this way that the Mysteries came to be of benefit; it is in this way that we came to realize that all these things were instituted by the ancients for the education and correction of our lives.[16]

> καὶ παρὰ τόπον ταῦτα ὠφελεῖ καὶ παρὰ καιρόν: καὶ μετὰ θυσίας δὲ καὶ μετ᾽ εὐχῶν καὶ προηγνευκότα καὶ προδιακείμενον τῇ γνώμῃ, ὅτι ἱεροῖς προσελεύσεται καὶ ἱεροῖς παλαιοῖς. οὕτως ὠφέλιμα γίνεται τὰ μυστήρια, οὕτως εἰς φαντασίαν ἐρχόμεθα, ὅτι ἐπὶ παιδείᾳ καὶ ἐπανορθώσει τοῦ βίου κατεστάθη πάντα ταῦτα ὑπὸ τῶν παλαιῶν.

Here, Epictetus offers an important and, to my knowledge, so far unremarked upon,[17] acceptance of primitivism and the didactic function of civic religion that it often envisages. While he unfortunately does not detail the component(s) of the mysteries that help to secure this end, he asserts that they were set down (καθίστημι) by the ancients to be beneficial (ὠφέλιμος) for humanity, and states that they provide education and correction (παιδείᾳ καὶ ἐπανορθώσει) for their participants.

It can be observed that Seneca offers a discussion on this theme when he considers Etruscan religion, which is also worthy of some consideration. When noting that the Etruscans hold that by observing lightning bolts they can ascertain certain aspects of Jupiter's thoughts or intentions, he argues:

> Up to this point the Etruscans and the philosophers share the same ideas, but they differ when they think that lightning-bolts are sent by Jupiter, and they give him three *manubiae.* . . . They describe the things to look for in lightning-flashes in a disorganized, rambling fashion, although they could classify them as they were classified by Attalus the philosopher.[18]

*Haec adhuc Etruscis philosophisque communia sunt. In illo, Dissentiunt quod
fulmina a Ioue dicunt mitti et tres illi manubias dant. . . . Quae inspicienda sint
in fulgure, passim et uage dicunt, cum possint sic diuidere quemadmodum ab
Attalo philosopho.*

In this section, Seneca manages to sustain issuing a firm critique of the
inadequacies of Etruscan theology along with crediting elements of it as
being in alliance with philosophical thought, even going so far as to claim
that they share (*commune*) some of the same conclusions. The primary area
of consilience for him appears to center around the conviction that everything in the universe is connected and ordered by the divine[19]; but he even
highlights that the way in which the Etruscans approach classifying lightning
partially matches the taxonomy of the phenomenon which his teacher Attalus
had established.[20] Seneca also proceeds to helpfully disclose the mechanism
that he believes transmitted this understanding to Etruscan society, positing
a scenario that is redolent of the one Epictetus supplies above to explain the
beneficial features of the mystery cults, namely that their religion was formulated by wise ancients:

> If you ask me for my own view, I do not think that they [the ancients] were so
> stupid as to believe that Jupiter's choices were unfair or that his aim was not
> very good. . . . So what was their purpose when they said this? In order to control
> the minds of the ignorant, those very wise men pointed to an inescapable object
> of fear. In order that we should be afraid of something superior to us . . . . But
> those most eminent men were not guilty of the error of thinking that Jupiter
> sometimes uses <heavier, sometimes> lighter lightning-bolts, like weapons used
> for training. But they wanted to warn those who have to hurl lightning-bolts
> against human wrong-doings that they should not all be struck in the same way:
> some should be grazed, some shot down and shattered, some given a warning.[21]

*Si a me quaeris quid sentiam, non existimo tam hebetes fuisse ut crederent
Iouem iniquae uoluntatis aut certae minus peritiae . . . Quid ergo secuti sunt,
cum haec dicerent? Ad coercendos imperitorum animos sapientissimi uiri iudi-
cauerunt ineuitabilem. metum, ut aliquid supra nos timeremus . . . Illos uero
altissimos uiros error iste non tenuit, ut existimarent Iouem modo leuioribus
fulminibus et lusoriis telis uti. Sed uoluerunt admonere eos quibus aduersus
peccata hominum fulminandum est non eodem modo omnia esse percutienda;
quaedam. frangi debere, quaedam allidi ac destringi, quaedam admoueri.*

Seneca holds that Etruscan religion was established by the ancients so that
Etruscan citizens would continue to be in contact with robust ethical thought
that they would otherwise have been isolated from. Even those elements of
their religion, which when viewed against the assured results of philosophical

thought are sentiently false, are nevertheless understood by him to tacitly transmit underlying truths to the populace.[22] Seneca's attempts to highlight the numerous inaccuracies which are embedded within Etruscan civic religion are not, therefore, being raised by him so that its deficiencies can be exposed, or so he can establish their religion's redundancy. In this regard, he later reiterates the compatibility of the Etruscans' religious beliefs with certain philosophical conclusions:

> They [the ancients] recognized the same Jupiter as we do, the ruler and guardian of the universe, the mind and breath of the world, the master and the craftsman of this creation, for whom every name will be appropriate.[23]

> *sed eundem quem nos louem intellegunt, rectorem custodemque uniuersi, animum ac spiritum mundi, operis huius dominum. et artificem, cui nomen omne conuenit.*

For Seneca, the ancients who fashioned these myths recognized (*intellego*) the same theological principles that he and his fellow Stoics have managed to obtain by means of philosophical deduction, in particular that the Etruscans' conception of divination and lightning has enabled them to adopt correct ideas about the flexibility of justice and the purpose and suitability of redressive punishments.

Returning to Epictetus, we can see that in a further section he issues a remark regarding another religious group's ability to induce correct behavior in humanity. When instructing his students that they should not fear the swords of tyrants, he asks:

> then is it possible that a person can arrive at such an attitude towards these things through madness, or as in the case of the Galileans, by mere habit, and yet that no person can be able of learning through reason and demonstration that god has made everything in the universe, and indeed the entire universe itself, to be free from hindrance and to be self-sufficient, and that all its parts serve the needs of the whole?[24]

> εἶτα ὑπὸ μανίας μὲν δύναταί τις οὕτως διατεθῆναι πρὸς ταῦτα καὶ ὑπὸ ἔθους οἱ Γαλιλαῖοι· ὑπὸ λόγου δὲ καὶ ἀποδείξεως οὐδεὶς δύναται μαθεῖν, ὅτι ὁ θεὸς πάντα πεποίηκεν τὰ ἐν τῷ κόσμῳ καὶ αὐτὸν τὸν κόσμον ὅλον μὲν ἀκώλυτον καὶ αὐτοτελῆ, τὰ ἐν μέρει δ᾽ αὐτοῦ πρὸς χρείαν τῶν ὅλων.

If, as seems to be the consensus, Epictetus is referring to the recently incepted Christian movement, then we have a further example of a religious group that he holds can lead people to absorb correct attitudes.[25] It is not possible to definitely ascertain what form of Christianity Epictetus was familiar with, but it can be highlighted that the book of Titus depicts the Apostle Paul planning to spend the winter in Nicopolis, and with the dates of Epictetus' remarks (ca. 110–115 CE) falling within/close to the normally assigned dating range for Titus (early second century CE), it is possible that Epictetus has observed Christians who had some association with Pauline Christianity.[26] In this regard, as per Epictetus' comments, we might note that guidance on anticipating and being able to endure physical threats is found within Pauline literature.[27] In any case, while this non-Greco-Roman and (at the time) largely marginal religious movement might seem to be an unusual group from which to draw a moral comparison, the choice for Epictetus' concern is apposite. Both Stoicism and Christianity (generally regardless of the particular strain) demanded that their adherents effect a dramatic and consistently upheld moral change in their lives. Of importance for our concern is that these Christians' lack of concern for their bodies, that is, a stance that Epictetus believes they have acquired from mere habit (ἔθος)[28] and are able to maintain to the point of martyrdom, meshes with the attitude that Epictetus argues his students should hold through reason.[29] Although possibly an interpolation in the text, Epictetus' stance is almost identically expressed in Marcus Aurelius' *Meditations*, where he states that the readiness to be released from the body: "must spring from a specific judgment, rather than mere contrariness as with the Christians," τὸ δὲ ἕτοιμον τοῦτο, ἵνα ἀπὸ ἰδικῆς κρίσεως ἔρχηται, μὴ κατὰ ψιλὴν παράταξιν [ὡς οἱ Χριστιανοί].[30] Aside from questions of what particular group is in view, or whether they can be classified as a religious one, in any case Epictetus' belief in the ability of correct opinions to spread outside of philosophical education is nevertheless still demonstrated.

Epictetus, Divination, and Laypeople

A final aspect of Epictetus' view regarding religion that warrants extended discussion is the stance he adopted toward the art (τέχνη) of divination—the belief that the course of future events can be made known.[31] I have explored this issue broadly in a recent article, where I argued that despite the prevailing scholarly opinion, Epictetus is convinced that divination can be beneficially utilized by people.[32] The narrower question to be addressed here though is whether he holds that divination can impact laypeople, and specifically whether he believes it can reveal truths to people even if they have never been introduced to philosophical instruction.

In the first text for our consideration (*Diss.* III.1), Epictetus is depicted as being approached by a young student of rhetoric who is seeking advice from

him on how he might live according to virtue. It becomes clear, however
(10-14), that Epictetus assesses that the young man lacks the disposition
and understanding that is required to allow him to benefit from the instruction he has requested. Although Epictetus considers ceasing this likely futile
conversation, he nevertheless deliberates: "[but] if you should at some future
time lay this charge [of silence] against me, what defense could I make?,"
τοῦτό μοι ὕστερον ἂν ἐγκαλῇς, τί ἕξω ἀπολογήσασθαι; ναί· ἀλλ᾽ ἐρῶ καὶ οὐ
πεισθήσεται.[33] He compares this situation with those who faced Apollo and
Socrates:

> You may as well ask, why is he Apollo, and why does he deliver oracles, why
> has he placed himself in such a post as a prophet and fountain of truth, for the
> inhabitants of the whole civilized world to resort to? Why is "Know Thyself"
> inscribed on the front of his temple, even if nobody heeds it. Did Socrates
> persuade all who came to him, to take proper care of themselves? Not one in a
> thousand.[34]

> διὰ τί δὲ Ἀπόλλων ἐστίν; διὰ τί δὲ χρησμῳδεῖ; διὰ τί δ᾽ εἰς ταύτην τὴν χώραν
> ἑαυτὸν κατατέταχεν, ὥστε μάντις εἶναι καὶ πηγὴ τῆς ἀληθείας καὶ πρὸς
> αὐτὸν ἔρχεσθαι τοὺς ἐκ τῆς οἰκουμένης; διὰ τί δὲ προγέγραπται τὸ γνῶθι
> σαυτὸν μηδενὸς αὐτὸ νοοῦντος; Σωκράτης πάντας ἔπειθε τοὺς προσιό ντας
> ἐπιμελεῖσθαι ἑαυτῶν; οὐδὲ τὸ χιλιοστὸν μέρος.

After reflecting upon their examples, Epictetus resolves to continue to
outline key philosophical tenets to the young man. Of significance for our
concerns is that while Socrates' role in confronting society with philosophy is well known, Epictetus' description of Apollo as serving a similar
function, but by giving prophecies/oracles (χρησμῳδέω) that are directed
to the whole civilized world and that are then disseminated in inscriptions
and maxims, is perhaps less so. We should note, however, that such an
understanding of Apollo's role is commonplace in the ancient perception
of divination.[35] The belief that the maxim "know thyself," γνῶθι σαυτόν,
which was famously inscribed on the temple at Delphi, was either given by
Apollo (as Epictetus suggests in this passage) or crafted by one, or all, of
the seven sages, is attested across numerous philosophical schools' writings,[36] as is the understanding that it commends an enterprise that should be
pursued through philosophical deliberation.[37] Epictetus, however, intimates
an awareness that only a slight uptake of its appeal for self-reflection will
ever likely occur within humanity. Several classical authors though credit
this aphorism with having prompted various individuals to commence their
philosophical vocations. For example, Plutarch succinctly comments: "how
many philosophic inquiries (ζητήσεις) have they [i.e., its words] set on foot,

and what a horde of discourses (λόγοι) has sprung up from each, as from a seed!"[38] This is an ability that, I suggest, significantly Epictetus references elsewhere:

> Is, then, the Delphic admonition, "Know thyself," superfluous?—"surely not," the man replies.—If one told the singer in a chorus to know himself, would he not attend to the order by paying regard to his partners in the chorus and taking care to sing in harmony with them?—"Yes"—and likewise with a soldier or a sailor.[39]

> μή τι οὖν καὶ τὸ ἐν Δελφοῖς παράγγελμα παρέλκον ἐστί, τὸ Γνῶθι σαυτόν;— τοῦτο δὲ μὲν οὔ, φησί.—τίς οὖν ἡ δύναμις αὐτοῦ; εἰ χορευτῇ τις παρήγγελλε τὸ γνῶναι ἑαυτόν, οὔκουν ἂν τῇ προστάξει προσεῖχε τῷ ἐπιστραφῆναι καὶ τῶν συγχορευτῶν καὶ τῆς πρὸς αὐτοὺς συμφωνίας;—φησίν.—εἰ δὲ ναύτῃ.

Far from being, as the question at the start of this dialectical exchange rhetorically poses, superfluous (παρέλκω), cognizance of this oracle's injunction is used by Epictetus to try to prompt a layperson to understand the need he has to examine his life and actions, and to seek the aid that philosophy can offer in this regard.[40] We can observe that in the philosophical tradition, oracular pronouncements are associated with having inaugurated the careers of figures such as Socrates, Diogenes of Sinope, Zeno, and Dio Chrysostom.[41] Furthermore, although it is rarely addressed by modern commentators of Stoicism, the belief that the mantic can be solicited to confirm an individual's philosophical career is present within numerous Stoic sources.[42] Importantly for our purposes I suggest that Epictetus appears to reference this phenomenon when, while expanding upon the qualifications that are required of philosophical teachers, he comments:

> it may well be that not even wisdom is a sufficient qualification for the care of the young; one should also have a particular predisposition, by Zeus, and aptitude for this, and the right bodily build, and, above all, the recommendation from god that one should occupy this office, as he recommended to Socrates that he should undertake that of cross-examining people, and to Diogenes that of rebuking people in kingly tones, and to Zeno that of instructing people and establishing doctrines.[43]

> ἀλλ᾽ οὐδὲ σοφὸν εἶναι τυχὸν ἐξαρκεῖ πρὸς τὸ ἐπιμεληθῆναι νέων: δεῖ δὲ καὶ προχειρότητά τινα εἶναι καὶ ἐπιτηδειότητα πρὸς τοῦτο, νὴ τὸν Δία, καὶ σῶμα ποιὸν καὶ πρὸ πάντων τὸν θεὸν συμβουλεύειν ταύτην τὴν χώραν κατασχεῖν, ὡς Σωκράτει συνεβούλευεν τὴν ἐλεγκτικὴν χώραν ἔχειν, ὡς Διογένει τὴν βασιλικὴν καὶ ἐπιπληκτικήν, ὡς Ζήνωνι τὴν διδασκαλικὴν καὶ δογματικήν.

As we have just seen, the three philosophers whom Epictetus mentions, Socrates, Diogenes, and Zeno, all had the commencement of their philosophical careers and their transition from being a layperson to philosopher credited by some classical authors as being prompted by the pronouncements of oracles. Epictetus almost certainly has this in mind when he remarks that they had been "recommended" (συμβουλεύω) by god to take up their positions: a qualification that he labors was quite separate from the skills or circumstances that otherwise commended them for their roles.[44] It is unlikely, though, that Epictetus expects that every person's decision to become a philosopher should be prompted in such an explicit manner; rather it is evident from elsewhere that he holds that philosophy's candidates should manifest sufficient aptitude for undergoing training, as well as an implacable and naturally invested compulsion to live under philosophy's supervision.[45] In some instances, and in line with broader ancient opinion, Epictetus appears, and significantly for our purposes, to believe that this confirmation can be obtained through divination.

In conclusion, in Epictetus' view civic religion's origins lie within the primeval, proto-virtuous epoch of humanity, and he is of the opinion that its ability to educate and amend people continues to be effective. With regards to divination its effects are understood by him to be mainly in inducing people to begin their philosophical careers/training. The belief that divination can orient people toward philosophical truths even if they are outside of philosophical education is significant, and should be integrated into our understanding of Epictetus' perception of laypeople, and the means whereby he believes that their differences from philosophers might be lessened.

CIVIC LAW

The next nonphilosophical means whereby I suggest that it is possible to explore whether Epictetus believes that laypeople can be profitably guided is civic law. Apprehending Epictetus' attitude toward the law can, however, be challenging. The topic is not made a matter of explicit deliberation in either the *Discourses* or the *Enchiridion*, and his stance toward it has only rarely been considered by his modern interpreters. In order to provide some context for understanding Epictetus' position on the law, I will briefly introduce some salient points and then proceed to document how his perception of it informs his views of laypeople.

Firstly, we should note that Epictetus finds frequent cause to critique the law, for example he lambasts the contradictory legislations that different states, such as those of the Jews, Syrians, Egyptians, and Romans, assume;[46] he lists courts alongside robbers (κλέπται) and tyrants (τύραννοι) as wrongly trying to control people by bringing force to bear against them[47]; and he implies that some legal officials have been selected for their positions because of their shrewd distribution of praise to individuals who hold positions of authority, rather than their ability to correctly discern and implement justice.[48] Moreover, Epictetus explicitly claims that it is philosophy and not the law which can set people free (ἐλευθερόω),[49] and states that our concentration on how to live should be directed to the parameters that have been established by philosophical insight, and not those that have been borne from legal deliberation, such as those of the Roman legal theorists Masurius and Cassius (the latter of whom Epictetus' near-contemporary Stoic Persius also critiques in a similar manner[50]).

I suggest that the above critiques, though, should be tensioned alongside numerous other passages in which Epictetus asserts that people should observe the law's ordinances. For example, he argues that it is the duty of good citizens (ἀγαθοὶ πολῖται) to obey the law,[51] broadly asserts that we should always endeavor to be follow/learn from (πείθεσθαι) the law,[52] and approvingly notes that his philosophical hero Socrates had a principle of always attempting to comply with state legislation.[53]

In trying to understand and bring these two positions together, I, firstly, suggest that Epictetus considers people's obedience to the law to be one of the numerous responsibilities that they should assume as part of their identity as citizens. In other words, Epictetus expects that people should tolerate the law's frequently faulty demands (although they should feel free to follow him in criticizing its failings), and only forgo adhering to them if the legislation *directly* contradicts their philosophical principles. Secondly, I argue that Epictetus believes that the law can, to some degree, be useful in aiding people to behave appropriately—a belief that I will now turn to explore now in more depth.

The Didactic Role of Civic Law and Laypeople

In turning to place Epictetus' reflections on civic religion within its proper context, firstly we can note a short remark he makes wherein he states that individuals with bad judgment have converted (καταλαμβάνω) courts into dens of robbers.[54] The choice of language here implies that Epictetus believes that the courts are not necessarily corrupt by nature, but, rather, that their integrity has been debased. Such language leaves open the possibility that Epictetus holds that if the corrupting individuals are removed, the law might be able to (at least partially) fulfill its task of beneficially regulating humanity's actions.

We have to look at another passage however, to which I will return to further consider in the following chapter, to see Epictetus specifying that a particular legal code is indeed of high philosophical worth, and where he again significantly appeals to the concept of the ancient and wise lawgiver. In this section, after citing numerous philosophical principles regarding the concepts of freedom, honor, and feelings of benevolence toward others, Epictetus argues while utilizing sarcasm:

> It was through principles like these that our well-governed cities flourished! It was upon these principles that Sparta was founded! These are the convictions that Lycurgus instilled into the Spartans through his laws and program of education: that slavery is no more base than noble, and freedom is no more noble than base! Those who fell at Thermopylae, died because they held such judgements as these! And from what principles but these did the Athenians abandon their city?[55]

> ἐκ τούτων τῶν λόγων ηὐξήθησαν ἡμῖν αἱ εὐνομούμεναι πόλεις, Λακεδαίμων διὰ τούτους τοὺς λόγους ἐγένετο, Λυκοῦργος ταῦτα τὰ πείσματα ἐνεποίησεν αὐτοῖς διὰ τῶν νόμων αὐτοῦ καὶ τῆς παιδείας, ὅτι οὔτε τὸ δουλεύειν αἰσχρόν ἐστι μᾶλλον ἢ καλὸν οὔτε τὸ ἐλευθέρους εἶναι καλὸν μᾶλλον ἢ αἰσχρόν, οἱ ἐν Θερμοπύλαις ἀποθανόντες διὰ ταῦτα τὰ δόγματα ἀπέθανον, Ἀθηναῖοι δὲ τὴν πόλιν διὰ ποίους ἄλλους λόγους ἀπέλιπον.

The opposite evaluation is, of course, intended to be made, namely that Spartan state's laws (νομοι), and significantly also those of the Athenian's, have been fashioned in a laudable manner, and that they had succeeded in training/rearing (παιδείας) well-governed cities (εὐνομούμεναι πόλεις) and instilling a profitable appreciation of freedom (ἐλεύθερος) into their populace.

Niko Huttunen though has suggested that Epictetus' argument here "however, is not entirely clear,"[56] for it praises dying for political freedom, which, Huttunen argues, Epictetus elsewhere downplays. In response to this, we can note that Epictetus' praise for the Spartan constitution is not restricted to the above remarks. He elsewhere commends the Spartans for apprehending that physical pain is not an evil,[57] and, as in the passage above, claims again that their ordinances had provided its people with proper social understanding.[58] Moreover, the propensity for members of the Stoa to present Spartan legal codes and individuals as displaying true freedom, and a range of other appropriate behaviors is seen across their writings, and is a habit that is commented upon by the school's observers.[59] In addition, in his treatise on the Stoic paradox *Only the Good Man is Free*, which is almost entirely drawn from Stoic arguments,[60] Philo of Alexandria praises the Spartans for giving up their lives for political freedom and for providing examples that allow the Stoic understanding of freedom—namely, the placing of principles above physical well-being—to be narrated.[61] Huttunen's caution, therefore, is not required.

Far from being unclear, Epictetus is appealing to a popular Stoic argument, and one that credits Spartan state polity as being in some way commensurate with philosophical ideals.

In other passages Epictetus appears to argue that there are instances where the law can broadly incline people to follow appropriate behavior. In the first comment for our consideration, Epictetus remarks:

> In the same way women are by nature common property, but when the legislator like the host at a feast has apportioned them, are you not willing like the rest to seek out your own portion and not grab somebody else's?[62]

> οὕτως καὶ αἱ γυναῖκες φύσει κοιναί. ὅταν δ᾽ ὁ νομοθέτης ὡς ἑστιάτωρ διέλῃ αὐτάς, οὐ θέλεις καὶ αὐτὸς ἴδιον μέρος ζητεῖν, ἀλλὰ τὸ ἀλλότριον ὑφαρπάζεις καὶ λιχνεύεις;

Here, the pronouncement of marriage by the legislator (νομοθέτης) is claimed by Epictetus to laudably restrain people's attempts to acquire another person's partner, a compulsion that he elsewhere credits as breaking down the social fabric of communities.[63] In another passage, he meanwhile refers to the connection between the state and the correct understanding of ownership, material possessions, and marital relationships that can be usually found present in its citizenry:

> You live in a city in the empire, you must exercise your authority and judge honorably, and keep your hands off what belong to others; consider no woman but your own wife to be beautiful, nor should any boy seem beautiful to you, nor any piece of silver or golden ware.[64]

> ζῆς ἐν ἡγεμονούσῃ πόλει· ἄρχειν σε δεῖ, κρίνειν δικαίως, ἀπέχεσθαι τῶν ἀλλοτρίων, σοὶ καλὴν γυναῖκα φαίνεσθαι μηδεμίαν ἢ τὴν σήν, καλὸν παῖδα μηδένα, καλὸν ἀργύρωμα μηδέν, χρύσωμα μηδέν.

Epictetus' view is that people broadly cannot help but be cognizant of the parameters that have been established by the state, whether that be regarding inappropriate sexual relations, or the theft of material goods, and the penalties that might have to be borne by individuals who transgress them. His remarks that his interlocutor lives in an imperial city "ζῆς ἐν ἡγεμονούσῃ πόλει," is hard to interpret. The verbal form of ἡγεμονία, which is used here, ἡγεμονέω, is a rarely used word in classical literature, but conveys the exercising of authority. We can observe that in light of the other injunction that he raises to his dialogue partner, namely that he should exercise his office and judge uprightly it appears that Epictetus is intending to communicate that humans have a responsibility to behave correctly and make use of their judgments as a vocational judge would.

It is worthwhile at this juncture to highlight that although this issue has never, to my knowledge, been commented upon in scholarship,[65] Epictetus' views in this regard are in continuity with those of other Stoic thinkers who credit the civic law as serving a profitable, even virtuous role within society. Cleanthes, Diogenes of Babylon, Posidonius, Rufus, Seneca, Arius Didymus, Persius, Cornutus, Dio Chrysostom, and Marcus Aurelius all aver that a state requires laws in order to render its populace civilized and not vicious.[66] For instance, Arius Didymus argues that it is the duty of a wise man to try and craft laws to help educate his fellow countrymen,[67] while Posidonius holds that the constitutions of Sparta, Athens, and Sicily were wisely established.[68] Significantly, for this book's thesis Posidonius also asserts that, provided they are carefully structured, legal pronouncements can aid the uneducated to behave appropriately.[69] Similarly, Marcus Aurelius argues that political communities, household assemblies, treatises, and truces have profitably regulated human societies,[70] while Rufus remarks on lawgivers who research what is good (ἀγαθός) for a city and the common good, and whose legislation we should look to observe,[71] and he further asserts that monarchs should study philosophy in order to correctly dispense justice.[72] This suggests that, as we have argued above, the opinions Epictetus holds regarding the value of the law should not be surprising to us. He is expressing a commonly held Stoic view.

Finally, with regards to Epictetus' views of civic law, and specifically relating to its implementation, we can note that Epictetus records that his friend:

> Agrippinus, when he was governor, would try to persuade the people whom he sentenced that it was proper for them to be sentenced. "For it is not as their enemy," he said, "or as a thief, that I pass my sentence against them, but as their overseer and guardian, just as the physician likewise encourages the person he is operating on, and persuades him to offer himself up to treatment."[73]

> ὁ Ἀγριππῖνος ἡγεμονεύων ἐπειρᾶτο τοὺς καταδικαζομένους ὑπ᾽ αὐτοῦ πείθειν, ὅτι προσήκει αὐτοῖς καταδικασθῆναι. οὐ γὰρ ὡς πολέμιος αὐτοῖς, ἔφη, οὐδ᾽ ὡς λῃστὴς καταφέρω τὴν ψῆφον αὐτῶν, ἀλλ᾽ ὡς ἐπιμελητὴς καὶ κηδεμών, ὥσπερ καὶ ὁ ἰατρὸς τὸν τεμνόμενον παραμυθεῖται καὶ πείθει παρέχειν ἑαυτόν.

Here, Epictetus approvingly notes that when Agrippinus Paconius served as a governor,[74] he was able to exercise his judicial responsibilities in such a way as to attempt (πειράω), encourage, and persuade (παραμυθέομαι καὶ πείθει) people to apprehend their errant behavior and to seek the moral reform of their lives. The word that Epictetus uses to describe their "treatment" is τεμνόμενον, the participle form of the verb τέμνω, which means to cut, or to operate upon. It is, therefore, a word that connotes that deep and painful methods of seeking remedy should be attempted, an understanding that should remind us of the material in chapter 1 regarding the significant effort that Epictetus believes undergoing moral advancement requires. Furthermore, aside from acting like a physician (ἰατρός), through the law Epictetus believes that Agrippinus had the opportunity to act as if he was the criminals' protector (ἐπιμελητής) and guardian (κηδεμών). It is, therefore, apparent that it is not just the state's legal doctrines that Epictetus views as having the potential to affect a change in people, but also the act of dispensing justice itself. This message would no doubt be particularly well received by Epictetus' students, many of whom appear to intend to assume positions of political responsibility once their formal philosophical training has ceased.[75]

In conclusion, although Epictetus believes that the law is frequently flawed or inadequately formed, he is also of the opinion that, like religion, it can have a useful role in establishing correct boundaries of behavior across society, and to influence individuals to act according to virtuous precepts. At no point does he portray philosophical education or awareness being required by people before the beneficial effects of the law can function. We can, therefore, reasonably conclude that the law is a means whereby Epictetus believes that differences between philosophers and laypeople can to some extent be attenuated.

NOTES

1. On Stoic theology, see Sedley (2001), Algra (2003), Brennan (2009b), and the selection of essays assembled in Salles (2009).

2. For example, see the comments at Cicero *Nat. D* 3.60. Ullucci (2011, 65): "The Stoics, for example, argue against popular anthropomorphic conceptions of the gods; however, their support of sacrifice is well known. There is nothing wrong with animal sacrifice in the Stoic view, so long as correct (i.e., Stoic) interpretations were maintained . . . To describe these comments as critiques of sacrifice is misleading and inaccurate. Most importantly, this interpretation masks the reality of what these writers (be they Platonists, Stoics, or Epicureans) are attempting to do—that is impose their own interpretation on a key religious ritual." See also the discussion in Frede (2001, 102). Gill (2013b, 79) further valuably comments: "This is not a very easy question [the Stoic attitude toward civic religion] to answer, particularly as the Stoics claimed that their theology was compatible with conventional religion. More precisely, they present their theology as offering a more systematic and theorized account of beliefs and practices found in different human societies, including Greek and Roman culture." On the extent of the Stoics' use of allegory, see Ramelli (2004, 79–145, 275–375), (2014, 486–496), and Van Sijl (2010, 99–105, 209–212, 242).

On early Stoics positive (re-)interpretation of traditional religion, see Jedan (2009, 9, 23, 29).

3. Consider the useful discussions in Algra (2007, 238–242), Vogt (2008, 59–62, 128), and particularly Seneca's comments at *Ep.* 90.28, 95.47 and *Phae.* 489-490. Brennan (2009, 110) notes: "the Stoics were frequently treated by later sources as natural allies and defenders of traditional religion. But the case is rather more complicated; their philosophical commitments led them to oppose and reject much of traditional religion, or to support it in name only."

4. *Diss.* II.8.12-13. Huttunen (2009, 48) claims that Epictetus "ridicules the desire to see a statue of Zeus in Olympia."

5. *Diss.* I.6.23-24.

6. Long (2002, 178–179) comments that Epictetus "undercuts the language and conventions of popular religion by transferring them into his own theology. Emotional collapse is 'impiety' because it flouts our God-given resources for coping with circumstance (1.6.39, cf. 2.23.2) . . . Lifeless images of gods are pointless when God's living works are available for contemplation (2.8.20, cf. 2.19.25), and, while all the mythological stories about Hades are nonsense, yet it remains true that the world is 'full of gods', as Stoically conceived (3.15)." Johnson (2009, 71), meanwhile, argues that Epictetus does not "express either intellectual dismissal or moral disapproval" toward common religious practices.

7. This present chapter is, I believe, the first attempt to explore Epictetus' opinions on civic religion in any detail. Indeed, it is noticeable that this topic has gathered very little attention from scholars; for example, Long's monograph on Epictetus has only one paragraph dedicated to it, where he presents Epictetus as having a rather negative conception of popular religion (see n.6 above). Moreover, in his study that considers the Stoic attitudes toward divination, Hankinson (1988) makes no mention of Epictetus, despite, as we shall see, Epictetus offering the most thorough reflection on it than any other extant Stoic thinker provides. However, see Johnson (2009, 71–72, 74–75), who catalogues many of Epictetus' references to popular religious practices, as well as the valuable reflections from scholars listed here at n.17.

8. *Diss.* II.8.26-27. On this passage, Algra (2009, 249) notes: "it provides us with yet another instance of a Stoic assessment of an anthropomorphic cult statue as being more than just 'childish': the way in which Pheidias has managed to convey the moral, exemplary aspect of Zeus apparently compensates for the fact that the Stoic Zeus strictly speaking does not look like a man."

9. *Diss.* I.18.15.

10. *Diss.* II.18.13; see also *Diss.* I.19.25, II.18.13, 20-22. On Epictetus and the Stoic understanding of prayer, see the discussion in Algra (2007, 49–51).

11. *Ench.* 31.5, cf. Diog. Laert. 7.119.

12. *Diss.* I.4.31-32.

13. *Diss.* I.16.15-18.

14. At *Ench.* 31, before he outlines the appropriateness of observing traditional religious practices, Epictetus also maintains that his students should "realize that the most important factor in piety toward the gods is to form right opinions about them as beings that exist and govern the universe well and justly, and to have set yourself to obey them, and to submit to all that happens, and willingly follow it, as something

that is being brought to pass by the most perfect intelligence," τῆς περὶ τοὺς θεοὺς εὐσεβείας ἴσθι ὅτι τὸ κυριώτατον ἐκεῖνό ἐστιν, ὀρθὰς ὑπολήψεις περὶ αὐτῶν ἔχειν ὡς ὄντων καὶ διοικούντων τὰ ὅλα καλῶς καὶ δικαίως καὶ σαυτὸν εἰς τοῦτο κατατεταχέναι, τὸ πείθεσθαι αὐτοῖς καὶ εἴκειν πᾶσι τοῖς γινομένοις καὶ ἀκολουθεῖν ἑκόντα ὡς ὑπὸ τῆς ἀρίστης γνώμης ἐπιτελουμένοις.

15. Van Sijl (2010, 134, n.119) comes close to articulating this view when she comments: "The attitude adopted by Epictetus (*Ench*. 31.5) and Balbus (Cic. *Nat. D* 2.71), for instance, suggests that there is a conservative strand in Stoicism that is prepared to let traditional religion co-exist with philosophical truth about god." Algra (2007, 24), remarking upon Epictetus, Seneca, and Cicero's Balbus, also states: "And it is true that some sources suggest that at least in some contexts some Stoics were prepared to talk about philosophy and traditional religion as two separate realms, with the implication that the former could leave the later completely intact . . . philosophical truth on the hand hand [*sic*] and the tradition on the other (i.e., what he [Seneca] calls *res* and *mos*) should co-exist. . . . This is an attitude familiar from other ancient philosophers: overall, as I noted in my introduction, the religious tradition was strong and influential, and few people were prepared to question its value openly or explicitly." Later Algra (25) refers to "Epictetus' suggestion of a peaceful *Nebeneinander* of philosophical theology and conventional religion."

16. *Diss.* III.21.14-15.

17. The few comments that have been issued on this section, for example Long (2002, 120–121) and Algra (2007, 55), focus on Epictetus' intention of urging his students to be dedicated to the pursuit of philosophical study.

18. *Nat. Quest.* 41.1, 48.2, trans. Hine (2010, 183, 186). On the Etruscan belief regarding lightning, see the useful discussion at Williams (2012, 312 n.63).

19. See the comments at Williams (2012, 312), *Nat. Quest.* 45.1 (discussed further on in this chapter), as well as Seneca's argument at *Nat. Quest.* 2.37.2 that the Etruscans' belief in the usefulness of vows demonstrates that they have a correct understanding of fate.

20. Hine (1981, 340, 420) argues that for Seneca Etruscan religion "is elevated to the level of a genuine, enlightened religion, grounded on true philosophy. . . . [He] saw Etruscan religion as a valid and successful attempt to discover something of the workings of the universe and of god." See also Williams (2012, 297, 312).

21. *Nat. Quest.* 42.2, 3; 44.2, trans. Hine (2010, 184–185).

22. See Inwood (2005, 198). On this concept in ancient philosophy, and in particular in the Platonic tradition, see Schofield (2007).

23. *Nat. Quest.* 45.1, trans. Hine (2010, 185).

24. *Diss.* IV.7.6.

25. See Incigneri (2003, 62–63) and Dunn (2009, 55–56). It is beyond the scope of this book to address the question of how Epictetus might have identified the early Christian movement; on the category of superstition and religion in antiquity, though, see Martin (2004), and especially his comments (128) regarding Seneca's understanding of the two concepts. We can observe at *Diss.* II.6.19-21 that Epictetus might, however, present Christianity as being a subset of Judaism. In this regard, see the study by Huttunen (2007) who responds to the view that Epictetus is referring to Gentile converts to Judaism, for example see Stern (1974, 1.541–543). Given that the

firm separation of Christianity and Judaism had largely yet to occur then the possible conflation of the two is understandable.

26. Titus 3.12.

27. For example, see 1 Cor 4.12, 2 Cor 4.9, and 2 Tim 3.10-12.

28. As Huttunen (2017, 313) notes regarding this passage, for Epictetus: "Habit emerges in thinking and acting without elaborated consideration. Habits are developed from birth, and as they are strongly rooted, it is difficult to change them."

29. As Engberg-Pedersen (2010b, 133, 137) notes: "Epictetus' reference to the 'habit' of the Galileans is mysterious. Perhaps he means that the Christians were brought up more or less blindly, that is, without 'reason and demonstration', to have their strange beliefs. But he also implies that it is one and the same attitude to worldly affairs that one may acquire either from madness or from Christian 'habit' or, indeed, in Epictetus' own proper way: from reason and demonstration . . . Epictetus knew that there was a similarity between what the 'Galileans' believed 'from habit' and what he himself thought could be proved."

30. *Med.* 11:3, trans. Gill and Hard (2011, 104–105). On this, see Incigneri (2003, 62–63), cf. Edwards (2012). We can further note that Galen (Marcus' one-time physician) argues that, through its use of parables rather than demonstrative arguments, Christianity is able to make some people act like philosophers.

31. For introductions to the ancient belief in divination in the philosophical schools, see Mikalson (2010, 110–139) and Struck (2016 *passim*). Notably, however, Epictetus is never mentioned in the above works.

32. MacGillivray (2020).

33. *Diss.* III.1.16.

34. *Diss.* III.1.18-19. On Epictetus' comments here, see also Sevenster (1966, 252) and Lipsey (2001, 247).

35. On the Stoics holding that divination can come through oracles, dreams, and prophecies, see *Acad.* 2.107, and the discussion in Struck (2016, 174). Mikalson (2010, 119) notes: "the Delphic Oracle and some other forms of divination [had a] surprisingly respected place" in the philosophic tradition; see also his discussion on Apollo and divination in Hellenistic philosophy at pp. 131–138. In his study on the Delphi oracles, Fontenrose (1978, 314), meanwhile, observes: "the usual philosopher's legend" that "the philosopher received his first impulse to philosophy from the Delphic Oracle."

36. Lipsey (2001, 230–231). See also Plato *Prt.* 343a, 343b.

37. For example, see Plato *Phaed* 229e, *Phlb.* 48c, Xenophon *Mem.* 4.2.24, *Cyr* 7.2.20, Dio. *Or.* 72.12. On the history of the saying, and particularly the citation of it in the Platonic tradition, see Tortzen (2002).

38. *De E* 2 trans. Babbitt (1936, 205). See also the discussion in Lispey (2001, 230–231) and Sellars (2003, 38 n.23).

39. *Fr.* 1.

40. Dio portrays the Cynic Diogenes arguing in similar language: "Have you ever heard of the inscription at Delphi: 'Know thyself?' 'I have.' 'Is it not plain that the god gives this command to all, in the belief that they do not know themselves?,'" trans. Cohoon (1932). See also *Or.* 4.57.

41. Socrates: Xenophon *Ap.* 14, Plato *Ap.* 22a6-8. On the pivotal nature of this divine calling for Socrates' conception of his role as a philosopher, see Doyle (2012). Bowden (2005, 82) also comments: "the fact that two disciples of Socrates include this story at the heart of their account of Socrates' defence suggests that Delphic approval of Socrates as something valued by his followers. Both Plato and Xenophon see Delphi as important in their works." Diogenes: Diog. Laert. 6.2.20; Zeno: Philo *Prob.* 160, Diog. Laert. 7.2; Dio: *Or.* 13.9.

42. See MacGillivray (2020, especially pp. 8–9). On the compatibility of such occurrences with Stoic physical theory in which god is held to not supervene within creation, namely that such events are understood to be the unfolding of a naturalistic causal chain which have been fated by god, see Brittain (2019).

43. *Diss.* III.21.18-19.

44. On this, consider also Schofield (2007, 76). On the importance of Epictetus' understanding that people are assigned different roles by god/nature, see the article by Johnson (2012).

45. So see *Diss.* III.6.9-10.

46. See *Diss.* I.11.12-14.

47. *Diss.* I.9.15, III.22.94.

48. *Diss.* III.7.31.

49. *Diss.* IV.7.17.

50. *Diss.* IV.3.12. See Persius *Sat.* 5.890.

51. *Diss.* I.12.7.

52. Diss. III.24.107.

53. *Diss.* IV.1.159-161.

54. *Diss.* II.22.28.

55. *Diss.* II.20.26. See also *Diss.* I.2.1-2.

56. Huttunen (2009, 86).

57. *Diss.* I.2.2.

58. *Diss.* III.7.19-20.

59. On Perseus and Sphaerus, see the comments from Brunt (2013, 91–92); Posidonius *apud* Seneca *Ep.* 77.14-15, 90.6; Muson. *Fr.* 1.4-5; Plutarch *Lyc.* 31; and *Med.* 11.24.

60. On this paradox, see Diog. Laert. 7.121, Dio *Or.* 80, and regarding Philo's treatise, see the discussions in Petit (1974, 54–57) and Engberg-Pedersen (2009). Stowers (1981, 69) has even argued that were it not for the handful of allusions to the Jewish scriptures in the text, *Prob.* 29, 43, 57, 68, 69, it might have been reasonably assumed that its author was a committed proponent of Stoic philosophy.

61. See *Prob.* 114, 116-120.

62. *Diss.* II.4.10.

63. *Diss.* II.4.2-5.

64. *Diss.* III.7.21. On the Stoics and the legal ruling against adultery, see Brunt (2013, 47).

65. This gap in our knowledge can lead scholars, for example such as Atkins (2013, 193), in an otherwise insightful study, to come to the erroneous understanding that the Stoics hold that state laws are void of use. This misapprehension precludes

Atkins from, I suggest, seeing several lines of comport between Stoicism and Cicero's views on Roman laws and politics.

66. On Cleanthes, see *Stob.* 2.103,14-17 and Diog. Laert. 6.72. Arius Didymus *Epit.*11d, 11i, Sen. *Ep.* 14.14, 94.39, *De Clem.* 1.22-23. Furthermore, we can observe that at *Ep.* 95.29-31, while Seneca argues that civic law can help keep murder and manslaughter in check, he also remarks that state-sanctioned warfare can legitimize mass killings, and posits that the law can bring various vices to the public's attention and, therefore, unwittingly corrupt them—on this, see the brief comments from Griffin (2013, 9) and Brunt (2013, 69–72). On Cornutus' positive attitude toward civic law, see the reassessment at Boys-Stones (2007b, 81–83). For Dio's comments on the substantial benefits that can come from the law, see *Or.* 69.6, 80.4, and especially his comments at *Or.* 75 *passim.*

67. Arius Didymus *Epit.* 11b.

68. *Ep.* 90.6.

69. See Seneca *Ep.* 94.38.

70. *M. Aur. Med* 9.9.

71. *Muson.* 15A. 1, 2. See also *Muson.* 20.5c.

72. *Muson.* 8.1-4. See also Chrysippus' comments at *SVF* 3.114.

73. F22.

74. See also Tacitus, *Ann.* 16.28, 29, 33, and Epictetus' further praise for him at *Fr.* 23.

75. For example, see *Diss.* IV.4.19; 10.8; 13.22, and *Ench.* 33.

Chapter 7

Exempla

EXEMPLA IN GRECO-ROMAN SOCIETY AND THE STOIC TRADITION

This chapter will begin by observing the popularity and extensive use of exempla in antiquity, and in Stoic writings in particular. Focusing upon Epictetus, it will then be observed who he cites as moral exempla, especially the appeals he makes to individuals in the philosophical tradition and to lay-people, and it is then considered whether the latter might provide evidence of his belief in the capacity of nonphilosophers to be morally creditworthy. Proceeding to highlight the widely held belief in antiquity that exempla can relay ethical principles to people without them having to undertake formal instruction, I will then explore if, and to what extent, Epictetus shares this view.

Epictetus' teachings are marked by their engaging style, with him presenting his audience with energetic expositions on philosophical themes, dialogues that are held with a variety of interlocutors, philosophical points that are drawn from everyday situations, all of which are delivered by a scholar that is evidently attuned and responsive to his audience's struggles and motivations. This had the result, as Arrian recalled in the prologue to the *Discourses*, that "when Epictetus himself spoke them [his lectures] his listener was compelled to feel just what Epictetus wanted him to feel," ἀλλ' ἐκεῖνο ἴστωσαν οἱ ἐντυγχάνοντες ὅτι, αὐτὸς ὁπότε ἔλεγεν αὐτούς, ἀνάγκη ἦν τοῦτο πάσχειν τὸν ἀκροώμενον αὐτῶν ὅπερ ἐκεῖνος αὐτὸν παθεῖν ἠβούλετο.[1] Undoubtedly, one of the most useful assets that helped Epictetus to achieve this effect was his custom of employing exempla, an anecdote that is intended to illustrate a broader—usually moral—point, to amplify the force of his statements. For instance, when he exhorts his pupils to be noble, he directs them to consider the actions of Sarpedon, the son of Zeus, which reveal that he valued honor (τιμή) above all else, or Socrates who avoided quarrelling even though he experienced aggravating domestic circumstances.[2]

Such exempla are consistently found accompanying Epictetus' arguments, being used, to my count, over a hundred times in the extant records of his discussions. It is evident that while Epictetus has several select situations and figures that he favors drawing exempla from, he is nevertheless prepared to scour an impressively wide range of source material in order to place a suitable exemplum before his audience: including from literature, mythology, Greek and Roman history, the lives of notable philosophers, and the political struggles that scarred the preceding generation.

The extensive and varied use of exempla is, it should be noted, a noticeably Classical enterprise.[3] As well as being an integral part of rhetorical training,[4] exempla are, as has been frequently observed,[5] prominent features in the writings of authors such as Cicero, Dio Chrysostom, Maximus of Tyre, Livy, Tacitus, and Suetonius and, perhaps most conspicuously, by Valerius Maximus in his *Memorable Deeds and Sayings*. Moreover, for almost a thousand years Greek and Roman inhabitants were presented with exempla that were embedded into their literature, drama, monuments, coinage, and education (from elementary childhood instruction[6] through to supervision in philosophy and rhetoric),[7] and can be found being appealed to at the opening of Classical literature in Homer's *Odyssey* and *Iliad*, to (arguably) its close in Boethius' *Consolation of Philosophy*.[8] In time even Epictetus himself would come to be cited by others as an exemplum.[9]

A portrayal that typifies the ancient presentation of exempla, and that also highlights their frequently intended role of inculcating correct behavior in their recipients, is recorded by Seneca the Elder, who depicts Gavius Silo (an orator during the Augustan era) recalling to his father "you were accustomed, father to narrate the exempla of famous men," *solebas mihi, pater, insignium uirorum exempla narrare*.[10] Meanwhile, Epictetus portrays a well-attended philosophy lecture as almost entirely revolving around commenting upon the lives of notable people, specifically the characters in Homer's *Iliad*:

> To achieve this is it necessary that a thousand benches be set out, an audience invited, and you, in fancy gown or cloak, ascend the podium and describe how Achilles died? . . . one person says to another: "That part about Xerxes was elegantly expressed," to which the other replies, "No, I preferred the part about Thermopylae."[11]

> τοῦτο ἵνα γένηται, δεῖ τεθῆναι χίλια βάθρα καὶ παρακληθῆναι τοὺς ἀκουσομένους καὶ σὲ ἐν κομψῷ στολίῳ ἢ τριβωναρίῳ ἀναβάντα ἐπὶ πούλβινον διαγράφειν, πῶς Ἀχιλλεὺς ἀπέθανεν; . . . λέγει πρός τινα 'κομψῶς ἔφρασεν τὰ περὶ τὸν Ξέρξην,' ἄλλος 'οὔ: ἀλλὰ τὴν ἐπὶ Πύλαις μάχην.'

Exempla appear to have enjoyed this period of fecund employment during the Classical era because of the combining of their ability to encapsulate
the value that an author might wish to commend to his/her audience, along
with the esteem that was credited in antiquity to previous generations, from
where exempla were, of course, most readily drawn.[12] As Clive Skidmore
notes, this meant that for the Romans in particular: "rather than struggle
with intellectual concepts of justice or moderation, one had merely to think
of Camilius or Publicola."[13] The, now unknown, author of *Rhetorica ad
Herennium* (dated to the first century BCE) also comments upon the aug-
menting power that supporting a position by appealing to an exemplum
could have, saying:

> it makes something more illustrious when it is employed with a view to enhanc-
> ing its status; more transparent when it makes that which is rather obscure more
> clear; more plausible when it makes it more probable; it gives a graphic repre-
> sentation of something when it expresses all details so clearly that one could so
> to speak almost touch the thing represented.[14]

> *Rem ornatiorem facit cum nullius rei nisi dignitatis causa sumitur; apertiorem,
> cum id quod sit obscurius magis dilucidum reddit; probabiliorem, cum magis
> veri similem facit; ante oculos ponit, cum exprimit omnia perspicue ut res prope
> dicam manu temptari possit.*

It is within this milieu of the Classical confidence and enthusiasm for
the power of the exemplum that Epictetus' lectures, which are so noticeably laced with their presence, find their context. We should note though
that the Stoics have been frequently singled out as being a group who
have a particular, perhaps even distinctive, avidity to appeal to exempla.[15]
Maren Niehoff indeed has argued that the Stoics primarily evaluated their
students' progress in philosophy not through their comprehension of the
school's texts or arguments, but by observing their adoption of the principles and behaviors which were exemplified in a series of normative role
models.[16] Whether or not one can fully accept her conclusion, Niehoff's
observation is valuable in that it recognizes the didactic strength that the
Stoics believed exempla could possess, and that they might hold them to be
able to influence a person irrespective of their ability to correctly parse or
comprehend intricate philosophical teachings—an issue that I will return
to consider shortly. In this regard, we receive a particularly memorable
insight from Seneca on the capacity that exempla could have for enthusing
Stoic adherents. In one of his *Moral Letters to Lucilius*, he recounts that
after reading narrations of great bravery and reflecting upon exempla, he
often feels compelled to rush into the forum and offer philosophical advice
to the people he would happen to meet[17]—although it is an urge he implies

he does not act upon. Elsewhere, he also discloses his custom of collecting the busts of honorable people so that he can be regularly reminded of the examples they have set,[18] and we can note Marcus Aurelius remarks upon his custom of keeping accounts of noble deeds of ancient Romans and Greeks to inspire him.[19]

Despite the importance of the exemplum for the Stoics, at least for their later adherents,[20] no study has yet sought to systematically understand or plot their use across the school, and there has been little reflection regarding their possible use as a pedagogical tool, rather than for just aiding efforts of paraenesis.[21] Furthermore, almost every, of the many, extended studies that have examined the Stoics' use of exempla have largely restricted themselves to consider Seneca's employment of them, and even believe that he uniquely pioneered their use within the school[22]—a peculiar situation given that Epictetus appeals to them with a similar frequency. William Turpin, however (although, again, almost exclusively while depending upon Seneca's writings), has helpfully posited that six features broadly mark the Stoics' utilization of exempla:

1) They believe the moral inspiration that exempla offer is as effective as doctrinal arguments or moral precepts.
2) The person/group that the exemplum is drawn from does not have to be perfect for it to offer inspiration.
3) Deterrence offered by noting the consequences of foolish/immoral behavior can be just as beneficial as portraying a noble exemplum that inspires emulation.
4) They are particularly effective when they record the dignified response of an individual to their impending death.
5) They are useful vehicles for reflecting upon the broader moral points they seek to highlight.
6) Each person can (and should) aspire to become an exemplum.[23]

It is not my intention to explore to what extent Epictetus' employment of exempla conforms to the above model, although areas of compatibility should become apparent as I work my way through the rest of this chapter.[24] My focus will rather be upon expanding elements that are related to Turpin's first two points: namely, whether some of Epictetus' exempla might relay information to us about his views of the moral capacity of laypeople, and whether he believes that exempla are able to not just inspire Stoic adherents (a belief that Turpin has ably shown is held by Seneca), but also motivate people who have no affiliation or familiarity with Stoicism to attempt to behave in a virtuous manner.

OVERVIEW OF EPICTETUS' USE OF EXEMPLA

Apart from the frequency of Epictetus' use of exempla, we can gauge his confidence in their importance for instructing and sustaining people to live according to philosophical ideals from several passages. In one of these, after having highlighted several events from Socrates' life, he incorporates the study of exempla alongside the more conventional areas of deliberation he suggests should mark his students' education, advising them to "study these points, these judgements, these arguments, contemplate these examples, if you wish to be free, if you desire freedom in accordance with its true value," ταῦτα μελέτα, ταῦτα τὰ δόγματα, τούτους τοὺς λόγους, εἰς ταῦτα ἀφόρα τὰ παραδείγματα, εἰ θέλεις ἐλεύθερος εἶναι, εἰ ἐπιθυμεῖς κατ᾽ ἀξίαν τοῦ πράγματος.[25] His expectation that reflecting upon exempla should be incorporated into his students' repertoire of philosophical exercises is also apparent in the *Enchiridion*, where he advises them to "lay down from this moment a certain character and pattern of behavior for yourself, which you will preserve when you are alone and also when you are in company," τάξον τινὰ ἤδη χαρακτῆρα σαυτῷ καὶ τύπον, ὃν φυλάξεις ἐπί τε σεαυτοῦ ὢν καὶ ἀνθρώποις ἐντυγχάνων.[26] Meanwhile, in the *Discourses* he counsels:

> It is sufficient even if you withdraw to the society of noble and virtuous men, and examine your life by comparison with theirs, whether you choose as your pattern one from the living or from the dead [Socrates, Heracles] . . . If you set these thoughts against your impression, you will triumph and not be swept away by it.[27]

> ἀρκεῖ κἂν ἐπὶ τὰς τῶν καλῶν καὶ ἀγαθῶν ἀνδρῶν συνουσίας ἀποχωρήσας πρὸς τούτῳ γίνῃ ἀντεξετάζων, ἄν τε τῶν ζώντων τινὰ ἔχῃς ἄν τε τῶν ἀποθανόντων . . . ταῦτα ἀντιθεὶς νικήσεις τὴν φαντασίαν, οὐχ ἑλκυσθήσῃ ὑπ᾽ αὐτῆς.

Epictetus even chastises his pupils because their lack of progress is precluding the ability of exempla to be drawn from the current generation of Stoic adherents.[28]

Furthermore, he holds exempla to be so effective at conveying philosophical truths that he even demurs that the memory of Socrates can be just as, or perhaps even *more*, profitable for us than his living presence would be,[29] a belief that Seneca also expresses when he asserts that the memory of great people can be as useful as their physical presence.[30] It is evident that exempla are, therefore, not merely used by Epictetus to add rhetorical flourish to his discussions, or to act as appendages to help boost or restate his arguments. For Epictetus, they are rather in and of themselves carefully considered pieces of philosophical explication, and should be paid close attention to by the interpreters of his thought: an enterprise that I shall now endeavor to fulfill in the rest of this chapter.[31]

EXEMPLA DRAWN FROM PHILOSOPHY

Before we proceed to understand Epictetus' appeals to laypeople as exempla, we need to be able to place his appeal to them in some context. Of first interest to me, several key founders of the Stoic tradition are (perhaps unsurprisingly) highlighted by Epictetus as being examples who are worthy of his students' consideration.[32] For instance, he brings Zeno's calm disposition when he met with people of high rank to their attention.[33] When Epictetus is depicted as reflecting upon the same theme in the *Enchiridion*, he again turns to Zeno's life, advising his audience that when they meet with figures of authority they should ask themselves what Zeno would have done in their situation, so that "you will not having trouble in making proper use of the occasion," καὶ οὐκ ἀπορήσεις τοῦ χρήσασθαι προσηκόντως τῷ ἐμπεσόντι.[34] He also attempts to counter a student who showed more desire to learn philosophy for scholastic reasons, rather than for the moral amendment of his life, by appealing for him to reflect upon the contrasting attitude that Zeno assumed when he pursued philosophical inquiry.[35] The Stoic philosopher Cleanthes is also referred to once by Epictetus because of his noteworthy resolve to dedicate himself to philosophical study, even though he was in penury.[36] Yet apart from these instances, and despite the extensive use of exempla throughout Epictetus' lectures, the founding figures of Stoicism do not receive further mention from him, and he does not refer once to the life of one of the most prominent members of this group, namely Chrysippus, as providing an example of appropriate behavior.

While the relatively slight use of Stoic thinkers as exempla is perhaps unexpected (although this tallies with the lack of Stoic exempla in popular moral literature while other philosophers such as Socrates, Plato, and Aristotle are relatively well represented),[37] Epictetus does reference a series of politicians who were alive in his youth who were affiliated with the school, and all of whom upheld their principles despite the hostility this aroused in the emperor.[38] Epictetus draws particular attention to this group in two passages: *Diss.* I.1.19-30 and I.2.12-24. He appeals to the example of Plautius Lateranus (*Diss.* I.1.19-20), a champion of republican government who was sentenced to death during the reign of Nero[39]; Thrasea Paetus (*Diss.* I.1.26), who like Epictetus had been a pupil of Rufus[40] and who became well known because of his opposition to Nero and was also executed[41]; Agrippinus Paconius (*Diss.* I.1.28-30, I.2.12-18) ,who was forced into exile by Nero around 67 CE[42] and who, as we have already seen, is praised by Epictetus because of his wise adjudication of trials during his tenure as a governor[43]; and, finally, Helvidius Priscus (*Diss.* I.2.19-24), who was exiled under Nero and executed on the orders of Emperor Vespasian.[44]

While Epictetus does not specify the progress that the members of this group have made, his portrayal of their actions align with those we would expect of sages, and as representing the key ideals of the school being put into practice.[45] Moreover, after citing the examples of Thrasea and Agrippinus, he offers the fulsome evaluation that "this is what it means to have studied what one ought to study; to have rendered one's desires and aversions incapable of being restrained, or incurred," τοῦτ' ἔστι μεμελετηκέναι ἃ δεῖ μελετᾶν, ὄρεξιν ἔκκλισιν ἀκώλυτα ἀπερίπτωτα παρεσκευακέναι.[46]

Aside from the three references to Agrippinus above, additional evidence that Epictetus held him in particular esteem has been preserved by Stobaeus, who records Epictetus noting the disregard that Agrippinus had for experiencing hardship or discomfort:

[Agrippinus] was a man of such a kind, said Epictetus, that if he was struck by any difficulty he would write in praise of it: if he had a fever, in praise of fever; if he suffered disrepute, in praise of disrepute; if he was exiled, in praise of exile. And once, when he was about to have breakfast, a messenger interrupted him with news that Nero had ordered him go into exile: "Well, then," said Agrippinus, "we will eat our meal at Aricia."[47]

οὗτος δ', ἔφη, ὁ ἀνὴρ τοιοῦτος ἦν, ὥστε τοῦ συμβαίνοντος ἀεὶ ἑαυτῷ δυσκόλου ἔπαινον γράφειν: εἰ μὲν πυρέττοι, πυρετοῦ: εἰ δὲ ἀδοξοῖ, ἀδοξίας: εἰ δὲ φεύγοι, φυγῆς. καὶ ποτε μέλλοντι, ἔφη, αὐτῷ ἀριστήσειν ἐπέστη ὁ λέγων, ὅτι φεύγειν αὐτὸν κελεύει Νέρων, καὶ ὃς ἔφη 'οὐκοῦν,' εἶπεν, 'ἐν Ἀρικίᾳ ἀριστήσομεν.'

We can find Epictetus again referring to Helvidius when he appeals to the example he set when he faced execution, stating: "Did not Socrates, then, fare badly? No; but his judges and accusers.—'Nor Helvidius at Rome?' No; but his murderer," ὥστε Σωκράτης οὐκ ἔπραξε κακῶς;—Οὔ, ἀλλ' οἱ δικασταὶ καὶ οἱ κατήγοροι.—Οὐδ' ἐν Ῥώμῃ Ἐλουίδιος;—Οὔ, ἀλλ' ὁ ἀποκτείνας αὐτόν.[48] Citing his death in combination with Socrates' is significant given that the latter event was credited in antiquity as being the paradigmatic instance of a philosopher remaining true to their principles (which we can see Epictetus also does[49]) despite them knowing the exacting consequences that would likely follow.[50] This means that Helvidius' example is being held against the most penetrating of lights, and implies that Epictetus must consider Helvidius' actions to have been a true and palpable expression of his virtuously inclined character and to reflect the noblest of the Stoic school's moral expectations.

Aside from the above references to a number of the school's founders and the notable stance that was assumed by some Stoic politicians during the preceding half century, the focus of Epictetus' attention when he was crafting exempla is unambiguously focused upon two figures: Diogenes of Sinope and Socrates.

As for Diogenes, supporting Stoic philosophy by appealing to instances from his life is a compulsion that can be observed from across the school's discourse.[51] The Stoics' proclivity to cite him as an exemplum can, I suggest, be accounted for by two factors. Firstly (although there was some divergence over this[52]), having instructed Zeno, Diogenes was reassuringly part of the Stoics' assumed philosophical lineage; secondly, his conspicuous disregard for external contingencies was concomitant with their own philosophical principles. Through both intellectual consanguinity and because of his renowned unconstrained lifestyle, with the two (of course) being connected, the various traditions that narrate Diogenes' life, therefore, appear to have been viewed by the Stoics as providing them with a legitimate and profitable resource that they could elucidate their philosophy from.[53]

Epictetus cites Diogenes as being an exemplum, to my count, on seven occasions.[54] In the most extended of these appeals, at *Diss.* IV.1.152-158, he provides his students with a plotted summary of Diogenes' activities as a Cynic and underscores how his persistent disregard for externals enabled him to acquire genuine freedom.[55] He also cites Diogenes, along with Socrates and Cleanthes, as being individuals who were "genuine philosophers" (γνησίως φιλοσοφοῦντες) and whose lives are worthy of his audience's emulation.[56] Diogenes is linked with Socrates again when Epictetus attempts to help his students conquer their misplaced affection for their favorite people and places by asking them to reflect:

> Can you imagine either of these crying or becoming aggravated, because he will not see such a person or such a person; nor will reside any longer at Athens or at Corinth, but rather at Susa or at Ecbatana?[57]
>
> ἐπινοεῖς τούτων τινὰ κλάοντα ἢ ἀγανακτοῦντα, ὅτι τὸν δεῖνα οὐ μέλλει βλέπειν οὐδὲ τὴν δεῖνα οὐδ᾽ ἐν Ἀθήναις ἔσεσθαι ἢ ἐν Κορίνθῳ, ἀλλ᾽, ἂν οὕτως τύχῃ, ἐν Σούσοις ἢ ἐν Ἐκβατάνοις;

Elsewhere, he utilizes the account of Diogenes being captured by pirates and being sold into slavery to raise a series of questions that are predicated upon the good example that he had set, namely where a succession of events that would usually be viewed by people as being unfortunate (e.g., being captured by pirates and sold into slavery) are not judged by Diogenes to be troublesome.[58]

It is, however, Diogenes' occasional partner in the above exempla, and an individual who was also held to be part of the Stoics' philosophical lineage, Socrates—who dominates Epictetus' attention when he resolves to set an exemplum before his pupils.[59] He will, in fact, reference Socrates' example three times more than he will Diogenes'.[60] A good illustration of the type of appeal he makes to Socrates' life, as well as providing us with a useful reflection on the inestimable value he holds Socrates has as an example (παράδειγμα) regards his well-known restraint from entering into quarrels (μάχομαι):

> a good and noble person neither quarrels with anyone, nor, so far as he can, does he permit others to. The life of Socrates provides us with an example of this too, as well as so much else, who not only consistently avoided quarrelling himself, but also tried to prevent others quarrelling.[61]

> ὁ καλὸς καὶ ἀγαθὸς οὔτ᾽ αὐτὸς μάχεταί τινι οὔτ᾽ ἄλλον ἐᾷ κατὰ δύναμιν. παράδειγμα δὲ καὶ τούτου καθάπερ καὶ τῶν ἄλλων ἔκκειται ἡμῖν ὁ βίος ὁ Σωκράτους, ὃς οὐ μόνον αὐτὸς πανταχοῦ ἐξέφυγεν μάχην, ἀλλ᾽ οὐδ᾽ ἄλλους μάχεσθαι εἴα.

Furthermore, elsewhere Epictetus also appears to twice cite Socrates as being the apogee of the moral exemplum, chiding a hypothetical tyrant by asking him: "Who would wish to be like you? Who would desire to imitate you, as he would Socrates," τίς σοι θέλει ὅμοιος γενέσθαι, τίς σου ζηλωτὴς γίνεται ὡς Σωκράτους.[62] In the *Enchiridion*, Epictetus is portrayed as counseling his readers: "and even if you are not yet a Socrates, you should live as one who does indeed wish to be a Socrates," σὺ δὲ εἰ καὶ μήπω εἶ Σωκράτης, ὡς Σωκράτης γε εἶναι βουλόμενος ὀφείλεις βιοῦν.[63] The latter account also seems to imply that Epictetus views Socrates' life to be *the* tangible expression of the philosophical tenets that he is attempting to coach his audience to accept, and that he believes characterizes his school's ethos. Indeed, from both the rate at which Socrates' example is set before them, as well as from his remarks about Socrates' value as an exemplum, it appears that Epictetus views him as being the moral exemplum *par excellence*; that, as Eleni Tsalla notes, "when he [Epictetus] needed to point out what it means to be a Stoic, he resorted to Socrates."[64] In this way, the exemplum of Socrates exemplum is being skillfully deployed by Epictetus to exhibit the group identity and values of the school.

With regards to philosophers from rival schools, as I have briefly noted in the opening chapter, Epictetus is comfortable in citing their opinions to help strengthen his arguments; however, unlike Seneca and Marcus Aurelius, he does not appear to search the accounts of their lives in order to find instances of noble behavior being exhibited. The only clear exception to this can be found at *Ench.* 15, where Epictetus references the pre-Socratic philosopher Heraclitus (ca. 535–475 BCE.) along with Diogenes as being figures whose behavior reveals that they have a proper understanding of what belongs to them, especially with regards to public offices, wealth, and children, and he proceeds to laud them by claiming "[they] and others like them, were deservedly divine and deservedly called so," Διογένης καὶ Ἡράκλειτος καὶ οἱ ὅμοιοι ἀξίως θεῖοί τε ἦσαν καὶ ἐλέγοντο.[65] The Stoic interest in Heraclitus and his teachings—and particularly his propositions on cosmology—has been helpfully documented by A. A. Long.[66] The evidence for their admiration of him, though, is largely restricted to Cleanthes and Marcus Aurelius' writings,[67] making the brief encomium of him in Epictetus' remarks here an important, if often overlooked, indication that there was a broad Stoic appreciation of him. For us, though, this passage is significant as it establishes that, while generally ignored as a resource for finding suitable exempla, Epictetus can consider the lives of philosophers from outside of the Stoic tradition to exemplify notable philosophical virtues.

Over a century ago, Percy E. Matheson also suggested in passing that Epictetus might allude to the examples of Anaxarchus and Zeno the Eleatic,[68] both of whom affiliated themselves with pre-Socratic philosophers. In his translation of the *Discourses*, Matheson drew attention to the following remark that Epictetus raises to support his contention that his students should not be alarmed by any threats that governing authorities might make against them:

> That person, therefore, whom neither pleasure nor suffering, nor glory nor riches, can get the better of, and who is able when he believes appropriate, to spit his whole body into his tormentor's face and depart from life, whose slave can he ever be? To whom can he still be subject?[69]
>
> οὗτινος οὖν οὐχ ἡδονὴ κρείττων ἐστίν, οὐ πόνος, οὐ δόξα, οὐ πλοῦτος, δύναται δ᾽, ὅταν αὐτῷ δόξῃ, τὸ σωμάτιον ὅλον προσπτύσας τινὶ ἀπελθεῖν, τίνος ἔτι οὗτος δοῦλός ἐστιν, τίνι ὑποτέτακται.

Due to the similarities of their deaths Anaxarchus and Zeno are often referenced alongside one another by ancient authors.[70] Both were reputed to have been put to death on the orders of tyrants, and to have expressed their disregard for the punishing torture that their bodies were undergoing by biting off and spitting out their tongues at their tormentors.[71] The similarity between the account of these philosophers' deaths and Epictetus' comments above about being prepared to spit out our entire bodies if we are faced with threats from irate authorities makes it likely, at least to my mind, that he is intending to bring Anaxarchus' and Zeno's examples to his students' attention, and they can rightly be included in our list of non-Stoic philosophers who Epictetus cites as moral exempla.[72] In closing, we might surmise that Epictetus either envisages that these non-Stoic philosophers' moral insights were established through the same processes that impact laypeople, or, more likely, that rival philosophies can instill some measure of correct thought into their followers—and so supports the conclusion that was reached in chapter 1 regarding his views of philosophers from other schools.

LAYPEOPLE AS EXEMPLA

Given that many luminary figures that are associated with classical philosophy receive such little or no attention from Epictetus, it is, I suggest, striking that he so frequently presents *laypeople* as being worthy of his students' emulation. For instance, he notes the accepting disposition that slaves and laborers assume in order to help them cope with the numerous strains that are placed upon their lives. Indeed, he seems to imply that there is some correspondence between their mindset and the ones which can be seen in Socrates, Diogenes, and Cleanthes:

> This is your dread, that you may not be able to live the life of an invalid. You should learn how the healthy live by reflecting upon how slaves live, how laborers, how those who are genuine philosophers live, how Socrates lived, even with a wife and children; how Diogenes lived, how Cleanthes who studied at the same time as drawing water lived . . . [do this] and you can live with confidence. In what? In the only thing that a person can properly have confidence in; what is trustworthy, what is free from hindrance and what can never be taken away—your own choice.[73]

> τοῦτο φοβῇ, μὴ οὐ δύνῃ ζῆν ἀρρώστου βίον, ἐπεί τοι τὸν τῶν ὑγιαινόντων μάθε, πῶς οἱ δοῦλοι ζῶσιν, πῶς οἱ ἐργάται, πῶς οἱ γνησίως φιλοσοφοῦντες, πῶς Σωκράτης ἔζησεν, ἐκεῖνος μὲν καὶ μετὰ γυναικὸς καὶ παίδων, πῶς Διογένης, πῶς Κλεάνθης ἅμα σχολάζων καὶ ἀντλῶν . . . καὶ ζήσεις θαρρῶν. τίνι; ᾧ μόνῳ θαρρεῖν ἐνδέχεται, τῷ πιστῷ, τῷ ἀκωλύτῳ, τῷ ἀναφαιρέτῳ, τοῦτ' ἔστι τῇ προαιρέσει τῇ σεαυτοῦ.

Though Epictetus believes that slaves (δοῦλοι) and laborers (ἐργάται) are pressured by their circumstances into embracing this accepting attitude, rather than establishing it through intellectual deliberation, these laypeople's understanding is compared by him to the notable trio of philosophers of Socrates, Diogenes, and Cleanthes, and what he calls "the legitimate philosophers," οἱ γνησίως φιλοσοφοῦντες; they are further praised by him for being able to exercise their faculty of choice/moral will (προαιρέσει) (a key concept in his philosophy[74]), and are cited by Epictetus as being examples for his students to follow. Interestingly, Turpin notes with some surprise that Seneca will appeal to slaves as exempla (see *Ben.* 3.23-24).[75] Epictetus' similar reference to them in this passage, however, supplies evidence that Seneca's move to highlight the commendable moral actions of laypeople such as slaves was in-step with the sentiments of the school.

Turning back to Epictetus, following his teacher Rufus,[76] he not only highlights that the Spartans have grasped the truth about the irrelevance of pain and that they exhibit their willingness to endure it, but he argues the Spartans find it reasonable (εὔλογος), an adjective that is used in Stoic works to designate something that is done with reasonable justification:[77]

> blows are not by nature unendurable.—" "How so?"—See how the Spartans bear a whipping, after they have learned that it is a reasonable thing.[78]

> πληγαὶ οὐκ εἰσὶν ἀφόρητοι τῇ φύσει.—τίνα τρόπον;—ὅρα πῶς: Λακεδαιμόνιοι μαστιγοῦνται μαθόντες ὅτι εὔλογόν ἐστιν.

Elsewhere, when attempting to convince an adherent of Epicureanism that his philosophy severs the natural bonds and structures of human society, Epictetus proceeds to further argue:

> it was upon these [Epicurean] principles that made our well-governed cities grow to greatness! It was upon these principles that Sparta was founded! Lycurgus instilled these convictions into the Spartans by his laws and system of education: that to be slaves is no more shameful than noble, and to be free is no more noble than shameful! Those who died at Thermopylae, died because they held such judgements as these.[79]

> ἐκ τούτων τῶν λόγων ηὐξήθησαν ἡμῖν αἱ εὐνομούμεναι πόλεις, Λακεδαίμων διὰ τούτους τοὺς λόγους ἐγένετο, Λυκοῦργος ταῦτα τὰ πείσματα ἐνεποίησεν αὐτοῖς διὰ τῶν νόμων αὐτοῦ καὶ τῆς παιδείας, ὅτι οὔτε τὸ δουλεύειν αἰσχρόν ἐστι μᾶλλον ἢ καλὸν οὔτε τὸ ἐλευθέρους εἶναι καλὸν μᾶλλον ἢ αἰσχρόν, οἱ ἐν Θερμοπύλαις ἀποθανόντες διὰ ταῦτα τὰ δόγματα ἀπέθανον.

The inverse is, of course, intended to be communicated. By accustomizing people to discomfort and exalting the concepts of freedom and honor, Epictetus argues that the Spartan state was able to instill (ἐμποιέω) numerous virtues into its citizenry and to steel them with a resolve to remain compliant with them: features that were most strikingly displayed by the 300 Spartans' sacrifice at Thermopylae to which Epictetus draws attention.

We should not conclude that the above argument was fashioned by Epictetus to merely score a point in a cross-ideological debate. Elsewhere, we find him valorizing the discernment of Sparta's founder, Lycurgus,[80] and the belief that Sparta had trained its citizens to act appropriately can be found being asserted by thinkers from across the ancient philosophical spectrum,[81] and was, as I noted before, a belief that was given particular emphasis by Epictetus' teacher Rufus. We might also usefully observe that Seneca highlights the example of a Spartan boy, where he usefully reflects upon the seemingly modest subject that his exemplum is based around, stating: "You think, I suppose that it is now in order for me to cite some examples of great men. No, I shall cite rather the case of a boy. The story of a Spartan lad has been preserved," *Exempla nunc magnorum virorum me tibi iudicas relaturum? Puerorum referam. Lacon ille memoriae traditur inpubis adhuc.*[82] He then proceeds to relay how the boy had killed himself rather than endure a life in shameful servitude.

Laypeople from Greek history are also presented by Epictetus as exempla. So, for instance, he challenges the view that death is always bad by remonstrating with his audience:

In god's name is it not possible to benefit even from death? And from lameness too? Do you think that Menoeceus gained only a small benefit through his death? May the person who talks like that gain the same kind of benefit as he did! Look here, did not he preserve his patriotism, his magnanimity, his faithfulness, his noble spirit? And, if he had lived on, would he not have lost all of this? And would he not have gained the very opposite? Would not cowardice, mean-spiritedness, and hatred of his country, and love of life? Well do you think he gained only a little benefit from his death?[83]

τὸν θεόν σοι, ἀπὸ θανάτου γὰρ οὐκ ἔστιν; ἀπὸ πληρώσεως γὰρ οὐκ ἔστιν, μικρά σοι δοκεῖ ὁ Μενοικεὺς ὠφεληθῆναι, ὅτ᾽ ἀπέθνῃσκεν;—τοιαῦτά τις εἰπὼν ὠφεληθείη ἢ οἷα ἐκεῖνος ὠφελήθη—ἔα, ἄνθρωπε, οὐκ ἐτήρησεν τὸν φιλόπατριν, τὸν μεγαλόφρονα, τὸν πιστόν, τὸν γενναῖον; ἐπιζήσας δὲ οὐκ ἀπώλλυεν ταῦτα πάντα; οὐ περιεποιεῖτο τὰ ἐναντία; τὸν δειλὸν οὐκ ἀνελάμβανεν, τὸν ἀγεννῆ, τὸν μισόπατριν, τὸν φιλόψυχον; ἄγε δοκεῖ σοι μικρὰ ὠφεληθῆναι ἀποθανών.

Here, Menoeceus of Thebes, who was reputed to have sacrificed himself in order to save his home city from destruction,[84] is presented by Epictetus as having correctly ascertained that death can be used to benefit (ὠφελέω) him. According to Epictetus, this realization allowed Menoeceus to display a range of appropriate behaviors and mindsets, namely "patriotism" (φιλόπατρις), "magnanimity" (μεγαλόφρονα), "fidelity" (πιστόν), and a "noble spirit" (γενναῖος), while conversely to avoid enacting a range of opposing vices.[85]

A further example of a virtuously inclined layperson might also be found in the following passage, where Epictetus again argues with an Epicurean interlocutor:

> now hardly any one denies that there are three things that make us humans: soul, body, and externals. It remains for you to answer which is best. What shall we tell people? The flesh? And was it for this that Maximus sailed in winter all the way to Cassiope to accompany his son? Was it for the pleasure of the flesh?[86]

> ὅτι μὲν γὰρ τρία ἐστὶ περὶ τὸν ἄνθρωπον, ψυχὴ καὶ σῶμα καὶ τὰ ἐκτός, σχεδὸν οὐδεὶς ἀντιλέγει· λοιπὸν ὑμέτερόν ἐστιν ἀποκρίνασθαι, τί ἐστι τὸ κράτιστον. τί ἐροῦμεν τοῖς ἀνθρώποις; τὴν σάρκα; καὶ διὰ ταύτην Μάξιμος ἔπλευσεν μέχρι Κασσιόπης χειμῶνος μετὰ τοῦ υἱοῦ προπέμπων, ἵν᾽ ἡσθῇ τῇ σαρκί;

Maximus' decision to undertake a lengthy journey in winter by boat so that he could accompany his son is used by Epictetus in an attempt to reveal the shortcomings of Epicureanism. The point that is intended to be communicated, as Epictetus helpfully summarizes at the end of the discussion,[87] is that it is not the pleasure of the flesh (or externals, ἐκτός) but properly governed and understood relationships with one's family and community that can help human beings to secure happiness. We are, though, unfortunately prevented from fully apprehending the force of his point as the subject of the exemplum is otherwise unknown to us. Though apparently familiar enough to Epictetus and his conversation partner (and, presumably, Arrian), Maximus' identity and the account of his unseasonable journey to Cassiope has not been transmitted beyond antiquity.[88] I must concede then that Maximus might have been a known advocate of philosophy; however, if his actions or disposition could be attributed to his philosophical affiliation, this would rather seem to denude the force of Epictetus' argument. So, while not an assured interpretation, the most natural conclusion seems to be that this is another instance of a layperson being presented by Epictetus as being a moral exemplum.[89]

Returning to consider *Diss.* I.2, after highlighting the notable perseverance of the politicians Agrippinus and Priscus, we can observe that Epictetus continues to describe in a similar manner how an injured athlete had decided to kill himself—in this case, so he could avoid castration.[90] The reason for the athlete's judgment, Epictetus implies, is that this procedure would have prevented him from continuing to realize his identity as a sportsman, presumably because, as a eunuch, he would have been prohibited from participating in numerous athletic events, and the decrease in his testosterone in any case would have rendered him uncompetitive.[91] Recently, though, and against the prevailing interpretation of this passage,[92] Stephen White has argued that Epictetus is not intending to raise an ethical point from this exemplum, but rather:

if Epictetus expressed a verdict on the athlete's decision, Arrian does not record it. The point of the anecdote, and its ethical basis, is rather to illustrate the power of personal commitment in decision-making . . . (the athlete) was *psychologically* unable to decide contrary to what he considered most reasonable, so Helvidius and Agrippinus were *morally* incapable of submitting to tyranny.[93]

According to White, the story of the athlete is recounted by Epictetus to merely demonstrate that a person can fix their identity to a role/position so firmly that their desire to successfully fulfill it enables them to transcend their fear of death. White argues that it was this aforementioned conviction that allowed the Stoically affiliated politicians I mentioned earlier to act with moral defiance in the face of external threat, and for the athlete to achieve an action of apparently unstated ethical worth. White's conclusion, therefore, implies that to present this exemplum as highlighting a laudable layperson is to risk misinterpreting it.

There are, though, I believe, several considerations that should cause us to hesitate before we accept White's position, and which allow us to affirm that the story of the athlete is indeed intended by Epictetus to be a moral exemplar: namely, his wider thought on the influence that roles should exert upon our ethics, and the language he chooses to frame the athlete and his decision in. In fact, I believe that this is one of the most clear and expansive accounts where Epictetus assigns exemplary moral worth to a layperson's actions, and so is a passage that is worthy of some extended deliberation.

Firstly, the relevance that a person's role (in Latin *personae*, and in Greek πρόσωπον, a word that usually refers to a mask, often worn by actors, but holds broader significance in philosophical literature) should have in informing their ethical decision-making is a topic that is given particular attention in two extant classical sources: Cicero's *On Duties* 1.107-118—which is presumed to have been derived to some extent from the Stoic Panaetius' teachings[94]—and the records of Epictetus' discussions.[95] Both postulate a division of ethics where our moral obligations are constituted by universal principles (i.e., those that affect everyone, regardless of their circumstances) as well as by our individual roles and occupations.[96] On this, Epictetus helpfully remarks by referencing the universal (κοινός) and particular (ἴδιος) obligations that each person must assume:

> For in all that we do, if we do not refer it to some standard, we shall be acting at random; if to a wrong standard, we shall not succeed. There is, besides, a *general* and a *particular* standard. First, for acting as a human. What does this involve? Not to be, though gentle, like a sheep; nor to act injuriously like an untamed beast. The particular end relates to each person's specific occupation and moral choice.[97]

ἕκαστον γὰρ τῶν γινομένων ὑφ᾽ ἡμῶν ἂν μὲν ἐπὶ μηδὲν ἀναφέρωμεν, εἰκῇ
ποιήσομεν: ἐὰν δ᾽ ἐφ᾽ ὃ μὴ δεῖ, διεσφαλμένως. λοιπὸν ἡ μέν τίς ἐστι κοινὴ
ἀναφορά, ἡ δ᾽ ἰδία. πρῶτον ἵν᾽ ὡς ἄνθρωπος. ἐν τούτῳ τί περιέχεται; μὴ ὡς
πρόβατον, εἰ βλαπτικῶς καὶ ἐπιεικῶς, ὡς θηρίον. ἡ δ᾽ ἰδία πρὸς τὸ ἐπιτήδευμα
ἑκάστου καὶ τὴν προαίρεσιν.

Consider also Cicero's comments at *De Off.* 1.107, which likewise assert
that the various identities and responsibilities we have been born with, or
have come to assume over the course of our lives (including, significantly,
our careers[98]), present us with a set of principles that we should adhere to.
Consequently, according to this understanding, to live appropriately each
person needs to be conscious of the various roles they hold and the behavior
that is commensurate with them. This awareness is important as actions that
might be appropriate for one individual to pursue might be wholly unsuitable
for another, that is, some behavior that is expected of a young woman might
not be appropriate if they are adopted by an elder statesman, and the accept-
able conduct of a bachelor might become a vice if he still observes them if he
transitions to become a husband and/or father.[99]

This determinative nature that our roles should have upon our ethics is
particularly evident in Epictetus' exposition on the calling of the Cynic. This
is a role, which Epictetus emphasizes, that removes its holder from having
ties to a family or community[100]; for this reason, it would be a position that
it would be wholly unsuitable for everyone to adopt. Indeed, a broad uptake
of the Cynic's role would seem to result in a society that would share many
of the features (though not intentions) of the imagined Epicurean community
that Epictetus so frequently lampoons during the course of his discussions.[101]
For those people though who have correctly deduced that this occupation
is suitable/intended for them, following the Cynic's distinctive lifestyle,
according to Epictetus, is an appropriate vocation for them to pursue.[102] In
this regard, we can also observe that a similar explication of how our roles
assign our ethical responsibilities is crafted by Cicero with reference to the
actions of Cato after the battle of Thapsus, wherein he argues that it was not a
universal principle that necessitated that he should commit suicide, but rather
the demands of his individual *persona*.[103]

Returning to consider the exemplum of the athlete, it should be apparent
just how steeped it is in the parlance of the proper observance of roles:

In this manner [as with Agrippinus and Priscus' example] a certain athlete also
acted, who was in danger of dying unless his genitals were amputated. His
brother, who was a philosopher, came to him and said, "Well brother, what are
you planning to do? Are we going to cut off this part of you, and return again to
the gymnasium?" But he would not submit to that, and so he awaited his death.

Someone inquired: "How was it that he [the athlete] did so? As an athlete or a philosopher?" As a man, Epictetus replied; and as a man who had contended at Olympia and been proclaimed a victor, and who had passed a good deal of time in such places and had not merely been rubbed with oil in Bato's training-ground. But if it were possible for him to live without it, another person would have had his very head cut off! This is what it means to act according to one's true character; and such is its weight for those who have acquired the habit of deliberately introducing this consideration when they examine how they should behave.[104]

τοῦτον τὸν τρόπον καὶ ἀθλητής τις κινδυνεύων ἀποθανεῖν, εἰ μὴ ἀπεκόπη τὸ αἰδοῖον, ἐπελθόντος αὐτῷ τοῦ ἀδελφοῦ (ἦν δ᾽ ἐκεῖνος φιλόσοφος) καὶ εἰπόντος ᾽ἄγε, ἀδελφέ, τί μέλλεις ποιεῖν; ἀποκόπτομεν τοῦτο τὸ μέρος καὶ ἔτι εἰς γυμνάσιον προερχόμεθα;᾽ οὐχ ὑπέμεινεν, ἀλλ᾽ ἐγκαρτερήσας ἀπέθανεν. πυθομένου δέ τινος· πῶς τοῦτο ἐποίησεν; ὡς ἀθλητὴς ἢ ὡς φιλόσοφος; ὡς ἀνήρ, ἔφη, ἀνὴρ δ᾽ Ὀλύμπια κεκηρυγμένος καὶ ἠγωνισμένος, ἐν τοιαύτῃ τινὶ χώρᾳ ἀνεστραμμένος, οὐχὶ παρὰ τῷ Βάτωνι ἀλειφόμενος. ἄλλος δὲ κἂν τὸν τράχηλον ἀπετμήθη, εἰ ζῆν ἠδύνατο δίχα τοῦ τραχήλου. τοιοῦτόν ἐστι τὸ κατὰ πρόσωπον· οὕτως ἰσχυρὸν παρὰ τοῖς εἰθισμένοις αὐτὸ συνεισφέρειν ἐξ αὐτῶν ἐν ταῖς σκέψεσιν.

Epictetus' praise of the athlete, who he specifically notes is not a philosopher, is clearly manifest. He exclaims that this is what he means by respecting one's true character and emphasizes that the athlete's resolution and courage (ἐγκαρτερέω) was enabled because of his habit of examining (σκέψις) how he should act. It is, indeed, hard to conceive how Epictetus could emphasize the athlete's appropriate attention to his role more without the point becoming wearisome. Moreover, immediately after this exemplum, the following exchange between Epictetus and his imagined interlocutor is depicted as taking place:

"Come now, Epictetus, shave off your beard"—If I am a philosopher, I will reply, I will not shave it off.—"Then I will have you beheaded"—If it will do you any good, behead me.[105]

ἄγε οὖν, Ἐπίκτητε, διαξύρησαι.᾽ ἂν ᾦ φιλόσοφος, λέγω ᾽οὐ διαξυρῶμαι.᾽ ᾽ἀλλ᾽ ἀφελῶ σου τὸν τράχηλον.᾽ εἰ σοὶ ἄμεινον, ἄφελε.

So, just as the athlete concludes that he cannot continue living if he underwent ablation, Epictetus resolves likewise with regards to any enforced removal of his beard (with the beard by this time being a mark of a philosopher[106]). For both men, then, these respective bodily parts should be an inviolate component of their identity, and sustaining them is an ethical duty.[107]

EXEMPLA DRAWN FROM LITERATURE

Epictetus also draws upon the lives of laypeople that are depicted in popular mythology and literature to help him construct suitable exempla. While they are occasionally raised to show the negative consequences of certain actions or presumptions, for example the failings of Paris, Achilles, and Agamemnon are highlighted to serve this end,[108] more often than not Epictetus recounts events from such figures' lives in order to present appropriate actions or dispositions to his audience. So, for instance, he uses Homer's account of Sarpedon as an exemplum when he attempts to place death within its proper philosophical context by noting that Sarpedon is portrayed as trying to persuade his companion Glaucus that they should join their fellow countrymen in the fray of a heated battle so that their honor (or κατορθόω, to accomplish something successfully) will be maintained.[109] Epictetus argues that this speech is articulating the same principle that he is endeavoring to coach his students to accept: namely, the need for them to maintain their virtue above all other, ultimately specious, concerns—even bodily well-being.

It seems, therefore, that Epictetus finds this passage to articulate a compelling and eloquent defense of the worth of self-sacrifice. He even argues that Sarpedon displays a resolve that is beyond his students' and, indeed his, present capabilities. Whether this is a genuine conviction, or is uttered by Epictetus to merely reinforce the appropriate nature of Sarpedon's actions, describing an exemplum as being beyond his, and his audience's, ability to emulate is an accolade that is normally reserved by Epictetus for the actions of figures such as Socrates,[110] yet it is given here to someone who had no apparent interest or training in philosophical thought.

There are two characters from popular literature and mythology that Epictetus frequently cites as exempla—Odysseus and Hercules. Narrowing my concentration to Odysseus,[111] in contrast to the prevailing popular opinion in antiquity, which (at least until imperial times) saw him as being a largely villainous individual who would readily manipulate situations and deceive others if he anticipated that he could gain some advantage,[112] numerous classical philosophers appear to have attempted to absolve him from such charges and to assert that the stories of his life, in actuality, depict some of their school's key tenets in narrative form.

While several studies have considered aspects of this positive reception and appropriation of Odysseus in the philosophical tradition,[113] the subject has been particularly well served by Silvia Montiglio's monograph on the history of his broad reception in antiquity. Montiglio in particular usefully draws attention to the interpretations that different schools use to explain Odysseus' story: from being recast as a reformer of humanity, who had little concern for external contingencies by Antisthenes; an individual who has an unenviable control over his irrational impulses according to Plato; or the ideal role model for monarchs according to the Epicurean philosopher Philodemus.[114]

Aligning with Antisthenes, proponents of Stoicism presumed that, provided the proper interpretative framework is assumed the life of Odysseus can offer its readers with a compelling account that demonstrates external factors are not requisite features of a contented life.[115] That, they assert, Odysseus' ability to remain composed when he went through numerous challenging circumstances displays an internal disposition that is akin to the one which their philosophy aims to ready its adherents to adopt.[116] As Seneca plainly states:

> We Stoics have declared that these [Odysseus and Hercules] were wise men, because they were unconquered by struggles, were despisers of pleasure and victors over all terrors.[117]
>
> *Hos enim Stoici nostri sapientes pronuntiaverunt, invictos laboribus et contemptores voluptatis et victores omnium terrorum.*

For Epictetus, it is also Odysseus' consistent adaptability and calm resolve which allows his virtuously inclined constitution to become evident. So, in one discussion he appeals to the broad sweep of the story of the *Odyssey* to challenge his students' misplaced desire to stay rooted or connected to certain places (an evidently pressing concern given the frequency with which he addresses this issue).[118] He also draws attention to Odysseus' apparent ability to endure the itinerant lifestyle, wherein Epictetus argues that his ability to adjust to each new location and circumstance without experiencing bewilderment or melancholy (although Epictetus acknowledges that there might be one possible exception to this[119]) is the same attitude that philosophers are attempting to instill in their pupils.[120] Similarly, he also alludes to the strikingly different types of clothing that Odysseus is said to have worn, asking: "Shall he [the man of noble character] not imitate Odysseus, who was no less distinguished in rags than in a fine purple robe?," οὐδὲ τὸν Ὀδυσσέα μιμήσεται, ὃς καὶ ἐν τοῖς ῥάκεσιν οὐδὲν μεῖον διέπρεπεν ἢ ἐν τῇ οὔλῃ χλαίνῃ τῇ πορφυρᾷ; Ἀρριανοῦ.[121] The account of Odysseus being shipwrecked at Nausicaa, meanwhile, provides Epictetus with a further instance of how he was able to assume a modest position with apparent ease:

> What did he put his trust in? Not in reputation, or wealth, or office, but in his own strength, that is to say, in his judgements about what things are in our power and what are not. For these judgements only are what make us free, make us impervious from hindrance, raise the head of those who have been made low, and make them look into the faces of the rich with steady eyes, and into the faces of tyrants. And this was what the philosopher could give.[122]

τίνι πεποιθώς; οὐ δόξῃ οὐδὲ χρήμασιν οὐδ᾽ ἀρχαῖς, ἀλλ᾽ ἀλκῇ τῇ ἑαυτοῦ, τοῦτ᾽ ἔστι δόγμασι περὶ τῶν ἐφ᾽ ἡμῖν καὶ οὐκ ἐφ᾽ ἡμῖν. ταῦτα γάρ ἐστι μόνα τὰ τοὺς ἐλευθέρους ποιοῦντα, τὰ τοὺς ἀκωλύτους, τὰ τὸν τράχηλον ἐπαίροντα τῶν τεταπεινομένων, τὰ ἀντιβλέπειν ποιοῦντα ὀρθοῖς τοῖς ὀφθαλμοῖς πρὸς τοὺς πλουσίους, πρὸς τοὺς τυράννους. καὶ τὸ τοῦ φιλοσόφου δῶρον τοῦτο ἦν.

Odysseus is again portrayed as not becoming dispirited at the dramatic changes in his circumstances, but as adopting the mindset that philosophy offers as a gift (δῶρον): namely, freedom (ἐλεύθερος) from concerns over obtaining good reputation (δόξα), money (χρῆμα), or office (ἀρχαῖς), and gaining the apprehension that it is only our internal disposition that is ours to control and that we should dedicate ourselves to perfect.[123] The phrase "what is in our power, and what is not" appeals to the key Stoic concept of ἐφ᾽ ἡμῖν (what is up to us), whereby they understand that a person can choose to give assent to follow a particular course of action.[124]

In addition, in a discussion on varying approaches to theology, Epictetus draws upon the figures of Socrates and Odysseus to represent the Stoic position, claiming:

> and there is a fifth group, to which both Socrates and Odysseus belonged, who say, "Not a move of mine goes unseen by you."[125]

> πέμπτοι δ᾽, ὧν ἦν καὶ Ὀδυσσεὺς καὶ Σωκράτης, οἱ λέγοντες ὅτι οὐδέ σε λήθω κινύμενος.

Here, Odysseus is credited as having understood a key Stoic position—specifically the importance of divine oversight.[126] As William Stephens notes this: "Agreement with Socrates on this important theological point elevates Odysseus to an estimable rank among the Homeric heroes."[127] He is, therefore, an important example of a layperson who exhibits notable virtuous qualities.

Before proceeding, I should highlight that the lack of scholarly appreciation of the Stoics stance regarding the possibility of laypeople setting commendable moral examples, for instance, is apparent in David Mehl's 2002 study. Mehl asserts that since Cicero's *Parad* frequently portrays non-Stoic figures' lives as exemplifying truths of paradoxes, such as the one that the sage alone is free, he should be understood to be challenging the Stoics' stance regarding the rareness of the sage. The results of this chapter should, however, demonstrate that Cicero's pattern of use of exempla, which has a heavy focus upon laypeople, was a conventional one within Stoicism, and should decidedly not be interpreted as tendering any implied criticism of the philosophy.

EPICTETUS AND DIDACTIC EXEMPLA

It is apparent that, while Epictetus expects his students will routinely seek the assistance of exempla to help them further their intended moral advance, on several occasions he also relays his belief that exposure to them can effect a change in people who have no such philosophical objective in mind, that is, laypeople. As opposed to his students, whose attention he normally directs toward the actions of notable historical figures, Epictetus seems to believe that laypeople are more readily impacted by reflecting upon the behavior of living people. For instance, we can observe that when the Procurator of Epirus is portrayed as approaching the philosopher for advice after he was jeered at by a crowd because of the partiality he had displayed toward a certain comic actor, Epictetus responds:

> When they saw was you, their governor, and the associate and Procurator of Caesar, expressing his favor in that way, surely it should be expected that they should show their partiality in a similar way? For if it is not right to show such favor, you should not do so yourself; and, if it is, why are you angry at them for imitating you? For whom else have the multitude to imitate but you their superiors? Whom are they to look to when they come into the theater but you? "Look at how Caesar's Procurator behaves while he is watching the show. He cries out," "Well, he is shouting, I will shout too. He jumps from his seat: I too will jump from mine."[128]

> σέ, ἔφη, βλέποντες τὸν αὐτῶν ἄρχοντα, τοῦ Καίσαρος φίλον καὶ ἐπίτροπον, οὕτως σπουδάζοντα οὐκ ἔμελλον καὶ αὐτοὶ οὕτως σπουδάζειν; εἰ γὰρ μὴ δεῖ οὕτως σπουδάζειν, μηδὲ σὺ σπούδαζε· εἰ δὲ δεῖ, τί χαλεπαίνεις, εἴ σε ἐμιμήσαντο; τίνας γὰρ ἔχουσιν μιμήσασθαι οἱ πολλοὶ ἢ τοὺς ὑπερέχοντας ὑμᾶς; εἰς τίνας ἀπίδωσιν ἐλθόντες εἰς τὰ θέατρα ἢ ὑμᾶς; 'ὅρα πῶς ὁ ἐπίτροπος τοῦ Καίσαρος θεωρεῖ· κέκραγεν· κἀγὼ τοίνυν κραυγάσω. ἀναπηδᾷ· κἀγὼ ἀναπηδήσω.

He attempts to persuade the governor that, whether he intends it or not, his position has instituted him to be a living exemplum for the public, and that they will instinctively attune their actions to match the ones he manifests. Epictetus, therefore, candidly suggests that it is the Procurator who is responsible for the crowd's inappropriate behavior, and that the people are merely reflecting his own vice back to him.

While the above passage relays Epictetus' belief on the corrupting influence that an official's example can have upon the moral constitution of a population, he also importantly holds that the public's impulse to imitate their leaders can allow patterns of good behavior to be inculcated into society. So, in the dialogue between Epictetus and the Epicurean commissioner at *Diss* III.7, he appeals for him to:

> Show us what is to our interest, and we will pursue it; show us what is against our interest, and we will turn away from it. Make us imitators of yourself, as Socrates made people imitators of him. He was truly a governor of men, who made people to subject to him their desires and aversions, and their impulses to act and not to act.[129]

> ὡς λογικῶν ἡμῶν ἄρξον δεικνὺς ἡμῖν τὰ συμφέροντα καὶ ἀκολουθήσομεν: δείκνυε τὰ ἀσύμφορα καὶ ἀποστραφησόμεθα. ζηλωτὰς ἡμᾶς κατασκεύασον σεαυτοῦ ὡς Σωκράτης ἑαυτοῦ. ἐκεῖνος ἦν ὁ ὡς ἀνθρώπων ἄρχων, ὁ κατεσκευακὼς ὑποτεταχότας αὐτῷ τὴν ὄρεξιν τὴν αὐτῶν, τὴν ἔκκλισιν, τὴν ὁρμήν, τὴν ἀφορμήν.

Again, Epictetus posits that it is not just this official's formal rulings which have the power to encourage and sanction certain behavior in society, but also the example they set—a concept that is also found in other Classical authors—[130] and to remind him that the people review/consider (θεωρέω) his actions. With this reality in mind, Epictetus continues to appeal for the commissioner to consider educating people as Socrates had done, not through issuing pronouncements or outlining detailed moral codes, but by endeavoring to induce the many (οἱ πολλοὶ) to emulate/imitate (μιμέομαι) him. Perhaps, Epictetus is thinking of the following sort of appraisal that Xenophon offers of Socrates' teaching method: "To be sure he never professed to teach this [the desire for goodness]: but by letting his own light shine, he led his disciples to hope that they through imitation of him would attain such excellence," καίτοι γε οὐδεπώποτε ὑπέσχετο διδάσκαλος εἶναι τούτου, ἀλλὰ τῷ φανερὸς εἶναι τοιοῦτος ὢν ἐλπίζειν ἐποίει τοὺς συνδιατρίβοντας ἑαυτῷ μιμουμένους ἐκεῖνον τοιούτους γενήσεσθαι.[131] Regarding the use of the verb ἀφορμάω, it should perhaps be highlighted that it usually means to start an action, but in philosophical idiom means aversion, that is, Epictetus appeals to the governor to behave in a way whereby those people who follow his behavior will avoid certain courses of (unwise) action. We might further note that Seneca, too, appeals to Nero in a similar manner by arguing that he can set the moral tone for his kingdom just as the head can influence the rest of the body:

> That this will largely come to pass, Caesar, we hope with joyful confidence. The mildness of your spirit will be handed on and spread through the whole framework of our dominion, and all things will be modelled on your likeness. Good health starts from the head: all else is energetic and alert, or drooping in exhaustion, to the degree that the mind is full of life or enfeebled.[132]

Futurum hoc. Caesar, ex magna parte sperare et confidere libet. Tradetur ista animi tui mansuetudo diffundeturque paulatim per omne imperii corpus, et cuncta in similitudinem tuam formabuntur. A capite bona valetudo: inde omnia vegeta sunt atque erecta aut languore demissa, prout animus eorum vivit aut marcet.

As well as government officials, Epictetus further believes that philosophers, or at least noted adherents of philosophy, can impact laypeople through their example. He discloses this belief in passing in two passages. In the first, comparing Priscus' noble example (παράδειγμα) with the purple in the senatorial toga, he opines:

Why, what good does the purple do to the tunic? What else than standing out as purple, and setting a fine example to the rest?[133]

τί δ᾽ ὠφελεῖ ἡ πορφύρα τὸ ἱμάτιον; τί γὰρ ἄλλο ἢ διαπρέπει ἐν αὐτῷ ὡς πορφύρα καὶ τοῖς ἄλλοις δὲ καλὸν παράδειγμα ἔκκειται;

While, in the other, he pointedly asks:

Is god so negligent of his own creatures, of his servants, his witnesses, whom alone he makes as examples to the uneducated.[134]

οὕτως ὁ θεὸς ἀμελεῖ τῶν αὑτοῦ ἐπιτευγμάτων, τῶν διακόνων, τῶν μαρτύρων, οἷς μόνοις χρῆται παραδείγμασιν πρὸς τοὺς ἀπαιδεύτους.

These two statements imply that Epictetus believes people who are committed to philosophy can extend their influence beyond observing the formal activities that are associated with it, such as explicating philosophical doctrines or texts to an assembled audience, or assuming the supervision of a body of students. He believes that their very lives can be used as a model (παράδειγμα) to convey the truths of philosophy to laypeople or, as referred to above, the uneducated/uninstructed (ἀπαίδευτοι).

Epictetus' conviction that philosophers can influence laypeople by their example is restated with more clarity in the following passage. Here he responds to a student who expresses a desire to start proffering salient philosophical advice to people around him by commenting:

But you want to benefit them? Show them, through your own example, what kind of people philosophy produces, and abstain from vacuous talk. When you eat, be of benefit to those who eat with you, when you drink, to those who drink with you. Be of benefit to them, by giving way to all, deferring to them, bearing with them; and not throwing your phlegm upon them.[135]

σὺ γὰρ προτέτρεψαι; θέλεις αὐτοὺς ὠφελῆσαι. δεῖξον αὐτοῖς ἐπὶ σεαυτοῦ, οἵους ποιεῖ φιλοσοφία, καὶ μὴ φλυάρει. ἐσθίων τοὺς συνεσθίοντας ὠφέλει, πίνων τοὺς πίνοντας, εἴκων πᾶσι, παραχωρῶν, ἀνεχόμενος, οὕτως αὐτοὺς ὠφέλει καὶ μὴ κατεξέρα αὐτῶν τὸ σαυτοῦ φλέγμα.

Epictetus argues that the most effective means that this student has for benefiting people (and he does so by using the verb ὠφελέω three times in this short passage) is not by trying to verbalize philosophy's contents, but by bringing them to light/showing them (δείκνυμι) through his actions in daily life.[136] In this way, Epictetus tries to persuade the student that his personal example holds the capacity to lead people to apprehend what he will otherwise struggle to articulate.

He elsewhere further argues the awareness that they have the ability to represent philosophy to outsiders through their life, should be a constantly modifying force upon his students' actions:

For we should not scare the world away from philosophy through our bodily appearance, but show ourselves cheerful and untroubled, in our body as in everything else.[137]

δεῖ γὰρ μηδὲ κατὰ τὴν ἀπὸ τοῦ σώματος ἔμφασιν ἀπὸ φιλοσοφίας ἀποσοβεῖν τοὺς πολλούς, ἀλλ᾽ ὥσπερ τὰ ἄλλα εὔθυμον καὶ ἀτάραχον ἐπιδεικνύειν αὐτὸν οὕτως καὶ ἀπὸ τοῦ σώματος.

We can see that Epictetus wants not only his pupils to *be* cheerful and untroubled, but, precisely for the sake of onlookers, that they should *appear* cheerful and untroubled: a feature of Stoicism that we can note, a generation later, Lucian will describe as attracting people to affiliate themselves with the school.[138] Moreover, Epictetus also issues an extended commentary on how philosophers might be called upon to reveal the truths of philosophy to others through their example:

For there is a reason he [god] now brings me here, and then sends me there; shows me to humanity, poor, without office, sick; sends me to Gyara, puts me in prison: not that he hates me; heaven forbid! For who hates the best of his servants? Nor that he neglects me, for he does not neglect even the least of his creation; but because he is exercising me, and making us of me as a witness to others . . . Only, do not make a parade of it, or boast about it, but demonstrate it in your actions; and, even if no one perceives it, be content in yourself to live a healthy and happy life.[139]

ἐπὶ τούτοις με νῦν μὲν ἐνταῦθα ἄγει, νῦν δ᾽ ἐκεῖ πέμπει, πένητα δείκνυσι τοῖς ἀνθρώποις, δίχα ἀρχῆς, νοσοῦντα: εἰς Γύαρα ἀποστέλλει, εἰς δεσμωτήριον

εἰσάγει. οὐ μισῶν: μὴ γένοιτο: τίς δὲ μισεῖ τὸν ἄριστον τῶν ὑπηρετῶν τῶν
ἑαυτοῦ; οὐδ᾽ ἀμελῶν, ὅς γε οὐδὲ τῶν μικροτάτων τινὸς ἀμελεῖ, ἀλλὰ γυμνάζων
καὶ μάρτυρι πρὸς τοὺς ἄλλους χρώμενος . . . μόνον μὴ πόμπευε αὐτὴν μηδ᾽
ἀλαζονεύου ἐπ᾽ αὐτῇ, ἀλλ᾽ ἔργῳ δείκνυε: κἂν μηδεὶς αἰσθάνηται, ἀρκοῦ αὐτὸς
ὑγιαίνων καὶ εὐδαιμονῶν.

Epictetus encourages his pupils to consider incidents such as exile, illness, and incarceration as providing them with the perfect backdrop against
which the virtues that philosophy has steeled within them can be revealed to
others, signified again by his use of the verb δείκνυμι, "bring to light/show."
In this regard, we can reflect that many of Epictetus' chosen exempla are
figures whose sincerity and strength of conviction became particularly
evident, or were highlighted because of such occurrences, for example the
reaction of Socrates and members of the "Stoic opposition" when they were
confronted by threats of exile and death. Epictetus' injunction, however,
that philosophers should not make an exhibition of themselves in order
to set an example is an important one. Epictetus evidently does not hold
that philosophers should engineer scenarios so that their philosophically
informed behavior and attitudes can be visibly exercised; indeed, he even
suggests that they should not be concerned if no one recognizes their good
behavior. This perspective matches with the conclusion of chapter 3 regarding Epictetus' view of the selective engagement of laypeople. He seems
to expect that philosophers will resolve to quietly disclose to others how
philosophy is impacting their lives by their daily manner of eating, drinking, and comporting themselves. The role of *exerting* oneself to become an
exemplum to others is a task that he decidedly leaves for another group of
people to fulfill—Cynics.

With regards to the Cynics, as is evident by the frequency with which
he refers to them, as well as by the fact that the largest extant discourse is
devoted to explore their role, Epictetus holds that they are charged with fulfilling an important function: that of presenting philosophical truths to the
general public and of being a messenger (ἄγγελος) and scout (κατάσκοπος)
that has been sent by god to humanity.[140] For this reason, he will refer to
them—and not, we must note, professional philosophers—as being the
"teacher of the public," (ὁ παιδευτὴς ὁ κοινός).[141] Although he will occasionally portray the Cynics as attempting to engage individuals in conversation,[142] the primary method he depicts them employing to help further their
mission is their practice of making themselves and their inoculation against
shame and the false esteem for external conditions arrestingly visible to
the people around them.[143] So, Epictetus will claim that Cynics are to make
themselves disgraced in the view of the world,[144] and depicts one of them
stating:

Behold I have been sent to you from god as an example, having neither property nor house, nor wife nor children, nor even a bed, or cloak, or household possessions. And see how fit I am. Test me, and, if you see me free from distress, hear the remedies, and by what means I was cured.[145]

ἰδοὺ ἐγὼ ὑμῖν παράδειγμα ὑπὸ τοῦ θεοῦ ἀπέσταλμαι μήτε κτῆσιν ἔχων μήτε οἶκον μήτε γυναῖκα μήτε τέκνα, ἀλλὰ μηδ᾽ ὑπόστρωμα μηδὲ χιτῶνα μηδὲ σκεῦος: καὶ ἴδετε, πῶς ὑγιαίνω: πειράθητέ μου κἂν ἴδητε ἀτάραχον, ἀκούσατε τὰ φάρμακα καὶ ὑφ᾽ ὧν ἐθεραπεύθην.

Elsewhere, he also frames their mission, to which they have been dispatched (ἀποστέλλω) by god to fulfill, as being:

to show them [humanity] that they have gone astray, and are seeking the true nature of good and evil where it is not, without ever reflecting upon where it really is.[146]

ὑποδείξων αὐτοῖς, ὅτι πεπλάνηνται καὶ ἀλλαχοῦ ζητοῦσι τὴν οὐσίαν τοῦ ἀγαθοῦ καὶ τοῦ κακοῦ, ὅπου οὐκ ἔστιν, ὅπου δ᾽ ἔστιν, οὐκ ἐνθυμοῦνται.

So, we can see that while Epictetus believes that philosophers should quietly comport themselves and offer almost passive testimony to their principles, he conversely expects that Cynics will strive to provide as evident a witness as they can.[147] They are caused to wander (πλανάω) to be a ὑποδείκνυμι, a compound verb, formed by δείκνυμι that is prefixed with the preposition ὑπο, which means to display or indicate, but can more readily connote the idea of "setting an example/to show them" than the verb δείκνυμι does on its own. The adverb ἀλλαχοῦ is an infrequently used one in ancient literature, but holds the sense of people who are elsewhere, that is, individuals who are far removed from the disposition of these wandering Cynics, that is, people who are philosophically (not spatially) lost. Epictetus' understanding is, therefore, that the Cynic's life and their wandering is designed so that the protreptic power of the personal exemplum can be utilized, and people who do not have a familiarity with philosophical tenets will be confronted with their principles in the most striking and memorable of ways.[148] It is unlikely though that Epictetus understands the Cynics to be engaged in gaining new adherents for Cynicism, as in an act of proselytism, but rather that he is framing them as offering a protreptic, or instructive service to the people around them.[149]

In conclusion, as well as being a tactic through which the school's key attributes were relayed, Epictetus' appeal to exempla highlights his conviction that nonphilosophers can act and think in morally beneficial ways. Throughout the records of Epictetus' discussions, his understanding that the examples which people set, either through interpersonal relationships or by more abstract routes such as historic or heroic narratives, are an important means whereby the moral worth of laypeople (as well as non-Stoics) is also demonstrated. Furthermore, regardless of their lack of philosophical education individuals can be profitably prompted to evaluate the appropriateness of their deeds and actions through exempla.[150]

NOTES

1. *Praef* 5.

2. *Diss.* I.27.8, IV.5.1-3.

3. On the exemplum's importance in Greek and Roman education, see especially Barchiesi (2009) and Seo (2013).

4. On exempla and rhetoric, see Cosby (1988, 93–105) and Nuffelen (2012, 63–92).

5. Chaplin (2000), Roller (2004, 2009), and O'Gorman (2011).

6. See Fiore (1986) and *Prt.* 325d-e, as well as comments from Jaegar (1945, 1.310). On the use of inscriptions to encourage the imitation of good examples, see the discussion at Harrison (2013, 233–238).

7. On the importance of using exempla, consider Isocrates' comments at *Antid* 277; cf. *Ep. ad Dem* 36, *Ep. ad. Nic* 38, 61, and a discussion on their place in rhetoric at *Rhet Her.* IV.1.1-7.10.

8. On Homer's use of exempla, see Skidmore (1996, 3); on Boethius', see his remarks at *Cons. Phil.* II.2.

9. For example, see Origen *C. Cels* 7.53.

10. *Controv.* 10.2.16. See further Virg. *Aen.* XII 435-40, along with the comments from Barchiesi (2009, 43), and *Pers.* 3.44-47 and Cicero *Arch.* 6.

11. *Diss.* III.23.35, 38.

12. So Mayer (1991, 167) comments with regards to their use in Roman society that being "drawn from the past which was common to all Romans the exemplary figure was hallowed by tradition. Reference to him or her made common ground between the moralist and his audience. The philosopher above all, whose essentially Greek intellectual discipline might render his doctrine suspect to some of his fellow Romans, would welcome the historical exemplum for this very reason."

13. Skidmore (1996, 18).

14. *Rh. Her.* 4.66, trans. Tieleman (2008, 134).

15. See, for example, the discussion in Nussbaum (1994, 338–340), who (339) comments: "in Stoic teaching narratives and examples will play a central role. There is no moral philosophy in the Western tradition in which this is more evident; it is a constant practice, and it is also a part of the official theory." See also Sedley (1999, 151).

16. Niehoff (2012, 376): "the Stoics acknowledged an impressive variety of exemplary figures, including philosophers from other schools, politicians, and heroes

mentioned in ancient texts. Moral authority was not based on a canonical text or a particular school allegiance, but rather followed from the usefulness of the model." See also Vogt (2008, 10).

17. *Tranq.* 1.12.

18. *Ep.* 64.9. On this see the very useful discussion in Staley (2010, 282–283). Furthermore, at *Ann.* 15.62 Tacitus reports that Seneca was said to have exclaimed at his death that the best gift he could give to his friends was the example of his life.

19. *Med.* 3.14.

20. We should note, though, that it is not clear if exempla were utilized in the first few generations of the school. On this, Sedley (1999, 151) argues: "to see the difference that this development [of using exempla] makes, it is instructive to compare Seneca's account of how the god is conceived in *Letter* 120.3-11, based on extrapolation from exemplary individuals, with Cicero's much more austere early Stoic account in *Fin.* 3.33-4, where the purely general considerations are invoked." See the wider discussion at Sedley (1999, 150–151). On this, see also the comments by Montliglio (2011, 66). We might, I suggest, suppose that the earlier generations' focus upon the sage might have had fulfilled the function exempla would later come to have—as Sorabji (2012, 138) and Brunt (2013, 106, 168) have also proposed. The earliest Stoic proponent, whom we can credit with using historical exempla, is Panaetius, so see the comments from Brunt (2013, 84, 118).

21. See the brief discussion in Sellars (2003, 30–31).

22. Mayer (1991), Staley (2002), Turpin (2008), Long (2009), Fantham et al. (2010), Niehoff (2012), and Roller (2015). Mayer (1991, 165), Braund (2004, 61), and Wildberger (2014b, 317–318) appear to suggest that the use of exempla as a didactic tool within the Stoic school was unique to Seneca. Presently, no study has sought to catalogue and understand Epictetus' use of exempla; however, see some valuable comments from Hijmans (1959, 72–77) and Huttunen (2009, 127–139). We can perhaps also note Seo's (2013, 66–93) discussion of Lucan's use of exempla to highlight Stoic themes.

23. Turpin (2008, 365). On Seneca's belief that keeping company with a virtuous friend can aid/prompt a person to make moral progress, consider the discussion at Long (2013a, 228–235)—an advantage that we can reasonably infer that exempla are intended to replicate.

24. We might add Langlands' (2011, 101–103) observation that in antiquity exempla were not cited to provide rigid interpretations of how to act, but to rather help people deduce what the correct course of action they should pursue might be. On this understanding in Seneca's use of exempla, see Inwood (2005, 295–296). I can perhaps also add that Epictetus occasionally uses animals as exempla; for example, he highlights the bravery that some fighting-cocks display (*Diss.* II.2.14), animal devotion to their offspring (*Diss.* I.23.7-8), their self-sufficiency (*Diss.* I.9.9), and freedom (*Diss.* IV.24-31). On Epictetus' use of animal exempla, see Stephens (2014a) and, in wider Stoic theory, Cooper (2004, 231–232). Wildberger (2014b, 308), though, has argued that Seneca did not believe animals should be used as exempla.

25. *Diss.* IV.1.170.

26. *Ench.* 33.1.

27. *Diss.* II.18,21,23.

28. *Diss.* I.29.56-57. Seneca, *Ep.* 98.13, argues that we should aim to become examples to others. This was a common theme in the Roman understanding of the exemplum; for example, Blom (2010, 79) observes that Cicero expresses a similar aim.

29. *Diss.* IV. 1.169.

30. *Ep.* 98.13.

31. Turpin (2008, 365) notes: "the Roman Stoics clearly regarded exemplum as more than mere decorations or illustrations. They could be flexible and powerful elements in moral instruction." See also Hijmans (1959, 77).

32. We should also observe that Epictetus will occasionally find it useful to direct his students to consider his own example. So Yieh (2008, 233), when commenting upon Epictetus' habit of drawing attention to his own life and circumstances in his teaching (e.g., *Diss.* I.29.22-29,40; 6.1-2; 16.5, 15-21, 19; 30.1; II.6.20-25; III.20.4; IV.1.151; 8.30-31), argues: "By presenting himself as a personal example for emulation, he [Epictetus] could show his pupils how to make progress in their moral exercises. Since he was the only teacher, the most significant person of authority in his school, he served as the most powerful example to help his pupils resist the influence of their reference groups from the upper social classes and focus on moral purpose." See also *Muson.* 9.9 and 11.5. On Seneca's use of himself as an exemplum, consider also Schafer (2009, 90, 109; 2011, 43 n.43). Tieleman (2010, 280) also comments that in the classical philosophical schools: "The scholarch not only explained the teaching of the founder through oral and written instruction but was also supposed to set a personal example, i.e. to embody the school's teaching through his whole demeanor."

33. *Diss.* II.13.14.

34. *Ench.* 33.

35. *Diss.* III.23.32.

36. *Diss.* III.26.23. See also Diog. Laert. 7.168, 174.

37. See Morgan (2007, 277–278).

38. On the so-called "Stoic opposition" in general, see Griffin (1976, 339–366).

39. See Rudich (1993, 96).

40. See Fergus (2004, 106). On Marcus Aurelius' similar admiration for Thrasea Paetus, see *M. Aur. Med* 1.14.

41. Tacitus, *Ann.* 13. 49, 14. 12, 48; 15. 20-22, 16. 21-35, *Hdt.*, 2. 91, 4. 5.

42. See Tacitus, *Ann.* 16.28, 29, 33.

43. *Fr.* 23 Gill and Hard (1995).

44. On Helvidius Priscus and his surrounding political context, see Tacitus, *Hist.* iv. 5, *Dial.*, 5; Dio Cassius lxvi. 12, lxvii. 13; Suetonius *Vesp.* 15; and Pliny *Ep.* vii. 19 I.2.19-21, as well as Frede (2010, 154–155) and Mann (2015) regarding Epictetus' account of him.

45. White (2010, 124) remarks on Epictetus' discussion on Helvidius: "this miniature dialogue and its concluding sermon exhibit the 'reasonable' response of an exemplary Stoic, if not sage, at least a committed 'progressor' well advanced on the path to virtue." On this group as a whole, see Gill's (2005, 610), comments on their "sage-like attitudes," and see also the discussion at White (2010, 121–126).

46. *Diss.* I.1.31.

47. *Fr* 21.

48. *Diss.* IV.1.123. On his position as governor, see *CIG* 2570.

49. So at *Diss.* II.16.35 Epictetus explains: "what claim do I have to be called of Socrates, who lived and died in the way he did": ποῦ γάρ μοι μέτεστι τούτου τοῦ πράγματος, οὗ Σωκράτει μετῆν τῷ οὕτως ἀποθανόντι, οὕτως ζήσαντι; οὗ Διογένει μετῆν; See also Tsalla (2005, 1).

50. See a useful study on this by Wilson (2007).

51. For example, *Muson.* 9.4; 11.6; *Ep.* 47.12; 90.14; *Tranq.*8.7-8; *Ben.* 5.4.3-4, and *M. Aur. Med* 8.3. Plutarch can also cite Diogenes as an exemplum (*De exil* 606C), as can Cicero (*Tusc.* 5.92).

52. For example, see Long (2018).

53. On Epictetus' effort to present Diogenes according to Roman sensibilities, see Billerbeck (1978).

54. Apart from those passages highlighted below, we can also cite *Diss.* II.16.35-36, III.22.91-92; and 24.65-68.

55. *Diss.* IV.1.152.

56. *Diss.* III.26.23, and *Diss.* IV.1.152-158.

57. *Diss.* II.16.36.

58. *Diss.* IV.1.115, 116.

59. So Tsalla (2005, 30) argues: "if we use the frequency of references as a qualitative criterion, it shows that, for Epictetus, Socrates is more important as the model of philosopher than any other Stoic sage." Apart from those passages mentioned below, we could also include *Diss.* I.9.1,22; 12.23;19.6; 25.31; 29.16-18; II.2.8, 15; 2.15-16; 5.18; 6.26; 12.5, 14-16; 16.34-36; 18.22; 26:6-7; III.1.42; 16.5; 24.60; IV.4.21; 5.33; *Ench.* 5; 33, and 46. Long (1996, 2) comments: "in the *Discourses* of Epictetus, Socrates is *the* philosopher, a figure canonised more than any other Stoic saint, whether Diogenes, Antisthenes or Zeno (emphasis his)." Brennan (2006, 286), meanwhile, remarks: "Epictetus seems to have invoked Socrates' name and fate on a daily basis; he quotes or refers to Socrates more than to any other figure, even more than the leaders of the Stoic school to which he belonged, and clearly models his own life and ways on the ways and life of Socrates." See also Hijmans (1959, 74) and Schofield (2007, 71).

60. An important qualification, though, should be raised. This difference in attention might also reflect Epictetus' stated awareness that Socrates' circumstances align more with his students' lives than they do with Diogenes'. So consider Epictetus comments at *Diss.* IV.1.159. Stephens (1996, 1) also notes: "Socrates is Epictetus' favorite hero because Socrates, as husband, father, soldier, Athenian citizen and member of the council, who calmly faced execution rather than breaking the law, embodies a true *Stoic* exemplar in contrast to Diogenes the Cynic, the childless, stateless, and often indecorous bachelor." See also Huttunen (2009, 133).

61. *Diss.* IV.5.1-2.

62. *Diss.* I.19.6.

63. *Ench.* 51.

64. Tsalla (2005, 32). See also Hijmans (1959, 76).

65. *Ench.* 15.

66. Long (1996, 35–57).

67. Long (1996, 46–56). On Heraclitus' influence on Marcus Aurelius, consider also Stephens (2012, 43–58).

68. Matheson (1916, 57 n.3).

69. *Diss.* III.24.71.

70. For example, see Philodemus *De Mort.* 35.33, Plutarch *De garrul* 8 (*Mor.* 505D); and *Stoic repgun.* 37 (*Mor.* 1051CD); *Adv. Col.* 32 (*Mor.* 1126D), Tertullian *Apol.* 50.6-9, and Origen *C. Cels.* 7.53, and see the discussion at Henten and Avemarie (2002, 12).

71. For example, see Diog. Laert. 9.27, 59.

72. Other more recent commentators, all curiously not mentioning the above more overt reference, have drawn attention to a trio of passages (*Diss.* I.29.18, II.2.15, and III.23.21) in which Epictetus posits that people should not fear individuals such as Antus and Meletus (the accusers of Socrates), who can chain your bodies, but cannot control your *proairesis*, and have noted the resonance of this claim with the stories that circulated regarding Anaxarchus and Zeno's lives; see Henten and Avemarie (2002, 13) and Sorabji (1997, 206 n.55), as well as Crabbe (1998, 18), who comments on *Diss.* I.1.22 and links this with the account of Anaxarchus' torture.

73. *Diss.* III.26.23, 24.

74. See, for example, Dobbin (1991).

75. Turpin (2008, 367).

76. See *Muson.* 10.1 and 20.5. See also Cicero *Tusc.* 2.34, 46, and 5.77.

77. See *Stob.* 2.85, and Diog. Laert. 7.107, and the discussion in Dobbin (1998, 81).

78. *Diss.* I.2.2. See the brief discussion of this section at Brunt (2013, 91).

79. *Diss.* II.20.26.

80. *Fr* 5, see also *Diss.* III.7.19-20, we can note that Cicero also comments at *Fin.* II.67: "I have never heard Lycurgus mentioned in Epicurus' school, or Solon, Miltiades, Themistocles or Epameinondas, all of whom receive due acknowledgement from other philosophers" trans. Rackham (1914, 157): *numquam audivi in Epicuri schola Lycurgum, Solonem, Miltiadem, Themistoclem, Epaminondam nominari, qui in ore sunt ceterorum omnium philosophorum.*

81. See Stob. 3.13.43, *M. Aur. Med* 11.24, Diog. Laert. 6.59, and Manilius *Astron.* I.770-774 on Solon and Lycurgus. At *Lyc.* 31, Plutarch also notes the Stoics' admiration for the Spartan state. On the Stoics Persaeus' and Sphaerus' writings on Sparta, see Brunt (2013, 91–92, 287). On the veneration of the Spartan educational system during the first century CE, see also Jaegar (1939, 84). It is important to note, however, that, especially during the earlier Hellenistic period, the Spartans were not always cited as representing the apex of virtue; for example, at Diog. Laert. 6:27 it is recorded that Diogenes remarked: "Being asked where in Greece he saw good men, he replied Good men nowhere, but good boys at Lacedaemon. [Sparta]." trans. Hicks (1925, 29): Ἐρωτηθεὶς ποῦ τῆς Ἑλλάδος ἴδοι ἀγαθοὺς ἄνδρας, ἄνδρας μέν, εἶπεν, οὐδαμοῦ, παῖδας δ' ἐν Λακεδαίμονι. See also Aristotle's critique of the Spartans at *Pol.* 1271a41-10 and *Eth. Eud* 1248b28-9, and the comments of Antiochus of Ascalon *apud* Cicero *Acad.* 2.136.

82. *Ep.* 77.14, trans. Gummere (1920, 177). This passage is also recorded by Plutarch at *Apoph.* 69.38. It is possible, as Babbit (1931, 407) has suggested, that at *Diss.* I.2.2-3 Epictetus is alluding to the above story (or a variant of it) when he comments on the Spartans' willingness to endure suffering and he proceeds to comment on the appropriate circumstances that can permit a person to commit suicide.

83. *Diss.* III.20.4-6. We can also note that Antisthenes produced two treatises on the Persian King Cyrus, in which he drew attention to the monarch's hard labor—see the discussion in Gruen (2011, 55).

84. Euripides *Phoen.* 913, 930, and Pseudo-Apollodorus *Bibl.* 3.73-75.

85. A similar exemplum is highlighted by Seneca at *Ep.* 120.7 regarding the valor of Horatius Cocles, who defended a bridge over the Tiber during Rome's war with Clusium.

86. *Diss.* III.7.2-3.

87. *Diss.* III.7.25-28.

88. On theories regarding his identity, see Matheson (1916, 14 n.2) and Oldfather (1928, 50 n.1).

89. Another exemplum that Epictetus makes is regarding Epameinondas—the famed statesman and general of Thebes. On him, Epictetus comments, *Diss.* III.22.78: "And from whom did the Thebans derive the greater benefit: from all those who left them children, or from Epaminondas, who died childless?": καὶ Θηβαίους μείζονα ὠφέλησαν ὅσοι τεκνία αὐτοῖς κατέλιπον Ἐπαμινώνδου τοῦ ἀτέκνου ἀποθανόντος. As I have noted (p. 175 n.80), Cicero remarks that Epameinondas was esteemed in various philosophical traditions; however, his reputed philosophical (especially Pythagorean) training in his youth means we cannot firmly designate him as being a layperson—see the useful discussion on his background at Buckler (1993).

90. *Diss.* I.2.25.

91. See White (2012, 126). On this belief, see Galen *De Sem. Lib.* II, and Stephens (2014b, 10). Cosan (2000, 244) also usefully notes: "Given that the body was the tool with which the man gained honor on the athletic field, he may have felt a duty to treat it with such respect that he would risk his life before seeing it mutilated."

92. For example, see Xenakis (1969, 17), Cosan (2000, 224), Stephens (2002; 2014, 8–10), Hill (2004, 257), Sorabji (2007, 143–144), Tsalla (2010, 26; 2014, 107–108, 127–128), and Johnson (2014, 43 176).

93. White (2010, 127—emphasis his). See his wider discussion on this passage at White (2010, 125–127).

94. The influence of Stoicism on Cicero and his philosophical writings is well known and is the subject of much scholarly interest. See in particular a succession of recent studies, namely Caspar (2011) and Schmitz (2014), which argue for a more complex relationship between Cicero's writings and Stoicism than is sometimes, and traditionally, presumed. On Cicero's use of the Stoic theory of roles in *De Off.* and the impact this has on his use of exempla, see Langlands (2011, especially pp. 107–108). See also Gill (1988).

95. Although there are disagreements over the precise understanding of this principle in different Stoic writers, see the discussions in De Lacy (1977), Gill (1988, 1990, 1994), Stephens (1998), Sorabji (2006, 157–171), Frede (2007, 153–168),

Tieleman (2007, 130–140), and especially Johnson (2012a, 2012b, 2014). On Aristo of Chios' concept of roles, see Diog. Laert. 7.160.

96. It should be noted that Cicero's account envisages four *personae*, including the position that is given to us by birth, as well as the responsibilities we assume by choice. On the differences between Panaetius' and Epictetus' conception of roles, see Frede (2007, 166–167). Johnson (2014, 135–173) also helpfully summarizes Cicero's/Panaetius' division of roles as being between "humanity, personality, social standing and career choice," while Epictetus' is more broadly divided between: "universal and specific (nature, relationships, choices . . .)"

97. *Diss.* III.23.3-5.

98. So at *Diss.* III.23.1-8 Epictetus highlights the occupations of lyre-player, carpenter, philosopher, and orator as being examples of roles that a person can fulfill. On careers as roles, see also the discussion in Sorabji (2006, 161) and Frede (2007, 157). Johnson (2014, 15) also notes: "Epictetus discusses the case of an athlete who must choose who he wishes to be ([*Diss.*]3.23.1-2), suggesting that he would plausibly include being an athlete as an *epitêdeuma*. . . . Epictetus understands 'each man's pursuit [*epitêdeuma*]' as some sort of role."

99. See Epictetus' comments at *Diss.* II.10.10-11.

100. *Diss.* III. 22.69-71, 83-85. On the Stoic attitude toward marriage and family, and especially according to Musonius Rufus and Epictetus, see the valuable discussion at Bosman (2010).

101. See *Diss.* III.22.67-76.

102. *Diss.* III.22.1-8, 86-109.

103. For more on this passage and its relevance to Cicero's wider theory of roles, see Gill (2008, 41–45) and Sorabji (2012, 112).

104. *Diss.* I.2.25-28.

105. *Diss.* I.2.29.

106. For a discussion on the link between beards and philosophers in antiquity, see Hahn (1989, 33–39) and Sellars (2003, 15–19). This association is, as Stephens (2002) likewise notes, also apparent in Epictetus' remarks at *Diss.* II.23.21, III.1.24, and IV.8.12, 8.15. See also the discussion at Brunt (2013, 132).

107. Cosan (2000, 244) notes: "Epictetus considers this [the athlete's] case as a paradigm of holding 'regard for one's proper character (*prosopon*)' (*Discourses* I.2.28); he likens the man's resolve to that of Helvidius Priscus, a Stoic senator who was executed because he spoke out for what he believed was right despite the Emperor's threats," and Tsalla (2014, 127, 128): "Epictetus confidently claims that the athlete who died refusing to amputate his genitals acted reasonably ([*Diss.*]1.2.25-26.) . . . the athlete was reasonable because by embracing death to maintain his manliness, he gave perfect evidence to his abiding by logos."

108. *Diss.* I.28.22-25, and II.24.21-27. On this, see Stephens (2002).

109. *Diss.* I.27.8, quoting *Il.*12.310-328. See also Cicero's comments at *De Fin.* III.64. On the perception that showing courage in battle is appropriate, see, for instance, Seneca *Ep.* 67.9, Dio Chrysostom's *Or.* 31.17, and, tying it with the theory of *oikeiosis* Cicero's comments at *De Fin.* III.64.

110. For example, see *Diss.* II.6.26-27.

111. Space constraints prevent us from considering Heracles as well. Epictetus presents him as being an exemplum on at least six occasions: *Diss.* I.6.36; II.18.22; III.26.32; 22.57, 16.44; and IV.10.10. See also Seneca *Constant.* 2.1, *Benef.* 1.13.3; Aetius 1.15; Cicero *Fin.* 2.118, 3.66; *Tusc.* 1.32 De *Off.* 1.118, and 3.25. On Epictetus' portrayal of Heracles as an exemplum of selflessness, courage, and the successful suppression of desires, see Huttunen (2009, 136–139) and Montiglio (2011, 81); and in the wider Cynic-Stoic tradition, consider Desmond (2008, 153–154) and Montiglio (2011, 86).

112. Montiglio (2011, 2–12).

113. For example, see Barnouw (2004) Levystone (2005).

114. However, see a useful overview of Aristotle's critique of Odysseus and the reasons that motivated it at Montiglio (2011, 60–65).

115. For example, *Muson.* 9.6, Dio *Or.* 8.21; 15.330-332; 32.88; and 33.19-22. On the Stoic portrayal of Odysseus, see Montiglio (2011, 66–94).

116. See Montiglio (2011, 35–36).

117. *Constant.* 1.2, trans. Basore (1928, 51).

118. See especially *Diss.* IV.4.34-35, and also I.9.1-2; 25.19-20; and II.16.32.

119. See *Diss.* III.24.18-21.

120. *Diss.* III.24.9,12-13. See a similar statement from Dio at *Or.* 13.9-11, as well as the comments from Montiglio (2011, 84).

121. *Fr* 11: On his clothing in purple, see *Od.* 19.28, and see *Od.* 16-22 on Odysseus disguising himself as a beggar. The latter account, understandably, proved to be particularly appealing for Cynics, or Cynic-leaning authors; see De Jong (1998, 35–36), and Montiglio (2011, 69–73).

122. *Diss.* III.26.34-36.

123. See also comments from Montiglio (2011, 139).

124. For example, see the useful discussion in Dobbin (1998, 65).

125. *Diss.* I.12.3.

126. On the importance of this topic for Epictetus, see, for instance, *Diss.* I.3;14, and II.8.

127. Stephens (2002).

128. *Diss.* III.4.2-4.

129. *Diss.* III.7.33.

130. Pliny, *Paneg* 45.6, and Tacitus *Ann.* 3.55. Tsalla (2005, 119) comments: "That Epictetus understands leadership as care of the citizens is verified by [*Diss.*] 3.22.35—where Epictetus likens the position of a king to his citizens to that of a shepherd over his sheep."

131. *Mem.* 1.2.3, trans. Marchant (1923, 15).

132. Seneca, *Clem.* 2.2.1 trans. Kaster and Nussbaum (2010, 171).

133. *Diss.* I.2.22.

134. *Diss.* III.26.28: On this passage, Ierodiakonou (2007, 67, 68) comments: "Epictetus explicitly says in the *Discourses* that philosophers are sent by God as examples to the uninstructed . . . This is also the reason why Epictetus himself makes frequent use in his lectures of particular episodes taken from the lives of paradigmatic philosophers, like for instance Socrates or Diogenes; and he repeatedly stresses that they should be treated as examples for other men to follow."

135. *Diss.* III.13.22-23. A similar point might also be expressed at *Diss.* II.1.36-39, although at *Diss.* IV.8.17-20 Epictetus implies that this attitude should also be adopted by mature philosophers.

136. We can note that Jim Stockdale, an American Air Force officer who was held as a prisoner of war in Vietnam from 1965 to 1973, and who wrote an account about how the teachings of Epictetus had sustained him during his time in captivity, comments from his experience, Stockdale (1993, 19): "Did I preach these things [Stoic philosophy] in prison? Certainly not . . . You soon realized that when you dared to spout high-minded philosophical suggestions through the wall, you always got a very reluctant response. No, I never tapped or mentioned Stoicism once. But some sharp guys read the signs in my actions."

137. *Diss.* IV.11.22.

138. Lucian, *Herm.* 18.

139. *Diss.* III.24.113, 118. See also *Diss.* I.29.33, 46, 49.

140. See this explored expertly by Ierodiakonou (2007).

141. *Diss.* III.22.12, 68.

142. So see *Diss.* II.13.24 and IV.1.115-121.

143. Schofield (2007, 85), meanwhile, argues that for Epictetus: "He [the Cynic] makes philosophy compelling by exhibiting in the way he lives the moral truth that philosophy enables us to discover in the Cynic lifestyle . . . Diogenes' life gives him a special authority when it comes to protreptic—to getting people to *see* that and how we should care for our souls . . . His life *shows* us how things could be different, how empty are the commonly accepted valuation of things, and above all how happiness, is something entirely in our own hands" (emphasis his).

144. *Diss.* III.22.52, although as Griffin (1996, 204) has noted, in Epictetus' depictions of the Cynic: "impudence and immodesty have been removed, while just those qualities are retained that I have argued above would seem advantageous in the Roman context—concentration on practical instruction by example, eloquence, physical toughness, general austerity. The result is an ideal clearly admirable by Roman standards."

145. *Diss.* IV.8.31. See also *Diss.* III.22.45-46.

146. *Diss.* III.22.23.

147. See also *Diss.* I.24.7; III.22.26, 46-47, 49, 57-59, 66-68; and IV.8.30-31, as well as comments from Schofield (2007, 78, 82).

148. Brunt (2013, 104, 105) remarks: "Epictetus must have thought that the Cynic could convey truth to the masses who were incapable of comprehending the doctrines by which Stoics were persuaded that virtue is man's sole good, men who lacked leisure and intelligence to take the long and circuitous path of reason, which the pupils in Epictetus' own school were to follow . . . by his [the Cynics'] example who could teach others to do likewise." Note in particular that Schofield (2007, 84, 85) comments: "I suggest that what Epictetus offers us is something modern scholars have not by and large succeeded in producing: a deeply pondered interpretation of Cynicism which makes sense of Diogenes' philosophical project as philosophy, and which deserves serious consideration as a historically viable account of what he saw himself as doing . . . if our conception of philosophy has no room for the idea of protreptic as a philosophical project, then Epictetus' argument that the Cynic's paradigmatic life is

such a project will not be able to get a purchase on us. But here Epictetus' philosophical categories clearly have the historical edge over more restrictive modern rivals. Diogenes is above all a practitioner of the philosophical life. He makes philosophy compelling by exhibiting in the way he lives the moral truth that philosophy enables us to discover—in the Cynic lifestyle."

149. Regarding Epictetus' views of the exclusive nature of the Cynic's position, see MacGillivray (2020). On the Cynic's lack of engaging in widespread proselytism, see Goodman (1994, 33–37) and Bosman (2017) *passim*, but especially his brief remarks (at p. 44) that "his [Epictetus] ideal Cynic is a special case with a special calling to guide and correct humankind, but certainly not a model for any popular movement among the socially uneducated and unrefined."

150. On other Stoics who believe in the didactic ability of exempla for laypeople, see *Med.* 1.1-2, 6.48, *Ep.* 6.5-6, c.f. *Tusc.* 3.50, and *Arch* 6.14, and especially Strabo *Geog.* 1.2.3-8. Regarding *Med.* 6.30, Gill (2013b, 78) argues that "One implication is that Antonius acquired, without the support of philosophy, the kind of emotional stability attributed to the Stoic wise person and Socrates, who often served as an exemplar for the Stoic wise person." See also Sellars (2003, 31, n.82), and Reydams-Schils (2011, 321).

Conclusion and Suggestions for Future Research

Given that several distinct areas of research have been explored with some depth over the course of this book's discussion, I believe that it is worthwhile for me to recount the various conclusions that have been made, and to comment upon how they help to illuminate Epictetus' views of laypeople. In closing I will then comment upon some broader themes of relevance that emerge from this book, and propose areas where future research might be profitably directed.

In chapters 1–3, it was established that in antiquity philosophical identity was subjectively established on the basis of an individual's knowledge and praxis, that the affiliates of philosophical schools could exhibit in-group characteristics, and that Epictetus believed various factors compounded to render the majority of humanity philosophically unaware. Epictetus' concern that philosophical teaching should not be actively promoted to laypeople because of the futility and distracting nature of this goal, and the discouraging stance he adopted when he interacted with nonphilosophers were also documented.

While the above chapters reveal that Epictetus and the Stoics more broadly perceive that the differences between laypeople and philosophers are stark and difficult to ameliorate, in chapters 4–7 more positive sentiments are seen to be expressed within our source material. Firstly, the Stoics' understanding of primeval humanity, wherein it was seen that they believe early humans were able to act according to virtue not because of any epistemic or theoretical awareness, but because certain conditions and institutions induced them to behave in this way. Significantly, it was argued that the Stoics held that these mechanisms remained to some extent operational in their own societies.

Taking the above insight to the records of Epictetus' remarks, it was argued that he believes preconceptions, civic law, religion, and exempla can aid laypeople people to improve their moral awareness. Therefore, although we have seen that he is of the opinion that laypeople have substantial misapprehensions, that the surrounding society threatens to subvert his students' moral ambitions, and he never attempts to advance any theodicy to explain why such a large portion of humanity never move beyond their lay status, Epictetus decidedly does not hold that the vast majority of humanity who are unschooled by philosophy are left completely vulnerable to vice's advance. Through the abovementioned envisaged processes and institutions, he rather believes that at least some positive effect is being exerted on nonphilosophers' attitudes and patterns of behavior.

FURTHER KEY THEMES

I suggest that two broader points emerge from this book's discussion which merit highlighting. Firstly, its conclusions can be used to inform and extend the recent scholarly reappraisal of Epictetus' philosophy, which has highlighted his distinctive focus upon ordinary people. In particular his interpreters have observed that Epictetus directs his attention away from ruminating upon the flawless attributes of the likely nonexistent sage who had characterized the discourse of early generations of Stoics, to deliberate upon practical ethics and to exhort his students to make continual (although almost certainly faltering) moral improvement,[1] Furthermore, how Epictetus' theory of roles positions itself against prevailing Stoic doctrine by maintaining that goodness can be obtained by philosophically informed individuals in their "ordinary life" and without them having to master logical studies has been recently studied.[2] This book hopefully demonstrates that the horizons of Epictetus' awareness and consideration of average people and their circumstances extend much further than scholarship has apprehended until now.

Secondly, this book's conclusions confirm the suggestion which has been occasionally raised in passing by scholars that while the Stoics hold that their philosophy offers the clearest articulation of natural truths, they might believe these principles can be observed in ideas, customs, and figures which have no association with their school.[3] This book's conclusions, therefore, continue to clarify the context which accounts for the Stoic school's distinctive lack of interest in venerating their founding figures,[4] and their disclination to assign these individuals with unassailable authority or to maintain the conceit that they have explicated otherwise incomprehensible truths.[5]

FUTURE RESEARCH

As I noted at the start, there has been a distinct lack of attention in scholarship to consider the Stoics' views of laypeople, and it would be a missed opportunity were I not to briefly highlight where I believe future research on this topic might be beneficially expended. In particular I would anticipate that increased attention on this topic might clarify where Epictetus' perspective on laypeople might draw upon antecedents in Stoic thought, and perhaps disclose additional reflections from within the school on how nonphilosophers might come to apprehend or act according to aspects of natural truth. In this regard, reflecting upon the results of some already-existing work should prove profitable. For example, Linda Woodward's masterful dissertation upon Diogenes of Babylon's theory of music briefly explores his conviction that poetry and music can have a didactic effect even upon people who are uninformed about philosophy.[6] Likewise, Gregory A Staley's monograph on Seneca's views on drama reaches a conclusion regarding his belief of the impact it can have upon people, which appears to cohere with Epictetus' perspective regarding exempla.[7] In addition, although he does not frame it around laypeople, within John Schafer's book, which explores Seneca's views of precepts, he asserts that Seneca holds poetry and precepts can positively affect peoples' understanding, without them requiring arguments, evidence, or doctrinal exposition to be presented, which is a process that Schafer calls "mysterious." Schafer later reasons that Seneca must have held that precepts worked on a "pre-rational" basis, and by "incit[ing] our inborn propensity of goodness."[8] Such conclusions can, I suggest, be usefully explained by reference to the framework that has been delineated in this book, especially those within chapters 4 and 5.

NOTES

1. On the distinctive nature of Epictetus' focus upon practical ethics, see Gill (2012b, 41), and the references he cites at n.21. As Long (2002, 31–32, 33) astutely notes: "We hear nothing in the discourses [of Epictetus] about the 'equality' of all faults or the ignorance and misery of everyone who has failed to achieve infallible knowledge. . . . We might call his Stoicism an ethics of the interval between wisdom and its contrary, a philosophy for persons who are fallible but completely committed to doing the best they can to live as free, thoughtful, self-respecting, and devoted family members and citizens. . . . [Epictetus has a] gentleness and tolerance towards those who err." See also Johnson (2014, 76–79), who (p. 64) argues that Epictetus "downplays Stoic sages—relegating them to a kind of appendix." On Panaetius', an earlier Stoic philosopher, decision to pivot Stoic ethical teaching away from focusing upon the sage toward highlighting the concept of making moral progress, consider, for example, Griffin and Atkins (1991, 168).

2. See Johnson (2014, 63–84), who argues that Epictetus allows for appropriate acts (καθήκοντα) and not just perfect acts (κατορθώματα) to be considered good, and so posits that goodness can be gained by the nonsage. Johnson also argues that within Epictetus' tripartite system of education (e.g., see *Diss.* II.17.29-34, 3.2.1-6, and *Ench.* 52) he believes that learning the first two topics, namely (1) desire and

aversion and (2) appropriate action and roles, enables a person to be good and that the third topic, logic, should be subsequently learned by the student that if mastered with allow them to obtain (p. 69) "perfection and certainty" in their moral understanding and actions.

3. Aside from the remarks we noted at p. 88, consider also Gill's (2012b, 50) comments that the Stoics "do not distinguish between practical and intellectual wisdom in a way that is normal in Platonic-Aristotelian thought; their ideal of wisdom can embrace both aspect. . . . The role of philosophy is not to serve as the unique pathway to human perfection. Rather, philosophy analyses with the unique clarity—for instance—human progress towards ethical perfection, though, this process is not itself necessarily dependent on philosophy as its instrument."

4. On the difference between the Stoic and the Epicurean school in this regard, see Seneca *Ep.* 33.4 and Epictetus' comments at *Diss.* I.4.30 along with the insightful remarks of Inwood (2019, 161–162). See also the first-century BCE Epicurean philosopher Philodemus' statement at *On Frankness of Speech*, fr. 45.8-1, that "the fundamental and most vital principle is that we will obey Epicurus, according to whom we have chosen to live," πειθαρχήσομεν Ἐπικούρῳ, καθ' ὃν ζῆν ᾑρήμεθα, and the useful study by Clay (1986).

5. For more on this, consider the discussion at the opening of chapter 4 and consider the conclusions of Synder (2000) and Reydams-Schils (2011).

6. Woodward (2010, 218–219).

7. Staley (2010, 67–69, 90–95).

8. Schafer (2009, 17, 94, 108).

References

Ahlholm, Tuuli. 2017. "Philosophers in Stone: Philosophy and Self-Representation in Epigraphy of the Roman Empire." MPhil thesis, University of Oxford.

Ahonen, Marke. 2014. *Mental Disorders in Ancient Philosophy*. Berlin: Springer Verlag.

Algra, Keimpe. 2003. "Stoic Theology." In *The Cambridge Companion to the Stoics*, edited by Brad Inwood, 152–79. Cambridge: Cambridge University Press.

———. 2007a. *Conceptions and Images: Hellenistic Philosophical Theology and Traditional Religion*. Amsterdam: Koninklijke Nederlandse Akademie van Wetenschappen.

———. 2007b. "Epictetus and Stoic Theology." In *The Philosophy of Epictetus*, edited by Anthony Mason and Theodore Scaltas, 32–56. Oxford: Oxford University Press.

———. 2009. "Stoic Philosophical Theology and Graeco-Roman Religion." In *God and Cosmos in Stoicism*, edited by Ricardo Salles, 224–52. Oxford: Oxford University Press.

Annas, Julia. 2007. "Epictetus on Moral Perspectives." In *The Philosophy of Epictetus*, edited by Anthony Mason and Theodore Scaltas, 140–53. Oxford: Oxford University Press.

Armisen-Marchetti, Mireille. 2014. "Ontology and Epistemology." In *Brill's Companion to Seneca: Philosopher and Dramatist*, edited by Gregor Damschen and Andreas Heil, 217–38. Leiden: Brill.

Asmis, Elizabeth. 2015. "Seneca's Originality." In *The Cambridge Companion to Seneca*, edited by Shadi Bartsch and Alessandro Schiesaro, 224–38. Cambridge: Cambridge University Press.

Atkins, Jed W. 2013. *Cicero on Politics and the Limits of Reason: The Republic and Laws*. Cambridge: Cambridge University Press.

Babbit, Frank C. 1931. *Plutarch. Moralia Volume III LCL* 305. Cambridge, MA: Harvard University Press.

Baltzy, Dirk. 2014. "Plato's Authority and the Formation of Textual Communities." *Classical Quarterly* 64.2: 793–807.

Barchiesi, Alessandro. 2009. "Exemplarity: Between Practice and Text." In *Latinitas Perennis. Volume II: Appropriation and Latin Literature*, edited by Yanick Maes and Jan Papy, 41–64. Leiden: Brill.

Barnes, John. 1997. *Logic and the Imperial Stoa*. Leiden: Brill.

———. 2002. "Ancient Philosophers." In *Philosophy and Power in the Graeco-Roman World*, edited by Gillian Clark and Tessa Rajak, 293–306. Oxford: Oxford University Press.

Barnouw, Jeffrey. 2004. *Odysseus, Hero of Practical Intelligence: Deliberation and Signs in Homer's Odyssey*. Lanham, MD: University of America Press.

Bartoš, Hynek. 2015. *Philosophy and Dietetics in the Hippocratic On Regimen a Delicate Balance of Health*. Leiden: Brill.

Bartsch, Shadi. 2015. *Persius: A Study in Food, Philosophy, and the Figural*. Chicago: University of Chicago Press.

Basore, John W. 1928–1935. *Moral Essays, LCL*, three vols. Cambridge, MA: Harvard University Press.

Becker, Adam H. and Annette Y. Reed. 2003. *The Ways That Never Parted: Jews and Christians in Late Antiquity and the Early Middle Ages*. Tübingen: Mohr Siebeck.

Belliotti, Raymond A. 2009. *Roman Philosophy and the Good Life*. Lanham, Maryland: Lexington.

Bénatouïl, Thomas A. 2006. "Philosophic Schools in Hellenistic and Roman Times." In *A Companion to Ancient Philosophy: Blackwell Companions to the Ancient World*, edited by Mary L. Gill and Pierre Pellegrin, 415–29. Hoboken, New Jersey: Wiley-Blackwell.

———. 2013. "Theoria and Schole in Epictetus and Marcus Aurelius: Platonic, Stoic or Socratic?" In *Plato and the Stoics*, edited by Alex G. Long, 147–73. Cambridge: Cambridge University Press.

———. 2014. "The Stoic System: Ethics and Nature." In *The Routledge Companion to Ancient Philosophy*, edited by James Warren and Frisbee Sheffield, 423–37. London: Routledge.

Bendlin, Andreas. 2011. "On the Uses and Disadvantages of Divination: Oracles and Their Literary Representations in the Time of the Second Sophistic." In *The Religious History of the Roman Empire: Pagans, Jews, and Christians*, edited by. John A. North and Simon R. F. Price, 175–252. Oxford: Oxford University Press.

Beniston, Richard J. 2017. *Seneca's Natural Questions: Platonism, Physics, and Stoic Therapy in the First Century*. PhD Thesis, Durham University.

Bett, Richard. 2006. "Stoic Ethics." In *A Companion to Ancient Philosophy: Blackwell Companions to the Ancient World*, edited by Mary L. Gill and Pierre Pellegrin, 530–48. Hoboken, New Jersey: Wiley-Blackwell.

———. 2009. "Stoicism." In *Oxford Encyclopedia of Ancient Greece and Rome*, edited by Michael Gagarin, 389–95. Oxford: Oxford University Press.

Billerbeck, Margarethe. 1978. *Epiktet, vom Kynismus*. Leiden: Brill.

———. 1979. *Der Kyniker Demetrius: Ein Beitrag zur Geschichte der frühkaiserzeitlichen Popularphilosophie*. Leiden: Brill.

———. 1996. "The Ideal Cynic." In *The Cynics: The Cynic Movement in Antiquity and Its Legacy*, edited by R. Bracht Branham, 205–21. Berkeley: University of California Press.

Blankert, Samuel. 1940. "Seneca (Epist. 90) over Natuur en Cultuur en Posidonius als Zijn Bron." Diss. Amsterdam, Utrecht University.

Blom, Henriette Van Der. 2010. *Cicero's Role Models: The Political Strategy of a Newcomer*. Oxford: Oxford University Press.

Blundell, Sue. 1984. *The Origins of Civilization in Greek and Roman Thought*. London: Routledge.

Bobzien, Susan. 1998. *Determinism and Freedom in Stoic Philosophy*. Oxford: Oxford University Press.

Bonhöffer, Adolf F. 1996. *The Ethics of the Stoic Epictetus: An English Translation*. Trans William O. Stephens. New York: Peter Lang.

Booth, Alan D. 1979. "The Schooling of Slaves in First-Century Rome." *Transactions of the American Philological Association* 109: 11–19.

Bosman, Philip. 2010. "Utopia, Domestication and Special Status: Marriage and Family in the Stoic Tradition." *Acta Patristica et Byzantina* 21.2: 5–18.

———. 2017. "Ancient Cynicism: Elitist or for the Masses?" In *Mass and Elite in Antiquity*, edited by Richard J. Evans, 34–48. London: Routledge.

Boter, Gerard. 1999. *The Encheiridion of Epictetus and Its Three Christian Adaptations: Transmission and Critical Editions*. Leiden: Brill.

———. 2010. "Evaluating Others and Evaluating Oneself in Epictetus' Discourses." In *Valuing Others in Classical Antiquity*, edited by Ralph M. Rosen and Ineke Sluiter, 323–52. Leiden: Brill.

———. 2017. "From Discourses to Handbook: The Encheiridion of Epictetus as a Practical Guide to Life." In *Knowledge, Text and Practice in Ancient Technical Writing*, edited by Marco Formisano and Philip van der Eijk, 163–99. Cambridge: Cambridge University Press.

Bowden, Hugh. 2005. *Classical Athens and the Delphic Oracle: Divination and Democracy*. Cambridge: Cambridge University Press.

Bowersock, Glen W. 2002. "Philosophy in the Second Sophistic." In *Philosophy and Power in the Graeco-Roman World*, edited by Gillian Clark and Tessa Rajak, 157–70. Oxford: Oxford University Press.

Boyle, Anthony J. 2014. *Seneca: Medea Edited with Introduction, Translation, and Commentary*. Oxford: Oxford University Press.

Boys-Stones, George R. 2001. *Post-Hellenistic Philosophy: A Study of Its Development from the Stoics to Origen*. Oxford: Oxford University Press.

———. 2003. "The Stoics' Two Types of Allegory." In *Metaphor, Allegory and the Classical Tradition: Ancient Thought and Modern Revisions*, edited by George R. Boys-Stones, 189–216. Oxford: Oxford University Press.

———. 2007a. "Physiognomy and Ancient Psychological Theory." In *Seeing the Face, Seeing the Soul Polemon's Physiognomy from Classical Antiquity to Medieval Islam*, edited by Simon Swain, 121–53. Oxford: Oxford University Press.

———. 2007b. "Fallere Sollers. The Ethical Pedagogy of the Stoic Cornutus." In *Greek and Roman Philosophy, 100BC to 200AD*, edited by Richard Sorabji and Robert W. Sharples, 77–88. London: Institute of Classical Studies.

———. 2013. "Seneca against Plato: Letters 58 and 65." In *Plato and the Stoics*, edited by Alex G. Long, 128–46. Cambridge: Cambridge University Press.

———. 2018. *L. Annaeus Cornutus: Greek Theology, Fragments, and Testimonia: 42 (Writings from the Greco-Roman World)*. Atlanta, GA: SBL Press.

Braicovich, Rodrigo S. 2014. "On the Notion of Ethical Exercises in Epictetus." *Prometeus Filosofia* 7: 126–38.

Branham, R. Bratch. 2018. "Cynicism: Ancient and Modern." In *Diogenes Laertius. Lives of the Eminent Philosophers*, edited by James Miller, trans. Pamela Mensch, 597–602. Oxford: Oxford University Press.

Braund, Susan M. 1992. *Lucan's Civil War*. Oxford: Oxford University Press.

———. 2004. *Juvenal and Persius. Satires, LCL* 91. Cambridge, MA: Harvard University Press.

———. 2009. *De Clementia. Edited with Text, Translation, and Commentary*. Oxford: Oxford University Press.

Brennan, Tad. 2006. "Socrates and Epictetus." In *A Companion to Socrates: Blackwell Companions to the Ancient World*, edited by Sara Ahbel-Rappe and Rachana Kamtekar, 285–97. Hoboken, New Jersey: Wiley-Blackwell.

———. 2009a. "Stoic Souls in Stoic Corpses." In *Body and Soul in Ancient Philosophy*, edited by Dorothea Frede and Burkhard Reis, 389–408. Berlin: Walter De Gruyter.

———. 2009b. "The Stoics." In *Ancient Philosophy of Religion*, edited by Graham Oppy and Nick N. Trakakis, 105–17. Durham: Acumen.

Brittain, Charles. 2011. "Posidonius' Theory of Predictive Dreams." *Oxford Studies in Ancient Philosophy* 40: 213–36.

Brookins, Timothy A. 2014. *Corinthian Wisdom, Stoic Philosophy, and the Ancient Economy*. Cambridge: Cambridge University Press.

Brouwer, Rene. 2012. "Stoic Sympathy." Draft Paper, *Oxford Philosophical Concepts at the Jepson School of Leadership, University of Richmond*. Accessed November 8, 2018: <http://jepson.richmond.edu/conferences/sympathy2012/BrouwerStoic%20Sympathy.pdf>/.

———. 2014. *The Stoic Sage: The Early Stoics on Wisdom, Sagehood, and Socrates*. Cambridge: Cambridge University Press.

Brown, Malcolm K. 2002. *The Narratives of Konon: Text, Translation and Commentary on the Diegesis*. Berlin: Walter De Gruyter.

Brunt, Peter A. 1977. "From Epictetus to Arrian." *Athenaeum* 55: 19–48.

———. 2013. *Studies in Stoicism*. Edited by Michael H. Crawford, Miriam T. Griffin, and Alison Samuels. Oxford: Oxford University Press.

Buckler, John. 1993. "Epameinondas and Pythagoreanism." *Historia: Zeitschrift für alte Geschichte* 42.1: 104–8.

Caplan, Harold. 1954. *Rhetorica ad Herennium, LCL* 403. Cambridge, MA: Harvard University Press.

Carrier, Richard. 2016. *Science Education in the Early Roman Empire*. Charlottesville: Pitchstone Publishing.

Caspar, Timothy W. 2011. *Recovering the Ancient View of Founding: A Commentary on Cicero's De Legibus*. Lanham, MD: Lexington.

Celkyte, Aiste. 2018. "The Soul and Personal Identity in Early Stoicism: Two Theories." *Aperion*, pre-publication version, accessed August 6, 2018.

Chaplin, Jane D. 2009. *Livy's Exemplary History*. Oxford: Oxford University Press.

Cohoon, James W. and Lamar H. Crosby. 1940. *Dio Chrysostom Volume III Loeb Classical Library 358*. Cambridge, MA: Harvard University Press.

Colish, Marcia L. 2014. "Seneca on Acting against Conscience." In *Seneca Philosophus*, edited by Jula Wildberger and Maria L. Colish, 431–65. Berlin: De Grutyer.

Conradie, Irene M. 2010. *Seneca in his Cultural and Literary Context: Selected Moral Letters on the Body*. Utrecht: Zeno, the Leiden-Utrecht Research Institute of Philosophy.

Cooper, John M. 2004. *Knowledge, Nature, and the Good: Essays on Ancient Philosophy*. Princeton, NJ: Princeton University Press.

———. 2012. *Pursuits of Wisdom: Six Ways of Life in Ancient Philosophy from Socrates to Plotinus*. Princeton, NJ: Princeton University Press.

Cosans, Christopher E. 2000. "Facing Death Like a Stoic: Epictetus on Suicide in the Case of Illness." In *Bioethics: Ancient Themes in Contemporary Issues*, edited by Mark G. Kuczewski and Ronald M. Polansky, 229–49. Cambridge, MA: MIT Press.

Cosby, Michael R. 1988. *The Rhetorical Composition and Function of Hebrews 11: In Light of Example Lists in Antiquity*. Macon, GA: Mercer University Press.

Crabbe, James M. C. 1999. *From Soul to Self*. London: Routledge.

Cribiore, Raffaella. 2007. *The School of Libanius in Late Antique Antioch*. Princeton, NJ: Princeton University Press.

Cuany, Monique. 2015. "Ἄγνοια in Hellenistic Philosophy: Illuminating the Paradoxes of Athenian Ignorance (Acts 17:30)." Paper delivered at *the British New Testament Society Conference*, Edinburgh, copy forwarded to myself on request.

Curnow, Trevor. 2006. *The Philosophers of the Ancient World*. Bristol: Bristol Classical Press.

Damon, Cynthia. 1997. *The Mask of the Parasite: A Pathology of Roman Patronage*. Ann Arbor: University of Michigan Press.

De Jong, Irene J. F. 1998. *Homer: Critical Assessments*. London: Routledge.

De Lacy, Philip H. 1977. "The Four Stoic Personae." *Illinois Classical Studies* 2: 163–72.

Desmond, William D. 2008. *Cynics*. Durham: Acumen.

———. 2009. "Low Philosophy." In *The Oxford Handbook of Hellenistic Studies*, edited by Boys-Stones George, Barbara Graziosi, and Phiroze Vasunia, 518–29. Oxford: Oxford University Press.

Dillon, John. 1981. "A Review of J. Glucker's '*Antiochus* and the Late Academy.'" *The Classical Review* 31: 60–62.

———. 1982. "Self-Definition in Later Platonism." In *Self-Definition in the Graeco-Roman World*, edited by Benjamin F. Meyer and Ed P. Sanders, 60–75. Philadelphia: Fortress Press.

———. 2002. "The Social Role of the Philosopher in the Second Century C.E.: Some Remarks." In *Sage and Emperor: Plutarch, Greek Intellectuals, and the Roman Power in the Time of Trajan (98-117A.D.)*, edited by Philip A. Stadter and Luc Van Der Stockt, 29–40. Leiden: Leuven University Press.

————. 2004. "Philosophy as a Profession in Late Antiquity." In *Approaching Late Antiquity*, edited by Simon Swain and Mark Edwards, 401–18. Oxford: Oxford University Press.

————. 2008. "The Essenes in Greek Sources: Some Reflections." In *Jews in Hellenistic and Roman Cities*, edited by John R. Bartlett, 117–28. London: Routledge.

Dobbin, Robbin. 1998. *Discourses Book 1: Claredon Later Ancient Philosophers*. Oxford: Oxford University Press.

Donaldson, Terence L. 2007. *Judaism and the Gentiles: Jewish Patterns of Universalism (to 135 CE)*. Waco, TX: Baylor University Press.

Donini, Pierluigi. 1999. "Stoic Ethics." In *The Cambridge History of Hellenistic Philosophy*, edited by Algra Keimpe, John Barnes, Jaap Mansfeld, and Malcolm Schofield, 675–738. Cambridge: Cambridge University Press.

————. 2011. "The History of the Concept of Eclecticism." In *Commentary and Tradition: Aristotelianism, Platonism, and Post-Hellenistic Philosophy*, edited by Mauro Bonazzi, 197–210. Berlin: Walter de Gruyter.

Dorandi, Tiziano. 1999. "Organisation and Structure of the Philosophical Schools." In *The Cambridge History of Hellenistic Philosophy*, edited by Jonathan Barnes and Malcolm Schofield, 54–62. Cambridge: Cambridge University Press.

Doyle, James. 2012. "Socratic Methods." *Oxford Studies in Ancient Philosophy* 42.2: 39–75.

Dunn, James D. G. 2009. *Beginning from Jerusalem*. Grand Rapids, MI: William B. Eerdmans Publishers.

Dunson, Benjamin. 2012. *Individual and Community in Paul's Letter to the Romans*. Berlin: De Grutyer.

Dupont, Florence. 2017. "Comédies et conférences Le spectacle de la philosophia." In *Philosophari Usages romains des savoirs grecs sous la République et sous l'Empire*, edited by Pierre Vesperini, 153–82. Paris: Classiques Garnier.

Dyson, Henry. 2009. *Prolepsis and Ennoia in the Early Stoa*. Berlin: Walter De Gruyter.

Edwards, Catharine. 1993. *The Politics of Immorality in Ancient Rome*. Cambridge: Cambridge University Press.

————. 1999. "The Suffering Body: Philosophy and Pain in Seneca's Letters." In *Constructions of the Classical Body*, edited by James I. Porter, 252–68. Ann Arbor: University of Michigan Press.

————. 2015. "Absent Presence in Seneca's *Epistles*: Philosophy and Friendship." In *The Cambridge Companion to Seneca*, edited by Shadi Barstch and Alessandro Schiesaro, 41–53. Cambridge: Cambridge University Press.

Edwards, Mark J. 1988. "Scenes from the Later Wanderings of Odysseus." *The Classical Quarterly* 38.2: 509–21.

————. 2012. "Religion in the Age of Marcus Aurelius." In *A Companion to Marcus Aurelius*, edited by Marcel Van Ackeren, 200–16. Chichester: Blackwell-Wiley.

Engberg-Pedersen, Troels. 2010a. "Setting the Scene: Stoicism and Platonism in the Transitional Period in Ancient Philosophy." In *Stoicism in Early Christianity*, edited by Tuomas Rasimus, Troels Engberg-Pedersen, and Ismo Dunderberg, 1–14. Grand Rapids: Baker Academic.

———. 2010b. *Cosmology and Self in the Apostle Paul: The Material Spirit*. Oxford: Oxford University Press.

Eshleman, Kendra. 2012. *The Social World of Intellectuals in the Roman Empire: Sophists, Philosophers, and Christians*. Cambridge: Cambridge University Press.

Esler, Philip F. 2003. *Conflict and Identity in Romans: The Social Setting of Paul's Letter*. Philadelphia: Fortress Press.

———. 2014. "An Outline of Social Identity Theory." In *T&T Clark Handbook to Social Identity in the New Testament*, edited by J. Brian Tucker and Coleman A. Baker, 13–39. London: Bloomsbury.

Fairclough, H. Rushton. 1926. *Horace. Satires. Epistles. The Art of Poetry, LCL* 194. Cambridge, MA: Harvard University Press.

Falconer, William A. 1932. *On Old Age. On Friendship. On Divination, LCL* 154. Cambridge, MA: Harvard University Press.

Fantham, Elaine H. M. 1982. *Seneca's Troades: A Literary Introduction with Text, Translation, and Commentary*. Princeton, NJ: Princeton University Press.

———. 2010. *Selected Letters*. Oxford: Oxford University Press.

Fantham, Elaine, Harry M. Hine, James Ker, and Gareth D. Williams. 2014. *Hardship and Happiness Hardship and Happiness. The Complete Works of Lucius Annaeus Seneca*. Chicago: Chicago University Press.

Fink, Jakob L. 2012. "Introduction." In *The Development of Dialectic From Plato to Aristotle*, edited by Jakob L. Fink, 1–23. Cambridge: Cambridge University Press.

Fiore, Benjamin. 1986. *The Function of Personal Example in the Socratic and Pastoral Epistles*. Rome: Biblical Institute.

Fisher, Jeffrey J. 2014. "Epictetus's Moral Epistemology." In *Epictetus: His Continuing Influence and Contemporary Relevance*, edited by Dane R. Gordon and David B. Suits, 77–88. New York: RIT Press.

Fitch, John G. 2002. *Seneca, Tragedies Volume I LCL* 62. Cambridge, MA: Harvard University Press.

Fitzgerald, John T., editor. 2008. *Passions and Moral Progress in Greco-Roman Thought*. London: Routledge.

———. 2013. "Greco-Roman Philosophical Schools." In *The World of the New Testament: Cultural, Social, and Historical Contexts*, edited by Joel B. Green and Lee M. McDonald, 135–48. Michigan: Baker Publishing.

Fontenrose, Joseph E. 1978. *The Delphic Oracle, Its Responses and Operations, with a Catalogue of Responses*. Berkeley: University of California Press.

Frede, Dorothy. 2001. "Theodicy and Providential Care in Stoicism." In *Traditions of Theology: Studies in Hellenistic Theology, Its Background and Aftermath*, edited by Dorothy Frede and André Laks, 85–117. Leiden: Brill.

Frede, Michael. 1999. "Epilogue." In *The Cambridge History of Hellenistic Philosophy*, edited by Keimpe Algra, Jonathan Barnes, Jaap Mansfeld, and Malcolm Schofield, 771–97. Cambridge: Cambridge University Press.

———. 2007. "A Notion of a Person Epictetus." In *The Philosophy of Epictetus*, edited by Theodore S. Scaltsas and Andrew S. Mason, 153–68. Oxford: Oxford University Press.

Frede, Michael and Anthony A. Long. 2011. *A Free Will: Origins of the Notion in Ancient Thought*. Berkeley: University of California Press.

Gill, Christopher. 1988. "Personhood and Personality: The Four-Personae Theory in Cicero *De Officiis* 1." *Oxford Studies in Ancient Philosophy* 6: 169–99.

———. 1990. "The Human Being as an Ethical Norm." In *The Person and the Human Mind: Issues in Ancient and Modern Philosophy*, edited by Christopher Gill, 137–61. Oxford: Oxford University Press.

———. 1994. "Peace of Mind and Being Yourself: Panaetius to Plutarch." In *ANRW* II.36.7, 459–640. Berlin: Walter De Gruyter.

———. 2004. "The Stoic Theory of Ethical Development: In What Sense Is Nature a Norm?" In *Was ist das für den Menschen Gute?/ What Is Good for a Human Being?* edited by Jan Szaif and Matthias Lutz-Bachmann Berlin, 101–25. Walter De Gruyter.

———. 2005. "Stoic Writers of the Imperial Era." In *The Cambridge History of Greek and Roman Politcal Thought*, edited by Malcolm Schofield, 597–615. Cambridge: Cambridge University Press.

———. 2006. *The Structured Self in Hellenistic and Roman Thought*. Oxford: Oxford University Press.

———. 2007a. "Marcus Aurelius." In *Greek and Roman Philosophy, 100 BC-100 AD*, edited by Richard Sorabji and Robert W. Sharples, 175–87. London: Institute of Classical Studies.

———. 2007b. "Marcus Aurelius' Meditations: How Stoic and How Platonic?" In *Platonic Stoicism-Stoic Platonism: The Dialogue between Platonism and Stoicism in Antiquity*, edited by Mauro Bonazzi and Christoph Helmig, 189–207. Leuven: Leuven University Press.

———. 2008. "The Ancient Self: Issues and Approaches." In *Ancient Philosophy of the Self*, edited by Pauliina Remes and Juha Sihvola, 35–56. New York: Springer.

———. 2012a. "Marcus and Previous Stoic Literature." In *A Companion to Marcus Aurelius: Blackwell Companions to the Ancient World*, edited by Marcel Van Ackeren, 382–95. London: Wiley-Blackwell.

———. 2012b. "Marcus Aurelius: Philosophy and the Rest of Life." In *Selbstbetrachtungen und Selbstdarstellungen – Meditations and Representations: Der Philosoph und Kaiser Marc Aurel im interdisziplinären Licht*, edited by Marcel Van Ackeren and Jan Opsomer, 35–64. Wiesbaden: Reichert Verlag Wiesbaden.

———. 2013. *Meditations, Books 1–6: Translated with an Introduction and Commentary*. Oxford: Oxford University Press.

Gill, Christopher and Robin Hard. 1995. *The Discourses, the Handbook, Fragments*. London: Everyman.

Girdwood, Allan B. 1998. "Innovation and Development in the Psychology and Epistemology of Epictetus." PhD thesis, Oxford University.

Gloyn, Elizabeth. 2014. "My Family Tree Goes Back to the Romans: Seneca's Approach to the Family in the *Epistulae Morales*." In *Seneca Philosophus*, edited by Jula Wildberger and Marcia L. Colish, 229–68. Berlin: De Grutyer.

Glucker, John. 1978. *Antiochus and the Late Academy*. Göttingen: Vandenhoeck und Ruprecht Verlag.

Goodman, Martin. 1994. *Mission and Conversion: Proselytizing in the Religious History of the Roman Empire*. Oxford: Oxford University Press.

Gould, Josiah B. 1970. *The Philosophy of Chrysippus*. Albany: SUNY Press.

Goulet, Richard. 2013. "Ancient Philosophers: A First Statistical Survey." In *Philosophy as a Way of Life: Ancient and Moderns. Essays in Honor of Pierre Hadot*, edited by Michael Chase and Stephen R. L. Clark, 10–39. Chichester: Blackwell-Wiley.

Goulet-Cazé, Marie-Odile. 2019. *Cynicism and Christianity in Antiquity*. Grand Rapids: Eerdmans.

Gourinat, Jean-Baptiste and Jonathan Barnes. 2009. *Lire les Stoïciens*. Paris: Presses Universitaires De France.

———. 2012. "Was Marcus Aurelius a Philosopher?" In *Selbstbetrachtungen und Selbstdarstellungen – Meditations and Representations: Der Philosoph und Kaiser Marc Aurel im interdisziplinären Licht*, edited by Marcel Van Ackeren and Jan Opsomer, 65–85. Wiesbaden: Reichert Verlag Wiesbaden.

Gowers, Emily. 1993. *The Loaded Table: Representations of Food in Roman Literature*. Oxford: Oxford University Press.

Graver, Margaret. 2012. "Cicero and the Perverse: The Origins of Error in *De Legibus* 1 and *Tusculan Disputations* 3." In *Cicero's Practical Philosophy*, edited by Walter Nicgorski, 113–32. Notre Dame, IN: University of Notre Dame Press.

———. 2015. "The Emotional Intelligence of Epicureans: Doctrinalism and Adaptation in Seneca's *Epistles*." In *Roman Reflections: Studies in Latin Philosophy*, edited by Gareth D. Williams and Katharina Volk, 192–210. Oxford: Oxford University Press.

Griffin, Miriam T. 1996. "Cynicism and the Romans: Attraction and Repulsion." In *The Cynics: The Cynic Movement in Antiquity and Its Legacy*, edited by R. Bracht Branham and Marie-Odile Goulet-Cazé, 190–204. Berkeley: University of California Press.

———. 2013. *Seneca on Society: A Guide to De Beneficiis*. Oxford: Oxford University Press.

Griffiths, John G. 1958. "Did Hesiod Invent the Golden Age." *Journal of the History of Ideas* 19.1: 91–3.

Gruen, Erich. 2011. *Rethinking the Other in Antiquity*. Princeton, NJ: Princeton University Press.

Gummere, Richard M. 1917–1925. *Seneca. Epistles, LCL*, 75–77. Cambridge, MA: Harvard University Press.

Haake, Matthias. 2015. "Philosophical Schools in Athenian Society from the Fourth to the First Century BC: An Overview." In *Private Associations and the Public Sphere. Proceedings of a Symposium held at the Royal Danish Academy of Sciences and Letters, 9–11 September 2010*, edited by V. Gabrielsen and C. A. Thomsen, 57–91. Copenhagen: Det Kongelige Danske Videnskabernes Selskab.

Hadas, Moses. 1951. *Aristeas to Philocrates: Letter of Aristeas*. New York: Harper.

Hadot, Ilsetraut. 2014. "Getting to Goodness: Reflections on Chapter 10 of Brad Inwood, 'Reading Seneca.'" In *Seneca Philosophus*, edited by Jula Wildberger and Marcia L. Colish, 9–41. Berlin: De Grutyer.

Hadot, Pierre. 1987. "Theologie, Exegese, Revelation, Ecriture, dans la Philosophic Grecque." In *Les regies de l'interpretation*, edited by Michel Tardieu, 13–34. Paris: Le Cerf.

————. 1995. *Philosophy as a Way of Life: Spiritual Exercises from Socrates to Foucault*. London: Wiley-Blackwell.

————. 1998. *The Inner Citadel: The Meditations of Marcus Aurelius*. Cambridge, MA: Harvard University Press.

————. 2002. *What Is Ancient Philosophy?* Cambridge, MA: Harvard University Press.

Hagland, Benedicte. 2010. "Formation and Function of Stoic Conceptions." Ann Harbour, UMI Dissertation.

Hahn, Johannes. 1989. *Der Philosoph und die Gesellschaft: Selbstverständnis, öffentliches Auftreten und populäre Erwartungen in der hohen Kaiserzeit*. Stuttgart: Franz Steiner Verlag.

Hankinson, Robert J. 1988. "Stoicism, Science and Divination." *Apeiron* 21.2: 123–60.

Hard, Robin. 2012. *Diogenes of Sinope. Sayings and Anecdotes with Other Popular Moralists*. Oxford: Oxford University Press.

Hard, Robin and Christopher Gill. 2011. *Marcus Aurelius. Meditations: With Selected Correspondence*. Oxford: Oxford University Press.

————. 2014. *Discourses, Fragments, Handbook*. Oxford: Oxford University Press.

Harmon, Alan M. 1913. *The Works of Lucian, LCL* 14. Cambridge, MA: Harvard University Press.

Harvey, Graham. 1996. *The True Israel: Uses of the Names Jew, Hebrew, and Israel in Ancient Jewish and Early Christian Literature*. Leiden: Brill.

Hatzimichali, Mytro. 2011. *Potamo of Alexandria and the Emergence of Eclecticism in Late Hellenistic Philosophy*. Cambridge: Cambridge University Press.

Hayes, Christine. 2015. *What's Divine about Divine Law?: Early Perspectives*. Princeton, NJ: Princeton University Press.

Helmig, Christoph and Mauro Bonazzi. 2007. *Platonic Stoicism: The Dialogue between Platonism and Stoicism in Antiquity*. Leuven: Leuven University Press.

Henten, Jan W. Van and Friedrich Avemarie. 2002. *Martyrdom and Noble Death: Selected Texts from Graeco-Roman, Jewish, and Christian Antiquity*. London: Routledge.

Hicks, Robert D. 1925. *Diogenes Laertius. The Lives of Eminent Philosophers, Volume II: Books 6–10, LCL* 185. Cambridge, MA: Harvard University Press.

Hijmans, Benjamin L. 1959. *Askesis: Notes on Epictetus' Educational System*. Assen: Van Gorcum.

Hill, Timothy. 2004. *Ambitiosa Mors: Suicide and the Self in Roman Thought and Literature*. London: Routledge.

Hilton, Alan. 2018. *Illiterate Apostles Uneducated Early Christians and the Literates Who Loved Them*. The Library of New Testament Studies. London: Bloomsbury.

Hine, Harry M. 1981. *Natural Questions, Book Two: An Edition with Commentary of Seneca*. New York: Arno.

————. 2010. *Natural Questions. The Complete Works of Lucius Annaeus Seneca*. Chicago: Chicago University Press.

————. 2015. "Philosophy and *Philosophi*: From Cicero to Apuleius." In *Roman Reflections: Studies in Latin Philosophy*, edited by Gareth D. Williams and Katharina Volk, 13–29. Oxford: Oxford University Press.

Hock, Ronald F. 1992. "By the Gods, It's My One Desire to See an Actual Stoic': Epictetus' Relations with Students and Visitors in His Personal Network." *Semeia* 52: 121–42.

Hoof, Lieve V. 2010. *Plutarch's Practical Ethics: The Social Dynamics of Philosophy*. Oxford: Oxford University Press.

Horster, Marietta and Christiane Reitz. 2011. *Condensing Texts, Condensed Texts*. Stuttgart: Franz Steiner Verlag.

Huttunen, Niko. 2007. "Stoalaisfilosofi Epiktetoksen Näkemys Kristityistä." *Teologinen Aikakauskirja* 112: 387–403.

———. 2009. *Paul and Epictetus on Law: A Comparison*. London: T & T Clark.

Ierodiakonou, Katerina. 2007. "The Philosopher as God's Messenger." In *The Philosophy of Epictetus*, edited by Andrew Mason and Theodore Scaltas, 56–70. Oxford: Oxford University Press.

———. 2014. "The Stoic System: Logic and Knowledge." In *Routledge Companion to Ancient Philosophy*, edited by James Warren and Frisbee Sheffield, 438–54. London: Routledge.

Incigneri, Brian J. 2003. *The Gospel to the Romans: The Setting and Rhetoric of Mark's Gospel*. Leiden: Brill.

Inwood, Brad. 1985. *Ethics and Human Action in Early Stoicism*. Oxford: Oxford University Press.

———. 2001. "God and Human Knowledge in Seneca's Natural Questions." In *Traditions of Theology: Studies in Hellenistic Theology, Its Background and Aftermath*, edited by Dorothy Frede and André Laks, 119–57. Leiden: Brill.

———. 2005. *Reading Seneca: Stoic Philosophy at Rome*. Oxford: Oxford University Press.

———. 2007. *Seneca: Selected Philosophical Letters*. Oxford: Oxford University Press.

———. 2009. "Why Physics." In *God & Cosmos in Stoicism*, edited by Ricardo Salles, 201–23. Oxford: Oxford University Press.

———. 2018. *Stoicism: A Very Short Introduction*. Oxford: Oxford University Press.

———. 2019. "The Pitfalls of Perfection Stoicism for Non-Sages." *Politeia* 1.4: 148–82.

Jackson-McCabe, Matt. 2004. "The Stoic Theory of Implanted Preconceptions." *Phronesis* 49.4: 323–47.

Jaegar, Werner. 1945. *Paideia: The Ideals of Greek Culture*, vol. 3. Oxford: Blackwell.

Jedan, Christoph. 2009. *Stoic Virtues: Chrysippus and the Religious Character of Stoic Ethics*. London: Continuum.

Jenkins, Richard. 1994. "Rethinking Ethnicity: Identity, Categorization and Power." *Ethnic and Racial Studies* 17.2: 197–223.

Johnson, Brian E. 2012a. "Ethical Roles in Epictetus." *Epoché* 16.2: 287–316.

———. 2012b. "Socrates, Heracles and the Deflation of Roles in Epictetus." *Ancient Philosophy* 32.1: 125–45.

———. 2014. *The Role Ethics of Epictetus: Stoicism in Ordinary Life*. Lanham: Lexington.

Johnson, Luke T. 2009. *Among the Gentiles: Greco-Roman Religion and Christianity*. New Haven: Yale University Press.

Johnson, William A. 2010. *Readers and Reading Culture in the High Roman Empire A Study of Elite Communities*. Oxford: Oxford University Press.

Jones, Madeleine. 2014. "Seneca's *Letters to Lucilius*: Hypocrisy as a Way of Life." In *Seneca Philosophus*, edited by Jula Wildberger and Marcia L. Colish, 393–429. Berlin: De Grutyer.

Judge, Edwin A. 2012. "What Makes A Philosophical School?" In *New Documents Illustrating Early Christianity Vol. 10*, edited by S. R. Llewelyn, James R. Harrison, and Edward J. Bridge, 1–5. Grand Rapids: Eerdmans.

Kamtekar, Rachana. 1998. "*Aidos* in Epictetus." *Classical Philology* 93.2: 136–60.

Kaster, Robert A. and Martha C. Nussbaum. 2010. *Lucius Annaeus Seneca. Anger, Mercy*. Chicago: University of Chicago Press.

King, J. E. 1927. *Tusculan Disputations, LCL* 141. John E. King. Cambridge, MA: Harvard University Press.

King, Cynthia. 2011. *Musonius Rufus, Lectures and Sayings*. Charleston, SC: CreateSpace.

Klein, Jacob. 2012. "Stoic *Eudaimonism* and the Natural Law Tradition." In *Reason, Religion, and Natural Law: From Plato to Spinoza*, edited by Jonathan A. Jacobs, 57–80. Oxford: Oxford University Press.

Korstange, Ryan. 2018. "Intellectual Virtue and the Non-Sage in Stoicism." In *The Bright and the Good: The Connection between Intellectual and Moral Virtues*, edited by Audrey L. Anton, 77–90. Lanham, Maryland: Rowman & Littlefield International.

Kraus, Thomas J. 1999. "'Uneducated', 'Ignorant', or Even 'Illiterate'? Aspects and Background for an Understanding of ΑΓΡΑΜΜΑΤΟΙ (and ΙΔΙΩΤΑΙ) in *Acts* 4.13." *New Testament Studies* 45.3: 434–49.

Langlands, Rebecca. 2011. "Roman Exempla and Situation Ethics: Valerius Maximus and Cicero *De Officiis*." *Journal of Roman Studies* 101: 100–22.

Lauwers, Jeroen. 2013. "Systems of Sophistry and Philosophy: The Case of the Second Sophistic." *Harvard Studies in Classical Philology* 107: 331–63.

———. 2015. *Philosophy, Rhetoric, and Sophistry in the High Roman Empire*. Leiden: Brill.

Lee, Desmond P. 1936. *Zeno of Elea: A Text with Translation and Notes*. Cambridge: Cambridge University Press.

Lefèvre, Eckard. 2001. *Panaitios' und Ciceros Pflichtenlehre: vom philosophischen Traktat zum politischen Lehrbuch*. Stuttgart: F. Steiner.

Lévystone, David. 2005. "La figure d'Ulysse chez les Socratiques: Socrate *polutropos*." *Phronesis* 50.3: 181–214.

Lipsey, Roger. 2001. *Have You Been to Delphi?: Tales of the Ancient Oracle for Modern Minds*. Albany: State University of New York Press.

Long, Anthony A. 1968. "The Stoic Concept of Evil." *Philosophical Quarterly* 18.73: 329–43.

———. 1974. *Hellenistic Philosophy; Stoics, Epicureans, Sceptics*. New York: Scribner.

———. 1996. *Stoic Studies*. Cambridge: Cambridge University Press.

————. 2002. *Epictetus: A Stoic and Socratic Guide to Life*. Oxford: Oxford University Press.

————. 2003. "Roman Philosophy." In *The Cambridge Companion to Greek and Roman Philosophy*, edited by David N. Sedley, 184–210. Cambridge: Cambridge University Press.

————. 2009. "Seneca on the Self: Why Now?" In *Seneca and the Self*, edited by Shadi Bartsch and David Wray, 20–36. Cambridge: Cambridge University Press.

————. 2013a. "Friendship and Friends in the Stoic Theory of the Good Life." In *Thinking About Friendship: Historical and Contemporary Philosophical Perspectives*, edited by Damian Calnori, 218–40. Basingstoke: Palgrave Macmillan.

————. 2017. "Seneca and Epictetus on Body, Mind and Dualism." In *From Stoicism to Platonism: The Development of Philosophy, 100 BCE- 100 CE*, edited by Troels Engberg-Pedersen, 214–30. Cambridge: Cambridge University Press.

————. 2018. "Zeno of Citium: Cynic Founder of the Stoic Tradition." In *Diogenes Laertius. Lives of the Eminent Philosophers*, edited by James Miller, trans. Pamela Mensch, 603–9. Oxford: Oxford University Press.

Long, Alex G., editor. 2013b. *Plato and the Stoics*. Cambridge: Cambridge University Press.

————. 2019. *Death and Immortality in Ancient Philosophy*. Cambridge: Cambridge University Press.

Long, Anthony A. and David N. Sedley, editors. 1987. *The Hellenistic Philosophers*, two vols. Cambridge: Cambridge University Press.

Lovejoy, Arthur O. and George Boas. 1935. *Primitivism and Related Ideas in Antiquity*. New York: Octagon.

MacGillivray, Erlend D. 2009. "Re-evaluating Patronage and Reciprocity in Antiquity and New Testament Studies." *Journal of Greco-Roman Christianity and Judaism* 6: 37–81.

————. 2012. "The Popularity of Epicureanism in Elite Late-Republican Roman Society." *The Ancient World* 43: 151–72.

————. 2015. "Philosophical Epitomes and the Critique of Epicurean Popularizers." *Journal of Ancient History* 3.1: 22–55 (based on 2010 Master's thesis: *Epicurean Mission and Membership from Early Garden to the Late-Roman Republic*).

————. 2016. "Fall Narratives in Classical Stoicism." In *Fall Narratives: An Interdisciplinary Perspective*, edited by Aine Larkin and Zohar Hadromi-Allouche, 51–62. Farnham: Ashgate Publishers.

————. 2019. "Reassessing Epictetus' Opinion of Divination." *Apeiron: A Journal for Ancient Philosophy and Science*, published online, ahead of publication.

————. 2020. "The Stoics and the Cynic Shortcut." *Classical Quarterly* (forthcoming).

MacMillan, Duane J. 1979. *The Stoic Strain in American Literature*. Toronto: University of Toronto Press.

Mann, Wolfgang-Rainer. 2011. "On Two Stoic 'Paradoxes' in Manilius." In *Forgotten Stars: Rediscovering Manilius' Astronomica*, edited by Steven Green and Katharina Volk, 85–103. Oxford: Oxford University Press.

————. 2015. "'You're Playing You Now': Helvidius Priscus as a Stoic Hero." In *Roman Reflections: Studies in Latin Philosophy*, edited by Gareth D. Williams and Katharina Volk, 213–37. Oxford: Oxford University Press.

Mansfeld, Jaap. 1983. "Zeno and Aristotle On Mixture." *Mnemosyne* 36.1: 306–10.

———. 1988. "Philosophy in Service of Scripture: Philo's Exegetical Strategies." In *The Question of Eclecticism Studies in Later Greek Philosophy*, edited by Anthony A. Long and John M. Dillon, 70–102. Berkeley: University Press of California.

Marchant, Edgar C. 1923. *Xenophon, Memorabilia. Oeconomicus. Symposium. Apology LCL* 168. Cambridge, MA: Harvard University Press.

Martin, Dale B. 2004. *Inventing Superstition: From the Hippocratics to the Christians*. Cambridge, MA: Harvard University Press.

Mason, Andrew S. 2007. "Introduction." In *The Philosophy of Epictetus*, edited by Theodore Scaltsas and Andrew S. Mason, 1–8. Oxford: Oxford University Press.

Matheson, Percy E. 1916. *The Discourses and Manual, Together with Fragments of his Writings*. Oxford: Oxford University Press.

Mattern, Susan P. 2013. *The Prince of Medicine: Galen and the Roman Empire*. Oxford: Oxford University Press.

Maxwell, Jaclyn L. 2006. *Christianization and Communication in Late Antiquity: John Chrysostom and His Congregation in Antioch*. Cambridge: Cambridge University Press.

Mayer, Ronald G. 1991. "Roman Historical Exempla in Seneca." In *Sénèque at la Prose Latine*, edited by Pierre Grimal, 141–69. Vancouver: Fondation Hardt.

McCabe, Mary M. 2013. "The Stoic Sage in the Original Position." In *Politeia in Greek and Roman Philosophy*, edited by Verity Harte and Melissa Lane, 251–74. Cambridge: Cambridge University Press.

Mehl, David. 2002. "The Stoic Paradoxes According to Cicero." In *Vertis in Usum: Studies in Honor of Edward Courtney*, edited by John F. Miller, Cynthia Damon, and K. Sara Myers, 39–46. Berlin: De Gruyter.

Meinwald, Constance. 2011. "Two Notions of Consent." *Oxford Studies in Ancient Philosophy* 50: 361–80.

Méndez-Moratalla, Fernando. 2004. *The Paradigm of Conversion in Luke*. London: Bloomsbury.

Mikalson, Jon D. 2010. *Greek Popular Religion in Greek Philosophy*. Oxford: Oxford University Press.

Millar, Fergus. 1965. "Epictetus and the Imperial Court." *Journal of Roman Studies* 55: 141–8.

Millet, Paul. 1988. "Encounters in the Agora." In *Kosmos: Essays in Order, Conflict and Community in Classical Athens*, edited by Paul Cartledge, Paul Millet and Sitta von Reden, 203–28. Cambridge: Cambridge University Press.

Montiglio, Silvia. 2005. *Wandering in Ancient Greek Culture*. Cambridge: Cambridge University Press.

———. 2011. *From Villain to Hero: Odysseus in Ancient Thought*. Ann Arbor: University of Michigan Press.

Morford, Mark P. O. 2002. *The Roman Philosophers: From the Time of Caro the Censor to the Death of Marcus Aurelius*. London: Routledge.

Morgan, Tessa. 2007. *Popular Morality in the Early Roman Empire*. Cambridge: Cambridge University Press.

Newmyer, Stephen T. 2011. *Animals in Greek and Roman Thought: A Sourcebook.* London: Routledge.

Nguyen, V. Henry. 2008. *Christian Identity in Corinth: A Comparative Study of 2 Corinthians, Epictetus, and Valerius Maximus.* Tübingen: Mohr Siebeck.

Niehoff, Maren R. 2012. "Philo and Plutarch on Homer." In *Homer and the Bible in the Eyes of Ancient Interpreters*, edited by Maren R. Niehoff, 127–53. Leiden: Brill.

Nock, Arthur D. 1933. *Conversion: The Old and the New in Religion from Alexander the Great to Augustine of Hippo.* Oxford: Oxford University Press.

Nussbaum, Martha C. 1994. *The Therapy of Desire: Theory and Practice in Hellenistic Ethics.* Princeton, NJ: Princeton University Press.

Oakes, Peter. 1993. "Epictetus (And the New Testament)." *Vox Evangelica* 23: 39–56.

Okell, Eleanor R. 2005. "Hercules *Furens* and Nero: The Didactic Purpose of Senecan Tragedy." In *Heracles/Hercules in the Ancient World: Exploring a Graeco-Roman Divinity*, edited by Louis Rawlings and Hugh Bowden, 185–204. Swansea: Classical Press of Wales.

Oldfather, William A. 1928. *The Discourses as Reported by Arrian, the Manual, and Fragments.* London: Heinemann.

Orlando, Antonello. 2014. "Seneca on Prolepsis: Greek Sources and Cicero's Influence." In *Seneca Philosophus*, edited by Jula Wildberger and Marcia L. Colish, 43–64. Berlin: De Gruyter.

Papas, Nickolas. 2015. *The Philosopher's New Clothes: The Theaetetus, the Academy, and Philosophy's Turn against Fashion.* London: Routledge.

Pavie, Xavier. 2012. *Exercices spirituels: Leçons de la philosophie antique.* Paris: Les Belles Lettres.

Pedersen, Fritz S. 1976. *Late Roman Public Professionalism.* Odense: Odense University Press.

Petit, Françoise. 1978. *Quaestiones in Genesim et in Exodum. Fragmenta Graeca.* Paris: Cerf.

Pitts, Andrew W. 2016. "Paul in Tarsus: Historical Factors in Assessing Paul's Early Education." In *Paul and Ancient Rhetoric: Theory and Practice in the Hellenistic Context*, edited by Stanley E. Porter and Bryan B. Dyer, 43–67. Cambridge: Cambridge University Press.

Pomeroy, A. 1999. Arius Didymus, *Epitome of Stoic Ethics.* Atlanta, GA: Society of Biblical Literature.

Rackham, Henry. 1914. *Cicero, On Ends* LCL 40. Cambridge, MA: Harvard University Press.

———. 1933. *On the Nature of the Gods. Academics, LCL* 268. Cambridge, MA: Harvard University Press.

Radice, Betty. 1969. *The Letters of the Younger Pliny.* Harmondsworth: Penguin.

Ramelli, Illaria. 2008. *Stoici romani minori.* Milano: Bompiani.

———. 2000. *Allegoria Temi metafisici e problemi del pensiero antico. Studi e testi.* Milan: Vita E Pensiero.

————. 2014. "Valuing Antiquity in Antiquity by Means of Allegoresis." In *Valuing the Past in the Greco-Roman World: Proceedings from the Penn-Leiden Colloquia on Ancient Values VII*, edited by Christoph Pieper, 485–507. Leiden: Brill.

Ramelli, Ilaria and David Konstan. 2009. *Hierocles. Elements of Ethics, Fragments and Excerpts*. Atlanta: Society of Biblical Literature.

Ramelli, Ilaria and Giulio A. Lucchetta. 2004. *Allegoria: L'età classica*. Milano: V & P Università.

Ranocchia, Graziano. 2012. "The Stoic Concept of Proneness to Emotion and Vice." *Archiv für Geschichte der Philosophie* 94.1: 74–92.

Rawson, Elizabeth. 1985. *Intellectual Life in the Late Roman Republic*. London: Gerald Duckworth.

Reydams-Schils, Gretchen. 2005. *The Roman Stoics: Self, Responsibility, and Affection*. Chicago: University of Chicago Press.

————. 2010a. "Philosophy and Education in Stoicism of the Roman Imperial Era." *Oxford Review of Education* 36.5: 561–75.

————. 2010b. "Seneca's Platonism: The Soul and Its Divine Origin." In *Models of Mind: Studies in Human and Divine Rationality*, edited by Andrea Nightingale and David N. Sedley, 196–215. Cambridge: Cambridge University Press.

————. 2011. "Authority and Agency in Stoicism." *Greece, Rome and Byzantine Studies* 51: 296–322.

————. 2015. "Hellenistic and Roman Philosophy." In *A Companion to Ancient Education*, edited by W. Martin Bloomer, 123–36. Hoboken, New Jersey: Wiley-Blackwell.

Richter, Daniel S. 2011. *Cosmopolis: Imagining Community in Late Classical Athens and the Early Roman Empire*. Oxford: Oxford University Press.

Rist, John M. 1982. "Are You a Stoic? The Case of Marcus Aurelius." In *Jewish and Christian Self-Definition*, edited by Benjamin F. Meyer and Ed P. Sanders, 23–45. Philadelphia: Fortress Press.

Robertson, Donald. 2010. *The Philosophy of Cognitive-Behavioural Therapy (CBT): Stoic Philosophy as Rational and Cognitive Psychotherapy*. London: Karnac.

Robertson, Paul M. 2016. *Paul's Letters and Contemporary Greco-Roman Literature*. Leiden: Brill.

Rolfe, Jhon C. 1927. Aulus Gellius *Attic Nights, Volume II, Books 6–13, LCL* 200. Cambridge, MA: Harvard University Press.

Roller, Duane W. 2014. *Strabo. The Geography of Strabo: An English Translation with Introduction and Notes*. Cambridge: Cambridge University Press.

Roller, Matthew B. 2004. "Exemplarity in Roman Culture: The Cases of Horatius Cocles and Cloelia." *Classical Philology* 99.1: 1–56.

————. 2009. "The Exemplary Past in Roman Historiography." In *The Cambridge Companion to the Roman Historians*, edited by Andrew Feldherr, 214–30. Cambridge: Cambridge University Press.

————. 2015. "Precept(or) and Example in Seneca." In *Roman Reflections: Studies in Latin Philosophy*, edited by Gareth D. Williams and K. Volk, 129–56. Oxford: Oxford University Press.

Roskam, Geert. 2005. *On the Path to Virtue: The Stoic Doctrine of Moral Progress and Its Reception in (Middle) Platonism*. Leuven: Leuven University Press.

Rosen, Ralph M. and Ineke Sluiter, editors. 2010. *Valuing Others in Classical Antiquity*. Leiden: Brill.

Rosenmeyer, Thomas G. 2000. "Seneca and Nature." *Arethusa* 33.1: 99–119.

Rousseau, Philip. 1996. "Conversion." In *Oxford Classical Dictionary*, 3rd ed, 386–87. Oxford: Oxford University Press.

Rudd, Niall P. 1998. *The Republic and the Laws*. Oxford: Oxford University Press.

Rudich, Vasily. 1993. *Political Dissidence Under Nero: The Price of Dissimulation*. London: Routledge.

Russell, Daniel C. 2012. *Happiness for Humans*. Oxford: Oxford University Press.

Russell, Donald A. 2002. *Quintilian. The Orator's Education, Volume V: Books 11–12, LCL* 494. Cambridge, MA: Harvard University Press.

Salles, Ricardo. 2005. *The Stoics on Determinism and Compatibilism*. Aldershot: Ashgate.

———. 2012. "Oikeiosis in Epictetus." In *Oikeiosis and the Natural Bases of Morality. From Classical Stoicism to Modern Philosophy*, edited by Georg Olms, 95–120. Chicago: Georg Olms Verlag.

Sandbach, F. H. 1971. "Ennoia and Prolepsis in the Stoic Theory of Knowledge." *Classical Quarterly* 24: 44–51.

Scaltsas, Theodore and Andrew S. Mason. 2007. *The Philosophy of Epictetus*. Oxford: Oxford University Press.

Schafer, John. 2009. *Ars Didactica: Seneca's 94th and 95th Letters*. Göttingen: Vandenhoeck & Ruprecht.

———. 2011. "Seneca's Epistulae Morales as Dramatized Education." *Classical Philology* 106.1: 32–52.

———. 2014. "The Philosophical Ambitions of Seneca's Letters." In *Strategies of Argument. Essays in Ancient Ethics, Epistemology, and Logic*, edited by Mi-Kyoung Lee, 282–96. Oxford: Oxford University Press.

Schmitz, Philip. 2014. *'Cato Peripateticus' - Stoische und Peripatetische Ethik im Dialog Cic. Fin. 3 und der Aristotelismus des Ersten Jh. v. Chr*. Berlin: Walter De Gruyter.

Schofield, Malcolm. 1991. *The Stoic Idea of the City*. Cambridge: Cambridge University Press.

———. 2007. "Epictetus on Cynicism." In *The Philosophy of Epictetus*, edited by Theodore Scaltsas and Andrew S. Mason, 71–86. Oxford: Oxford University Press.

———. 2015. "Seneca on Monarch and the Political Life: *De Clementia, De Tranquillitate Animi, Do Otio*." In *The Cambridge Companion to Seneca*, edited by Shadi Barstch and Alessandro Schiesaro, 68–81. Cambridge: Cambridge University Press.

Seddon, Keith. 2005. *Epictetus' Handbook and the Tablet of Cebes: Guides to Stoic Living*. London: Routledge.

Sedley, David N. 1989. "Philosophical Allegiance in the Greco-Roman World." In *Philosophia Togata*, edited by Miriam Griffin and Jonathan Barnes, 97–119. Oxford: Oxford University Press.

———. 1999. "The Stoic-Platonist Debate on *Kathêkonta*." In *Topics in Stoic Philosophy*, edited by Katerina Ierodiakonou, 128–52. Oxford: Oxford University Press.

———. 2003a. "Roman Philosophy." In *The Cambridge Companion to Greek and Roman Philosophy*, edited by David N. Sedley, 184–210. Cambridge: Cambridge University Press.

———. 2003b. "Philodemus and the Decentralisation of Philosophy." *Cronache Ercolanesi* 33: 31–41.

———. 2010. "Socrates Speaks in Seneca, *De Vita Beata* 24–28." In *Ancient Models of Mind: Studies in Human and Divine Rationality*, 180–95. Cambridge: Cambridge University Press.

———. 2018. "Stoics and Their Critics on Diachronic Identity." *Rhizomata* 6.1: 24–39.

Sedley, David and A. Laks. 2001. "The Origins of Stoic God." In *Traditions of Theology*, edited by D. Frede, 41–83. Leiden: Brill.

Sellars, John. 2003. *The Art of Living: The Stoics on the Nature and Function of Philosophy*. Aldershot: Ashgate.

———. 2007. "Stoic Practical Philosophy in the Imperial Period." In *Greek and Roman Philosophy, 100 BC-200 AD*, edited by R. Sorabji and R. W. Sharples, 115–40. London: Institute of Classical Studies.

———. 2014. "Seneca's Philosophical Predecessors and Contemporaries." In *Brill's Companion to Seneca, Philosopher and Dramatist*, edited by G. Damschen and A. Heil, 97–112. Leiden: Brill.

———. 2016. "The Stoics." In *The History of Evil in Antiquity*, edited by T. Angier, 175–86. Abington: Routledge.

Seo, J. M. 2013. *Exemplary Traits: Reading Characterization in Roman Poetry*. Oxford: Oxford University Press.

Setaioli, A. 2014a. "Epistulae Morales." In *Brill's Companion to Seneca: Philosopher and Dramatist*, edited by G. Damschen and A. Heil, 191–200. Leiden: Brill.

———. 2014b. "Ethics I: Philosophy as Therapy, Self-Transformation, and 'Lebensform.'" In *Brill's Companion to Seneca: Philosopher and Dramatist*, edited by G. Damschen and A. Heil, 239–56. Leiden: Brill.

———. 2014c. "Ethics III: Free Will and Autonomy." In *Brill's Companion to Seneca: Philosopher and Dramatist*, edited by G. Damschen and A. Heil, 277–99. Leiden: Brill.

———. 2014d. "Physics III: Theology." In *Brill's Companion to Seneca: Philosopher and ~ Dramatist*, edited by G. Damschen and A. Heil, 379–401. Leiden: Brill.

Sevenster, J. N. 1966. "Education or Conversion: Epictetus and the Gospels." *Novum Testamentum* 8.2: 247–62.

Sharpe, M. 2014. "How it's Not the Chrysippus you Read: On Cooper, Hadot, Epictetus, and Stoicism as a Way of Life Philosophy Today." *Philosophy Today*. Published Online First May 7, 2014.

Shogry, S. 2019. "The Stoic Appeal to Expertise: Platonic Echoes in the Reply to Indistinguishability." *Apeiron* 52.1: 29–64.

Sidebottom, H. 2009. "Philostratus and the Symbolic Roles of the Sophist and the Philosopher." In *Philostratus*, edited by E. Bowie and J. Elsner, 69–100. Cambridge: Cambridge University Press.

Skidmore, C. 1996. *Practical Ethics for Roman Gentlemen: The Work of Valerius Maximus*. Exeter: University of Exeter Press.

Sneddon, Keith. 2005. *Epictetus' Handbook and the Tablet of Cebes. Guides to Stoic Living*. London and New York: Routledge.

Snyder, H. Gregory. 2000. *Teachers and Texts in the Ancient World: Philosophers, Jews and Christians*. London: Routledge.

Sorabji, Richard. 1997. "Is Stoic Philosophy Helpful as Psychotherapy?" *Bulletin of the Institute of Classical Studies* 41: 197–209.

———. 2002. *Emotion and Peace of Mind: From Stoic Agitation to Christian Temptation; the Gifford Lectures*. Oxford: Oxford University Press.

———. 2006. *Self: Ancient and Modern Insights About Individuality, Life, and Death*. Chicago: University of Chicago.

———. 2012. *Gandhi and the Stoics: Modern Experiments on Ancient Values*. Oxford: Oxford University Press.

Staley, Gregory A. 2010. *Seneca and the Idea of Tragedy*. Oxford: Oxford University Press.

Stanton, G. R. 1973. "Sophists and Philosophers: Problems of Classification." *The American Journal of Philology* 94: 350–64.

Stephens, William O. 1996. "Epictetus on How the Stoic Sage Loves." *Oxford Studies in Ancient Philosophy* 14: 193–210.

———. 1998. "Masks, Androids, and Primates: The Evolution of the Concept 'Person.'" *Etica & Animali* 9: 111–27.

———. 2002a. "Epictetus on the Irrationality of Fearing Death and Reasons for Suicide." Accessed December 9, 2015: <http://puffin.creighton.edu/phil/Stephens/Epictetus%20on%20Death%20and%20Suicide.htm#_ednref19>.

———. 2002b. "Socrates: Epictetus' Stoic Hero." Accessed December 9, 2012: <http://puffin.creighton.edu/phil/Stephens/Socrates-Epictetus' -Stoic-Hero.htm>.

———. 2007. *Stoic Ethics: Epictetus and Happiness as Freedom*. London: Continuum.

———. 2012. *Marcus Aurelius: A Guide for the Perplexed*. London: Continuum.

———. 2013. "The Roman Stoics on Habit." In *A History of Habit: From Aristotle to Bourdieu*, edited by Tom Sparrow and Adam Hutchinson, 37–65. Lanham, MD: Lexington Books.

———. 2014a. "Epictetus on Beastly Vices and Animal Virtues." In *Epictetus: His Continuing Influence and Contemporary Relevance*, edited by Dane R. Gordon and David B. Suits, 205–38. New York: RIT.

———. 2014b. "Epictetus on Fearing Death: Bugbear and Open Door Policy." Accessed July 6, 2014: <http://apaclassics.org/sites/default/files/documents/abstracts/stephens.pdf>.

Stock, Brian. 1982. *The Implications of Literacy: Written Language and Models of Interpretation in the 11th and 12th Centuries*. Princeton, NJ: Princeton University Press.

Stockdale, James B. 1993. *Courage under Fire: Testing Epictetus' s Doctrines in a Laboratory of Human Behavior*. Stanford, CA: Hoover Institution, Stanford University Press.

Stojanovic, Pavle. 2014. "Epictetus and Moral Apprehensive Impressions in Stoicism." In *Epictetus: His Continuing Influence and Contemporary Relevance*, edited by Dane R. Gordon and David B. Suits, 165–96. New York: RIT.

Stowers, Stanley K. 1981. *The Diatribe and Paul's Letter to the Romans*. Chicago: Scholars Press.

———. 2011. "Does Pauline Christianity Resemble a Hellenistic Philosophy?" In *Redescribing Paul and the Corinthians*, edited by Ron Cameron and Merrill P. Miller, 219–44. Atlanta, GA: Society of Biblical Literature.

Striker, Gisela. 1996. *Essays on Hellenistic Epistemology and Ethics*. Cambridge: Cambridge University Press.

Struck, Peter T. 2016. *Divination and Human Nature: A Cognitive History of Intuition in Classical Antiquity*. Princeton, NJ: Princeton University Press.

Swain, Simon. 1998. *Hellenism and Empire: Language, Classicism, and Power in the Greek World, AD 50-250*. Oxford: Oxford University Press.

———. 2000. "Dio's Life and Works." In *Dio Chrysostom: Politics, Letters, and Philosophy*, edited by Simon Swain, 13–52. Oxford: Oxford University Press.

Swain, Simon, George R. Boys-Stones, Jas Elsner, Antonella Ghersettia, Robert Hoyland, and Ian Repath. 2007. *Seeing the Face, Seeing the Soul: Polemon's Physiognomy from Classical Antiquity to Medieval Islam*. Oxford: Oxford University Press.

Thom, Johan. 2005. *Hymn to Zeus: Text, Translation, and Commentary, STAC* 33. Tübingen: Mohr Siebeck.

———. 2012. "Popular Philosophy in the Hellenistic-Roman World." *Early Christianity* 3.3: 279–95.

Thorsteinsson, Runar M. 2010. *Roman Christianity and Roman Stoicism: A Comparative Study of Ancient Morality*. Oxford: Oxford University Press.

Tieleman, Tuen. 1996. *Galen and Chrysippus on the Soul: Argument and Refutation in the De Placitis, Books II–III*. Leiden: E.J. Brill.

———. 2007. "Panaetius' Place in the History of Stoicism. With Special Reference to His Moral Psychology." In *Pyrrhonists, Patricians and Platonizers. Hellenistic Philosophy in the Period 155–86 BC, Proceedings of the Tenth Symposium Hellenisticum*, edited by Anna M. Ioppolo and David N. Sedley, 103–42. Naples: Bibliopolis.

———. 2008. "Onomastic Reference in Seneca. The Case of Plato and the Platonists." In *Platonic Stoicism—Stoic Platonism The Dialogue between Platonism and Stoicism in Antiquity*, edited by Christoph Helmig and Mauro Bonazzi, 133–49. Leuven: Leuven University Press.

———. 2010. "Orality and Writing in Ancient Philosophy: Their Interrelationship and the Shaping of Literary Forms." In *The Interface of Orality and Writing: Speaking, Seeing, Writing in the Shaping of New Genres. Studies in Honour of Antoinette Clark Wire*, edited by Annette Weissenrieder and Robert B. Coote, 19–35. Tubigen: Mohr Siebeck.

Todd, Robert B. 1973. "The Stoic Common Notions: A Re-Examination and Reinterpretation." *Symbolae Osloenses* 48: 47–75.

Tortzen, Chr. G. 2002. "Know Thyself- A Note on the Success of a Delphic Saying." In *Noctes Atticae: Articles on Greco-Roman Antiquity and Its Nachleben*, edited by Pernille Flensted-Jensen, Thomas H. Nielsen, Adam Schwartz, and Chr. H. Tortzen, 302–14. Copenhagen: Museum Tusculanum.

Trapp, Michael B. 1997. "On The Tablet of Cebes." *Bulletin of the Institute of Classical Studies* 41: 159–78.

———. 2007. *Philosophy in the Roman Empire: Ethics, Politics and Society*. Aldershot: Ashgate.

———. 2014. "Philosophia between Greek and Roman Culture: Naturalized Immigrant or Eternal Stranger?" In *Three Centuries of Greek Culture Under the Roman Empire*, edited by Francesa Mester and Pillar Gomez, 29–48. Barcelona: Universitat de Barcelona.

———. 2017. "Philosophical Authority in the Imperial Period." In *Authority and Expertise in Ancient Scientific Culture*, edited by Jason König and Greg Woolf, 27–57. Cambridge: Cambridge University Press.

Trembley, Michael. 2016. "Spiritual Exercises in Epictetus: Difficult but Justified." MA Thesis, Carleton University.

Tsalla, Eleni. 2005. "Socrates as the Paradigm of the Ethical Personality in Epictetus." Diss., University of South Florida.

———. 2010. "Epictetus on Plato: The Philosopher as an Olympic Victor." *Philosophical Inquiry* XXXII.1: 21–42.

———. 2014. "Epictetus on the Meaning of Names and on Comprehensive Impressions." In *Epictetus: His Continuing Influence and Contemporary Relevance*, edited by Dane R. Gordon and David B. Suits, 55–75. New York: RIT.

Tsouna, Voula. 2007. *The Ethics of Philodemus*. Oxford: Oxford University Press.

Turpin, William. 2008. "Tacitus, Stoic Exempla, and the Praecipuum Munus Annalium." *Classical Antiquity* 27.2: 359–404.

Ullucci, Daniel. 2014. "Contesting the Meaning of Animal Sacrifice." In *Ancient Mediterranean Sacrifice*, edited by Jennifer W. Knust and Zsuzsanna Varhelyi, 57–74. Oxford: Oxford University Press.

Usher, Stephen. 1985. *Critical Essays, Volume II: On Literary Composition. Dinarchus. Letters to Ammaeus and Pompeius, LCL* 466. Cambridge, MA: Harvard University Press.

Van Houte, Maarten S. A. 2010. *Seneca's Theology in its Philosophical Context*. Utrecht: Zeno, the Leiden-Utrecht Research Institute of Philosophy.

Van Nuffelen, Peter. 2011. *Rethinking the Gods: Philosophical Readings of Religion in the Post-Hellenistic Period*. Cambridge: Cambridge University Press.

Van Nuffelen, Peter and Lieve Van Hoof. 2013. "Posidonius and the Golden Age: A Note on Seneca, *Epistulae* Morales 90." *Latomus* 72: 186–95.

Vander Waerdt, Paul A. 2003. "The Original Theory of Natural Law." *The Studia Philonica Annual* 15: 17–34.

Van Sijl, Claartje. 2010. *Stoic Philosophy and the Exegesis of Myth*. Utrecht: Zeno, the Leiden-Utrecht Research Institute of Philosophy.

Vogt, Katja. 2007. *Law, Reason, and the Cosmic City: Political Philosophy in the Early Stoa*. Oxford: Oxford University Press.

———. 2008. "The Good Is Benefit. On the Stoic Definition of the Good." *Proceedings of the Boston Area Colloquium in Ancient Philosophy* XXIII: 155–74.

Von Arnim, J. 1903–1924. *Stoicorum Veterum Fragmenta (SVF)*, 4 vols. Leipzig: Teuber.

Von Staden, Heinrich. 1982. "Hairesis and Heresy: The Case of the *haireseis iatri- kai*." In *Jewish and Christian Self-Definition: Self Definition in the Graeco-Roman World*, edited by Benjamin F. Meyer and Ed P. Sanders, 76–100. London: SCM Press.

Walsh, Patrick G. 2000. *On Obligations*. Oxford: Oxford University Press.

Ware, James. 2008. "Moral Progress and Divine Power in Seneca and Paul." In *Passions and Moral Progress in Greco-Roman Thought*, edited by John Fitzgerald, 267–83. London: Routledge.

———. 2017. "The Salvation of Creation: Seneca and Paul on the Future of Humanity and of the Cosmos." In *Paul and Seneca in Dialogue. Ancient Philosophy and Religion*, vol. 2, edited by Joseph R. Dodson and David E. Briones, 285–306. Leiden: Brill.

Walsh, Peter G. 1997. *The Nature of the Gods*. Oxford: Oxford University Press.

Watts, Edward J. 2006. *City and School in Late Antique Athens and Alexandria*. Oakland, CA: University of California Press.

Wendt, Heidi. 2016. *At the Temple Gates: The Religion of Freelance Experts in the Roman Empire*. Oxford: Oxford University Press.

White, Michael L. 2003. "Stoic Natural Philosophy (Physics and Cosmology)." In *The Cambridge Companion to the Stoics*, edited by Brad Inwood, 124–52. Cambridge: Cambridge University Press.

White, Stephen. 2007. "Posidonius and Stoic Physics." In *Greek & Roman Philosophy 100 BC- 200 AD Vol 1*, edited by R. Sorabji and R. W. Sharples, 35–76. London: Institute of Classical Studies.

———. 2010. "Stoic Selection Objects, Actions, and Agents." In *Ancient Models of Mind: Studies in Human and Divine Rationality*, edited by Andrea Nightingale and David N. Sedley, 110–29. Cambridge: Cambridge University Press.

White, L. Michael and John T. Fitzgerald. 2003. "Quod est Comparandum: The Problems of Parallels." In *Early Christianity and Classical Culture*, edited by John Fitzgerald T. Olbricht, and L. Michael White, 13–39. Leiden: Brill.

Wildberger, Jula. 2008. "Beast or God? – The Intermediate Status of Humans and the Physical Basis of the Stoic *Scala Naturae*." In *Mensch und Tier in der Antike*, edited by A. Alexandridis, L. Winkler Horacek, and M. Wild, 47–70. Wiesbaden: Reichert Verlag.

———. 2013. "Delimiting a Self by God in Epictetus." In *Religious Dimensions of the Self ~ in the Second Century CE*, edited by Jörg Rüpke and Greg Woolf, 23–45. Tübingen: Mohr Siebeck.

———. 2014a. "The Epicurean Trope and the Construction of a 'Letter Writer' in Seneca's *Epistulae Morales*." In *Seneca Philosophus*, edited by Jula Wildberger and Marcia L. Colish, 431–65. Berlin: De Grutyer.

———. 2014b. "Ethics IV: Wisdom and Virtue." In *Brill's Companion to Seneca, Philosopher and Dramatist*, edited by Gregor Damschen and Andreas Heil, 301–22. Leiden: Brill.

———. 2018. *The Stoics and the State: Theory, Practice, Context*. Berlin: Nomos Verlagsgesellschaft.

Williams, Gareth D. 2012. *The Cosmic Viewpoint: A Study of Seneca's Natural Questions*. Oxford: Oxford University Press.

Wilson, Emily R. 2007a. *The Death of Socrates*. Cambridge, MA: Harvard University Press.

Wilson, Marcus. 2007b. "Rhetoric and the Younger Seneca." In *A Companion to Roman Rhetoric: Blackwell Companions to the Ancient World*, edited by William Dominik and Jon Hall Hoboken, 425–38. New Jersey: Wiley-Blackwell.

Wilson, Walter T. 1994. *The Mysteries of Righteousness: The Literary Composition and Genre of the Sentences of Pseudo-Phocylides*. Tübingen: Mohr Siebeck.

Woodward, Linda H. 2009. "Diogenes of Babylon: A Stoic on Music and Ethics." Master's Thesis, University College London.

Wray, David. 2015. "Seneca's Shame." In *The Cambridge Companion to Seneca*, edited by S. Barstch and A. Schiesaro, 199–211. Cambridge: Cambridge University Press.

Wright, Rosemary. 2009. *Introducing Greek Philosophy*. London: Routledge.

Xenakis, Iason. 1969. *Epictetus Philosopher-Therapist*. The Hague: Martinus Nijhoff.

Yieh, John Y.-H. 2003. *One Teacher Jesus' Teaching Role in Matthew's Gospel*. Berlin: Walter De Gruyter.

Zanker, Paul. 1995. *The Mask of Socrates: The Image of the Intellectual in Antiquity*. Berkeley: University of California.

Index

About the Author

Erlend D. MacGillivray received his PhD from the University of Aberdeen, Scotland, in 2018. His work has been published in journals such as the *Journal of Ancient History*, *Apeiron: A Journal for Ancient Philosophy and Science*, and *Ancient World.* He is also the editor of www.ancientphilosophy-timeline.org.

Printed in Great Britain
by Amazon